Epiphanius of Cyprus

CHRISTIANITY IN LATE ANTIQUITY
THE OFFICIAL BOOK SERIES OF THE NORTH
AMERICAN PATRISTICS SOCIETY

Editor
Christopher A. Beeley, Yale University

Associate Editors
Elizabeth A. Clark, Duke University
Robin Darling Young, The Catholic University of America
International Advisory Board
Lewis Ayres, Durham University • John Behr, St Vladimir's Orthodox Theological Seminary, New York • Brouria Bitton-Ashkelony, Hebrew University of Jerusalem • Marie-Odile Boulnois, École Pratique des Hautes Études, Paris • Kimberly D. Bowes, University of Pennsylvania and the American Academy in Rome • Virginia Burrus, Syracuse University • Stephen Davis, Yale University • Elizabeth DePalma Digeser, University of California Santa Barbara • Mark Edwards, University of Oxford • Susanna Elm, University of California Berkeley • Thomas Graumann, Cambridge University • Sidney H. Griffith, Catholic University of America • David G. Hunter, University of Kentucky • Andrew S. Jacobs, Scripps College • Robin M. Jensen, University of Notre Dame • AnneMarie Luijendijk, Princeton University • Christoph Markschies, Humboldt-Universität zu Berlin • Andrew B. McGowan, Berkeley Divinity School at Yale • Claudia Rapp, Universität Wien • Samuel Rubenson, Lunds Universitet • Rita Lizzi Testa, Università degli Studi di Perugia

1. *Incorruptible Bodies: Christology, Society, and Authority in Late Antiquity*, by Yonatan Moss
2. *Epiphanius of Cyprus: A Cultural Biography of Late Antiquity*, by Andrew S. Jacobs
3. *Melania: Early Christianity through the Life of One Family*, by Catherine M. Chin and Caroline T. Schroeder

Epiphanius of Cyprus

A Cultural Biography of Late Antiquity

Andrew S. Jacobs

UNIVERSITY OF CALIFORNIA PRESS

University of California Press, one of the most
distinguished university presses in the United States,
enriches lives around the world by advancing scholarship
in the humanities, social sciences, and natural sciences. Its
activities are supported by the UC Press Foundation and
by philanthropic contributions from individuals and
institutions. For more information, visit www.ucpress.edu.

University of California Press
Oakland, California

© 2016 by The Regents of the University of California

First Paperback Printing 2021

Library of Congress Cataloging-in-Publication Data

Names: Jacobs, Andrew S., 1973- author.
Title: Epiphanius of Cyprus : a cultural biography of late
   antiquity / Andrew S. Jacobs.
Description: Oakland, California : University of
   California Press, [2016] | "2016 | Includes
bibliographical references and index.
Identifiers: LCCN 2015048170 (print) | LCCN 2015050963
   (ebook) | ISBN 9780520291126 (cloth : alk. paper) |
   9780520385702 (pbk. : alk. paper) | 9780520964983 (ebook)
Subjects: LCSH: Epiphanius, Saint, Bishop of Constantia
   in Cyprus, approximately 310–403. | Orthodox Eastern
   Church—Bishops—Biography. | Christian saints—
   Cyprus—Biography. | Church history—Primitive and
   early church, ca. 30–600.

Classification: LCC BX395.E65 J33 2016 (print) | LCC

BX395.E65 (ebook) | DDC 270.2092—dc23

LC record available at http://lccn.loc.gov/2015048170

*To Elizabeth A. Clark, emeritissima—mentor,
inspiration, and friend*

CONTENTS

Acknowledgments ix

List of Abbreviations xiii

Introduction: Epiphanius, Now and Then
1

1. Celebrity
31

2. Conversion
65

3. Discipline
97

4. Scripture
132

5. Salvation
176

6. After Lives
221

Conclusion
263

Bibliography 279
Index 309

ACKNOWLEDGMENTS

This book caught me by surprise. I had expected, after finishing my book on the circumcision of Christ, to begin a project on conversion, specifically a study of narratives about Jewish conversion to Christianity and the role they played in ancient Christianity and in modern scholarship. I began by looking at three early Christian ex-Jews: Romanos, Ambrosiaster, and Epiphanius. The long, but mostly forgotten, history of Epiphanius's ex-Jewishness struck me as particularly indicative of the twists and turns the study of ancient Christianity has taken in the modern and postmodern era.

This book is not that book on early Christian ex-Jews, although pieces of that initial foray have found their way into chapter 6, and I hope soon to return to that book on conversion. Instead I found myself drawn to explore Epiphanius in his fourth-century context. Epiphanius of Cyprus had figured significantly in my first two books, but I had never stepped back to consider him on his own merits. I had first encountered Epiphanius as one of the "bad guys" of the Origenist controversy, and then turned to him as a somewhat odd but surprisingly useful resource for thinking about Christian attitudes toward Jews and Judaism. But for the first time now I asked, "Why do modern scholars have such disdain for Epiphanius when he was so influential in his own time and place?" This book is my attempt to answer that question.

I was incredibly fortunate when beginning this project to discover the 2006 University of Michigan dissertation of Young Richard Kim ("The Imagined Worlds of Epiphanius of Cyprus"). When I reached out to Professor Kim, now at Calvin College, I found a generous, smart, and creative scholar who has acted as my guide and colleague in the world of Epiphaniana. From his invaluable translation of Epiphanius's *Ancoratus* (published in 2014) to his numerous articles and now his impressive book (*Epiphanius of Cyprus: Imagining an Orthodox World*) to his support and encouragement of my own project, I have to thank Young Kim first and foremost here for helping this project to come to fruition. Our end results are very different, but I think complementary in useful and important ways.

I should also thank the growing cadre of scholars who work on Epiphanius from even more diverse perspectives: Todd Berzon, Richard Flower, David Maldonado, and Scott Manor have all been important interlocutors and discussion partners during the writing of this book. I must also thank Claudia Rapp, whom I had the great fortune to get to know while we both lived in Southern California, for sharing her enormously impressive University of Oxford dissertation on the Greek *Vita Epiphanii* with me in the early days of this project and for continuing to give impeccable scholarly counsel.

I was fortunate to be invited to present pieces of this work before generous and thoughtful audiences. My thanks to the Center for the Study of Religion at The Ohio State University, and my hosts, David Brakke, J. Albert Harill, and Kristina Sessa; and to Stephen J. Shoemaker, who invited me to deliver the Ira E. Gaston Lecture at the University of Oregon. I must also thank the very patient and helpful audiences at the annual North American Patristics Society and the quadrennial International Conference on Patristic Studies, Oxford, who listened to pieces of this work in progress. I am particularly grateful to have been invited to participate in the "Origenist Textualities" workshop of the 2011 Oxford conference with such brilliant colleagues as Catherine Chin, Rebecca Krawiec, Jeremy Schott, and Blossom Stefaniw. Previous versions of these earlier presentations, now revised as chapters 2 and 4, appeared in print as "Matters (Un-)Becoming: Epiphanius of Salamis on Conversion," *Church History* 81 (2012): 27–47, and "Epiphanius of Salamis and the Antiquarian's Bible," *Journal of Early Christian Studies* 21 (2013): 437–64, respectively. Thanks also to Kenneth Wolf, who allowed me to present some of my thoughts on Epiphanius and late antiquity at the Claremont Colleges Late Antiquity and Medieval Studies Colloquium "Religious Boundaries and Their Maintenance."

Thanks also to several colleagues who provided guidance to me as I ventured into new waters during this project: Mark DelCogliano, who graciously read a draft of chapter 5; Andrew Crislip, who shared his prepublication translation of Shenoute's *I Am Amazed*; David Brakke, Caroline Schroeder, and Rebecca Krawiec, most excellent guides to the world of Shenoute and Egyptian monasticism; and Christine Shepardson, who offered sage wisdom on the very complicated episcopal crises of fourth-century Antioch. Any remaining errors reflect my own failures as a student, not theirs as teachers.

Christopher Beeley, editor of the Christianity in Late Antiquity series, along with associate editors Elizabeth Clark and Robin Darling Young, gave incredibly helpful comments and editorial advice on early versions of the first chapters of this book, and it is a real pleasure to be part of this newly relaunched series. The people at the University of California Press have also been wonderful to work with: Maeve Cornell-Taylor, who has been unfailingly helpful in matters of preproduction; Cindy Fulton, a fantastic production editor; and Eric Schmidt, an editor with whom it has been a true pleasure to work. Enormous gratitude also to Marian Rogers for diligent copyediting and to Roberta Engleman for precise indexing.

Scripps College provided essential financial support and sabbatical leave at a crucial stage in the writing of this book. The staff of the Honnold/Mudd Library of the Claremont Colleges have a knack for finding even the most obscure article or essay. My students and colleagues at the Claremont Colleges demonstrate every day the vital importance of the humanities and a liberal arts education. I was able to learn more than I ever thought possible about niche Victorian literature and Anglo-Catholicism in the stacks of the Huntington Library, where I am lucky enough to be a Reader.

Every day I am grateful to my spouse, Catherine Allgor, who provides intellectual and emotional support and knows what it takes to get a book done.

Finally, I dedicate this book to my mentor, Elizabeth A. Clark, professor emerita of religion at Duke University. I met Epiphanius in my first semester as a graduate student, in Liz's course on the Origenist controversy and in her incomparable book on the same subject (*The Origenist Controversy: The Cultural Construction of an Early Christian Debate*). I could fill hundreds of pages explaining all the things I learned from Liz in that class, and since. Among the priceless lessons evident in *The Origenist Controversy* is that critical engagement with the ancient world springs from a place of deep awareness of and investment in one's own cultural debates. Thank you, Liz.

ABBREVIATIONS

The following abbreviations are used for critical editions, journals, and book series in the notes and bibliography.

BZ	*Byzantinische Zeitschrift*
CA	*Classical Antiquity*
CCL	Corpus Christianorum, Series Latina. Turnhout: Brepols, 1953–.
CH	*Church History*
CQ n.s.	*Classical Quarterly*, new series
CSCO	Corpus Scriptorum Christianorum Orientalium. Leuven: Secretariat du Corpus CSCO, 1903–.
CSEL	Corpus Scriptorum Ecclesiasticorum Latinorum. Vienna: Akademie Verlag, 1866–.
DOP	*Dumbarton Oaks Papers*
FC	Fathers of the Church. Washington, DC: The Catholic University of America Press, 1947–.
GCS n.F.	Griechischen Christlichen Schriftsteller. Neue Folge. Leipzig: J. C. Hinrichs, 1899–.
HTR	*Harvard Theological Review*
JAAR	*Journal of the American Academy of Religion*

JBL	*Journal of Biblical Literature*
JECS	*Journal of Early Christian Studies*
JLA	*Journal of Late Antiquity*
JR	*Journal of Religion*
JRS	*Journal of Roman Studies*
JTS n.s.	*Journal of Theological Studies*, new series
NHMS	Nag Hammadi and Manichaean Studies
OCM	Oxford Classical Monographs
OECS	Oxford Early Christian Studies
OECT	Oxford Early Christian Texts
OSLA	Oxford Studies in Late Antiquity
PG	Patrologia Graeca. Ed. J.-P. Migne. 162 vols. Paris: Migne, 1857–66.
PL	Patrologia Latina. Ed. J.-P. Migne. 217 vols. Paris: Migne, 1844–65.
PMS	Patristic Monograph Series
SC	Sources Chrétiennes. Paris: Cerf, 1943–.
SP	*Studia Patristica*
TCH	Transformation of the Classical Heritage
VC	*Vigiliae Christianae*
ZAC	*Zeitschrift für antikes Christentum*

Introduction

Epiphanius, Now and Then

> Tantae enim venerationis semper fuit, ut regnantes haeretici, ignominiam suam putarent, si talem virum persequerentur. He was always held in such great veneration that when heretics reigned they considered their own ignominy should they persecute so great a man.
>
> Jerome, *Contra Ioannem Hiersolymitanum* 4

"PASSIONATE PURITAN": EPIPHANIUS IN MODERNITY

Modern scholarship has very little use for Epiphanius, bishop of Constantia (Salamis) on the island of Cyprus ca. 367–403.[1] He is, at best, a source for otherwise lost documents pertaining to ancient debates

---

1. See Young Richard Kim, *Epiphanius of Cyprus: Imagining An Orthodox World* (Ann Arbor: University of Michigan Press, 2015), 1–3. Jon Dechow, *Dogma and Mysticism in Early Christianity: Epiphanius of Cyprus and the Legacy of Origen*, PMS 13 (Macon, GA: Mercer University Press, 1988), 26–27, summarizes modern (negative) reactions to Epiphanius. Pierre Nautin, "Épiphane (Saint), de Salamine," *Dictionnaire d'histoire et de géographie ecclésiastiques* 15 (1963): 617–31, provides a sober yet critical assessment of Epiphanius as having "défauts trop fréquents, qui s'accentuèrent avec l'âge, comme les jugements sommaires et définitifs, les partis pris, la facilité à s'aveugler sur soi et sur les autres" (626). Christos Simelidis, "Epiphanius," *Encyclopedia of Ancient History*, ed. Roger Bagnall et al. (London: Wiley/Blackwell, 2013), 2463–64, offers a balanced (although brief) account of Epiphanius's career.

about orthodoxy and heresy.² He is, at worst, an intransigent and prevaricating churchman and a meddlesome controversialist, whose most famous work—the massive encyclopedia of heresies called the *Panarion*, or "Cure-All"—stands as a monument to his narrowness and intolerance. Henry Chadwick, in his classic survey of early Christianity, describes the rigid bishop as a "passionate puritan" with a "rigorous hostility to every sort of intellectual pretension, including theological speculation."³ Modern scholars routinely describe Epiphanius as anti-intellectual—indeed, lacking any coherent intellect or education of his own.⁴ He is a poor writer, thinker, and person, about whom scholars are prepared to think the worst. "No patristic source is filled with more invective and distortion," Bart Ehrman recently wrote, in arguing that one of the most famous incidents in the *Panarion* (*Panarion* 26, on the Phibionites) was invented out of whole cloth.⁵ Epiphanius's generally sympathetic English translator, Frank Williams, wrote:

> Of all the church fathers, Epiphanius is the most generally disliked. It would be easy to assemble, from the writings of patrologists and historians of religion, a bill of particulars against him. He is a heresy hunter, a name caller, and "nasty." His judgments are uncritical. His theology is shallow and his manner of holding it intransigent.⁶

---

2. Scholars of Gnosticism, of Jewish-Christian movements, and of Trinitarian thought find Epiphanius's collection of documents and sources particularly useful, so much so that the only full translation into English of Epiphanius's masterwork, the *Panarion*, was published in the Nag Hammadi Studies series out of Brill Press (see below, n. 6).

3. Henry Chadwick, *The Early Church* (London: Penguin Books, 1967), 184. In the same decade Pierre Fraenkel, "Histoire sainte et hérésie chez Saint Épiphane de Salamine, d'après le tome I du *Panarion*," *Revue de Théologie et de Philosophie* 12 (1962): 175, writes of Epiphanius's "zèle puritain."

4. Calogero Riggi, one of the most prolific (and positive) European scholars on Epiphanius, writes when trying to decipher some confusing lines on divorce in the *Panarion*: "Dans ce texte il s'agit du style d'Épiphane, qui comme d'habitude écrit très mal" ("Nouvelle lecture du *Panarion* LIX, 4 [Épiphane et le divorce]," *SP* 12.1 [1975]: 130).

5. Bart D. Ehrman, *Forgery and Counterforgery: The Use of Literary Deceit in Early Christian Polemics* (Oxford: Oxford University Press, 2013), 22.

6. *The Panarion of Epiphanius of Salamis*, vol. 1, Book 1 (Sects 1–46), trans. Frank Williams, 2nd rev. ed., NHMS 63 (Leiden: Brill, 2009), xxxi.

Williams goes on to moderate these various negative assumptions about Epiphanius—his "nastiness," for example, can be understood in terms of the rhetorical norms of his day—but the initial accusation, that Epiphanius inevitably arouses general dislike, cannot be so easily dislodged.

Part of Epiphanius's disrepute in modernity arises in comparison with other figures deemed more worthy of study, who, it is assumed, are more representative of the heady intellectual, religious, and cultural times in which they lived. Aline Pourkier, author of one of the few modern studies of Epiphanius, draws a sharp contrast between the object of her study and the other luminaries of the "golden age" of patristics:

> Who was the author of the *Panarion?* Born between 310 and 320, having died in 402, he spans very precisely that fourth century which was the "golden age" of patristics. And yet what a contrast between Epiphanius and the other Fathers of this period! Next to Gregory of Nazianzus or John Chrysostom, Basil of Caesarea and Gregory of Nyssa, his brother, all raised in the purest tradition of Greek *paideia,* he cuts the figure of a man of little cultivation, barely knowing his own language, ignorant of the very pagan culture he condemns.[7]

We turn instead to Chrysostom, the Cappadocians, and Athanasius, and (in the West) Augustine and Ambrose in order to understand the full richness of Christianity in late antiquity. These theological and intellectual titans, building on the work of earlier titans, such as Clement of Alexandria and Origen, constructed a new Christian culture out of the remains of a fading pagan past. Epiphanius was a mere gadfly

---

7. Aline Pourkier, *L'hérésiologie chez Épiphane de Salamine,* Christianisme Antique 4 (Paris: Beauchesne, 1992), 29: "Qui était l'auteur du *Panarion?* Né entre 310 et 320, mort en 402, il couvre très exactement ce IVe siècle qui fut l' 'âge d'or' de la Patristique. Et pourtant quel contraste entre Épiphane et les autres Pères de ce temps! À côté de Grégoire de Nazianze ou de Jean Chrysostome, de Basile de Césarée et de Grégoire de Nysse, son frère, tous élevés dans la plus pure tradition de la παιδεία grecque, il fait figure d'homme peu cultivé, sachant mal la langue, ignorant et même condamnant la culture païenne." See also Kim, *Epiphanius,* 4.

among them, useful perhaps in a rancorous debate over orthodoxy, but easily and happily forgotten.

Yet whatever flaws we might find in the person and conduct of Epiphanius (and they are certainly legion) our distaste for him is particularly our own. In his own time among his peers, he was extraordinarily significant. His influence across the Mediterranean world, from Rome to Constantinople, is undeniable, and it is remarkable that an otherwise insignificant Palestinian monk rose to become the bishop of a small city on the island of Cyprus, and from there to cast his shadow across the eastern Mediterranean. (I outline the extent of his influence below.) Our objections to Epiphanius indicate rather the type of value we find in the transformative era we have come to call "late antiquity," and the kinds of cultures it produced. To the extent that history writing is always, in some respects, an exercise in self-reflection, it is no surprise that scholars have been drawn to historical figures particularly attuned to our own interests: learned, but often tortured, intellectuals, sometimes rancorous, often passionate, able to perceive dimly and insightfully the shape of a world beyond their own. Those "golden age" Fathers lauded by Pourkier possessed the brilliance to reshape a new Christian Roman Empire. Yet by focusing on this regular cast of characters, we have been reproducing the same kind of patristic canon that "the Fathers" themselves began to construct soon after the advent of imperial Christianity at the Council of Nicaea.[8] This is not to say that our regular cast of historical characters have nothing valuable to tell us about late antiquity and the rise of a Christian Roman Empire: obvi-

---

8. On the ways in which a patristic past began to be produced toward the end of the fourth century, see Mark Vessey, "The Forging of Orthodoxy in Latin Christian Literature: A Case Study," *JECS* 4 (1996): 495–513; Éric Rebillard, "A New Style of Argument in Christian Polemic: Augustine and the Use of Patristic Citations," *JECS* 8 (2000): 559–78. On the ways in which scholars reproduce this canonical early Christianity, see Karen King, *What Is Gnosticism?* (Cambridge, MA: Belknap Press of Harvard University Press, 2003), 15–18; and Ellen Muehlberger, "On Authors, Fathers, and Holy Men," *Marginalia Review of Books*, http://marginalia.lareviewofbooks.org/on-authors-fathers-and-holy-men-by-ellen-muehlberger/.

ously their continuing resonance makes them important figures for scholarly contemplation. I do think, however, that this intellectual reproduction has unnecessarily limited us.

One of my goals in this book is to broaden the framework within which we seek to understand Christian late antiquity. I begin from the simple premise that if Epiphanius was influential in his own time, we should take that influence seriously. I then use Epiphanius to reimagine certain core cultural concepts of late ancient Christianity. I do not suggest that we revise our modern opinion of Epiphanius, clasp him close, and rediscover in him a boon companion. He was, to be sure, a difficult and harsh figure—as were, we should recall, many transformative people in this era. Rather we should recognize that he speaks more representatively of his time and place than he is given credit for.

I call this project a "cultural biography" because I argue that, by studying the life and times of Epiphanius, we can gain a new, very different understanding of Christian culture in the pivotal last decades of the fourth century. By "culture" I mean all the multifarious ways Christians came to understand their material and intellectual particularity in their world: their views of politics, education, embodiment, and society, and how they relate this fallen, sinful world to the perfect world to come. As I noted above, the historical understanding of late ancient Christianity has, for much of the modern period, been dominated by certain key people who resonate more with our own cultural aspirations and anxieties. When we focus primarily on intellectuals like Augustine of Hippo or Basil of Caesarea, we are remaining largely in a world we find comforting and familiar. Even as the field of late antiquity itself shifts—from intellectual history to social history to cultural history, and so on—the persons who dominate our studies remain remarkably fixed.[9] When reading Peter Brown's eloquent epilogue, "New Directions," appended

---

9. For a concise but helpful view of these shifts since the 1960s, see Dale B. Martin, introduction to *The Cultural Turn in Late Antiquity: Gender, Asceticism, History*, ed. Dale B. Martin and Patricia Cox Miller (Durham, NC: Duke University Press, 2005), 1–21.

in the year 2000 to his original 1967 biography, *Augustine of Hippo*, we can be struck by two things. First, as Brown himself explains, we note the degree to which more recent studies of Augustine "challenge readers to realize the very real gap of time that lies between ourselves, in 1999, and the distant and distinctive age of Augustinian studies of the 1960s."[10] At the same time, we cannot help but note also that somehow Augustine, as a thinker—indeed, as a biography—can contain and encompass that "very real gap" with surprising ease. We may change, but Augustine (among others) remains constant, our historiographic North Star, in his centrality to our understanding of this period of time.

There are, to be sure, many reasons scholars of various stripes remain drawn to this canon of historical figures, and I address some larger themes in the conclusion. I do think, however, that one of the factors that has remained consistently appealing among these historical personages is their attitude toward culture generally. These "Fathers" looked with concern and anxiety over the fractures emerging in their new, Christian Roman world. They agonized over the transition from "pagan" to Christian empire; they worried over the value of "secular" culture; they wondered how to Christianize the knowledges that had come before, and how to end internal dissent and conflict. They saw their world as one in transition (as, indeed, we continue to view it), and their own literary remains seem, to us, preoccupied with how to navigate that transition. They understood—as we understand—the precipitous and intellectually fraught moment that constitutes "late antiquity."

Unlike Augustine or Basil, Epiphanius does not worry over the fractious anxieties of identity that characterized the early Christian Roman Empire. It may sound strange to say of an early Christian author whose signal achievement is the inscription of a new tradition of intolerant heresiology,[11] but Epiphanius—as we see in the chapters that follow—

---

10. Peter Brown, *Augustine of Hippo: A Biography*, 2nd ed. (Berkeley: University of California Press, 2000), 487.

11. A legacy that scholarship has only recently begun to take seriously; see Averil Cameron, "How to Read Heresiology," in Martin and Miller, *Cultural Turn*, 193–212.

is remarkably comfortable with division and difference. Indeed, his appeal in his particular time may very well have stemmed from his ability to weave an awareness of difference and otherness into his Christian culture. Epiphanius's culture is one of masterful fragmentation and recombination, of careful management of status and ideas, of visible authority and conflict in the name of an aspirational, but never achieved, unity. His world is full of "others" (Jews, pagans, heretics), and he casts a clear and confident gaze over their seemingly endless and multiplying ranks.

I have argued elsewhere that we can see in some streams of late ancient Christianity a particularly Roman imperial attention to otherness and difference: a focus on management and incorporation, rather than eradication and destruction, of "others."[12] Epiphanius's understanding of his own cultural situation, I suggest, coheres with this late Roman sensibility. The *Panarion* itself stands as witness to Epiphanius's attitude toward difference. As a "manual" of heresy it is, as many scholars have pointed out, somewhat lacking in utility: most of the heresies are unknown or invented, and the very notion of "heresy" contained therein is so capacious that it stretches back to Adam.[13] The goal cannot be to assist individual Christians in sniffing out and eradicating heretics, a sort of "Diagnostic and Statistical Manual of Heretical Disorders." Instead, the goals are larger, epistemological, and cultural: to craft a way of understanding difference, to show mastery over it, to incorporate it—from the dawn of time to the present moment—into a

---

12. Andrew S. Jacobs, *Christ Circumcised: A Study in Early Christian History and Difference*, Divinations (Philadelphia: University of Pennsylvania Press, 2013), 1–19.

13. Leading Frances Young to ask in *SP* 17 (1982): 199–205: "Did Epiphanius know what he meant by heresy?" See, more recently, Jeremy Schott, "Heresiology as Universal History in Epiphanius' *Panarion*," *ZAC* 10 (2006): 546–63; and Richard Flower, "Genealogies of Unbelief: Epiphanius of Salamis and Heresiological Authority," in *Unclassical Traditions*, vol. 2, *Perspectives from the East and West in Late Antiquity*. ed. Christopher Kelly, Richard Flower, and Michael Stuart Williams (Cambridge: Cambridge University Press, 2011), 70–87, for more sophisticated attempts to understand Epiphanius's project.

totalizing Christian world.[14] Of course, as I have also attempted to explore in previous work, we should understand the flip side of such discourses of masterful control as always rippling underneath the surface: anxiety about the cracks in totalized power that even so confident a figure as Epiphanius can never escape.

When we acknowledge that Epiphanius's masterful and eclectic management of difference appealed to many of his Christian contemporaries, things look markedly different. Throughout his career, Christian leaders solicited his opinions on a range of topics, and widely circulated his written responses. If, like his contemporaries, we take Epiphanius and his late Roman Christian culture seriously, we—as scholars of early Christianity, and historians of religion more broadly—will have to come to terms with how and why we continue to circulate certain kinds of narratives.

"FATHER OF BISHOPS": EPIPHANIUS IN ANTIQUITY

Who was this bishop who wielded so much influence during his ecclesiastical career, and whom modern scholars find so distasteful?[15] His biography is straightforward.[16] Epiphanius was born sometime in the early fourth century, probably to a relatively affluent Christian family.[17]

---

14. On Epiphanius and totalizing discourse, see Andrew S. Jacobs, *Remains of the Jews: The Holy Land and Christian Empire in Late Antiquity*, Divinations (Stanford, CA: Stanford University Press, 2004), 44–51; and Schott, "Heresiology," 563.

15. I do not mean to suggest Epiphanius was universally beloved until modernity; he certainly had his detractors in the fourth and fifth centuries (as I discuss in chapter 1), and throughout the premodern period. The disavowal of Epiphanius in the twentieth and twenty-first centuries, I suggest, is of a different caliber.

16. On his reconstructed biography, see Nautin, "Épiphane"; Dechow, *Dogma and Mysticism*, 31–43; and now Gabriella Aragione, "Una 'storia' universale dell'eresia: Il Panarion di Epifanio," in *Epifanio di Salamina: Panarion, Libro primo*, ed. Giovanni Pini, Letteratura Cristiana Antica, nuova serie 21 (Brescia: Morcelliana, 2010), 6–19.

17. Epiphanius was educated, and he had the means to travel to Egypt as a young man and the financial resources to pursue a monastic vocation (perhaps, as Nautin argues [see below], on his own estate).

Although the sources for determining the religion of his parents are complicated,[18] the later hagiographic tradition that he was raised Jewish but converted to Christianity as a young man seems unknown during his lifetime. He was born in Palestine but went (as he tells us) as a young man to Egypt, perhaps, like other young men of his age and class, to study rhetoric in Alexandria.[19] While there, he became attracted to the growing movement of Egyptian monasticism, eventually returning home and founding his own monastery near his hometown.[20] He remained in charge of this monastery throughout much of the 350s and 360s, becoming at some point allied—or at least sociable with—various Nicene partisans in exile throughout the eastern Roman Empire.[21] For reasons that remain unclear, Epiphanius was ordained in 367 as the new bishop of Constantia, the city formerly, and still popularly in his day, known as Salamis.[22] Perhaps he had already moved from Palestine to Cyprus following theological disagreements or professional

---

18. Primarily a fragment of a purported letter written by Epiphanius to the emperor Theodosius. On this fragmentary letter, see my discussion below and in chapter 6.

19. Epiphanius's biography shares several details with the life of his mentor, Hilarion, as outlined in Jerome's *Vita Hilarionis:* origin in Palestine; study (and then monastic conversion) in Egypt; return to Palestine; emigration to Cyprus. Whether Hilarion was an influence on Epiphanius during his career, or later their biographies became blurred, must remain unclear.

20. Nautin, "Épiphane," 681, even suggests that Epiphanius's monastery in Palestine was constructed on his family's estate.

21. Epiphanius recounts a visit to see the exiled bishop Eusebius of Vercelli in Palestine in the 350s or early 360s; see Daniel Washburn, "Tormenting the Tormentors: A Reinterpretation of Eusebius of Vercelli's Letter from Scythopolis," *CH* 78 (2009): 731–55; and Kim, *Epiphanius*, 85–88.

22. Nautin, "Épiphane," 617, asserts that Epiphanius died in 402, not 403, and therefore puts his elevation to the episcopacy in 366 instead of 367; but see now Kim, *Epiphanius*, 226. The old Greek harbor town of Salamis had been destroyed in earthquakes at the beginning of the fourth century, and refounded under Constantius II as Constantia. Even into the fifth century, however, Christian sources refer to Epiphanius as bishop of Salamis; likely the reference to Salamis in Acts 13:6 influenced common usage. Jerome refers to him as *Cypri Salaminae episcopus* (*De viris inlustribus* 114; *Hieronymus: Liber de viris inlustribus; Gennadius: Liber de viris inlustribus*, ed. E.C. Richardson, Texte und Untersuchungen zur Geschichte der altchristlichen Literatur 14.1a [Leipzig: J.C. Hinrichs, 1896], 51); *Vita Hilarionis* prologus [PL 23:29]; *Ep.* 127.5.1 [CSEL 54:149]);

disappointments;[23] perhaps he had been picked from afar by the Cypriot bishops due to his growing renown as a monastic leader.[24] Whatever the case, after being installed in the late 360s in his new and fairly obscure see, by the early 370s he had developed enough of a reputation that monastic and ecclesiastical leaders in other provinces of the eastern Roman Empire began turning to him for theological guidance. According to his own writings, he was a close colleague of Athanasius of Alexandria and possibly imagined taking up his mantle of Nicene authority after that bishop died in 373. He became engaged in multiple theological controversies, from Cyprus to Constantinople to Jerusalem to Rome, eventually dying on a sea voyage home from Constantinople in the early fifth century. By the sixth century, when an anonymous pilgrim from Piacenza, Italy, visited the city of Constantia on his way to the Holy Land, Epiphanius's saintly tomb was a site of veneration.[25]

Epiphanius was not a prolific writer. As far as our sources show, he never wrote except upon request from others. Only a few of his letters survive, either in fragments incorporated into later works of his own or translated into Latin by Jerome in the 390s. He wrote a major theological treatise in the early 370s, the so-called *Ancoratus*, at the request of monks and ecclesiastics in Syria and then, a few years later, completed the enormous and complex *Panarion*, which itself contains several

---

likewise the Greek historian Sozomen calls him Σαλαμῖνος τῆς Κύπρου ἐπίσκοπος (Sozomen, *Historia ecclesiastica* 6.32.2–3; 8.14.1 [GCS n.F. 4:282–88, 367]).

23. Some scholars speculate that Epiphanius had hoped to be named bishop of Eleutheropolis after the death of Eutychius or (alternately) that theological disputes with Eutychius before his death drove Epiphanius out of Palestine; see the summary of Young Richard Kim, "Epiphanius of Cyprus vs. John of Jerusalem: Improper Ordination and the Escalation of the Origenist Controversy," in *Episcopal Elections in Late Antiquity*, ed. Johan Leemans, Peter van Nuffelen, Shawn W.J. Keough, and Carla Nicolaye, Arbeiten zur Kirchengeschichte 119 (Berlin: De Gruyter, 2011), 412 n. 4.

24. Kim, *Epiphanius*, 141–57.

25. *Itinerarium Antonini Placenti* 1 (CCL 175:129): "We went out from Constantinople to the island of Cyprus, into the city of Constantia where Saint Epiphanius rests. It is a beautiful city, delightful, adorned with date palms." The Piacenza pilgrim probably made land in Cyprus around 570.

earlier works by Epiphanius, also at the request of distant ecclesiastics. Both of these works seem to have circulated widely, despite their rather rough Greek style. Indeed, their roughness gives us a sense of their production; Frank Williams, translator of the *Panarion*, has pointed out that

> the huge *Panarion*, begun and finished within three years, is for the most part oral Greek. It was chiefly dictated, we may suppose in haste, and taken down just as Epiphanius delivered it. His stenographer and scribe, the deacons Anatolius and Hypatius, sign their names at the end of *De Fide* [Epiphanius's long, concluding doxological chapter]. Presumably Epiphanius had notes before him, or copies of some of his sources, but much of his composition is plainly *ad lib*.[26]

This characterization of Epiphanius as hasty author, dictating but not editing his works before sending them off, stands in stark contrast to figures like Augustine or Gregory of Nazianzus, whose careful management of their own literary legacies can sometimes obscure their original contexts. The voice preserved in the pages of Epiphanius's writings is as close as we get to the living voice of an ancient bishop, grammatical mistakes and all.

After the production of the *Panarion* Epiphanius became involved in trying to resolve the complicated episcopal dramas of nearby Antioch, which, in the late 370s, had at least one too many bishops. Despite theological affinities, he does not seem to have been present at the Council of Constantinople in 381, or at least he is not among the signatories who stayed until the end. Scholars have posited that Epiphanius's opposition to the settlement of the tangled confusion surrounding the contested Antiochene episcopacy led to his absence.[27] Epiphanius supported the episcopacy of Paulinus, while the council chose his rival, Meletius, who even chaired the council until his sudden death. Soon after the council, Epiphanius traveled to Rome with Paulinus of Antioch to seek the support of the bishop there, Damasus. Their traveling companion and

26. Williams, *Panarion*, 1:xxix.
27. Nautin, "Épiphane," 622.

(perhaps) translator was Jerome, an ambitious monk from the West returning home after a sojourn among Syrian monks. During a long stay in the city of Rome, where they pleaded Paulinus's case to the sympathetic Damasus, Epiphanius convinced a wealthy widow named Paula to embrace the monastic life along with her household.[28]

Epiphanius's activities in the 380s are not particularly clear, but by the end of the decade we see him entangled in theological controversies in both Egypt and Palestine, spearheading a transprovincial movement against the teachings of Origen of Alexandria espoused by monks of the desert. During this period he also wrote at least two biblical commentaries, both of which survive only in Greek fragments and translations: *On Weights and Measures* and *On Twelve Gems*.[29] In the early 390s Epiphanius was ranging around his old Palestinian stomping grounds: illicitly ordaining local monks, angrily tearing down a church curtain with an image on it, and challenging Bishop John of Jerusalem during church services.[30] By the late 390s, the Origenist controversy roiled the major urban centers of the East, fueled largely by Epiphanius's rancor and influence.[31] The dawning years of the fifth century find the elderly bishop of Constantia in the capital of Constantinople, facing off against Bishop John Chrysostom. On a ship back to Cyprus, in 402 or 403, Epiphanius died—by now possibly in his eighties, a towering presence across the Christian Roman Empire, remembered by his longtime ally Jerome as "the father of nearly all the bishops" (*patrem paene omnium episcoporum*).[32]

---

28. Jerome recounts this story in his *Epitaphium Paulae* (*Ep.* 104), written at Paula's death in 404; I discuss these incidents in chapter 1.

29. See my discussion of these texts below.

30. Much of these aggressions is recounted in Epiphanius's letter to John of Jerusalem (surviving in a Latin translation by Jerome as his *Ep.* 51) and in Jerome's own treatise *Contra Ioannem Hierosolymitanum*.

31. On Epiphanius's role in the fourth-century Origenist controversy, see Elizabeth A. Clark, *The Origenist Controversy: The Cultural Construction of an Early Christian Debate* (Princeton, NJ: Princeton University Press, 1992), 86–104.

32. Jerome, *Contra Ioannem Hiersolymitanum* 12 (PL 23:365).

There is much, of course, that we do not know about Epiphanius's life and times. He nowhere gives a strict narrative account of his own *curriculum vitae*; he does little more than incorporate some sparse incidents here and there in his writing. What information we do have from Epiphanius and other contemporaries is no more reliable than what we can glean from any other highly rhetorical and artistic representations of famous men and women that survive from this period. We don't know about crucial moments in his life: Why did he become a monk? How did he end up in Cyprus? Was he at the Council of Constantinople and, if not, why not? What we know about Epiphanius is, seemingly, only what he wants us to know. From this careful persona we steal no glimpses into the interior psyche of a "great man"; I am arguing, however, that we can espy the cultural landscape of a dawning Christian Roman Empire.

EPIPHANIUS'S WRITINGS

Since we know Epiphanius only from his writings, it is worth surveying his surviving corpus and its extant remains. Epiphanius's corpus is quite narrow in comparison with his prolific contemporaries, but complicated enough in its transmission to merit some discussion at the outset. Here I briefly survey what we know about the circumstances of each of Epiphanius's surviving written works, and note the editions and translations cited in this book. While Epiphanius's most famous writings survive in reliable Greek versions, other texts survive in fragments, translations, or citations. I indicate those sources I discuss in the main body of the work with an asterisk (*); all others are included here for context. As far as we can tell, all of Epiphanius's extant writings date from after his ascendancy to the episcopal throne of Constantia (Salamis) in 367.

Letters

Very little of Epiphanius's correspondence survives, and almost none of it in the original Greek. Jerome, for instance, mentions a presumably well-known letter Epiphanius composed at the death of his monastic mentor Hilarion, but this letter is not extant.[33] Basil of Caesarea replies to correspondence from Epiphanius with both theological concessions and heresiological information; Epiphanius's side of the correspondence does not survive.[34] Pieces of some letters of Epiphanius survive quoted in two Syriac *florilegia*.[35] Fragments of three letters concatenated at the end of Severus of Antioch's *Contra impium Grammaticum* seem reasonably authentic and (according to Joseph Lebon) date to the early years of Epiphanius's episcopal career.[36] Since they have been extracted for a particular theological purpose (i.e., defending Severus's Monophysite Christology), their larger contexts are difficult to infer. Lebon also defends the authenticity of a letter of Epiphanius written against a certain "Dorotheus," who has Apollinarian sympathies, preserved in several fragments in another fifth-century Monophysite *florilegium*.[37]

We also possess a piece of an early letter in the original Greek, written possibly in 370,[38] concerning the appropriate date of Easter; but its

---

33. Jerome, *Vita Hilaronis* 1 (PL 23:29): "Sanctus Epiphanius Salamine Cypri episcopus, qui cum Hilarione plurimum versatus est, laudem eius brevi epistola scripserit."

34. Basil, *Ep.* 258 (PG 32:948–53). See my discussion in chapters 1 and 5.

35. On these fragments, see Nautin, "Épiphane," 628–29.

36. These fragments can be found in Joseph Lebon, *Seueri Antiocheni liber contra impium Gramamaticum*, CSCO 101-2 (Leuven: CSCO, 1938–52), 101:318–20 (Syr.) and 102:235–36 (Lat.). On the authenticity of these fragments, see Joseph Lebon, "Sur quelques fragments de lettres attribués à S. Épiphane de Salamine," in *Miscellanea Giovanni Mercati*, vol. 1, *Bibbia—Letteratura cristiana antica*, Studi e Testi 121 (Vatican City: Biblioteca Apostolica Vaticana, 1946), 146–58. Two of the fragments are tied to geographic locations in Syria (Pisidia and Antioch, presumably Antioch-on-the-Orontes): possibly Severus had access to a local collection of Epiphanius's letters? For the authenticity and date of the first fragment ("on the dating of the Pasch"), Lebon relies on a fragmentary letter from Athanasius to Epiphanius preserved in the *Chronicon Paschale* (PG 92:76) on the same subject. But on this letter, see David Brakke, "Athanasius' *Epistula ad Epiphanium* and Liturgical Reform in Alexandria," *SP* 36 (2001): 482–88.

37. The text is found in Ignaz Rucker, *Florilegium Edessenum Anonymum (Syriace ante 562)*, Sitzungberichte der Bayerischen Akademie der Wissenschaften, Phil.-Hist. Abteilung 5 (Munich: Verlag der Bayerischen Akademie der Wissenschaften, 1933). See Lebon, "Quelques fragments," 158–73; Lebon is agnostic on a date for this letter (173 n. 94).

38. So Dechow, *Dogma and Mysticism*, 54, following Lebon, "Quelques fragments," 154. Note, however, that Lebon bases his dating on the confluence of this Greek fragment,

circumstances (other than the immediate festival debate) are murky as well.[39] One other early letter survives complete in Greek. In this epistle to "beloved children and brothers in Arabia," Epiphanius defends the lifelong virginity of Mary against detractors. Epiphanius mentions this *Epistula ad Arabos* in his chapter against the Apollinarians in the *Panarion*,[40] and then includes a copy of the entire letter in the subsequent chapter of the *Panarion*.[41] This long letter is our only surviving letter by Epiphanius in the original Greek.

Two letters written by Epiphanius during the Origenist controversy survive translated into Latin by Jerome. The first, more substantive letter is Epiphanius's *Epistula ad Ioannem Hierosolymitanum** (Letter to Bishop John of Jerusalem), written in 394 at the beginning of hostilities between the two bishops. While the beginning of the letter constitutes a halfhearted apology for Epiphanius's improper ordination of a monk in John's episcopal jurisdiction, the bulk of the epistle lays out Epiphanius's charges against John as an Origenist heretic. Jerome later admitted, when criticized by his theological opponents, that his translation of this letter was rather loose (*ad sensum*). In a defense of his translation procedures, Jerome "confessed" that "when I translate Greek (except for the sacred Scriptures, where even the order of the words is a mystery), not word for word but sense for sense do I express," citing the

---

the Syriac fragment of a letter on the same subject preserved by Severus of Antioch (see above), and the letter of Athanasius to Epiphanius "the bishop" (thus, written between 367 and 373). The Athanasius letter is, thus, a linchpin of Lebon's dating, called into question by Brakke, "Athanasius' *Epistula*."

39. The portion of the letter survives in a single, fifteenth-century manuscript (Ambrosianus gr. 515, folios 237–39, surrounded by two empty pages), along with selections from Basil of Caesarea and Gregory of Nyssa on creation, Athanasius's *Life of Antony*, and Manuel Moschopoulos (a late Byzantine author); see the description in Aemidius Martini and Dominicus Bassi, *Catalogus codicum graecorum Bibliothecae Ambrosianae*, vol. 2 (Milan: Impensis u. Hoepli: 1906), 620.

40. Epiphanius, *Panarion* 77.36.3 (GCS 37:448), since some claim Apollinarius's followers deny the virgin birth.

41. Epiphanius, *Panarion* 78.2.1–24.6 (GCS 37:452–75); the letter forms the bulk of this chapter against the "defamers of Mary" (Ἀντιδικομαριαμιτῶν).

precedent of Cicero (*De optimo genere oratorum* 23).[42] Nonetheless, the Latin version still retains much of the flavor and tone of Epiphanius.

The final section of this letter also survives in a Greek version, comprising Epiphanius's *conclusio* and an addendum in which Epiphanius apologizes for tearing down a church curtain with a human image on it, also in John's jurisdiction.[43] These selections may be from the original Greek letter of Epiphanius (they accord rather closely with Jerome's Latin version), or they may be a Greek retranslation of Jerome's version. They first appear during the eighth-century iconoclast controversy, at which point Epiphanius's objection to an image of "Christ or one of the saints" on the Palestinian curtain was adduced against the iconophiles.[44] The iconophile patriarch Nicephorus of Constantinople, in the ninth century, claimed that both the Greek and the Latin postscripts of the *Epistula ad Ioannem* were forgeries, along with other supposedly iconoclastic texts of Epiphanius (see below).[45] I have only consulted the Latin translation of the *Epistula ad Ioannem* in this book, and do not discuss the incident recounted in the final chapter.

---

42. Jerome, *Ep.* 57.5.2 (CSEL 54:508). This letter in manuscripts bears the subtitle "On the best method of translating" (also an allusion to Cicero's "On the best type of orators"); see the commentary of G.J.M. Bartelink, *Hieronymus: Liber de optimo genere interpretandi (Epistula 57): Ein Kommentar*, Mnemosyne Supplement 61 (Leiden: Brill, 1980); and William Adler, "*Ad Verbum* or *Ad Sensum*: The Christianization of a Latin Translation Formula in the Fourth Century," in *Pursuing the Text: Studies in Honor of Ben Zion Wacholder on the Occasion of His Seventieth Birthday*, ed. John C. Reeves and John Kampen (Sheffield: Sheffield Academic Press, 1994), 321–48. On Jerome's translations in the context of the Origenist controversy, see my "'What Has Rome to Do with Bethlehem?' Cultural Capital(s) and Religious Imperialism in Late Ancient Christianity," *Classical Receptions Journal* 2 (2011): 29–45.

43. Epiphanius, *Ep. ad Ioannem* (= Jerome, *Ep.* 51) 8–9 (CSEL 54:410–12).

44. See the discussion of P. Maas, "Die ikonoklastische Episode in dem Brief des Epiphanios an Johannes," *BZ* 30 (1929–30): 279–86, who includes the Greek version of these chapters from the *Ep. ad Ioannem* on pp. 281–83. Note also that our surviving Latin copies of *Ep. ad Ioannem* also date to the ninth century, and later (CSEL 54:395, *app. crit.*).

45. Nicephorus's argument is summarized, and defended, by Steven Bigham, *Epiphanius of Salamis, Doctor of Iconoclasm? Deconstruction of a Myth*, Patristic Theological Library (Rollinsford: Orthodox Research Institute, 2008), 43–46, 127–32.

A second, very brief letter from Epiphanius directly to Jerome survives (written around 400), in Jerome's Latin translation, celebrating the condemnation of Origen at Theophilus of Alexandria's synod and directing Jerome to translate Theophilus's synodical letter, which had been sent to Epiphanius.[46]

Fragments of a letter to the emperor Theodosius also survive in Greek (*Epistula ad imperatorem Theodosium*), preserved in the refutation of Nicephorus of Constantinople (who claims this iconoclastic letter is another forgery) and in other writings that date from the eighth- and ninth-century iconoclast controversies. If authentic, this letter to Theodosius probably dates to the early 390s. Karl Holl extracted the fragments and published them in the early twentieth century, defending their authenticity, along with other iconoclastic writings ascribed to Epiphanius in later centuries.[47] These pieces of textual flotsam and jetsam have complicated constructions of Epiphanius's theology, activity, and politics in the years of the Origenist controversy, a period deeply concerned with images, materiality, and orthodoxy.[48]

For such an active bishop, with such a long tenure in his bishopric (more than thirty years), we might be surprised that so few of his letters

---

46. Epiphanius to Jerome: *Ep.* 91 (CSEL 55:145–56); Theophilus's synodical letter: *Ep.* 92 (CSEL 55:147–55).

47. The texts originally collated by Holl have been reordered, with a German translation, by Hans Georg Thümmel, "Die bilderfeindlichen Schriften des Epiphanius von Salamis," *Byzantinoslavica* 47 (1986): 169–88, texts on 181–88. These other iconoclastic fragments include a *Testament to the Citizens of Salamis* and an *Oration against Image-Makers*, both also excerpted in Nicephorus's refutation and in other documents from the iconoclastic councils (see Thümmel, "Bilderfeindlichen Schriften," 169–71). On these various fragments, see the negative assessments of Bigham, *Epiphanius of Salamis*, and the more positive viewpoint (placing Epiphanius's iconoclasm in both theological and political contexts) of Olga Solovieva, "Epiphanius of Salamis and His Invention of Iconoclasm in the Fourth Century A.D.," *Fides et Historia* 42 (2010): 21–46; and Solovieva, "Epiphanius of Salamis between Church and State: New Perspectives on the Iconoclastic Fragments," *ZAC* 16 (2012): 344–67.

48. Clark, *Origenist Controversy*, 103–4; Patricia Cox Miller, *The Corporeal Imagination: Signifying the Holy in Late Ancient Christianity*, Divinations (Philadelphia: University of Pennsylvania Press, 2009), 7, 22–23.

survive.⁴⁹ Several recent studies have explored the role that an author's desire to craft a self-conscious literary persona played in the compilation and circulation of letter collections.⁵⁰ It seem evident that Epiphanius kept copies of some of his letters (and thus was able to include his *Epistula ad Arabos* in the *Panarion*), as did some of his recipients (thus the cluster of letters preserved in Syriac). It seems equally clear that Epiphanius had little interest in fashioning a particular literary persona through epistolography, and so neither he nor his successors on Cyprus saw fit to collect or circulate his letters. I do not suggest Epiphanius was uninterested in crafting a literary legacy or persona; but rather his preferred literary ground was ultimately the treatise rather than the letter.

Treatises

Epiphanius has left two theological treatises that are still extant in Greek, and two biblical commentaries that survive in Greek fragments and more complete versions in non-Greek translations.

The *Ancoratus** was composed around 373–374.⁵¹ The title seems to be Epiphanius's, drawing on a metaphor in his prologue of a ship seeking safe harbor; furthermore, his secretary Anatolius mentions it in his subscription: "I, Anatolius, who wrote this book of the treatise named

---

49. Lebon, "Quelques fragments," 173, notes pensively: "La sort a été particulièrement cruel pour une correspondence qui, à en juger par le temperament curieux et combatif de son auteur, dut être considerable et variée."

50. See, recently, Andrew Cain, *Letters of Jerome: Asceticism, Biblical Exegesis, and the Construction of Christian Authority in Late Antiquity*, OECS (Oxford: Oxford University Press, 2009); Michele Renée Salzman, *The Letters of Symmachus*, Society of Biblical Literature Writings from the Greco-Roman World 30 (Leiden: Brill, 2012); Jennifer Ebbeler, *Disciplining Christians: Correction and Community in Augustine's Letters*, OSLA (Oxford: Oxford University Press, 2012).

51. See Oliver Kösters, *Die Trinitätslehre des Epiphanius von Salamis: Ein Kommentar zum "Ancoratus*," Forschungen zur Kirchen- und Dogmengeschichte 86 (Göttingen: Vandenhoek & Ruprecht), 77–116.

'Ancoratus.'"⁵² On what exactly is supposed to be "anchored" (the faith? the reader? the treatise?), I follow Oliver Kösters and Young Richard Kim, who think it makes most sense to understand the title (as conveyed by Anatolius) as *Ankurōtos logos*, "the well-anchored treatise."⁵³ The treatise was written upon request from ecclesiastics in Asia Minor whose community, or communities, had been disrupted by debates over the divinity of the Holy Spirit; in response, Epiphanius composed a wide-ranging exploration of the orthodox faith with particular attention to the erroneous theologies of Origen, Apollinarius, and so-called Spirit-Fighters. Material from the *Ancoratus* seems preparatory for (and is indeed reused) in the *Panarion*, suggesting overlap in composition. The *Ancoratus* circulated rather widely and was translated into Coptic by the sixth century, along with other works by Epiphanius.⁵⁴ The surviving Greek manuscripts come from the later middle ages,⁵⁵ when it seems to have been understood largely as a companion piece to the *Panarion*.⁵⁶

I cite the *Ancoratus* by volume and page number of the recently revised critical edition of the Griechischen Christlichen Schriftsteller series by Marc Bergermann and Christian-Friedrich Collatz, who repair and restore the earlier critical edition of Karl Holl.⁵⁷ All translations are my own, although I have frequently consulted the recent and invaluable translation of Young Richard Kim in the Fathers of the Church series.

---

52. Epiphanius, *Ancoratus* 119.16: ἐγὼ ὁ Ἀνατόλιος ὁ γράψας τοῦτο τὸ βιβλίον τοῦ Ἀγκυρωτοῦ ἐπονομασθέντος λόγου (GCS n.F. 10.1:149).

53. Kösters, *Trinitätslehre*, 107–11; and Young Richard Kim, *Saint Epiphanius of Cyprus, Ancoratus*, FC 128 (Washington, DC: Catholic University of America Press, 2014), 8.

54. Enzo Lucchesi, "Un corpus épiphanien en copte," *Analecta Bollandiana* 99 (1981): 95–99. To date, Coptologists have recovered significant portions of the *Ancoratus* and the treatise *De XII gemmis* (see below).

55. See the discussion of Kim, *Ancoratus*, 9; and Kösters, *Trinitätslehre*, 77–80.

56. Photius, *Bibliotheca*, codex 122 refers to the *Ancoratus* as "a sort of synopsis of the *Panarion*" (σύνοψις ὥσπερ τῶν Παναριῶν), in *Photius, Bibliothèque*, vol. 2, ed. René Henry, Collection Byzantine (Paris: Éditions 'Les Belles Lettres,' 1960), 97.

57. See especially GCS n.F. 10.2 outlining the *addenda* and *corrigenda* of GCS n.F. 10.1, which contains the entirety of the *Ancoratus* and the first thirty-three chapters of the *Panarion*; and Kim, *Epiphanius*, 6 n. 19.

Epiphanius must have started composing, or at least mapping out, the *Panarion**, or "Medicine Chest [against Heresies]," while he was still working on the *Ancoratus*. *Ancoratus* 12.7–13.8 (GCS n.F. 10.1:20–22) already lists the eighty heresies (twenty before Christ, sixty after) of the *Panarion*. The main composition of the *Panarion* took place roughly in the years 375–378. Like the *Ancoratus*, the *Panarion* was composed upon request: a certain Acacius and Paul had "heard the names applied by Your Honor to the heresies," and asked for a full explanation of them.[58] Whether they had read the *Ancoratus* and were puzzled by the (out-of-the-blue) list of heresies, or whether Epiphanius was publicizing his list by other means, we cannot know. Epiphanius composed the *Panarion* rather quickly (in under three years), considering its length, complexity, and (presumably) his other episcopal duties during this period. As is the case with the *Ancoratus*, Epiphanius's compositional style seems to have left little time for editing after his initial dictation.

The *Panarion* contains a wealth of other Christian documents (from both "heretics" and "orthodox"): our only Greek fragments of Irenaeus's *Against Heresies*, Ptolemy's *Letter to Flora*, and various documents pertaining to theological struggles during Epiphanius's own time, to name just a few. In addition to these texts, Epiphanius has also included writings of his own, dictated directly into the *Panarion*, including a lengthy "refutation" (*elenchos*) of Marcion's Bible, which he had written "some years before" (*apo etōn hikanōn*)[59] and later embedded in *Panarion* 42 (against the Marcionites),[60] and his aforementioned *Epistula ad Arabos*, in defense of Mary's virginity. These are merely the two earlier writings he names: given that he also copies material from the *Ancoratus* (sometimes without signaling that he is doing so[61]) we might also imagine

---

58. *Epistula Acacii et Pauli* 1.9 (GCS n.F. 10.1:154).
59. Epiphanius, *Panarion* 42.10.2 (GCS 31:106).
60. Epiphanius, *Panarion* 42.11–12 (GCS 31:107–82). Note that, although this *refutatio* is only two chapters of the *Panarion*, it covers 75 pages in the critical edition.
61. See, for instance, *Panarion* 70.7.6–8.4 (GCS 37:239–40), which repeats the argument of *Ancoratus* 54.1–7 (GCS n.F. 10.1:63–64).

Epiphanius economically recycling other earlier written materials at hand that have not otherwise survived. To the *Panarion* Epiphanius has appended a short treatise *De fide** (On Faith), which first dilates upon the central metaphor of the *Panarion* from Song of Songs 6:8–9,[62] then lists forty-four Greek philosophies (some of the "maidens without number" of Song 6:8), as well as various other philosophies and mysteries, before rehearsing the tenets of his orthodox faith. To the treatise *De fide* he also appends a (perhaps preexisting) mini-treatise *De regulis** (On Rules), which I discuss in chapter 3. The *Panarion* is, among modern scholars, Epiphanius's best-known work and was arguably such in late antiquity as well. It circulated throughout the Christian world even during Epiphanius's lifetime, and became the foundational text of subsequent premodern Christian heresiography.[63]

The various, mostly partial Greek manuscripts of the *Panarion* were collated and published in the early twentieth century by Karl Holl,[64] whose critical editions have been updated by Jürgen Dummer, Marc Bergermann, and Christian-Friedrich Collatz in the Griechischen Christlichen Schriftsteller series. I cite the *Panarion* by volume and page number from this series. All translations from the Greek are my own, in consultation with the revised two-volume English translation of Frank Williams.[65]

Later in his life, Epiphanius wrote two biblical commentaries. Neither survives in Greek, except in fragments. The treatise conventionally

---

62. Song 6:8–9: "There are sixty queens and eighty concubines, and maidens without number. My dove, my perfect one, is the only one, the darling of her mother, flawless to her that bore her" (NRSV). The "sixty queens" are the post-Christ heresies, and "eighty concubines" are all of the heresies since Adam. The single "dove" is orthodoxy.

63. See Averil Cameron, "How to Read Heresiology," in Martin and Miller, *Cultural Turn*, 193–212, esp. 197–200.

64. See his account of the various manuscripts and their families: Karl Holl, *Die handschriftliche Überlieferung des Epiphanius (Ancoratus und Panarion)*, Texte und Untersuchungen zur Geschichte der altchristlichen Literatur 36 (Leipzig: J. C. Hinrichs, 1910).

65. Williams, *Panarion, Book I*; and *The Panarion of Epiphanius*, vol. 2, *Books II and III, De fide*, trans. Frank Williams, 2nd rev. ed., NHMS 79 (Leiden: Brill: 2013).

titled *De mensuris et ponderibus** (On Weights and Measures) is actually a compendium of biblical information, which, at its core, contains a description of the different terms for measurement found in the Bible. In this treatise Epiphanius also describes the text of the Bible (including a detailed description of the sigla and columns of the Hexapla, Origen's six-column "critical edition" of the Septuagint), its translation history, and geographic information on biblical sites. The treatise can be dated to 392 based on Epiphanius's listing of the emperors and consuls at the time of composition (see *De mensuris et ponderibus* 20). According to the Syriac preface, Epiphanius wrote the treatise upon request from a "priest" (*qashisha*') of the "Persian race" (*persaya' begensa*') he met at the imperial court in Constantinople (*De mensuris et ponderibus* 1).[66]

The entire treatise survives in Syriac (*Epiphanius' Treatise on Weights and Measures: The Syriac Version*, ed. James Elmer Dean, Studies in Ancient Oriental Civilizations 11 [Chicago: University of Chicago Press, 1935]),[67] with significant fragments of the original Greek (E. Moutsoulas, "To Peri metrōn kai stathmōn ergon Epiphaniou tou Salaminos," *Theologia* 44 [1973]: 157–98), as well as selections in Georgian (*Les versions géorgiennes d'Épiphane de Chypre, Traité des poids et de mésures*, ed. Michel van Esbroeck, CSCO 460–61 [Leuven: Peeters, 1984]) and Armenian (*The Armenian Texts of Epiphanius of Salamis "De mensuris et ponderibus,"* ed. Michael Stone and Roberta Ervine, CSCO 583 [Leuven: Peeters, 2000]).[68] I cite primarily from the Greek and Syriac versions (using Dean's chapter numbers, English pages, and Syriac folio page numbers,

---

66. *Epiphanius' Treatise on Weights and Measures: The Syriac Version*, ed. James Elmer Dean, Studies in Ancient Oriental Civilizations 11 (Chicago: University of Chicago Press, 1935), 45a (Syr.).

67. As Dean notes (*Weights and Measures*, 3), the treatise survives complete only in Syriac, and in a manuscript dated to the seventh century which has a plausible claim to be "the oldest known manuscript of Epiphanius," even eighty years after Dean wrote. Dean also lists the fragmentary Greek texts that survive (*Weights and Measures*, 4–5).

68. On the interrelation of the texts, see Michael Stone and Roberta Ervine, eds., *The Armenian Texts of Epiphanius of Salamis, "De mensuris et ponderibus,"* CSCO 583 (Leuven: Peeters, 2000), 1–5.

with the lines of Moutsoulas's Greek in parentheses where available). I use Dean's translation from the Syriac, sometimes adapted for clarity or in light of the extant Greek.

Jerome makes mention of Epiphanius's treatise *De XII gemmis** (On Twelve Gems), of which he possessed a copy, describing it as "most full of knowledge" (*plenissimam scientiam*).[69] Assuming that Epiphanius personally gave Jerome a copy soon after its composition, many modern studies assert that *De XII gemmis* was written around 394, when we know Epiphanius visited Palestine.[70] According to the prologue, Epiphanius has written this treatise (like all of his others) at the request of a fellow cleric, this time one Bishop Diodore of Tyre.[71] The treatise comprises naturalist and allegorical interpretations of the twelve gemstones in the breastplate of the high priest (Exod 28:17–21), along with a survey of different biblical orderings of the sons of Israel.

Epiphanius's *De XII gemmis* does not survive in the original Greek, except in fragments and epitomes.[72] A partial, early Latin translation

---

69. Jerome, *Ep.* 64.21.1 (CSEL 54:613), in his letter to Fabiola, written around 397, providing a *terminus ante quem*. He also mentions his possession of the treatise in his commentaries on Isaiah and Ezekiel, written in the second decade of the fifth century (*Commentarius in Isaiam* 15.54.11/12 [PL 24:525]; *Commentarius in Ezechielem* 9.28.11 [PL 25:271]).

70. Dechow, *Dogma and Mysticism,* 249; but Nautin, "Épiphane," 628, is agnostic on this point. Modern editors of the Georgian (*Epiphanius De gemmis: The Old Georgian Version and the Fragments of the Armenian Version,* ed. Robert P. Blake and Henri de Vis, Studies and Documents [London: Christophers, 1934], xiii) and Armenian texts (*Epiphanius von Salamis, Über die zwölf Steine im hohepriesterlichen Brustschild [De duodecim gemmis rationalis],* ed. Felix Albrecht and Arthur Manukyan, Gorgias Eastern Christian Studies 37 [Piscataway, NJ: Gorgias Press, 2014], vii) also assume Epiphanius gave Jerome the copy during the visit to Palestine recounted in Jerome's *Contra Ioannem Hierosolymitanum*.

71. We know little about Diodore, except that (according to Rufinus, *Historia ecclesiastica* 11.21 [PL 21:527]) he had been consecrated bishop of Tyre by members of Paulinus of Antioch's (Epiphanius's theological ally) Nicene faction sometime before 373 (if the addressee of Athanasius's *Ep.* 64 [PG 26:1261–62, preserved in Latin by Facundus of Hermiane] is, indeed, the same Diodore). Other modern scholars assume the dedicatee must have been the more famous Diodore of Tarsus (e.g., Johannes Quasten, *Patrology* [Utrecht: Spectrum, 1966], 3:389).

72. On these epitomes, see Blake and Vis, *Epiphanius,* xiv–xvi and xxiii–xxv.

was preserved in the so-called *Collectio Avellana,* a sixth-century compendium of documents primarily dealing with the Roman episcopacy.[73] The Old Georgian text and Coptic fragments were published by Robert Blake and Henri de Vis in 1934,[74] with a survey of all known surviving fragments up to that point. In 2014, a previously unedited, extensive Armenian version, possibly translated from the original Greek in the seventh century, was edited and published with a German translation by Felix Albrecht and Arthur Manukyan.[75] The surviving versions disagree on the order of the treatise; the Old Georgian places the survey of tribes at the end, while the Coptic, Latin, and Armenian place it before the allegorical reading of the stones. Blake, who had not seen the Armenian version, assumed that the Old Georgian preserved the original order.[76] Albrecht and Manukyan, on the strength of their Armenian version and the Coptic and Latin versions (which are probably the oldest extant versions of the treatise), place the allegorical section at the end, after the ordering of the tribes.[77] I discuss these discrepancies and their relation to the nature of the treatise in chapter 4. To date, the Old Georgian version seems to be the most complete, and so I cite the text

---

73. *Epistulae imperatorum pontificum aliorum avellana quae dicitur collectio,* ed. Otto Günther, CSEL 35 (Vienna: F. Tempsky, 1898), 743–73. Epiphanius's *De XII gemmis* is the last document in the *Collectio.* Günther postulates (754n) that this treatise, which "barely pertains" (*minime pertinere*) to the rest of the collection, was added at a later date for "some reason" (*casu quodam*). The obscure nature of this treatise by Epiphanius led medievalist Patrick Amory to assume that the Constantia mentioned in Günther's footnote was the city in Scythia (former Tomis, the site of Ovid's exile), a region otherwise well represented in the *Collectio* (Amory, *People and Identity in Ostrogothic Italy, 489–554* [Cambridge: Cambridge University Press, 1997], 112 n. 18 and 130 n. 131); followed also by Kate Blair-Dixon, "Memory and Authority in Sixth-Century Rome: The *Liber Pontificalis* and the *Collectio Avellana,*" in *Religion, Dynasty, and Patronage in Early Christian Rome, 300–900,* ed. Kate Cooper and Julia Hillner (Cambridge: Cambridge University Press, 2007), 68 n. 8.

74. On the surviving Coptic pages, see Lucchesi, "Corpus épiphanien."

75. Albrecht and Manukyan, *Über die zwölf Steine,* xiii, note that Albrecht is preparing a new edition of the extant Greek texts.

76. Blake and Vis, *Epiphanius,* xxxviii.

77. Albrecht and Manukyan, *Über die zwölf Steine,* xi-xii, following the in-depth review of Blake and Vis by W. Hengstenberg in *BZ* 37.2 (1937): 400–408.

by the page numbers of Blake's English translation, which I have modified to update proper names in English and in consultation with the German translation of Albrecht and Manukyan.

Pseudepigrapha

Over the centuries various *spuria* have attached themselves to Epiphanius, often because of his reputation as a strict orthodox preacher and as an antiquarian author. All of these *spuria* were edited and translated into Latin, along with Epiphanius's own works and the Greek *Life of Epiphanius*, by the seventeenth-century French Jesuit Denis Pétau (Dionysius Petavius).[78] Pétau's editions and translations were reedited and republished by Migne in the nineteenth-century Patrologia Graeca (volumes 41–43). From very early on, capsule summaries of the *Panarion* circulated alongside the text, labeled *Anakephalaioses* (or *Epitomes*), and soon came to be considered the work of Epiphanius. In the Middle Ages, Epiphanius was often credited with authorship of the *Physiologus*, a naturalist treatise that, indeed, Epiphanius seems to have known and relied upon.[79] A book titled the *Lives of the Prophets* likewise passed under Epiphanius's name. In addition several homilies once ascribed to Epiphanius are now taken to be spuriously attributed, including a cluster on Easter Week (Palm Sunday, Christ's death, resurrection, and ascension) and "Mary Theotokos."[80]

---

78. Dionsyius Petavius [Denis Pétau], *Sancti Patris Nostri Epiphanii Constantiae sive Salaminis in Cypro, episcopi, opera omnia*, 2 vols. (Paris: Sumptibus Michaelis Sonnii, Claudii Morelli, et Sebastiani Cramoisy, 1622). The first volume contained Pétau's introduction and the Greek *vita* (see my discussion in chapter 6) along with the *Panarion*; the second volume contained the rest of Epiphanius's authentic and spurious works.

79. Alan Scott, "The Date of the *Physiologus*," *VC* 52 (1998): 430–41, esp. 433–34, and 440, where Scott notes that the generic similarities between *De XII gemmis* and the *Physiologus* may explain "why Epiphanius is among the attributed authors of the *Physiologus* in the Middle Ages." A version of the *Physiologus* is included among the *dubia et spuria* in the Patrologia Graeca (PG 43:517–34).

80. These homilies were collected in early modern editions and included in the Patrologia Graeca (PG 43:427–508).

This textually diverse corpus of writings that attached themselves to Epiphanius's name raises intriguing, but ultimately unanswerable, questions about Epiphanius's writerly production as well as his own self-image and self-presentation as a writer. For instance, we must assume that, as bishop of Constantia and archbishop of Cyprus, Epiphanius did, in fact, deliver sermons.[81] Yet Epiphanius did not (like many of his episcopal colleagues) have these sermons transcribed, edited, or published during his lifetime or arrange for their publication after his death. The dearth of authentic homilies by Epiphanius reminds us of the tremendous amount of invisible labor involved in the publication of sermons, from the amanuenses to the scribes to the copyists, as well as the material costs: it is not by chance that we can linger over the public speeches of Basil, Augustine, Jerome, or Gregory of Nyssa. These Christian intellectuals (or their sponsors) made provision for the public dissemination of their orations. Epiphanius was certainly not shy about sharing his opinions, so why didn't he use available resources to make his opinions known in this oratorical format? Did he draw a line between oral preaching and written works? Did he address more local concerns in his homilies that he felt were inappropriate for wider audiences? Did he simply lack the financial resources? When we consider the reach of Epiphanius's influence without the circulation of public letters and speeches (see chapter 1), his fame is perhaps even more impressive.[82]

We might also wonder, perhaps fruitlessly, about Epiphanius's library.[83] From what we can tell just from his surviving writings—especially the *Panarion*—Epiphanius must have had an impressive library

---

81. Jerome, at least, recalls seeing Epiphanius deliver a sermon in Jerusalem at the invitation of his rival Bishop John; Jerome, *Contra Ioannem Hierosolymitanum* 13–14 (PL 23:365–67).

82. For comparison, see Mark Vessey's analysis of Augustine's very self-aware attempts to "make a name" through literary channels in the late fourth century through letters: "Conference and Confession: Literary Pragmatics in Augustine's '*Apologia contra Hieronymum*,'" *JECS* 1 (1993): 175–213.

83. I plan to address Epiphanius's library in a forthcoming short study.

of Christian and non-Christian works by both "orthodox" and "heretics." Where did it come from, and what happened to it? Possibly he acquired copies of some of the works housed in the famous library of Caesarea of Palestine, built (ironically) on the remains of the personal library of Origen, whom Epiphanius condemned, while still a monk there.[84] Perhaps his bibliophilia was ignited even earlier, during his monastic youth in Egypt, when he encountered gnostic sects with "many books."[85] By the time he began to write the *Panarion* in the mid-370s, he had, at hand, a welter of texts spanning the history of Christianity to his day. No one has yet sat down to study the library of Epiphanius (although scholars make much secondhand use of it), nor have they ventured to guess what happened to Epiphanius's *thesaurus librorum* after his death. Even though Epiphanius's own written remains are comparatively modest, his work as an author raises many intriguing questions about the pace and production of Christian culture in the Theodosian age.

. . .

I have organized the chapters of this book according to several major themes of late ancient Christian culture: in this sense my cultural biography is not so much that of Epiphanius but rather of the times he reflected and shaped. My themes emerge from Epiphanius's own writings and are chosen to create a more complex picture of the culture assumed and perpetuated by Epiphanius among his contemporaries.

In chapter 1, "Celebrity," I use Epiphanius's career in order to raise questions about our assumptions about episcopal authority. I analyze Epiphanius's fame through the lens of modern celebrity studies, in which a celebrity's *function* in cultural analysis takes precedence over explaining *why* someone is famous. What cultural work did Epiphanius's

---

84. On this library, see Anthony Grafton and Megan H. Williams, *Christianity and the Transformation of the Book: Origen, Eusebius, and the Library of Caesarea* (Cambridge, MA: Harvard University Press, 2006), esp. 1–85.

85. Epiphanius notes of the "Gnostikoi" that "they have lots of books" (τὰ μὲν βιβλία αὐτῶν πολλά) (*Panarion* 26.8.1 [GCS n.F. 10.1:284]).

celebrity accomplish in his lifetime and after his death, particularly in the formation of a Christian Roman culture?

I then turn, in chapter 2, to the topic of "conversion." Epiphanius attends, throughout his corpus, to multiple changes in religious status, including conversion to the priesthood, or to heresy, as well as to and from Christianity. Instead of allowing us to view conversion as an internal psychological transformation, Epiphanius forces us to view changes in religious status along the lines of other forms of status change in the late Roman world: as the exteriorized management of difference.

Chapter 3, "Discipline," brings together Epiphanius's writings on bodily and institutional control to examine the analogous operations by which mastery and self-mastery construct Christian individuals and communities. Epiphanius's disciplinary thinking is notably improvisational, at times eschewing formal institutions and "rules" in favor of direct intervention and monitoring. The result is a series of systems (bodily, ecclesiastical, monastic, imperial) in which power is at once concealed and yet constantly exerted and contested.

Chapter 4, "Scripture," treats Epiphanius's seemingly disorganized approach to biblical interpretation as an instance of ancient antiquarianism, which operates by a very different logic than the philosophical scriptural interpretation favored by modern scholars. Loose, digressive, and idiosyncratic, Epiphanius's Bible is also a masterful demonstration of the power of knowledge in the late Roman Christian world.

Chapter 5, "Salvation," explores Epiphanius's theology of the human person and the Trinity. Both his anthropology and his theology operate according to the same logic: discrete elements (of the human or divine being) are united into a single moral unity. These theologies explain Epiphanius's particular heresiological enmities as well as his appeal: his theology of salvation is both monastic (creating space for human agency and continuity) and imperial (emphasizing masterful unity out of fragmentary diversity).

Chapter 6, "After Lives," compares two hagiographic treatments of Epiphanius: the late fifth-century or early sixth-century *Vita Epiphanii*, pseudonymously ascribed to his monastic followers; and the nineteenth-century novella *Epiphanius: The History of His Childhood and Youth, Told by Himself; A Tale of the Early Church* (1874), written by Anglo-Catholic historian Thomas Wimberley Mossman. Both *vitae* portray Epiphanius as a convert from Judaism (a story that has no parallel during his lifetime). In this final chapter I ask more broadly, what kinds of Christian cultures of difference and otherness can be constructed out of the remains of Epiphanius, and how did two very different empires—Byzantine and Victorian—make sense of him by thinking with difference?

I return, in a brief conclusion, to consider the implications of our new "cultural biography" of late antiquity: how did we end up with the field of late antiquity as it exists in the present Anglophone sphere, and what would change if we placed Epiphanius at its center?

CHAPTER ONE

Celebrity

A CELEBRITY IN LATE ANTIQUITY

In the late fourth century, caustic monk and scholar Jerome recalled to his bishop, John of Jerusalem, a recent confrontation between John and Jerome's mentor, Epiphanius:

> Is it not the case that, when you were going forth from the Resurrection Church to the cross, a crowd flowed together toward him, of every age and sex, holding up their children, kissing his feet, pulling at his fringes; and when he couldn't move forward a step, and in one place he could scarcely hold up against the sweeping flood of people, you—twisted with envy—shouted against this pompous old man (*gloriosum senem*)? And you did not blush to say to his face that he wanted and schemed to be held up.[1]

Epiphanius, the "pompous old man" (*gloriosus senex*, which we might also translate as "famous old man"), showed up his episcopal rival later that same day in his rival's church, rising after the sermon to more rejoicing (*risus*) and applause (*acclamatio*). The sheer frenzy of the crowds and the utter loathing of the rival bishop and his cronies are two sides of the same coin: Epiphanius is at one and the same time "an old

1. Jerome, *Contra Ioannem Hierosolymitanum* 11 (PL 23:364).

blowhard" (*fatuus senex*) and "the father of bishops" (*pater episcoporum*).[2] One way to describe Epiphanius, in this account—this double-sided figure of fame and renown who also draws down accusations of falseness and scheming for attention—is as a *celebrity*.

I am interested in this chapter in how we might use Epiphanius's particular form of prominence to reimagine authority in late ancient Christianity in ways distinct from more familiar terms like *status*, *authority*, or the nebulous but compelling term *power*.[3] When we frame our analyses of the authority of Christian figures in terms of *power*, we are often aiming to imagine a broader field of social relations in late antiquity.[4] Power allows us to compare Christian authorities (bishops, abbots, patriarchs, and so forth) to analogous Greek and Roman authorities (governors, emperors, and generals).[5] Applying such power or status analysis to individuals—such as Augustine, Athanasius, or John Chrysostom—coheres with our familiar narratives of continuity and transformation in late antiquity: their style of prominence makes sense in terms of larger trends and patterns.

An analysis grounded in celebrity, however, works differently. I delve more deeply into the nuances of fame and celebrity below, but for now let me point out two of the most useful and obvious connotations of the term. First, a focus on celebrity rather than authority shifts our emphasis away from cause to effect: we no longer imagine stable channels of

---

2. Jerome, *Contra Ioannem Hierosolymitanum* 11, 12 (PL 23:364, 365).

3. Charles Kurzman et al., "Celebrity Status," *Sociological Theory* 25 (2007): 363: "Celebrity is status on speed."

4. See Claudia Rapp, *Holy Bishops in Late Antiquity: The Nature of Christian Leadership in an Age of Transition*, TCH 37 (Berkeley: University of California Press, 2005), 6–18. Much of this work to position early Christian leaders into the sociocultural fabric relies (directly or indirectly) on Peter Brown's early essay, "The Rise and Function of the Holy Man in Late Antiquity," *JRS* 61 (1971): 80–101, which itself was influenced by British functionalism in sociology (see Peter Brown, "The Rise and Function of the Holy Man in Late Antiquity, 1971–1997," *JECS* 6 [1998]: 353–76).

5. An excellent example is Peter Brown, *Power and Persuasion in Late Antiquity: Toward a Christian Empire*, Curti Lectures (Madison: University of Wisconsin Press, 1992).

power producing figures of authority (bishops, governors, and so forth), but instead trace the effects of a person's prominence across multiple social fields. Once we stop asking where authority comes from, a question often slippery if not impossible to answer, we can attend instead to how it works. Second, and similarly, celebrity signifies (among other things) both immediacy and transience: the celebrity is that person with whom the crowds identify and whom they adore (or despise), but whose fame is fleeting and impermanent. Celebrities function, therefore, as condensed icons of precise historical moments.[6]

Epiphanius was, I argue, such a historically precise icon, whose shining omnipresence in the last third of the fourth century defies analysis through our standard rubrics of episcopal advancement.[7] His otherwise inexplicable fourth-century celebrity makes him historically valuable. Tracing the origins of his authority is practically impossible, but its effects are multiple and vivid. If we want to understand the cultural contours of imperial Christianity, we should take seriously those leaders who were famous in their time. Their transient fame might tell us more about their specific and contingent contexts than we might otherwise appreciate.

I am *not* arguing that Epiphanius was somehow more important or beloved in his time, raised up by talents far above his peers in ways now lost to us. He was, as my opening anecdote shows, as much despised as adored. But he was indisputably *known:* by the 370s Epiphanius was suddenly, it seems, everywhere. How he moved from a Palestinian monastery to the episcopacy of Constantia (Salamis) on Cyprus remains a mystery; modern historians guess he must have already gained some acclaim as an ascetic and vocal opponent of heresy.[8] Once bishop,

---

6. Jeffrey Alexander, "The Celebrity-Icon," *Cultural Sociology* 4 (2010): 323–36.

7. Rapp, *Holy Bishops,* draws on the ways in which bishops achieved prominence in late antiquity; when discussing Epiphanius, Rapp must rely on his posthumous *vita,* which fills in biographical lacunae that would explain his prominence through miraculous works (Rapp, *Holy Bishop,* 151, 202, 246, 259). I discuss this *vita* in chapter 6.

8. Jon Dechow, *Dogma and Mysticism in Early Christianity: Epiphanius of Cyprus and the Legacy of Origen,* PMS 13 (Macon, GA: Mercer University Press, 1988), 41: "It seems

Epiphanius not only reformed and united the churches of Cyprus,[9] but extended his hand throughout the Christian East, and even to Rome. He involved himself in disagreements over the date of Easter, the tangled episcopal elections in Antioch, theological debates on the Trinity (especially the newly controversial role of the Holy Spirit), and, eventually, conflicts over the speculative theology of Origen of Alexandria. We do not see Epiphanius rising through the ecclesiastical ranks, forging allegiances, establishing a reputation, courting supporters.[10] He is simply, all at once, *there*, from Constantinople to Rome,[11] well known (if not always well liked), riding a wave of episcopal celebrity.

---

likely that Epiphanius, before his election, was known to the Cyprus church at least from his monastic fame in Egypt and Palestine and, as Sozomen may be implying [see discussion below], his monastic reputation contributed to his election." Epiphanius's connection to Hilarion (who likewise moved from monastic fame in Palestine to Cyprus) may also have contributed, as might his various conflicts with anti-Nicene clergy in Palestine in the 360s; see Dechow, *Dogma and Mysticism*, 42–43.

9. Young Richard Kim, "The Imagined Worlds of Epiphanius of Cyprus" (PhD diss., University of Michigan, 2006), 29: "Thus under Epiphanius's administration, Cyprus became a sort of Nicene haven."

10. The one moment we see Epiphanius doing something like networking comes sometime in the late 350s or early 360s, when he and some fellow monks (presumably: ἐγώ τε καὶ οἱ ἄλλοι ἀδελφοί) visit Eusebius of Vercelli in his exile in Scythopolis; Epiphanius recounts this visit decades later in *Panarion* 30.5.2 (GCS n.F. 10.1:339), in a long digression in his chapter on the Ebionites. See Daniel Washburn, "Tormenting the Tormentors: A Reinterpretation of Eusebius of Vercelli's Letter from Scythopolis," *CH* 78 (2009): 731–55, esp. 747–78. It is difficult to interpret the significance of this event in light of Epiphanius's larger career, but either he was (somehow) already engaged in various pro-Nicene networks in Constantius II's largely anti-Nicene eastern empire, or his happenstance contact with Eusebius during his exile introduced him into these networks.

11. Epiphanius is not listed among the signatories of the Council of Constantinople in 381 (Pierre Nautin, "Épiphane [Saint], de Salamine," *Dictionnaire d'histoire et de géographie ecclésiastiques* 15 [1963]: 622), but several months later he accompanies the deposed bishop Paulinus of Antioch to Rome to support his case (see discussion of Dechow, *Dogma and Mysticism*, 87). Among their entourage was a young, Latin-speaking priest ordained by Paulinus, named Jerome (see Jerome, *Ep.* 108.6.1, 127.7.1 [CSEL 55:310–11, 56:150]). Epiphanius's last dramatic public appearances were in Constantinople, facing off against John Chrysostom, before dying aboard ship heading home (Socrates, *Historia ecclesiastica* 6.14–15 [GCS n.F. 1:335–38]).

In this chapter I reframe Christian authority in the late fourth century through this lens of celebrity: how can the fame of Epiphanius tell us how Christians during this crucial time grappled with major cultural and social issues? We find in Epiphanius not a stable model of a new Christian Roman Empire, but rather an amenable screen on which Christians of his time, and soon after, might imagine the fraught and often contradictory possibilities of Christian empire. The function of Epiphanius's celebrity, rather than the substance of his person, guides us toward new historical possibilities. I begin with a brief survey of the rich field of celebrity studies, which has likewise struggled since the 1960s to detach the social and cultural functions of celebrity from our (often) judgmental dismissal of the persons of celebrities. I then proceed to place Epiphanius's celebrity in its social context, among his peers in the last part of the fourth century. Finally, I explore the cultural deployment of Epiphanius's fame—his "celebrity-function"—in several major discourses of the fifth century.

THINKING CELEBRITY: CULTURE AND SOCIETY

The critical study of celebrity in the twentieth century began as a form of cultural critique of sudden forms of fame grounded in ephemeral popular culture. In the 1960s, in a caustic essay, Daniel Boorstin famously described the celebrity as *"a person who is known for his well-knownness.... He is neither good nor bad, great nor petty. He is the human pseudo-event. He has been fabricated on purpose to satisfy our exaggerated expectations of human greatness."*[12] By characterizing the celebrity as a "pseudo-event," Boorstin assumes and valorizes his or her

---

12. Daniel Boorstin, "From Hero to Celebrity: The Human Pseudo-event," in *The Image: A Guide to Pseudo-Events in America* (1961; repr., New York: Vintage Books, 2012), 57–58 (emphasis original). Graeme Turner, *Understanding Celebrity* (London: Sage, 2004), 5–7, and P. David Marshall, *Celebrity and Power: Fame in Contemporary Culture* (Minneapolis: University of Minnesota Press, 1997), 11–12, both place Boorstin in his particular cultural and theoretical context.

opposite: a "real" event, a "great" person who has achieved prominence for true and substantive reasons.[13] Such a reading asks us to separate the emptiness of celebrity from more durable and institutional forms of public recognition, such as status (Weber) or distinction (Bourdieu).[14] Some sociologists and theorists still persist in distinguishing between fame (which is earned) and celebrity (which is not).[15] Yet attempts to create language that distinguishes the pseudo-event of celebrity from the presumably more substantial categories of fame, status, or renown reflect contingent and particular presumptions and judgments about social meaning and merit: some prominent people we approve of (the famous) and others we do not (celebrities).[16] We can imagine how such presumptions would allow us to dismiss certain historical figures as unimportant while elevating others to become representatives of an age. If Epiphanius is simply "known for his well-knownness," why should we take him seriously? Epiphanius's lack of substance undermines his historical importance for us.

Yet other students in the growing field of celebrity studies have rejected this broad pronouncement; instead of judging "good" and "bad" forms of renown, these scholars focus on the way celebrity works, particularly by linking the phenomenon of celebrity to considerations of

---

13. Boorstin, "From Hero to Celebrity," lays the fault for the lamentable elision between "famous men and great men" (46) at the feet of the "Graphic Revolution" (47), i.e., mass media (especially television and movies).

14. Weber's concept of *charisma* provides a kind of foundation for contemporary celebrity studies, but often as a point of theoretical departure (see Kurzman et al., "Celebrity Status"). Murray Milner Jr. still insists that we can interpret modes of celebrity through Weberian ideas about status; see, most recently, Milner, "Is Celebrity a New Kind of Status System?," *Society* 57 (2010): 379–87 (his answer is no). For a general theoretical overview of the roots of celebrity studies (including Weber, Freud, Baudrillard, and Foucault), see Marshall, *Celebrity and Power*, 10–65.

15. Chris Rojek, *Celebrity* (London: Reaktion, 2001), 11–12; Stella Tillyard, "Celebrity in 18th-Century London," *History Today* 55.6 (2005): 22 and 25; Peter A. Lawler, "Celebrity Studies Today," *Society* 57 (2010): 419: "Celebrity, in the most obvious sense, is the lowest form of fame."

16. This judgmental note toward "celebrity," sounded already in Boorstin, is often reflected in the focus on popular culture as the "native" ground of celebrification.

culture and society.[17] Instead of focusing on the celebrity, we can look to the "celebrity-function."[18] Earlier critics like Boorstin judged celebrity based on its causes: why someone had achieved fame determined whether or not we should credit that fame. But the function of celebrity operates independently of its origins. While celebrities might become famous for something (e.g., acting in movies or being enmeshed in a public scandal), their ongoing celebrity, once launched onto a broader platform, transcends its original noteworthiness.[19]

Celebrities do not, however, remain contentless ciphers: rather, they become available receptacles for cultural production and critique. Indeed, precisely what Boorstin lamented in the 1960s—the seeming vacuity and transitoriness of the "famous person"—makes that person an ideal vehicle for great numbers of people to reflect on the cultural issues of their day. Celebrities become, as Leo Braudy notes, "vehicles of cultural memory and cohesion."[20] The celebrity does not merely reflect, but also potentially transforms, cultural identities. Graeme Turner, another theorist of celebrity, specifies "the celebrity's role as a location for the interrogation and elaboration of cultural identity."[21] Celebrities

---

17. For a useful collection of excerpts and sources on celebrity reaching back to Weber's writings on charisma, see P. David Marshall, ed., *The Celebrity Culture Reader* (London: Routledge, 2006).

18. Marshall, *Celebrity and Power*, 57: "The 'celebrity-function' is as important as Foucault's 'author-function' in its power to organize the legitimate and illegitimate domains of the personal and individual within the social." See Michel Foucault, "What Is an Author?," in *Textual Strategies: Perspectives in Post-Structuralist Criticism*, ed. Josué V. Harari (Ithaca, NY: Cornell University Press, 1979), 41–60.

19. Turner, *Understanding Celebrity*, 3: "The celebrity's fame does not necessarily depend on the position or achievements that gave them their prominence in the first instance. Rather, once they are established, their fame is likely to have outstripped the claims to prominence developed within that initial location."

20. Leo Braudy, *The Frenzy of Renown: Fame and Its History* (Oxford: Oxford University Press, 1986), 15. P. David Marshall, introduction to *Celebrity Culture Reader* (3), describes the celebrity as "a source of self and identity" and elsewhere notes: "The power of the celebrity is to represent the active construction of identity in the social world" (Marshall, *Celebrity and Power*, xi).

21. Turner, *Understanding Celebrity*, 24. See also Marshall, *Celebrity and Power*, 244.

delineate cultural spaces within which particular ideologies or cultural positions might be upheld, subverted, or destabilized. We see below how this emphasis on the cultural role of celebrity, rather than its validity or authenticity, can be useful in gauging the impact of Epiphanius in his time and soon after: it was precisely the fluidity and even seeming groundlessness of his fame throughout the eastern Mediterranean that allowed him to be so useful in cultural critique and debate.

Modern studies have also fleshed out the ways in which celebrity is a thoroughly social phenomenon, emerging out of the interaction between a celebrated persona and an audience (whether appreciative or disapproving).[22] To explore celebrity is to approach networks of social relations and locations from new angles.[23] To the extent that celebrities are commodified—integrated into economies of exchange and value—they can be shaped and reshaped, their signification transformed, by those who possess them.[24] Often fans are more interested in engaging their social world *through* that celebrity. Movie stars, to take the most current spectacular example, are rarely famous simply for the craft of filmmaking:[25] seemingly unrelated issues of power, identity, and social hierarchy can be projected onto the celebrity, and in

---

22. On "audience subjectivity," see Marshall, *Celebrity and Power*, 61–71. Turner, *Understanding Celebrity*, 24–25, notes: "The celebrity is not only a semiotic regime, but also the visible tip of a highly contingent field of power relations."

23. Scholars of early Christianity have made fruitful use of "network analysis" since the 1990s; see Elizabeth A. Clark, "Elite Networks and Heresy Accusations: Toward a Social Description of the Origenist Controversy," *Semeia* 56 (1991): 79–117; and Adam M. Schor, *Theodoret's People: Social Networks and Religious Conflict in Late Roman Syria*, TCH 48 (Berkeley: University of California Press, 2011).

24. See Marshall, introduction to *Celebrity Culture Reader*, 2: "Celebrities are part of a very elaborate media economy which is connected to audiences and value." On the commodification of celebrity, see Rojek, *Celebrity*, 15; Turner, *Understanding Celebrity*, 4; and Kathryn Lofton, "Religion and the American Celebrity," *Social Compass* 58 (2011): 346–52. Warholian pop art provides numerous examples of celebrity commodification and resignification.

25. See the classic study of Richard Dyer, *Stars* (London: British Film Institute, 1979); and more recently Samantha Barbas, *Movie Crazy: Fans, Stars, and the Cult of Celebrity* (New York: Palgrave, 2001).

that celebrity nexus these issues can be transformed, contested, and reframed.[26]

Many studies insist that fundamentally modern structures undergird celebrity, such as mass media, democracy, or capitalism.[27] I am not arguing that we should extend the modern genealogy of celebrity into late antiquity; rather, I am noting that several of the insights of this theoretical field prove useful when we turn to the premodern era.[28] Students of the Roman world are already attuned to the ways in which personas could be broadcast, popularized, and even commodified.[29] Classicist Thomas Habinek engages profitably with the celebrity of Seneca the Younger, a figure who, like the modern celebrity, was "famous at least in part for being famous."[30] By studying Seneca's fame, Habinek can access "aspects of Roman society not easily spelled out in

---

26. On fans and fandom, see Tyler Cowen, *What Price Fame?* (Cambridge, MA: Harvard University Press, 2000), 22–25.

27. David Marshall, arguably the dean of celebrity studies, is quite insistent on this point; see Marshall, *Celebrity and Power*, 4; and Marshall, introduction to *Celebrity Culture Reader*, 19: "Celebrity is a modern phenomenon." Rojek, *Celebrity*, 11, and Turner, *Understanding Celebrity*, 12, likewise see the requirement of modern mass media, especially the celebrification apparatus of cinema. Fred Inglis, *A Short History of Celebrity* (Princeton, NJ: Princeton University Press, 2010), insists on the modernism of celebrity, but places its birth in eighteenth-century London.

28. Robert Garland, "Celebrity in the Ancient World," *History Today* 55.3 (March 2005): 24–30; Garland, *Celebrity in Antiquity: From Media Tarts to Tabloid Queens*, Classical Inter/faces (London: Duckworth 2006); Garland, "Celebrity Ancient and Modern," *Society* 47 (2010): 484–88.

29. From the Republican period onward, public personalities in the Roman world engaged in various acts of self-promotion in texts and other media (such as statues and coins); see Eleanor W. Leach, "The Politics of Self-Presentation: Pliny's 'Letters' and Roman Portrait Sculpture," *CA* 9 (1990): 14–39; Carlos F. Noreña, "The Communication of the Emperor's Virtues," *JRS* 91 (2001): 146–68; John Dugan, *Making a New Man: Ciceronian Self-Fashioning in the Rhetorical Works* (Oxford: Oxford University Press, 2005); Andrew Cain, *The Letters of Jerome: Asceticism, Exegesis, and the Construction of Christian Authority in Late Antiquity*, OECS (Oxford: Oxford University Press, 2009).

30. Thomas Habinek, "Seneca's Renown: *Gloria, Claritudo,* and the Replication of the Roman Elite," *CA* 19 (2000): 264–303. Braudy, *Frenzy of Renown*, 146–68, discusses Seneca in the context of Roman imperial fame, and Habinek cites Braudy throughout.

a straightforward narrative of political history."[31] In the equally fraught context of the post-Constantinian Christian empire, personalities could also be magnified and circulated to embody crucial and historically specific tensions of Christian Roman cultural and social identity. Instead of pursuing the rutted paths of ancient "authority" in our explorations of episcopal power, I suggest insights from the notions of celebrity may allow us a more fluid approach to a period in flux. Epiphanius's prominence in the fourth century may be an enigma to the modern historian; for the ancient Christian, it was an opportunity.

CELEBRITY AND SOCIETY

As we have seen, modern celebrity studies in recent decades have shifted our focus from a reflexive rejection of "mere" celebrity to analyzing specific sites of society and culture through the magnified celebrity of an individual. In the same way, we do not need to figure out why Epiphanius was so well-known and influential, nor to gauge the substance and quality of his fame against others'. Rather, we can analyze his celebrity-function: how does the fame of Epiphanius give us access to particular modes of cultural and social critique?

We can approach the production of Epiphanius as a celebrity from two, complementary angles: the social and the cultural. First we can try to gain a sense of the social deployment of Epiphanius's celebrity:[32] the ways we see his celebrity being generated among his various friends and admirers. Incontestably, Epiphanius was—seemingly overnight—a famous bishop, "renowned for his renown." Only a few years after his ascendancy to the episcopal throne we see him involved with most of the major ecclesiastical controversies of his period. Certainly in his own

---

31. Habinek, "Seneca's Renown," 284.

32. Braudy, *Frenzy of Renown*, 150–89, discusses early Christianity and fame, but primarily from the perspective from those seeking adulation and fame, leading him to what strikes me as overly simplistic contrasts between Roman desire for renown and Christian desire for renunciation.

writings Epiphanius portrays himself as an influential participant in ecclesiastical politics: he consults with Athanasius of Alexandria;[33] he responds to theological disputes over the Virgin Mary in Arabia;[34] he presumes to vet the various contenders for the disputed episcopal see of Antioch.[35] We do not, however, have to rely on Epiphanius's own self-reporting to gauge his renown. Epiphanius's role as a player also emerges out of his surviving correspondence with episcopal colleagues. A letter from Athanasius of Alexandria survives in fragments, and even in its fragmentary form makes it clear that the two bishops desired to operate as allies.[36] A letter from Basil of Caesarea also survives in which he heaps praise on Epiphanius. To be sure, much of Basil's flowery obsequiousness is formulaic: Epiphanius is "your holiness," "your wisdom," and "your excellency,"[37] while Basil is "unworthy and insignificant" and

---

33. Epiphanius, *Panarion* 72.4.4 (GCS 37:259): "I myself, on some occasion, asked the blessed *papa* Athanasius about this Marcellus [of Ancyra]. He did not defend him nor again did he bear any hostility against him, only, with a smile on his face (διὰ τοῦ προσώπου μειδιάσας), he hinted that he had not been far from depravity, but he had acquitted himself." The "smile" in this incident conveys a certain intimacy, as I discuss in chapter 5.

34. Epiphanius, *Panarion* 78.1.1 (GCS 37:452) describes the heresy in Arabia (against Mary's virginity) as "referred to my humble self by some of those pious ones" (ἀνηνέχθη δὲ τῇ ἡμῶν ταπεινότητι περὶ τούτων ὑπό τινων εὐλαβῶν).

35. Epiphanius, *Panarion* 77.20.3 (GCS 37:434): "While I was in Antioch I met with their leaders." Epiphanius does not mention why he happened to be in Antioch, nor why the church leaders met with him, nor why they consented to his (unsuccessful) mediation (recounted in *Panarion* 77.20.4–24.5 [GCS 37:434–38]); I discuss this incident in more detail in chapter 5.

36. The fragment of Athanasius's letter is preserved in the *Chronicon Paschale* 26 (PG 92:76C), and seeks to enlist Epiphanius in endorsing Athanasius's calculation of the date for Easter. David Brakke, "Athanasius' *Epistula ad Epiphanium* and Liturgical Reform in Alexandria," *SP* 36 (2001): 482–88, argues that Athanasius's letter was actually written to one of his Alexandrian ecclesiastical subordinates, and not the bishop of Cyprus. Earlier scholars (such as Karl Holl, "Ein Bruchstück aus einem bisher unbekannten Brief des Epiphanius," in *Festgabe für Adolf Jülicher zum 70. Geburtstag*, ed. R. Bultmann and H. Soden [Tübingen: J.C.B. Mohr, 1927], 159–89) had supposed that Athanasius was responding in some fashion to Epiphanius's own letter to some persons concerning the timing of Holy Week from around the same time (Holl includes the text of his letter in his essay).

37. Basil, *Ep.* 258.1, 2, 4 (PG 32:948–49, 952–53). The letter probably dates from 376 (so Dechow, *Dogma and Mysticism*, 74; Nautin, "Épiphane," 621, dates it "vers 377").

"awestruck."[38] Basil is also gingerly seeking to put off several ecclesiastical and theological demands conveyed by Epiphanius's prior letter and his emissaries.[39] In gauging Epiphanius's celebrity, we should find Basil's tone more significant than any actual concessions he does or does not make to Epiphanius. As modern studies make clear, celebrity is produced in social interactions, a give-and-take between celebrity and audience. The conciliatory tone of one bishop to another, as well as the tacit acknowledgment of Epiphanius's right to intervene in various foreign episcopal venues, serves to affirm the stature of Epiphanius among his episcopal colleagues.[40]

In the thick of the Origenist controversy, Theophilus of Alexandria sent a letter to Epiphanius that was meant to serve as a cover letter for his circular letter to all the bishops of the East.[41] Again the tone is one of subservience and respect: Epiphanius is the hardened warrior who has preceded Theophilus into the battle they now wage together against heretics; Epiphanius should take charge and push the battle forward.[42] Even at the time people mistrusted Theophilus's motives, accusing him of duping Epiphanius, flattering him, and using him to strike out at his enemies.[43] Nevertheless, the very fact that Theophilus

---

38. Basil, *Ep.* 258.1, 2 (PG 32:948–49).

39. Nautin, "Épiphane," 621, describes Basil's tone as "courtoise mais ferme." Dechow, *Dogma and Mysticism,* 77, concurs: "Basil's answer to Epiphanius is somewhat flowery and flattering, bearing the marks of church diplomacy and reluctance to offend a respected acquaintance rather than of personal intimacy with a trusted friend."

40. Basil, *Ep.* 258.2 (PG 32:949), remarks approvingly of Epiphanius's intervention in disputes among the monks on the Mount of Olives. Right afterward (*Ep.* 258.3 [PG 32:949–50]) Basil attempts to prevent Epiphanius from intervening in the episcopal conflicts in Antioch. The juxtaposition of the two is telling: Basil clearly cedes to Epiphanius the right to impose himself in church politics generally, but begs restraint in certain circumstances.

41. Theophilus, *Ad Epiphanium* (= Jerome, *Ep.* 90) survives among Jerome's corpus of letters, translated into Latin (CSEL 55:143–45).

42. Theophilus, *Ad Epiphanium* (= Jerome, *Ep.* 90) 2 (CSEL 55:144).

43. Palladius, *Dialogus de vita sanctis Iohannis Chrysostomi* 16, 17 (SC 341:320–22, 349); Elizabeth A. Clark, *The Origenist Controversy: The Cultural Construction of an Early Christian Debate* (Princeton, NJ: Princeton University Press, 1992), 37–38, 45–46.

finds it useful to dupe Epiphanius speaks to Epiphanius's fame: he is someone whose value in the public sphere is worth exploiting.

As I noted in the introduction, Epiphanius seems to have composed all of his surviving writings upon request from monks and bishops from around the Greek-speaking world.[44] We do not know why these various parties chose to write to Epiphanius—that is, how he had become so famous that others might solicit his written advice. What we can trace, however, are the social networks through which Epiphanius's celebrity was channeled. As far as we know, Epiphanius had not published any theological treatises in the 370s when he received two different letters from clergy and monks in the city of Syedra in Pamphylia (south-central Asia Minor).[45] Yet the writers implore Epiphanius—"god-honored" and "master"—to provide for them "correct and healthy faith," particularly concerning the godhead of the Holy Spirit. The result, produced in 373/74 (less than a decade into Epiphanius's episcopacy), was the long and somewhat rambling *Ancoratus*, a work at once highly idiosyncratic and yet deeply embedded in the theological controversies raging in the years building up to the Council of Constantinople in 381.[46] The preexisting celebrity of Epiphanius results, in this instance, in a moment of theological solidarity among pro-Nicene partisans.

It seems likely that reading or hearing about the *Ancoratus* inspired some priests and monks not long afterward to request a heresiological treatise from Epiphanius. A certain Acacius and Paul, who were

---

44. Excluding his correspondence, which (by definition) is in response to other people.

45. On these letters, see Oliver Kösters, *Die Trinitätslehre des Epiphanios von Salamis: Ein Kommentar zum "Ancoratus,"* Forschungen zur Kirchen- und Dogmengeschichte 86 (Göttingen: Vandenhoeck & Ruprecht, 2003), 89–106; and my discussion in chapter 5.

46. The end of the treatise includes two versions of the creed; the second, longer version (*Ancoratus* 119.3–12 [GCS n.F. 10.1:148–49]) addresses contemporary heresies (such as the Pneumatomachoi and Apollinarians), and it seems (from his letter to Basil, at least [see above]) that Epiphanius made some attempts to popularize this expanded creed in the years leading up to the Council of Constantinople. On the first version, see my discussion in chapter 5.

probably monks in Syria,[47] appear to have been puzzled by a list of eighty heresies inserted early in the *Ancoratus*, and they wrote to Epiphanius for clarification and expansion.[48] Once again, Epiphanius's celebrity seems to be the determinative factor in his appeal to these distant monks. To Acacius and Paul, Epiphanius possesses a God-given grace similar to that of the apostles.[49] Since circumstances prevent them from receiving his wisdom in person, they plead for a written treatise explaining these diverse heresies.[50] Social interaction refracts Epiphanius's celebrity in a new direction: from theological master to heresiological expert. These two roles are not, of course, utterly distinct or unrelated, although the literary products themselves are quite different. Rather, I suggest that the only real link between these two works for the clergy who requested them (besides a stray line in the *Ancoratus*) is admiration for Epiphanius's ecclesiastical fame.

We do not have the letters requesting Epiphanius's two biblical commentaries, which were executed later in his career (in the 390s, most likely) and which survive primarily in fragments and translations. According to an editorial preface in the Syriac translation, the treatise *On Weights and Measures* was written at the request of a Persian priest whom Epiphanius met while "summoned by the pious emperors" to Constantinople.[51] Whether this represents at all the circumstances

---

47. Again, this information comes from the preface to Acacius and Paul's letter, inserted by a later editor, identifying them as "abbots in Chalcis and Beroea in Coele-Syria."

48. *Epistula Acacii et Pauli* 1.9 (GCS n.F. 10.1:154) ("We have heard names assigned to the heresies by your Honor") likely refers to *Ancoratus* 12.7–13.8 (GCS n.F. 10.1:20–22), a (digressive) list of eighty heresies, most of which Epiphanius's readers had probably never heard of. The preface added to the letter indicates that Acacius and Paul write to Epiphanius in 376; if this is correct, given the speed with which Epiphanius produced the *Panarion* (it was finished roughly a year later), he was doubtless already composing it when he received their letter.

49. *Epistula Acacii et Pauli* 1.1, 1.12 (GCS n.F. 10.1:153–54).

50. *Epistula Acacii et Pauli* 1.2 (GCS n.F. 10.1:153); they have sent "a member of their community" as a messenger with their letter.

51. *De mensuris et ponderibus* praef. 1 (Dean, *Weights and Measures*, 11 [Eng.], 45a [Syr.]). On the origins and date of this treatise, see my discussion in the introduction.

under which the treatise was composed we cannot know; that readers of Epiphanius could imagine such a scenario—involving crossed borders, imperial patrons, and Epiphanius as wise bishop on the spot—speaks clearly to assumptions about Epiphanius's reputation. In Epiphanius's preface to one of his last works, the treatise *On Twelve Gems,* written at the request of Bishop Diodore of Tyre, Epiphanius in a somewhat confusing analogy compares himself and Diodore to Jesus and the Samaritan woman at the well and to Elijah and the widow. Which bishop is supposed to be playing which role is not clear, but the general thrust is that Epiphanius—reluctantly—accepts the job of soliciting and transmitting gifts of divine wisdom.[52] Again, neither of these works was requested based on any widely acknowledged biblical expertise on Epiphanius's part: their dedicatees, it seems, reached out to the celebrated Christian and expected a noteworthy response.

Epiphanius's literary output was certainly not prodigious; nevertheless, we can glean from it some of the ways in which Epiphanius's celebrity was produced and expanded during his lifetime. Although we moderns recall Epiphanius primarily as a heresiologist and controversialist, the social domain of his celebrity was remarkably unfixed. His celebrity precedes the specific social locations of his ecclesiastical work. Epiphanius was, first and foremost, a man who spoke loudly, and whom people (some people, at least) wanted to hear from on a variety of topics. We have no clear sense of how Epiphanius became famous, but we see in these scattered sources how his fame continued to be reproduced in multiple social contexts during his lifetime.

CELEBRITY AND CULTURE

If we see the social production of celebrity in Epiphanius's own writings and networks, we see the cultural effects of his celebrity manifest

52. Blake and Vis, *Epiphanius,* 99–102. On the origins and date of this treatise, see my discussion in the introduction. The cover letter to Diodore also survives in an early Latin translation (CSEL 35:743–45).

in the writings of others during his life and after his death. We recall that the theorists of celebrity in our own time focus less on the contents of a person's celebrity ("Why is she famous?") than on the ways that celebrity functions in the wider culture: the "celebrity-function." While specific aspects of Epiphanius's writings and actions survived him, what also survived was the fact of his fame, which continued to be contemplated and manipulated as a source of cultural production. We do not derive the "real Epiphanius" from his posthumous celebrity, but rather insight into the key issues and concerns that later Christians thought about in light of his celebrity.

Our main sources for gauging the cultural effects of Epiphanius's celebrity during his life and in the decades following his death are Jerome, surely Epiphanius's most vocal fan during his lifetime; the ecclesiastical historians Socrates and Sozomen in the fifth century;[53] and the Greek versions of the *Apophthegmata Patrum* (Sayings of the Fathers), collections of monastic anecdotes that were compiled in the late fifth or early sixth century but may contain material dating back to earlier in the fifth century.[54] From these sources we can discern some major areas of cultural concern in the late fourth and early fifth centuries refracted through the person of Epiphanius. I break these cultural concerns into three broad categories: *imperium, paideia,* and *askesis.* By *imper-*

53. Theodoret does not mention Epiphanius in any of his works, although he must certainly have known of both Epiphanius's writings (his own treatise on heresies relies at points on the *Panarion*) and his role in the tangled episcopacy of Antioch in the 370s and 380s, about which he writes in his *Historia ecclesiastica*. Indeed, it seems from *Historia ecclesiastica* 5.34.2–3 (GCS 19:334) that Theodoret has consigned Epiphanius to a kind of *damnatio memoriae*, when he refuses to name those responsible for the condemnation of John Chrysostom. Either Epiphanius is among "those who wronged" John, whose "virtue" Theodoret otherwise admires; or he is one of the "wretched people" (δύστηνους) manipulated into accusing John of heresy.

54. I am not going to consider in this context the Greek *Life of Epiphanius*, which (according to its most diligent student, Claudia Rapp) likely dates to the end of the fifth century. While I certainly think the *Life* draws on many of the same cultural tropes as other circulating images of Epiphanius, it functions more as a distillation and commodification—perhaps like the modern celebrity "biography." I discuss the *Life* more fully in chapter 6.

ium I mean Epiphanius's utility for Christians exploring their own relation to empire. By *paideia* I mean Epiphanius's portrayal with respect to multiple forms of education (classical, Christian, scriptural). Finally, by *askesis* I mean Epiphanius's depiction as the guarantor of particular modes of religious and bodily discipline, particularly monastic life.

I am obviously not arguing that these cultural fields emerge only in the commodification of Epiphanius's persona in the fifth century: they are well-attested, and well-studied, aspects of late ancient Christianity. Instead, I am arguing that these cultural fields allow us to gauge the production and circulation of Epiphanius's image, his *celebrification*, and thereby resituate our approach to episcopal authority. Celebrity acts as a fun-house mirror for culture, reflecting and distorting at the same time. Our tendency in the cultural study of early Christianity is to move toward an almost teleological vision of Christian cultural formation. Our studies of power, knowledge, and discipline—as well as other facets of late ancient Christian culture that I explore in the other chapters of this book—thus often speak of *making, construction,* and *formation.*[55] Certain early Christian persons become reliable screens onto whom we project our historical syntheses. Epiphanius is not amenable to such historiographic projection and therefore seems—to us—to pale next to more representative early Christians.[56] Herein lies the value of an analysis of Epiphanius's celebrity: by focusing more specifically on how Epiphanius—in his particular time and place—was made to speak to power, knowledge, and discipline, we capture in a finer grain certain ambiguous moments at the dawn of the Christian Roman Empire. We cannot use Epiphanius to plot the progression of a nascent Christian culture under construction. Rather, in the celebrity of Epiphanius, we see the threads of that Christian culture deconstructed, entangled in ways that perhaps confound our own expectations.

---

55. See the remarks of Teresa M. Shaw, "*Askēsis* and the Appearance of Holiness," *JECS* 6 (1998): 485 and n. 1.

56. See my discussion in the introduction.

Imperium

What can the distorting mirror of Epiphanius tell us about the range of fears and desires that Christians held about imperial power?[57] When Christians think through the problem of empire using Epiphanius, they can envision multiple, contradictory possibilities. Even the very possibility of a Christian empire, a novelty during Epiphanius's early career, might be queried through the famous bishop. Epiphanius's elevation to the episcopacy took place only a few years after the death of the last pagan emperor; perhaps for this reason, the collators of the *Apophthegmata Patrum* ascribed to Epiphanius this story about Athanasius:

> Bishop Epiphanius recounted that, before the Blessed Athanasius the Great, crows flew around the temple of Serapis, crying out (*ekrazon*) without a rest, "*Kras, kras!*"[58] And those pagans (*Hellēnes*) standing opposite the Blessed Athanasius cried out (*ekraxan*): "Evil-doer, tell us what the crows are crying out!" And answering he said: "The crows are crying out, *Kras, kras,* for in the Western language [i.e., Latin], '*kras*' is *tomorrow*. For tomorrow you will see God's glory." In short order the death of the Emperor Julian was announced. And when this happened, they ran around crying out against Serapis: "If you didn't like him, why did you accept things from him?"[59]

Epiphanius here serves as a secondhand witness to the end of the pagan Roman Empire and the triumph of Christianity over paganism. We might also hear hints of a unified Christian Roman Empire in this apophthegm about Athanasius attributed to Epiphanius. Both the Cypriot and the Alexandrian bishops sought to exert their influence across the empire, even traveling all the way to Rome and learning Latin.

---

57. Obviously many fine studies of Christianity and empire have appeared in recent decades, seeking to trace—either in broad strokes or through the careers of individual clerics—the evolution of imperial power in the Christian Roman Empire. While these historical studies have their place, I am more interested in how the character of Epiphanius across a range of texts disrupts any coherent narrative.

58. "Kras" being the sound that crows make in Greek, from the verb κράζω, used of both crows and pagans in the apophthegm.

59. *Apophthegmata Patrum Epiphanius* 1 (PG 65:161–64).

Other sources placed Epiphanius in more direct contact with imperial power.[60] In his vituperative treatise *Against John of Jerusalem*, Jerome defends his hero, Epiphanius, against his rival, John. (This chapter's opening anecdote comes from this treatise, as Epiphanius and John square off in spectacular, public fashion.) Epiphanius is, of course, perfectly virtuous and orthodox (unlike John!), a stalwart against the tides of heresy, which, until so recently, swept through all of the Eastern provinces (and which continue to do so, now in secretive fashion). Jerome explicitly links the tides of heresy with the faithlessness of pre-Theodosian emperors. Jerome notes that orthodox bishops fell, one by one, into imperial exile, but the bishop of Constantia "was not touched by Valens. He was always of such great veneration that when heretics reigned, they considered their own disgrace if they should persecute such a man."[61] Epiphanius is so great a man, so staunch in his orthodoxy, that not even heretical emperors dare to act against him. Of course, Jerome wishes to praise Epiphanius (and demean John by comparison). But, in a larger sense, he is thinking through the politics of Christianity, imagining through an outsized Epiphanius an orthodox church always under threat from, but ultimately triumphant over, a potentially heretical *imperium*.

The fifth-century historians Socrates and Sozomen found different messages about *imperium* embedded in Epiphanius's famous orthodoxy. Both historians were writing in the mid-fifth century in Constantinople, and what we can infer about their backgrounds and motives comes almost entirely from their historical texts. In their treatment of Epiphanius, Socrates seems most interested in maintaining imperial peace against the troublesome antics of divisive bishops (such as Theophilus and Epiphanius), while Sozomen shows more interest in promoting certain monks, bishops, and other holy men as key figures of a new

60. We might also recall the (possibly apocryphal) story behind Epiphanius's composition of the treatise *De mensuris et ponderibus*, occasioned when Epiphanius was summoned by four emperors to Constantinople (see above, n. 51).

61. Jerome, *Contra Ioannem Hierosolymitanum* 4 (PL 23:358–59).

Christian empire.[62] In Socrates's *Church History*, Epiphanius possesses "extraordinary piety" (*huperballousan eulabeian*) but is also "easily influenced" (*tacheōs hupēchthē*) by the machinations of an insincere Theophilus.[63] Eventually Theophilus coaxes Epiphanius into traveling to Constantinople, where he inspires many but also makes numerous enemies, including the bishop, John Chrysostom.[64] Conflict escalates, and eventually Epiphanius storms out of the capital city. Socrates even records a tradition that the two bishops cursed each other—that Epiphanius should die before reaching home, and John should be deposed from his episcopal seat.[65] Epiphanius's part in John's complicated narrative ends here, but not before Socrates adds: "After Epiphanius sailed away, John learned from certain people that the empress Eudoxia had armed Epiphanius against him" (literally, Eudoxia "made Epiphanius her infantry soldier [hoplite] [*exōplisen*]").[66] It is a curious detail, neither elaborated nor supported by the preceding narrative, except to the extent that Socrates has portrayed Epiphanius as "easily influenced" by nefarious forces, and Eudoxia as opposed to John. It is enough for Socrates to suggest a link between Epiphanius and John Chrysostom's imperial nemesis. Much as in Jerome's diatribe against John of Jerusalem, Epiphanius's fame opens up an opportunity to think about *imperium*: but instead of becoming the face of an orthodoxy impervious to imperial heresy, Epiphanius here represents the vulnerability of the church to imperial scheming.

Sozomen, whose *Church History* drew on Socrates's, thought rather differently about *imperium* through Epiphanius. Already his version of

---

62. See Theresa Urbainczyk, "Observations on the Differences between the Church Histories of Socrates and Sozomen," *Historia* 46 (1997): 355–73.

63. Socrates, *Historia ecclesiastica* 6.10.4 (GCS n.F. 1:328). Socrates also describes Epiphanius as "famous for his piety" (ἐπ' εὐλαβείᾳ περιβόητον).

64. Young Richard Kim, *Epiphanius of Cyprus: Imagining an Orthodox World* (Ann Arbor: University of Michigan Press, 2015), 218–36, narrates the "machinations" of Theophilus.

65. Socrates, *Historia ecclesiastica* 6.14.1–2 (GCS n.F. 1:335–36).

66. Socrates, *Historia ecclesiastica* 6.15.1 (GCS n.F. 1:336).

Epiphanius is more sympathetic than Socrates's: while the bishop is still "easily led" (*rhadiōs prosetheto*) by Theophilus, it is only because he has already formed his own strong opinions against Origen's teachings.[67] Once in Constantinople, Epiphanius attempts to clean John's theological house, even threatening to publicly call for the excommunication of Dioscorus, one of the Origenist "Tall Brothers" who had been granted refuge by John. John's partisans persuade Epiphanius not to "cause a popular uprising" (*en tōi plēthei ē staseōs kinētheisēs*), and he temporarily desists.[68] At this point Eudoxia once more makes a sudden entrance. She asks Epiphanius to pray for her ill son, and the bishop replies that he would be happy to do so if she would simply cut her ties to the heretical Tall Brothers. Eudoxia's first response is to shame Epiphanius: she replies that she doubts he could do anything for her son anyway, a bishop unable to raise his own archdeacon from the dead. Sozomen then reports that companions of Ammonius, another one of the Tall Brothers, went to meet with Epiphanius and adds: "This was at the pleasure of the empress herself" (*touto gar autēi tēi basilidi edokei*).[69] Ammonius implores Epiphanius to be reasonable, and the bishop relents, "quite moderately persuaded" (*metriōteron pōs prosdialechtheis*).[70] Epiphanius, in this telling, sails away precisely to avoid further confrontation with John.

For Jerome, Epiphanius represents orthodox resistance to the force of a theologically suspect empire; for Socrates, he embodies the susceptibility of orthodoxy to devious *imperium*; for Sozomen, Epiphanius models moderation called for and enabled by empire. Our tendency, as historians, is normally to focus our attention on the authors and their particular cultural contexts, and to conclude, perhaps, that Sozomen is more sympathetic to Eudoxia than is Socrates. We recognize that we

---

67. Sozomen, *Historia ecclesiastica* 8.15.2 (GCS n.F. 4:369).
68. Sozomen, *Historia ecclesiastica* 8.14.10–11 (GCS n.F. 4:368–69). Once more, Sozomen portrays Epiphanius as less hotheaded and susceptible than Socrates. On the "Tall Brothers," see Clark, *Origenist Controversy*, 20–22 and 106–8.
69. Sozomen, *Historia ecclesiastica* 8.15.1–3 (GCS n.F. 4:369).
70. Sozomen, *Historia ecclesiastica* 8.15.4–5 (GCS n.F. 4:369–70).

can learn little to nothing about Epiphanius himself, refracted as his actions are into multiple, even contradictory significations. Because we cannot pin down the real Epiphanius, we dismiss him as historically unimportant. I suggest we should reverse our thinking: precisely because of his importance at a precise historical moment, and because his celebrity has come unmoored from his specific deeds, Epiphanius is available as a resource for thinking in multiple, contradictory ways about *imperium*. As he is a celebrity, Epiphanius's iconicity does not resolve but simply embodies cultural tensions. *Imperium*, in the opening decades of the fifth century, was not a problem to be solved but a tension to be explored within the relatively safe boundaries of a celebrated persona.

Paideia

Later authors writing about Epiphanius articulate similar cultural tensions through Epiphanius with respect to the appropriate bounds of education (*paideia*). Many modern scholars have taken to reading Epiphanius as being opposed to classical *paideia;* they view him as staking out a claim for theological expertise over and against "worldly" knowledge.[71] Yet during his lifetime, and soon after, Epiphanius enjoyed a reputation for multiple kinds of expertise, both secular and Christian. Augustine, pressed by the bishop of Carthage to compose a treatise on heresies, tries to refer his correspondent to the "very learned" Epiphanius, framing him as a paragon of specifically Christian

---

71. See, for instance, Kim, "Imagined Worlds," 144–48, and Kim, *Epiphanius*, 21 and 63–64, as well as several essays by J. Rebecca Lyman: "The Making of a Heretic: The Life of Origen in Epiphanius *Panarion* 64," *SP* 31 (1997): 445–51; "Origen as Ascetic Theologian: Orthodoxy and Authority in the Fourth-Century Church," in *Origeniana Septima*, ed. Wolfgang Bienert and Uwe Kühneweg (Leuven: Peeters, 1999), 187–94; and "Ascetics and Bishops: Epiphanius on Orthodoxy," in *Orthodoxie, Christianisme, Histoire/ Orthodoxy, Christianity, and History*, ed. Susanna Elm, Éric Rebillard, and Antonella Romano, Collections de l'École Française de Rome 270 (Paris: de Boccard, 2000), 149–61.

knowledge.⁷² Jerome, in his later biblical commentaries, refers to the "genius and erudition" (*ingenii et eruditionis*) of Epiphanius's exegetical treatise *On Twelve Gems*, comparing his work to a non-Christian classic like Pliny's *Natural History*.⁷³ Indeed, whatever his own attitudes toward Christian and non-Christian education may have been during his lifetime, the capacious celebrity of Epiphanius made him useful for thinking about Christian and secular *paideia* in various, even contradictory, ways.

Perhaps no statement is more representative of the multiple considerations of education than Jerome's surprisingly brief notice in his treatise *On Famous Men*:

> Epiphanius, bishop of Salamis in Cyprus, wrote books *Against All Heresies* and many others that are eagerly read by the learned on account of their subjects and by the more simple on account of their language. He survives until today, and in his extreme old age still composes various works.⁷⁴

We should note that, for Jerome at least, the fact that Epiphanius writes in a style that appeals to the "more simple" does not make his works any less "learned." While we moderns might praise such a compositional feat, this disengagement of elevated style from erudite content was

---

72. Augustine, *Ep.* 222.2 (CSEL 57:447), replying to Quodvultdeus's request for a treatise on heresies, writes of Epiphanius and describes him as "much more learned" (*longe ... doctior*) than his Latin counterpart, Filastrius. When Augustine (after relenting) does write his treatise *De haeresibus*, he cites Epiphanius as a source (*De haeresibus* prol. 10, 22, 25, 27, 28, 32, 37, 39, 41, 42, 43, 45, 49, 50, 51, 53, 57, 84 [PL 42:23, 27, 29, 30, 31, 32, 33, 34, 39, 40–41, 46]). Considering that he later in life refers to the *Panarion* as a "little book" (*opusculo: contra Iulianum opus imperfectum* 4.47 [PL 45:1366]), it is likely he had only a copy of the *Anakephalaioses* (or *Epitomes*) of the *Panarion* at his disposal. See Berthold Altaner, "Augustinus und Epiphanius von Salamis: Ein quellenkritische Studie," *Mélanges Joseph de Ghellinck* (Gembloux: J. Duculot, 1951), 265–75, who also suggests Augustine's familiarity with Epiphanius's treatise *On Weights and Measures*.

73. Jerome, *Commentarius in Isaiam* 15.54.11–12 (PL 24:525); *Commentarius in Ezekielem* 9.28:11ff. (PL 25:271).

74. Jerome, *De viris inlustribus* 114 (*De viris inlustribus* 114; *Hieronymus: Liber de viris inlustribus*; *Gennadius: Liber de viris inlustribus*, ed. E. C. Richardson, Texte und Untersuchungen zur Geschichte der altchristlichen Literatur 14.1a [Leipzig: J.C. Hinrichs, 1896], 51).

more counterintuitive in the late fourth and early fifth centuries.[75] Later Greek authors, not to mention modern scholars, disparaged Epiphanius for the exact thing that merited praise from Jerome: his poor style.[76] *Paideia* was a cultivation of both content and style, and portraying Epiphanius as both "learned" (*eruditus*) and speaking in the style of the "more simple" (*simpliciores*) risked cultural contradiction. The larger-than-life celebrity of Epiphanius allows for this impossible intersection of "simple" (perhaps, ascetic) style and cultivated scholarly wisdom. Jerome can project onto Epiphanius a posture he himself was eager to strike during the Origenist controversy, claiming (especially in his treatise *Against John of Jerusalem*) a kind of learned rusticity that counteracted his opponents' slick, but empty, arguments.[77] Through Epiphanius, Jerome can attempt a subtle reimagining of the bounds of learnedness.[78]

Other authors likewise used Epiphanius as an opportunity to interrogate the appropriate breadth and depth of Christian learning. In the *Apophthegmata Patrum*, Epiphanius issues vague but sincere recommendations of books, especially books of "Scripture."[79] We have already seen how Socrates portrays Epiphanius as zealous but simpleminded;

---

75. In fact, one of the social effects of *paideia* was precisely to separate out the *eruditi* from the *simpliciores*; see the discussion of Edward Watts, *City and School in Late Antique Athens and Alexandria*, TCH 41 (Berkeley: University of California Press, 2006), 7–23, who describes *paideia* as "a source of upper-class cultural unity" (21).

76. Photius, *Bibliotheca*, codex 122 remarks of Epiphanius's *Panarion:* "With respect to manner of expression he is lowbrow (τὴν δὲ φράσιν ταπεινός) and might seem to be unpracticed in Attic education (Ἀττικῆς παιδείας ἀμελέτητον)"; text in *Photius, Bibliothèque*, vol. 2, ed. René Henry, Collection Byzantines (Paris: Éditions 'Les Belles Lettres,' 1960), 96.

77. Jerome, *Contra Ioannem Hierosolymitanum* 21, 25, 32, 38 (PL 23:371–72, 375–76, 383–84, 390).

78. See Megan Hale Williams, *The Monk and the Book: Jerome and the Making of Christian Scholarship* (Chicago: University of Chicago Press, 2008); and more generally Werner Jaeger, *Early Christianity and Greek Paideia* (Cambridge, MA: Belknap Press of Harvard University Press, 1961); and Brown, *Power and Persuasion*, 35–70.

79. *Apophthegmata Patrum Epiphanius* 8–11 (PG 65:165), promoting possession of "Christian books" (τῶν Χριστιανῶν βιβλίων), reading of "Scriptures" (τῶν Γραφῶν), and knowledge of "divine laws" (τῶν θείων νόμων).

Sozomen makes Epiphanius slightly less zealous, but perhaps not less simple, as on Sozomen's telling Epiphanius admits to Ammonius that he has not actually read any of the Tall Brothers' supposedly heretical works.[80] Rufinus, in his treatise *On the Adulteration of the Works of Origen*, takes a swing at Epiphanius's learnedness. After claiming that Origen's detractors are actually secret plagiarists who warn people not to read Origen so that their literary crimes will not be discovered,[81] he singles out Epiphanius (without naming him):

> One of those, who thinks he has the burden—as if he were spreading the gospel through all the nations and through all the languages!—to speak ill of Origen, confessed before a great audience of monks that he had read 6,000 of his books. But if it is true that, as he is accustomed to say, he read them in order to recognize [Origen's] evil, then ten, or twenty, or at most thirty books should have certainly been sufficient to gain such knowledge![82]

Rufinus's blind swipe at Epiphanius is notable for the way it plays with Epiphanius's learned reputation. First, Epiphanius is famous enough to be preaching to "a great audience of monks." Rufinus does not even need to name Epiphanius: his fame is never at issue, merely its significance. The content of the statement, moreover, seems to be acknowledging Epiphanius's cleverness and even his learnedness: Epiphanius has read thousands of volumes of Origen—no mean feat.[83] We might at first think Rufinus is making fun of Epiphanius as boastful and perhaps even exaggerating. Yet Rufinus goes on to accept Epiphanius's zealous deployment of knowledge in order to twist it into something insidious and underhanded: the real reason he read so many of Origen's

---

80. Sozomen, *Historia ecclesiastica* 8.15.3 (GCS n.F. 4:369).
81. Rufinus, *De adulteratione librorum Origenis* 14 (SC 464:316–18).
82. Rufinus, *De adulteratione librorum Origenis* 15 (SC 464:318).
83. Compare Rufinus's sneering accusation with the later praise of his companion Melania the Elder by Palladius, *Historia Lausiaca* 55.3 (text in *The Lausiac History of Palladius*, ed. Dom Cuthbert Butler, Texts and Studies 6 [Cambridge: Cambridge University Press, 1898], 2:149), who notes that she was "most eloquent and loved study" (λογιωτάτη ἣ καὶ φιλήσασα τὸν λόγον) and read "three million lines of Origen," not just once but "seven or eight times."

supposedly tainted works was to plagiarize them. Jerome responds angrily to this insult in his *Apology against Rufinus*: first by denying that Origen even had 6,000 books to be read,[84] and second by trumpeting Epiphanius's linguistic prowess and dubbing him *pentaglossus*, master of "five languages."[85] Rufinus and Jerome are engaged in a decades-long struggle to come to terms with the appropriate Christian attitude toward *paideia*, and their differing representations of Epiphanius's knowledge (or lack thereof) serve their respective agendas.[86] Once again, Epiphanius's available celebrity makes him useful in debates about Christian learnedness. Because Epiphanius is famous for his fame, his relation to *paideia* can be appropriated and resignified by Christians with widely differing agendas. My point here is not to isolate and compare various Christian attitudes toward secular knowledge, but rather to show how easily they can be muddled and confounded in the famous bishop from Cyprus.

Askesis

Finally, I turn to consider how talk about Epiphanius condenses various concerns about *askesis*, the bodily and spiritual discipline that was increasingly exemplified in the fourth and fifth centuries in the rising tide of monasticism. Once again, we see how Epiphanius's celebrity-function enlarges to encompass diverse views about the ascetic life, and condenses the specific concerns of his fifth-century admirers. At times, Epiphanius is held up as a model of ascetic rigor. In the *Apophthegmata*

---

84. Jerome, *Apologia contra Rufinum* 2.16, 21–22 (SC 303:142, 160–64); at 3.23 Jerome refers to Rufinus's "6,000 books claim" but merely to point out Rufinus's hypocrisy in claiming sometimes that Epiphanius is well read and at other times a "silly old man" (*delirus senex*) (SC 303:274–76).

85. Jerome, *Apologia contra Rufinum* 2.22, 3.6 (SC 303:162–64, 230).

86. See my "'What Has Rome to Do with Bethlehem?' Cultural Capital(s) and Religious Imperialism in Late Ancient Christianity," *Classical Receptions Journal* 3 (2011): 29–45; Catherine M. Chin, "Rufinus of Aquileia and Alexandrian Afterlives: Translation as Origenism," *JECS* 18 (2010): 617–47.

Patrum, Epiphanius as bishop still directs at long distance his old monastery in Palestine. When his monks boast of their scrupulous attention to the canonical hours of prayer, Epiphanius chastises them: "You are clearly neglecting the other hours of the day, unoccupied with prayer!"[87] In another apophthegm, Epiphanius invites his monastic mentor, Hilarion, to dine at his episcopal table. When Hilarion piously refuses the bird Epiphanius offers, claiming not to have touched meat since taking the habit, Epiphanius replies: "Since I took the habit, I have not allowed anyone to go to sleep holding anything against me, nor have I gone to sleep holding anything against someone else." Hilarion, duly chastened, admits to Epiphanius: "Your way of life (*politeia*) is better than mine."[88] Both of these anecdotes showcase the ascetic prowess of Epiphanius, but not unambiguously: in a monastic collection that emphasizes humility and collaborative mentorship, Epiphanius displays neither.[89] Perhaps Epiphanius's ascetic celebrity here is used not only as a model but as a caution.

Jerome also plays with Epiphanius's ascetic fame in his letter written at the death of his monastic companion Paula. Jerome recounts how Epiphanius lodged with Paula during a legation to the bishop of Rome (when, presumably, Jerome also made her acquaintance). The mere

---

87. *Apophthegmata Patrum Epiphanius* 3 (PG 65:164) = *Apophthegmata Patrum collectio systematica* 12.6 ("Concerning praying continually and soberly") (SC 474:210–12).

88. *Apophthegmata Patrum Epiphanius* 4 (PG 65:164) = *Apophthegmata Patrum collectio systematica* 4.15 ("Concerning continence, and that not only should one abstain from meat but also from anything living thing") (SC 387:192). Epiphanius already during his life is associated with Hilarion, an older Palestinian monk who also studied in Egypt and resided in Cyprus. Jerome (who wrote a *Life of Hilarion*) notes that Epiphanius had circulated "a short letter read by the masses" in praise of Hilarion, presumably at his death (*Vita Hilarionis* prol. [PL 23:29]), and Sozomen (*Historia ecclesiastica* 6.32.2 [GCS n.F. 4:288]) associates Epiphanius with Hilarion's disciple Hesychius as famous Palestinian monks.

89. On humility in the *Apophthegmata*, see Douglas Burton-Christie, *The Word in the Desert: Scripture and the Quest for Holiness in Early Christian Monasticism* (Oxford: Oxford University Press, 1993), 236–60; on the centrality of the master-disciple relationship, see Graham Gould, *The Desert Fathers on Monastic Community*, OECS (Oxford: Oxford University Press, 1993), 26–87.

presence of Epiphanius and of his colleague Paulinus, who lodged elsewhere, was enough to convert Paula to the ascetic life: "Inflamed by their virtues, every moment she pondered leaving behind her homeland."[90] When Paula does leave her home, her toddler waving sadly from the port, her journey east brings her to Cyprus,

> where, rolling at the feet of the holy, venerable Epiphanius, she stayed with him for ten days; not in recovery, *as he had thought,* but in God's work, as the matter proved. For, visiting all the monasteries of that region as much as she could, she left behind replenishments of resources for the brothers, whose love of the sainted man drew them there from the entire world.[91]

On Jerome's telling, Epiphanius is a monastic exemplar whose sanctity has made Cyprus a haven of monasteries. Yet the novice Paula seems already to have outstripped her ascetic inspiration: when he assumes she needs to rest from her trip, she spends her time in tireless beneficence. Years later, Jerome reports, Paula was sick and refusing the doctor's advice to take a little wine:

> And I myself, in secret, beseeched *papa* Epiphanius that he might admonish her, even compel her to drink wine; but she, as she was prudent and of skillful genius, right away sensed the trap; and smiling, intimated that what he was saying was mine. What more? When the blessed *pontifex,* after many exhortations, came out, he answered (when I asked him how it went): "Only that I got to the point that she almost persuaded me—an old man—that I shouldn't drink wine!"[92]

---

90. Jerome, *Ep.* 108.6.1–2 (CSEL 55:310–11). Epiphanius and Paula seem to reenact an earlier inspirational meeting between Athanasius of Alexandria and a young girl named Marcella (later a wealthy widow in Rome and a monastic companion of Paula's), as reported, at least, by Jerome, *Ep.* 127.5.1 (CSEL 56:149). That Jerome is the source for both of these stories may indicate his inventiveness (or Epiphanius's), but certainly indicates Epiphanius's enormous ascetic reputation by the 400s.

91. Jerome, *Ep.* 108.7.2–3 (CSEL 55:312–13) (emphasis added). See now Andrew Cain, *Jerome's Epitaph on Paula: A Commentary on the "Epitaphium Sanctae Paulae" with an Introduction, Text, and Translation,* OECT (Oxford: Oxford University Press, 2013), 206–7.

92. Jerome, *Ep.* 108.21.2–3 (CSEL 55:337).

Jerome here emphasizes Epiphanius's institutional ecclesiastical authority by ascribing to him the preeminently respectful titles *papa* and *pontifex*, both used during this period of the most prominent bishops.[93] Yet Jerome's portrayal of Epiphanius's ascetic value is more ambiguous. Epiphanius remains Paula's monastic mentor, such that Jerome imagines Epiphanius alone can convince her to relax her punishing regimen, but he is also revealed to be a lesser ascetic talent than Paula herself.[94] Much as Epiphanius's rustic *paideia* reflected Jerome's own pretensions to learned simplicity, so too Epiphanius in this letter acts as a foil for Paula's ascetic superiority.

Epiphanius's ascetic fame also makes him useful for his contemporaries to imagine the relationship between asceticism and the episcopacy. We have already seen the monasteries under his episcopal supervision receiving Paula's generosity, and Palladius tells us that the aristocratic ascetic Olympias was equally generous to Epiphanius's monastic foundations.[95] Sozomen is generally quite flattering in his portrayal of Epiphanius, and he associates the fame Epiphanius acquired as a monk with his selection for the episcopacy. Writing about the notable monks of Palestine, Sozomen reports:

> Educated from his youth by the best monks (*hupo monachois aristois paideutheis*) and on this account having spent a great deal of time in Egypt, he became most famous for his monastic philosophy among the Egyptians and

---

93. Only much later would *papa* become restricted to the bishop of Rome; see John Moorhead, "*Papa* as 'Bishop of Rome,'" *JEH* 36 (1985): 337–50.

94. On this incident, see Cain, *Jerome's Epitaph on Paula*, 390–92. I discuss it from a different perspective in chapter 3. Elizabeth Clark has discussed the role that female ascetics play in male texts as "shaming" devices; Clark, "Sex, Shame, and Rhetoric: En-Gendering Early Christian Ethics," *JAAR* 59 (1991): 221–45.

95. Palladius, *Dialogus de vita sancti Ioannis Chrysostomi* 17 (SC 341:320–22); this passage is reproduced (slightly edited) in the anonymous *Vita Olympiadis* 14 (text in Hippolyte Delehaye, "Vita Sanctae Olympiadis et narratio Sergiae," *Analecta Bollandiana* 15 [1896]: 420), on which see Elizabeth A. Clark, "Introduction to the *Life of Olympias* and Sergia's *Narration Concerning St. Olympias*," in *Jerome, Chrysostom, and Friends: Essays and Translations*, Studies in Women and Religion 1 (New York: Edwin Mellen Press, 1979), 113–14, 124 n. 50.

Palestinians (*episēmotatos epi monastikēi philosophiai gegone para te Aiguptiois kai Palaistinois*), afterward also among the Cypriots, by whom he was chosen to be bishop of the capital of the island.⁹⁶

The progression from monastic excellence to episcopal service seems quite direct. The account becomes, however, a bit confused. Although Sozomen has already suggested that Epiphanius became "most famous" (*episēmotatos*) for his asceticism, which led to his selection as bishop, he also notes that he was such a successful bishop that "in a short time he became known (*gnōrimos*) to all the citizens and every kind of foreigner: to some who had looked upon him and received the experience of his way of life (*tēs autou politeias*); and to others who learned of it from them."⁹⁷ On the one hand, Sozomen tells us that Epiphanius's ascetic fame led to his episcopal status; on the other hand, his episcopal status led to his ascetic fame. Sozomen is not clear on the sequence of events. The only certain point is that Epiphanius's fame emerges at the nexus of ecclesiastical service and monastic excellence.

The mid-fifth century, when Sozomen wrote his history, was the period of the rise of the "monk-bishop." Recent studies have detailed how the institutional edifice of the church began to appropriate the sanctity of the ascetic holy man in both literature and life: hagiographies of holy monks who became bishops circulated as prominent monasteries became sites for the cultivation of new clergy.⁹⁸ So we should not be surprised to see the famous Epiphanius drafted as an exemplar of this new model of Christian leadership. Yet while Sozomen's praise of Epiphanius fits into this new monastic-ecclesiastical model, it also betrays a bit of ambivalence: which is superior, the monk or the bishop?

---

96. Sozomen, *Historia ecclesiastica* 6.32.3 (GCS n.F. 4:288).
97. Sozomen, *Historia ecclesiastica* 6.32.4 (GCS n.F. 4:288). The use of *politeia* here certainly indicates ascetic conduct.
98. Andrea Sterk, *Renouncing the World Yet Leading the Church: The Monk-Bishop in Late Antiquity* (Cambridge, MA: Harvard University Press, 2004); and Rapp, *Holy Bishops in Late Antiquity*.

A similar confusion between institutional and ascetic authority animates a story found in the *Apophthegmata Patrum*, which an *abba* tells a grumpy disciple in order to illustrate the value of humility, forgiveness, and repentance.[99] Two "worldly men" decide to become monks and, being zealous but ignorant, castrate themselves in order to become "eunuchs for the Kingdom of Heaven."[100] Their bishop, hearing of this forbidden action, excommunicates them. Incensed that their ascetic superiority has been disrespected, the two monks appeal their case up a circuitous chain of episcopal command: to Jerusalem, then Antioch, and finally to the bishop of Rome, who is "head of them all" (*kephalē pantōn*). When he, too, affirms their excommunication the monks decide that all of these bishops are just supporting each other because they are friends and colleagues "who go to synods together." They say: "Let us go to that holy man of God Epiphanius, the bishop of Cyprus, because he is a prophet and he doesn't take account of a person's status (*prosōpon anthrōpou*)." Epiphanius does not even meet with them: forewarned by a vision, he sends out an escort to bar them from entering his city. At this point, the monks realize their folly and repent. They wail: "It's true, we have sinned! Even if they [i.e., the other bishops] had excommunicated us unjustly, is he not a prophet? Behold, God has told him about us." Epiphanius, sensing their true repentance from a distance, sends them to an Egyptian monastery, along with a note of recommendation addressed to the bishop of Alexandria.[101] In this story Epiphanius is indeed a bishop and an ascetic expert, but the two are strangely disjointed: he is not like

---

99. The story also appears in the anonymous collection (*Apophthegmata Patrum collectio anonyma* 334); text and translation in John Wortley, ed., *The Anonymous Sayings of the Desert Fathers: A Select Edition and Complete English Translation* (Cambridge: Cambridge University Press, 2013), 216–18.

100. On the historical and discursive phenomenon of Christian self-castration, see Mathew Kuefler, *The Manly Eunuch: Masculinity, Gender Ambiguity, and Christian Ideology in Late Antiquity*, Chicago Series on Sexuality, History, and Society (Chicago: University of Chicago Press, 2001), 245–82. Kuefler does not discuss this particular apophthegm.

101. *Apophthegmata Patrum collectio systematica* 15.111 ("On Humility") (SC 474:352–56). Note that, with the inclusion of the bishop of Alexandria at the end of the anecdote, four of the five patriarchates of the Roman Empire are mentioned (Jerusalem, Antioch,

the other bishops, standing somehow above and apart from them, even the bishop of Rome, "the head of them all." His ascetic expertise here seems to exist in spite of his episcopal fame, and vice versa.

In all three of these aspects of Christian life—*imperium, paideia,* and *askesis*—the celebrity of Epiphanius opens up a space for cultural exploration, but in multiple, often contradictory ways. Precisely because his image is replicated and repossessed by diverse audiences, the commodified image of the celebrity will resist cultural resolution. Indeed, the imperviousness of the celebrity to fixity—the fact that his fame is so open and malleable—seems to be one of the appeals of a celebrity in cultural discourses: the fact that he can remain, in Graeme Turner's words, an indeterminate "location for the interrogation and elaboration of cultural identity."[102] Imperial power hovers around Epiphanius, whether it is regarded as being impotent, insidious, or imminently sensible. Epiphanius's engagement with knowledge is at once transparently simplifying and schemingly dishonest. His ascetic prowess is both rigorous and lax, embedded in the episcopal hierarchy and yet elevated far beyond it. That all of these contradictory attitudes and ideas can be embedded in the persona of Epiphanius within decades of his death is possible precisely because, as he was a celebrity, his fame was unmoored from his specific accomplishments. And because he was a celebrity, the ability of his person to speak in multiple voices in multiple social and cultural contexts was what mattered to fourth- and fifth-century audiences.

CELEBRITY-ICON

My goal in this chapter has not been to restore Epiphanius's reputation in the fourth century, nor even to try to understand why he was so

---

Rome, and Alexandria), leaving only Constantinople out. Is Epiphanius meant to stand in for the patriarch of Constantinople in this apophthegm?

102. Turner, *Understanding Celebrity,* 24.

prominent. Celebrity does not operate through a clear calculus of achievement and reward. Nor does an analysis of celebrity lend itself to an analysis of a historical figure's *longue durée:* the fame of Epiphanius the theologian and controversialist of the early fifth century is not the same as the fame of Epiphanius the wonderworking monk in the sixth century, or that of the defender of icons in the ninth.[103] Our own historiographic desires for solidity and continuity either link these images together or dismiss them all as wispy hagiographic fantasies that tell us nothing historical. Rather, I have sought to understand his celebrity-function during and after his life in the early decades of the Christian Roman Empire in order to enrich our ongoing discussions of authority and status in Christian late antiquity. By attending to the seemingly ephemeral and inconstant, the malleable and multifarious, fame of a late fourth-century bishop, we can attend more precisely to the issues and concerns animating his cultural context, to the functions of personal authority rather than its causes. When early Christian audiences looked at Epiphanius or read about him, they were willing to see in him reflections of their own cultural values and to appropriate his person to change or redirect those values.

It would be a mistake for us to read this multifarious celebrity-function as somehow indicating that the real Epiphanius lacked authority, that he was unimportant or insubstantial or merely a cipher. Our own unexamined assumptions about celebrity still often track with the critique leveled by Boorstin in the 1960s: we want to distinguish between real (earned, substantial, authentic) authority and "pseudo"-celebrity. The wave of cultural studies of celebrity since Boorstin has reversed this understanding: celebrities are real and substantial precisely in the way they can encompass the contradictions of culture at a particular historical moment. It is because of his tremendous importance—his celebrity—that Epiphanius could anchor so many seemingly contradictory and confounding cultural attitudes. Rather than

---

103. I approach these later refractions of Epiphanius in chapter 6.

indicating a wispy insubstantiality, Epiphanius's celebrity signals to us his concrete realness and centrality at a specific historical moment. In this way, we might consider Epiphanius-the-celebrity as analogous to the ancient icon.

In her study of the "material turn" in late antiquity, Patricia Cox Miller questions how scholars have traditionally viewed the highly stylized and even schematic way in which saints were depicted in icons. Art historians like Ernest Kitzinger look upon the isolated, less formally realistic portraits and interpret them as wraith-like and insubstantial, inanimate figures lacking real presence to viewers.[104] Miller objects: "The problem is that viewing icons as unrealistic portrayals flies in the face of what Byzantines themselves thought about these images."[105] We equate "lifelike" with "realistic," and impose our own mode of viewing. But, as Miller details, these seemingly flat and insubstantial images teemed with life, inspiring contemplation and reaction from their viewers. So, too, Epiphanius's celebrity—which seems to us so transient, wispy, and insubstantial—does not indicate that he was an insubstantial pseudo-event; rather, it shows the ways in which his substance was refracted and made open to more complicated attempts to grasp cultural values in his time and for his contemporaries.

---

104. Patricia Cox Miller, *The Corporeal Imagination: Signifying the Holy in Late Ancient Christianity*, Divinations (Philadelphia: University of Pennsylvania Press, 2009), 167–71, citing Ernest Kitzinger, *Byzantine Art in the Making: Main Lines of Stylistic Development in Mediterranean Art, 3rd–7th Century* (Cambridge, MA: Harvard University Press, 1977), and two earlier essays: Kitzinger, "Byzantine Art in the Period between Justinian and Iconoclasm," in *Berichte zum XI. internationalen Byzantinisten-Kongress, München 1958* (Munich: C.H. Beck, 1958), 4.1:1–50; and Kitzinger, "The Cult of Images in the Age before Iconoclasm," *DOP* 8 (1954): 83–150.

105. Miller, *Corporeal Imagination*, 172. She cites approvingly Henry Maguire, *The Icons of Their Bodies: Saints and Their Images in Byzantium* (Princeton, NJ: Princeton University Press, 1981).

CHAPTER TWO

Conversion

BOUNDARIES AND FRONTIERS

In his treatise *On Weights and Measures,* Epiphanius recounts a trio of noteworthy tales of religious conversion.[1] In the course of explaining the origins of the Greek translations of the Hebrew Bible, Epiphanius gives brief accounts of Aquila, Symmachus, and Theodotion. These three Greek-speaking converts were popularly credited with translating the Hebrew Bible into Greek after the circulation of the Septuagint. Aquila, Epiphanius explains, was a member of the imperial family stationed in the ruins of Jerusalem by a leprous Emperor Hadrian.[2] While there, he became so impressed by the local Christian disciples

---

1. On the origins and date of this treatise, see my discussion in the introduction.

2. Epiphanius, *De mensuris et ponderibus* 14 (Dean, *Weights and Measures,* 30 [Eng.], 54d [Syr.]; Moutsoulas, "Περὶ μέτρων," ll. 385) identifies Aquila as Hadrian's brother-in-law (πενθερίδης; *bar hemha'*). Much of the biographical material on Aquila in *De mensuris et ponderibus* also appears in the later *Dialogue of Timothy and Aquila;* Fred Conybeare, *The Dialogues of Athanasius and Zacchaeus and of Timothy and Aquila,* Anecdota Oxoniensia (Oxford: Clarendon Press, 1898), xxv-xxxiii, notes these similarities and posits an earlier common source, a conclusion upheld (tentatively) by Robert Kraft, *Exploring the Scripturesque: Jewish Texts and Their Christian Contexts,* Supplements to the *Journal for the Study of Judaism* 137 (Leiden: Brill, 2009), 183.

that he was baptized as a Christian.[3] Unable to give up his love of astrology (*astronomia*), however, he was ultimately excommunicated; he cursed Christianity and decided to be converted to Judaism and circumcised as a Jew (*prosēluteuei kai peritemnetai Ioudaios*). Now twice converted, Aquila learned Hebrew (he was already Hadrian's Greek translator) and executed a "perverse" (Syr.: *mepataltah*) Greek translation of the Hebrew Bible.[4]

Symmachus had been one of the "wise men" (*sophōn*) of the Samaritans, but felt spurned by his own people. To satisfy his "lust for power," he converted to Judaism and was "circumcised a second time." (Assuming his audience will be surprised to hear this, Epiphanius patiently explains that second circumcisions are routine in Samaritan-Jewish cross-conversion, as are, he adds, operations to undo circumcision altogether.[5]) To spite his former fellow Samaritans, we learn, Symmachus

---

[3]. That Aquila was a Christian before he was a Jew seems unique to Epiphanius; Irenaeus, *Adversus haereses* 3.21.1 refers to both Aquila and Theodotion simply as "Jewish proselytes" (Θεοδοτίων ὁ Ἐφέσιος καὶ Ἀκύλας ὁ Ποντικός, ἀμφότεροι Ἰουδαῖοι προσήλυτοι) (SC 211:398, preserved in Eusebius, *Historia ecclesiastica* 5.8.10 [GCS 9.1:446]). Ancient sources on the lives of the "Three" were collected by Henry Swete, *An Introduction to the Old Testament in Greek* (Cambridge: Cambridge University Press, 1900), 31–35 (Aquila), 42–44 (Theodotion), 49–51 (Symmachus). On more recent theories of their identities, see Sidney Jellicoe, *The Septuagint and Modern Study* (Oxford: Clarendon Press, 1968), 77–99; on a comparison of Jewish and Christian sources on Aquila specifically, see Jenny R. Labendz, "Aquila's Bible Translation in Late Antiquity: Jewish and Christian Perspectives," *HTR* 102 (2009): 353–88 (on Epiphanius, 381–83).

[4]. Epiphanius, *De mensuris et ponderibus* 13–15 (Dean, *Weights and Measures*, 29–32 [Eng.], 54a–55b [Syr.]; Moutsoulas, "Περὶ μέτρων," ll. 360–424). Aquila appears in rabbinic literature as well, where his translation is tied more directly to rabbinic resistance to Greek (presumably, Christian use of the Septuagint); see Naomi Seidman, *Faithful Renderings: Jewish-Christian Difference and the Politics of Translation* (Chicago: University of Chicago Press, 2006), 73–114; and Labendz, "Aquila's Bible," 354–70.

[5]. On this story, see Reinhard Pummer, *Early Christian Authors on Samaritans and Samaritanism: Texts, Translations, and Commentary*, Texts and Studies in Ancient Judaism 92 (Tübingen: Mohr-Siebeck, 2002), 134–38, including extensive discussion of the "double circumcision" of Symmachus; on p. 137, Pummer notes that Symmachus's second circumcision brings his story into parallel with those of Aquila and Theodotion (who, Epiphanius notes explicitly, undergo circumcision). In this quite detailed description

executed an additionally "perverse" (Gk.: *diastrophēn*; Syr.: *potlah*) translation of the Hebrew Bible into Greek.[6]

Epiphanius then arrives at the story of Theodotion. Theodotion was originally a follower of Marcion, "the heresiarch of Sinope," and like Marcion, and Aquila the translator, Theodotion came from Pontus on the Black Sea. Theodotion also "grew angry with his heresy" (we are not told why) and "turned aside to Judaism and was circumcised and learned the language of the Hebrews and their writings." More influenced than the other two by the Septuagint, Theodotion produced a Greek translation not notably "perverse" (*diastrophēn*) to orthodox Christian sensibilities, but doubtless unwelcome as such among his former Marcionite coreligionists.[7]

This trio of conversion narratives evokes many kinds of overlapping boundaries and borders. Epiphanius has initially brought up these three figures because of their illicit relationship to the linguistic border between biblical Hebrew and Greek: what the inspired "Seventy" had produced under God's watch, these three figures deformed and perverted. Other borders and boundaries amplify this linguistic boundary. Epiphanius asks us to imagine the translators crossing several different religious boundaries of late antiquity, moving back and forth between paganism, Judaism, Christian heresy, and even the more exotic Samaritanism. A kind of cluster forms in the conceptual space around orthodox Christianity: it is no one's final religious destination, but is rather

---

of circumcision reversal, Epiphanius also notes that Esau invented the procedure, a (perhaps anti-Roman?) notion also found in later rabbinic materials (see Nissan Rubin, "*Brit Milah:* A Study of Change in Custom," in *The Covenant of Circumcision: New Perspectives on an Ancient Jewish Rite*, ed. Elizabeth Wyner Mark [Hanover, NH: Brandeis University Press, 2003], 89–97, esp. 88–92 and 224 n. 20.)

6. Epiphanius, *De mensuris et ponderibus* 16 (Dean, *Weights and Measures*, 32–33 [Eng.], 55c-55d [Syr.]; Moutsoulas, "Περὶ μέτρων," ll. 429–48). Eusebius, *Historia ecclesiastica* 6.17 (GCS 9.2:554) says that Symmachus's "heresy was Ebionite" (αἵρεσις δέ ἐστιν ἡ τῶν Ἐβιωναίων).

7. Epiphanius, *De mensuris et ponderibus* 17 (Dean, *Weights and Measures*, 33 [Eng.], 55d-56a [Syr.]; Moutsoulas, "Περὶ μέτρων," ll. 450–56).

framed by these marginal beliefs.⁸ Geographical borders also shape these stories: from Pontus in the north (the original home of both Aquila and Theodotion) to Egypt in the south. At the center lies the liminal and multiply named space of Palestine/Judaea (and Jerusalem/Aelia),⁹ out of which these multiple Greek translations of the Bible emerge and spread across the Roman Empire.¹⁰ The series of stories ends with the imposition of textual boundaries. All of these heterodox and perverse translations, we learn, end up collected together into the uniform columns of Origen's Hexapla, surrounding the correct, and corrective, translation of the Septuagint.¹¹ These marginal, boundary-crossing, perverse translators are safely, even usefully, contained for orthodox Christian delectation.¹² Borders proliferate, boundaries blur, but Epiphanius contains them all within *his* text and creates a sense of control over these shifty matters.

In recent years, students of early Christianity and late antiquity more generally have made fruitful use of the concept of boundaries and borders, in order to dislodge the monological self-presentations of our

---

8. This quartet—Hellenism, Judaism, Samaritanism, heresy—recalls the formative quartet of "mother heresies" in Epiphanius's *Panarion* (barbarism, Hellenism, Scythism, Judaism). It is equally true, as Tessa Rajak notes, that "each of the 'Three' is assigned a role on the margins of Jewry" (Rajak, *Translation and Survival: The Greek Bible and the Ancient Jewish Diaspora* [Oxford: Oxford University Press, 2009], 310).

9. Epiphanius, *De mensuris et ponderibus* 14 (Dean, *Weights and Measures*, 30 [Eng.], 54c–54d [Syr.]; Moutsoulas, "Περὶ μέτρων," ll. 370–90) mentions "Palestine, which is called Judea," and describes Hadrian's renaming of Jerusalem after himself, Aelia.

10. On the role of geography in Epiphanius's *Panarion*, see Young Richard Kim, "The Imagined Worlds of Epiphanius of Cyprus" (PhD diss., University of Michigan, 2006), 27–99; and Kim, "Epiphanius of Cyprus and the Geography of Heresy," in *Violence in Late Antiquity: Perceptions and Practices*, ed. Harold Drake (Burlington, VT: Ashgate, 2006), 235–51.

11. Epiphanius, *De mensuris et ponderibus* 18–19 (Dean, *Weights and Measures*, 36–37 [Eng.], 57b–d [Syr.]; Moutsoulas, "Περὶ μέτρων," ll. 507–44).

12. Anthony Grafton and Megan Williams, *Christianity and the Transformation of the Book: Origen, Eusebius, and the Library of Caesarea* (Cambridge, MA: Harvard University Press, 2008), 85–132; they discuss Epiphanius's "polemical" envisioning of the order of the columns (to preserve the primacy of the Septuagint, at the center) on pp. 92–94.

ancient sources.[13] To think in terms of borders—both established and breached—is to imagine the point at which the "self" and "other" touch, merge, and even change places. Borders must be asserted, put into place, and so ancient attention to borders signals, ironically, an acute anxiety about the porousness of identity and community: "Borders themselves," Daniel Boyarin has written, "are not given but constructed by power to mask hybridity, to occlude and disown it."[14] Borders produce, and elide, difference and distinction. Roman borders—or, more properly, *limites,* or frontiers, sites of material and cultural exchange—were primarily sites for the exercise of control, where the authoritative logic of empire was most visibly, and anxiously, at work. Epiphanius's stories of the conversion of the Greek translators of the Hebrew Bible situate the act of religious transformation—that is, conversion—squarely within these anxious, frontier discourses.

When we follow Epiphanius's lead and situate our rhetorics of conversion in these borderlands, therefore, we can begin to rework our assumptions about the nature of religious transformation.[15] Just as the border is about the often uneasy management of social, cultural, and religious contact, so late ancient conversion can be viewed as a discourse of identity subject to structures of power and knowledge.[16] Reading late

---

13. See Judith Lieu, "'Impregnable Ramparts and Walls of Iron': Boundary and Identity in 'Judaism' and 'Christianity,'" *New Testament Studies* 48 (2002): 297–313; and my *Christ Circumcised: A Study in Early Christian History and Difference,* Divinations (Philadelphia: University of Pennsylvania Press, 2012).

14. Daniel Boyarin, *Border Lines: The Partition of Judaeo-Christianity,* Divinations (Philadelphia: University of Pennsylvania Press, 2004), 15.

15. "Borderlands" theory emphasizes the porosity and hybridity of cultural identities and emerges from studies of Latino/a and Chicano/a culture on the US-Mexican border (see Gloria Anzaldúa, *Borderlands/La Frontera* [Ann Arbor: University of Michigan Press, 1987]); it has been recently picked up by students of late antiquity, such as the Ancient Borderlands Research Focus Group (www.ihc.ucsb.edu/ancientborderlands).

16. So Zeba Cook, *Reconceptualising Conversion: Patronage, Loyalty, and Conversion in the Religions of the Ancient Mediterranean,* Beihefte zur Zeitschrift für die neutestamentlische Wissenschaft und die Kunde der älteren Kirche 130 (Berlin: De Gruyter, 2004), resists the "siren song of psychologism" (4) by reframing ancient conversion—

ancient conversion as an exterior form of knowledge and power, rather than as an interior, psychological change, disrupts some of our well-established historical narratives. Modern, Western understandings of conversion often attempt to locate their psychologizing roots in late antiquity: theorists of conversion, such as Arthur Darby Nock and William James,[17] famously relied on that supposed master of interior introspection, Augustine.[18] Such readings are, of course, partial: enamored by the affective display of his "introspective conscience" in the *Confessions*,[19] modern readers at times pay less attention to some of the social realities of conversion in Augustine's episcopal career, such as his use of violence to force the conversion of local Donatists.[20] Despite such

---

specifically that of the apostle Paul—in the social context of patron-client relations. Cook, like many contemporary Pauline scholars, draws inspiration from Krister Stendahl, "Paul and the Introspective Conscience of the West," *HTR* 56 (1963): 199–215.

17. A.D. Nock, *Conversion: The Old and the New in Religion from Alexander the Great to Augustine of Hippo* (Oxford: Oxford University Press, 1933), remains highly influential. Nock, in turn, was greatly influenced by William James, *The Varieties of Religious Experience* (New York: Longman & Green, 1902). On Nock's and James's continuing influence over interpretations of conversion in antiquity, see Peter Brown, "Conversion and Christianization in Late Antiquity: The Case of Augustine," in *The Past before Us: The Challenge of Historiographies of Late Antiquity*, ed. Carole Straw and Richard Lim (Turnhout: Brepols, 2004), 103–17. On the psychologizing view held by Nock and his fellow ancient historians that the high Roman Empire was a period of individual alienation, see Nicola Denzey, "'Enslavement to Fate,' 'Cosmic Pessimism,' and Other Explorations of the Late Roman Psyche: A Brief History of a Historiographical Trend," *Studies in Religion/Sciences Religieuses* 33 (2004): 277–99.

18. Paula Fredriksen, "Paul and Augustine: Conversion Narratives, Orthodox Traditions, and the Retrospective Self," *JTS* n.s. 37 (1986): 3–34, esp. 26–33, following closely on Stendahl, "Paul." In a later piece, Fredriksen calls for the "retirement" of the term "conversion" in studies of Paul: "Mandatory Retirement: Ideas in the Study of Christian Origins Whose Time to Go Has Come," *Studies in Religion/Sciences Religieuses* 35 (2006): 231–46.

19. Stendahl, "Paul," 205: "[Augustine's] *Confessions* are the first great document in the history of the introspective conscience." See, more recently, Brent Shaw, *Sacred Violence: African Christians and Sectarian Hatred in the Age of Augustine* (Cambridge: Cambridge University Press, 2011).

20. Fredrick H. Russell, "Persuading the Donatists: Augustine's Coercion by Words," in *The Limits of Late Ancient Christianity: Essays on Late Antique Thought and Culture in Honor of R.A. Markus*, ed. William Klingshirn and Mark Vessey (Ann Arbor:

overdetermined reliance on the *Confessions*, and its availability to modernist psychology, there are surprisingly few introspective narratives of religious conversion in antiquity: moments at which a subject invites us to witness his or her internal process of moving from one religious life to another.[21] More often, we read *about* religious transformation from the outside: authors like Epiphanius in my examples above circulate narratives of conversion, which then form part of the larger discursive social and religious fabric of late antiquity. To borrow an insight from Jeffrey Shoulson, a scholar of Victorian English literary culture,

> Conversion does not merely function as a figure for change; rather, these fictions of conversion serve as a nexus for the negotiation of various kinds of change, often in conflict with one another. Conversion becomes a means through which other technologies of transformation ... are figured during the period under consideration.[22]

I am similarly interested in how Epiphanius can help us revision late ancient "technologies of transformation."

More helpful than psychologizing attempts to track the inner movements of the soul may be readings of conversion that focus instead on

---

University of Michigan Press, 1999), 115–30, tries to circle the square of Augustine's acts of social management and psychological theories of sign and will: "Augustine's attack upon the Donatists was a precariously balanced blend of external discipline and inward nurturance" (125).

21. On some of the more "classic" first-person narratives of conversion, see Laura Nasrallah's discussion of Justin Martyr and Tatian: "The Rhetoric of Conversion and the Construction of Experience: The Case of Justin Martyr," *SP* 40 (2006): 467–74. The modern tendency to frame conversion as an entirely interiorized movement of the self was tackled sociologically by Rodney Stark and John Lofland, "Becoming a World-Saver: A Theory of Conversion to a Deviant Perspective," *American Sociological Review* 30 (1965): 863–74; for overview and critique, see Lorne L. Dawson, "Who Joins New Religious Movements and Why: Twenty Years of Research and What Have We Learned?," in *Cults and New Religious Movements: A Reader*, ed. Lorne L. Dawson (Oxford: Blackwell, 2003), 116–30; originally published in *Studies in Religion/Sciences Religieuses* 25 (1996): 141–61.

22. Jeffrey S. Shoulson, *Fictions of Conversion: Jews, Christians, and Cultures of Change in Early Modern England* (Philadelphia: University of Pennsylvania Press, 2013), 10–11.

its social and cultural locations.[23] Some recent studies of conversion in multiple historical contexts have already tried to dislodge our reigning view of religious conversion as primarily an internal, psychological event or process.[24] Laura Nasrallah, in an essay on ancient conversion, fruitfully applied to the late ancient Christian context Gauri Viswanathan's insights into the role of conversion as a colonial discourse.[25] For Viswanathan, conversion appears in the rhetoric of empire when the state desires to visibly grapple with, and masterfully overcome, the problems of identity and difference within its borders: "If conversion precipitates breaches within the fold, it also sets in motion a dynamic social process that confers a new power and role on the state."[26] I have argued elsewhere for the usefulness of colonial discourse analysis as a theoretical lens in the study of the late Christian Roman Empire. Of course, I am not suggesting that the British Empire, studied by Shoulson and Viswanathan, was functionally or materially identical to the Roman Empire, but rather that some of the insights from postcolonial theory may be useful in thinking through analogous issues in antiquity. Here I suggest it can help us rethink important cultural ideas about politics and religion.[27] In sum, in periods during which the interests of

23. See Arietta Papaconstantinou, introduction to *Conversion in Late Antiquity: Christianity, Islam, and Beyond*, ed. Arietta Papaconstantinou, with Neil McLynn and Daniel Schwartz (Burlington, VT: Ashgate, 2015), xv-xxxvii.

24. See the essay collections edited by Kenneth Mills and Anthony Grafton: *Conversion in Late Antiquity and the Early Middle Ages: Seeing and Believing* (Rochester, NY: University of Rochester Press, 2003) and *Conversion: Old Worlds and New* (Rochester, NY: University of Rochester Press, 2003); also Eugene V. Gallagher, "Conversion and Community in Late Antiquity," *JR* 73 (1993): 1-15; and Shane P. Gannon, "Conversion as a Thematic Site: Academic Representations of Ambedkar's Buddhist Turn," *Method and Theory in the Study of Religion* 23 (2011): 1-28 for a different theoretical approach to a "hermeneutics of conversion."

25. Nasrallah, "Rhetoric of Conversion," 467, 469-70, 473-74.

26. Gauri Viswanathan, *Outside the Fold: Conversion, Modernity, and Belief* (Princeton, NJ: Princeton University Press, 1998), 17.

27. Andrew S. Jacobs, *Remains of the Jews: The Holy Land and Christian Empire in Late Antiquity*, Divinations (Stanford, CA: Stanford University Press, 2003); "The Lion and the Lamb: Reconsidering 'Jewish-Christian Relations' in Antiquity," in *The Ways that Never Parted: Jews and Christians in Antiquity and the Middle Ages*, ed. Adam H. Becker and

the state overlap with those of religious institutions—the late Roman Empire, for instance—to think about conversion is to think about personhood. Just as empires grapple with the blurry boundaries that both define and threaten their coherence, so too their logic of control and power illuminates the ways in which persons cross various thresholds of religious status and being.[28]

In this chapter, I argue that Epiphanius allows us to consider conversion in a more expansive fashion: not simply or even primarily as the internal reorientation to a "new life," but as the exteriorized management of status and difference. That is, through Epiphanius we can think more *imperially* about the ways in which people underwent religious transformation in the late ancient Christian world. Epiphanius also encourages us to think more *expansively* about what we typically call "conversion." Once we relocate the discourse of conversion from the interior psyche to the exterior site of an imperial frontier zone,[29] a variety of types of religious transformation becomes relevant. When conversion is about an internal state, we are concerned with psychological categories such as belief or sincerity. When we think of changes in religious status as objects of exterior investigation and management,

---

Annette Yoshiko Reed, Texts and Studies in Ancient Judaism 95 (Tübingen: Mohr-Siebeck, 2003), 95–118; and *Christ Circumcised: A Study in Early Christian History and Difference*, Divinations (Philadelphia: University of Pennsylvania Press, 2012), 6–10.

28. On historically and geographically situating "conversion," see Averil Cameron, "Christian Conversion in Late Antiquity: Some Issues," in Papaconstantinou, McLynn, and Schwartz, *Conversion in Late Antiquity*, 3–21.

29. The concept of a "frontier zone" has been deployed in the history of religions by David Chidester, *Savage Systems: Colonialism and Comparative Religion in Southern Africa* (Charlottesville: University of Virginia Press, 1996), 20–26; "I define a frontier as a zone of contact, rather than a line, a border, or a boundary. By this definition, a frontier is a region of intercultural relations between intrusive and indigenous people. Those cultural relations, however, are also power relations. A frontier zone opens with the contact between two or more previously distinct societies and remains open as long as power relations are unstable and contested, with no one group or coalition able to establish dominance. A frontier zone closes when a single political authority succeeds in establishing its hegemony over the area" (20–21). See also Boyarin, *Border Lines*, 13–14, 202–9.

the category broadens. James Muldoon has written about what he calls "the conversion spectrum," an attempt to gather together in one analytic framework "a variety of transforming experiences."[30] Along with the intensely individual experience of Paul on the road to Damascus and the ostentatiously public conversion of a Constantine or a Clovis, Muldoon considers the move from lay to monastic life, or even spiritual advancement within the religious life. "At each point along the spectrum," he notes, "there is a process involved, not just an event."[31] When we further plot these events in the social and political space of Epiphanius's Christian empire, we see the contiguous operations between multiple forms of religious status change.

I explore through Epiphanius's writings three different types of religious conversion, each of which will give us some purchase on understanding the frontiers of Christian personhood, and each of which is informed by the logic of imperial identity. First, changes in status within Christian hierarchies (from priest to lay, and back again) illustrate the ways in which frontiers function as unstable zones of authoritative control. Next, in the conversion from orthodox to heretical Christian, we see the erratic ways in which religious and state power intersect in a Christian empire. Finally, by looking at the change from Jew to Christian we see how, in the very act of establishing boundaries, Christianity causes those religious boundaries to collapse in on themselves, as identity in the borderlands becomes totalizing.

BECOMING A LEADER: ASCETICS AND PRIESTS

In two very different episodes, Epiphanius describes changes of religious status within the Christian ecclesiastical hierarchy. In his letter to Bishop John of Jerusalem, written in 394 as part of an opening salvo

---

30. James Muldoon, "Introduction: The Conversion of Europe," in *Varieties of Religious Conversion in the Middle Ages* (Gainesville: University of Florida Press, 1997), 1–10, cited here at p. 1.

31. Muldoon, "Introduction," 1.

in the Origenist controversy,[32] Epiphanius tells the story of an unusual ordination. Through contact over the years, Epiphanius had become aware that a certain monastery in John's geographic jurisdiction had no one to administer the sacraments: the two priests already resident there, it seemed, "did not want to oversee the sacrifices which are owed to their rank."[33] A third potential priestly candidate, who had so far eluded ordination, serendipitously presented himself before Epiphanius with other monks wishing to "make satisfaction" for "some grudge (*tristitiae*)."[34] As Epiphanius tells it,

> I commanded him—unknowing, and having no suspicion within—to be seized by several deacons and that his mouth be held (lest perhaps desiring to be let go, he might swear at us through Christ's name); and first I ordained him a deacon, laying before him the fear of God and compelling him to minister; of course he struggled vigorously, shouting that he was unworthy, and protesting that this heavy burden exceeded his strength. Scarcely therefore had I compelled him, and I was able to persuade him with testimony from Scriptures, and by laying before him God's commands. And when he had ministered in the holy sacrifices, once more with his mouth held with remarkable difficulty, I ordained him presbyter.[35]

Epiphanius's victim here is Paulinian, Jerome's brother, an inhabitant of Jerome's monastery in Bethlehem, some miles from Jerusalem.[36] Paulinian's is not the only forcible clerical ordination we hear of during this period, or later: forcible (or, at least, coercive) ordination becomes something of a trope in hagiographic literature, part of the

---

32. On this letter, see my discussion in the introduction.

33. Epiphanius, *Ep. ad Ioannem* (= Jerome, *Ep.* 51) 1.3 (CSEL 54:396). One of those priests was Jerome himself. I discuss this incident from different vantage points in chapters 3 and 5. On this series of confrontations between John and Epiphanius, see Young Richard Kim, *Epiphanius of Cyprus: Imagining an Orthodox World* (Ann Arbor: University of Michigan Press, 2015), 211–17.

34. Epiphanius, *Ep. ad Ioannem* (= Jerome, *Ep.* 51) 1.5 (CSEL 54:396).

35. Epiphanius, *Ep. ad Ioannem* (= Jerome, *Ep.* 51) 1.5–6 (CSEL 54:396–97).

36. We know little about Paulinian apart from scant mentions by Jerome (and, here, by Epiphanius mediated through Jerome); see now Young Richard Kim, "Jerome and Paulinian, Brothers," *VC* 67 (2013): 517–30.

growing *mythos* of the saintly "monk-bishop."[37] Epiphanius's account is one of the few narratives we possess of forcible ordination from the hand of one of the direct participants,[38] and it is striking for its matter-of-factness.[39]

In this letter, Epiphanius is ostensibly responding to accusations that he had irregularly ordained Paulinian within Bishop John's jurisdiction without John's consent. In a broader sense, the story is about who exerts control over the boundaries of Christian status and selfhood. Mostly obviously, the poorly maintained ecclesiastical boundary of clergy and laity is managed and corrected by Epiphanius: for years, he reports, the monks of the monastery had been complaining about their clerical deficiency.[40] In an act of charity, Epiphanius had forcibly escorted Paulin-

---

37. Claudia Rapp, *Holy Bishops in Late Antiquity: The Nature of Christian Leadership in an Age of Transition*, TCH 37 (Berkeley: University of California Press, 2005), 141–47, discusses the political and rhetorical effects of monks protesting their ordination. Peter Norton, *Episcopal Elections, 250–600: Hierarchy and Popular Will in Late Antiquity*, OCM (Oxford: Oxford University Press, 2007), 191–96, provides a brief catalog of forced, or coerced, ordinations, mostly from hagiography and mostly to the episcopacy.

38. Augustine of Hippo is another direct witness, on two counts: in a much later sermon, he recounts how he was more or less conscripted into the priesthood ("apprehensus, presbyter factus sum") while visiting Hippo (*Sermo* 355.2 [PL 39:1569]; his ordination took place in 391, and this sermon was probably delivered toward the end of his life); and in a thoroughly apologetic letter, Augustine narrates the narrowly averted forcible ordination of Pinian, husband of Melania the Younger, during their stay in North Africa following the sack of Rome: *Ep.* 126 (written to Albina, Melania's mother; he also discusses the event in *Ep.* 125 to his friend and episcopal colleague Alypius) (CSEL 44:3–18). On these twin events, see Kate Cooper, "Poverty, Obligation, and Inheritance: Roman Heiresses and the Varieties of Senatorial Christianity in Fifth-Century Rome," in *Religion, Dynasty, and Patronage in Early Christian Rome, 300–900*, ed. Kate Cooper and Julia Hillner (Cambridge: Cambridge University Press, 2007), 165–67.

39. Although Epiphanius and other contemporary sources do not discuss the circumstance of his own ordination, his hagiography (from, perhaps, the late fifth century) presents Epiphanius's ordination to the priesthood as similarly forced and violent: *Vita Epiphanii* 60 (text in Claudia Rapp, "The *Vita* of Epiphanius of Salamis: An Historical and Literary Study" [D.Phil. thesis, Oxford University, 1991], 2:126–28).

40. Elsewhere Epiphanius remarks generally on the problem of staffing shortages among Christian clergy: *Panarion* 59.4.4 (GCS 31:367–68), *De fide* 21.8 (GCS 37:522).

ian—twice—across clerical borders to correct this deficiency.[41] Other boundaries and borders are implicated here as well. Epiphanius suggests that the monastery by its nature exists outside of episcopal authority, a free-floating island of sanctity that defies its own geography. He further notes that his action concerned "a monastery of brothers, of foreign brothers, who owe nothing to your province"; that is, they are not under John's jurisdiction.[42] Besides, Epiphanius chides, why should John be so precious about episcopal borders? In the "large and ranging" province of Cyprus, Epiphanius is grateful if other bishops ordain priests he has "been unable to capture" himself.[43] It is, somewhat paradoxically, a sign of control and mastery to allow others to intrude on these boundaries. Finally, John's overly conscientious attention to his own boundaries bespeaks an ironic loss of self-control: Epiphanius (somewhat cattily) implores John: "May fury not get the better of you, nor indignation overcome you."[44] John's anger threatens to spill beyond even the boundaries of the *oikoumene*: "I have heard you are puffed up against us, and you are enraged, and you threaten to write to the very ends of the world, even places and provinces without names!"[45] Epiphanius, by contrast, as he forced Paulinian across the borders of ecclesiastical hierarchy, is masterful and orderly.[46] Even as he writes this letter to John (the bulk of which accuses the Jerusalem bishop of being an

---

41. There is no sense in his letter about the amount of time that passed between Paulinian's diaconate and presbyterate; he notes: "I ordained one of the brothers deacon, and *after he had ministered as such*, admitted him to the priesthood" (*Ep. ad Ioannem* [= Jerome, *Ep. 51*] 1.3 [CSEL 54:396], emphasis added). Presumably the gap could have been as short as a single service, during which Paulinian was "convinced" to take up his diaconal duties.

42. Epiphanius, *Ep. ad Ioannem* (= Jerome, *Ep. 51*) 1.3 (CSEL 54:396).
43. Epiphanius, *Ep. ad Ioannem* (= Jerome, *Ep. 51*) 2.1 (CSEL 54:397–98).
44. Epiphanius, *Ep. ad Ioannem* (= Jerome, *Ep. 51*) 2.5 (CSEL 54:399).
45. Epiphanius, *Ep. ad Ioannem* (= Jerome, *Ep. 51*) 1.1 (CSEL 54:395).
46. Furthermore, in order to escape censure, it seems Paulinian took up "official" residence in Cyprus soon after; so Jerome, *Contra Ioannem Hierosolymitanum* 41 (PL 23:393): "You see that he is with his own bishop, that he has returned to Cyprus, that he comes to visit us occasionally (*interdum*), not as one of yours, but another's (*alienum*), indeed, belonging to the one who ordained him."

unrepentant heretic), Epiphanius underscores his own cool control: he might think uncharitable thoughts about John to himself, but would never "say such a thing openly."[47] The entire incident stands as a model of effective control of self and others.

Efforts to control clerical and geographic boundaries coincide in another story of religious status transformation that Epiphanius tells in the fortieth chapter of his *Panarion*, on the "Archontics."[48] (Like many of Epiphanius's eighty heresies, the "Archontics" are otherwise unattested among ancient Christians.) This story takes place before Epiphanius had become a bishop, while he still led his monastery in Palestine. Epiphanius recalls a monk named Peter, who lived in Palestine near Epiphanius's own home turf:

> At an early age he was enrolled in many heresies, but when Aetius was bishop, having been accused and refuted then for being part of the gnostic heresy, he was deposed from the presbyterate (for some time before he was ordained a presbyter). After his refutation he was exiled (*ediōchthē*) from that place by Aetius, and going off, he settled in Arabia at Kokabe.[49]

We might consider this a simple reversal of the story of Paulinian: a man is stripped of his presbyterate, forced by a masterful bishop back across a clerical boundary he had illegitimately transgressed. Once again, appropriate control of Christian frontiers is being exerted. But the story does not end there. A generation after his deposition (Aetius of Lydda was dead by the 340s), Peter returned to Epiphanius's neighborhood as an old man, although "bearing in him that secret poison." Peter began to "whisper" (*epsithurise*) his heresy until "having been

---

47. Epiphanius, *Ep. ad Ioannem* (= Jerome, *Ep. 51*) 3.2 (CSEL 54:399).
48. Kim, *Epiphanius*, 90–95. On the Archontics more broadly, see Roelof van den Broek, "Archontics," in *Dictionary of Gnosis and Western Esotericism*, ed. W.J. Hanegraaff (Leiden: Brill, 2006), 89–91.
49. Epiphanius, *Panarion* 40.1.5 (GCS 31:81). Aetius should not be confused with the "Anomoioan" heretic condemned by Epiphanius in *Panarion* 76; this elder Aetius was bishop of Diospolis (Lydda/Lod) in the early fourth century, and a signatory at the Council of Nicaea.

refuted by me he was anathematized and refuted by my insignificance."[50] Epiphanius seems to refer here to a monastic expulsion, since, as an abbot but not yet a bishop, he does not possess the power of excommunication. Forced once more across an internal ecclesiastical boundary, the ex-priest now becomes an ex-monk. Where the first religious status change failed to do its job, we might think, the second will be more successful.

A closer reading of the anecdote, however, reveals that Epiphanius has jumbled the order of events to make his own actions, and those of Aetius, seem more efficacious. When we first meet Peter in the *Panarion*, "he seemed to be an anchorite (*anachōrētēs*), dwelling in a certain cave, who seemingly (*dēthen*) drew many into renunciation (*eis apotaxin*) and seemingly (*dēthen*) was called 'father' on account of his age and his habit (*to schēma*)."[51] Since this ersatz hermit lives in the area of Epiphanius's own monastery (near Eleutheropolis[52]), we might imagine that Epiphanius rebuked and refuted him during this time. Yet later in the chapter Epiphanius seems to contradict himself, when he reports that *after* the false monk's expulsion "he dwelled in the cave, abhorred by all and forsaken (*monōtheis*) by the brotherhood."[53] That is, Peter becomes a "seeming" anchorite only *after* being expelled from Epiphanius's monastery, and while the brotherhood of Epiphanius's monks may have "forsaken" him, many others continued to venerate him and call him "Father."

Epiphanius's narrative therefore lacks the fully confident mastery of his ordination of Paulinian. For, Peter—ex-priest, ex-monk—has, seemingly, lost none of his religious status and remains a teacher and minister. From his deceptive anchoritic cave—in a sheepskin that

---

50. Epiphanius, *Panarion* 40.1.6 (GCS 31:81).
51. Epiphanius, *Panarion* 40.1.4 (GCS 31:81).
52. Epiphanius, *Panarion* 40.1.3 (GCS 31:81). Later sources identify this region as Epiphanius's birthplace and the site of his monastic community: Sozomen, *Historia ecclesiastica* 6.32.1 (GCS n.F. 4:282).
53. Epiphanius, *Panarion* 40.1.7 (GCS 31:81). Kim, *Epiphanius*, 94, suggests that Peter may have been living in the cave already while still a member of Epiphanius's monastic community.

makes him, according to Epiphanius, an actual wolf in sheep's clothing[54]—Peter passes his heretical teachings to one Eutactus, a visitor passing by from Egypt who will imbibe Peter's poison and go on to "sow his tare" in Armenia.[55] The failure to enforce internal ecclesiastical boundaries is echoed by porous geographic boundaries, as heresy oozes across the empire's fragile frontiers. If the story of Paulinian is one of the control of hierarchical boundaries, the story of Peter is about the loss of containment that threatens even the most well-managed frontier zone.

Even this account of failed control of clerical borders, however, serves the larger purpose of helping us envision this kind of conversion (from priest to layperson, and vice versa) as a question of status management and power rather than according to a more modern, romanticized notion of a priestly "calling." To be(come) a member of the Christian clergy in late antiquity was to participate in a very public and visible social class analogous to and even patterned upon other public offices in the Roman Empire.[56] Clerical management, then, was not a matter of conscience so much as a matter of human resource allocation and control. We can recall, alongside Epiphanius's narrative evidence, the great number of ecumenical canons in the fourth and fifth centuries devoted to precisely this question of clerical status, particularly questions of how to reintegrate formerly "heretical" clergy back into the fold.[57] Even when clerical border-crossings are illicit, they still

---

54. Epiphanius, *Panarion* 40.1.4 (GCS 31:81): "For truly on the outside he wore a sheep's fleece, and no one knew that on the inside abided a rapacious wolf."

55. Epiphanius, *Panarion* 40.1.8 (GCS 31:81–82).

56. Sabine Huebner, "Currencies of Power: The Venality of Offices in the Later Roman Empire," in *The Power of Religion in Late Antiquity*, ed. Andrew Cain and Noel Lenski (Burlington, VT: Ashgate, 2009), 167–79, outlines how clerical officeholding, particular high-status positions (in Constantinople) became commodified into the sixth century.

57. Council of Nicaea, canons 8, 19 (text and commentary in Karl Joseph von Hefele, *Histoire des conciles* [Paris: Letouzey et Ané, 1907], 1.1:576–87, 615–18); Council of Ephesus, canons 3, 4, 5 (text in Karl Joseph von Hefele, *Histoire des conciles* [Paris: Letouzey et Ané, 1908], 2.1:339–40).

inculturate Christians into a sort of life that understands changes in status as a form of management and control that *should* be exerted by authorities such as Epiphanius.

BECOMING A HERETIC

Among the many ways we can read Epiphanius's most famous work, the *Panarion,* is as a study both in the porous frontiers of religious identity and in Epiphanius's own role as the manager of those anxious frontiers. Of all the boundaries crossed by Christians, the threshold between orthodoxy and heresy looms largest in Epiphanius's imagination. In some respects, this is because of the all-encompassing view of the Christian universe that Epiphanius cultivates throughout his writings: in a totalized scheme in which there is no "outside"—everyone, from Adam to the present, exists on a spectrum of orthodoxy and heresy—the multifarious differences within stand in precipitously high relief.[58] Just as the movement across status lines within the clerical hierarchy speaks to issues of power and control, the movement of Christians from orthodoxy into heresy likewise evokes the lack of containment within that orthodoxy totality. The fluid failures of an individual's religious status mirror, and even contribute to, the instability of the community as a whole. Viswanathan notes that "conversion unsettles the boundaries by which selfhood, citizenship, nation-hood, and community are defined, exposing these as permeable borders."[59] To pass from orthodoxy to heresy, for Epiphanius, is to make visible one of a myriad of fault lines fracturing the facade of Christian community. It is also, in a way, to provide an opportunity for a masterful Christian heresiologist to map and control those faults.

---

58. See Jacobs, *Remains of the Jews,* 44–55; Jeremy Schott, "Heresiology as Universal History in Epiphanius's *Panarion,*" *ZAC* 10 (2006): 546–63; and Kim, "Imagined Worlds," passim.

59. Viswanathan, *Outside the Fold,* 16.

We witness several Christians passing from truth to error in the pages of the *Panarion*. In many of these biographical vignettes, the conversion to heresy comes not as the result of a psychological failure but in the peculiar circumstances of the heretics' lives. That is, their "conversion" to heresy does not result from an interior reorientation to a new set of beliefs, but rather responds to various external life events. Valentinus "had a bit of piety" (*meros ... eusebeias*) as he preached around the Roman Empire. But after suffering a shipwreck on his way to Cyprus, "he gave up the faith and changed his opinion (*ton noun*).... On Cyprus finally he arrived at the last impiety (*eis eschaton asebeias*)."[60] Theodotus, a "very learned shoemaker" from Byzantium, denied Christ during a persecution against Christians. "Deeply ashamed," he fled to Rome, where, confronted with his lapse in the face of martyrdom, he invented a christological heresy to cover his shame: "I did not deny God," he claimed. "I denied a man."[61] Bardesan was originally a member of "God's holy church," even risking martyrdom, before he "made the acquaintance (*prosphtheiretai*) of the Valentinians."[62] The suggestion here is that social ties led Bardesan off the path of holiness. Sometimes the circumstances are left vague: Hieracas "was Christian ... but did not remain in Christ's way of life (*tēi tou Christou politeiai*); for he went astray and, having slipped, he ran aground."[63] What caused Hieracas to "stray" and "slip"? The vagueness creates a sense of unease around the maintenance of orthodox identity. The borderlands of Christian orthodoxy are precarious indeed, across which faithful Christians can drift and morph into heresiarchs.

---

60. Epiphanius, *Panarion* 31.7.2 (GCS n.F. 10.1:396). Epiphanius is the only ancient source to place Valentinus on Cyprus, much less place his "conversion" to heresy there. Some scholars have suggested Epiphanius has inferred Valentinus's presence in Cyprus from the existence of Valentinian communities there in his own day; see Einar Thomasson, *The Spiritual Seed: The Church of the "Valentinians,"* NMHS 60 (Leiden: Brill, 2006), 419.

61. Epiphanius, *Panarion* 54.1.3–7 (GCS 31:317–18).

62. Epiphanius, *Panarion* 56.2.1 (GCS 31:340).

63. Epiphanius, *Panarion* 67.1.4 (GCS 37:133).

Epiphanius is more fulsome in his examination of the causes of this "slippage" in the longer chapters against more major heresiarchs. I focus more specifically in this section on two significant heretical border-crossers. Young Richard Kim has noted the degree to which biography structures the longer chapters of the bishop's heresiography.[64] Following Kim's lead, I delve into the heretical biographies of two major heresiarchs of the *Panarion:* Origen and Arius.[65] The ways in which these two Christians converted into heretics highlight a second aspect of Epiphanius's discourse of conversion: the erratic presence of empire in the management of Christian boundaries.

Origen, against whose teaching Epiphanius waged a protracted battle,[66] begins his life in *Panarion* 64 as a model Christian, the pious son of a martyr, himself subject to harassment in Alexandria for his Christianity. Although he lapses at the pagan altar before the threat of sexual violence,[67] once he is replanted in Caesarea he remains, Epiphanius says, "of the correct and catholic faith."[68] So, from the beginning, the shadow of empire, in the form of religious persecution, casts a chill over Origen's Christianity. Origen is studious to a fault, and his longing for knowledge leads him into heresy: "His wealth of learning (*polupeirias*) turned out to be his great downfall (*mega ptōma*)";[69] he was "bitten by a terrible viper, I mean worldly education (*tēs kosmikēs propaideias*), and became fatal to others."[70] The sexual violence of the state and

---

64. Kim, "Imagined Worlds," 100–178; and Kim, "Reading the *Panarion* as Collective Biography: The Heresiarch as Unholy Man," *VC* 64 (2010): 382–413.

65. Kim, "Imagined Worlds," also looks at the biography of Mani, which is probably the longest biography in the *Panarion* (based, primarily, on the scurrilous *Acta Archelai*). While Mani's biography is certainly rife with failed boundaries—of geography, status, and orthodoxy—he operates on the margins of all of these borders, never inhabiting "orthodoxy" in the way Origen and Arius do before their conversions to heresy.

66. I discuss Epiphanius's particularly scriptural anti-Origenism in more detail in chapter 4 and his theological anti-Origenism in chapter 5.

67. Epiphanius, *Panarion* 64.2.2–3 (GCS 31:404).

68. Epiphanius, *Panarion* 64.3.1 (GCS 31:405).

69. Epiphanius, *Panarion* 64.3.8 (GCS 31:409).

70. Epiphanius, *Panarion* 64.72.5 (GCS 31:523). Kim, "Imagined Worlds," highlights the "denunciation of classical culture" (8) throughout Epiphanius's oeuvre, particularly

the intellectual violence of worldly education are perhaps not unrelated in Epiphanius's mind, insofar as they both envision the boundaries of the person (body and mind) subject to the deteriorating outside influence of empire (political and cultural). As a consequence, Origen retrojects these negative influences back outward: in addition to producing "fatal (*thanasima*) words of interpretation,"[71] Origen was rumored to have devised unnatural ways of "dealing with his body," such as methods of neurological or chemical castration and medical memory-enhancement.[72]

Folded within the story of Origen's fall from orthodoxy to heresy is the story of Ambrose, his eventual patron. Origen is pressed to meet Ambrose, "who happened to be one of the luminaries of the imperial court," so that he might draw him from heresy (Epiphanius guesses Marcionite or Sabellian) to the proper orthodoxy, which, at that time, Origen professed.[73] Origen is seemingly successful: Ambrose is con-

---

in his attack on Origen (esp. 144–48); J. Rebecca Lyman, "Origen as Ascetic Theologian: Orthodoxy and Authority in the Fourth-Century Church," in *Origeniana Septima*, ed. Wolfgang Bienert and Uwe Kühneweg (Leuven: Peeters, 1999), also describes Epiphanius as "a man of limited education" (187) and sees in his attack on Origen a "populist" rejection of *paideia* (192–94). While it does seem clear that Epiphanius did not have formal philosophical education, it seems undeniable that he must have had grammatical and some rhetorical education; his attacks on "Hellenistic *paideia*" should therefore be understood as themselves highly rhetorical devices.

71. Epiphanius, *Panarion* 64.3.9 (GCS 31:409).

72. Epiphanius, *Panarion* 64.3.11–13 (GCS 31:409): "for some say that he severed a nerve so that he would not be troubled by pleasure (ἡδονῇ).... But others do not say this, but that he came up with some drug to apply to his [private] parts and dried them up." Eusebius of Caesarea, a partisan of Origen, recounts the castration in *Historia ecclesiastica* 6.8.1, in terms that seem to indicate a more mechanical act on Origen's part, described twice as "an action" (τοὔργον, ἔργοις) (GCS 9.2:534); certainly Epiphanius's younger contemporary Jerome envisioned something more straightforward: *ferro truncaret genitalia* (*Ep.* 84.8.1 [CSEL 55:130]). See Jon Dechow, *Dogma and Mysticism in Early Christianity: Epiphanius of Cyprus and the Legacy of Origen*, PMS 13 (Macon, GA: Mercer University Press, 1988), 128–29, who highlights Epiphanius's "skepticism" about Origen's castration.

73. Epiphanius, *Panarion* 64.3.1 (GCS 31:405). Epiphanius seems to be the only source that identifies Ambrose in this way (τινὶ συντυχὼν τῶν διαφανῶν ἐν αὐλαῖς βασιλικαῖς), affirming (again) the ambivalent role of empire in Origen's conversion to

verted from his "other heresy" to orthodoxy, and later bankrolls Origen's prodigious textual and exegetical criticism.[74] Yet, according to Epiphanius, it is precisely because Origen has acquired the support of Ambrose—the convert from heresy—that he can himself become so swallowed up in secular learning that he begins to produce his fatal exegeses. Origen's life becomes a case study in improperly maintained boundaries of orthodoxy: the life of Origen becomes a kind of Möbius strip, leading without clear transition from childhood orthodoxy to near apostasy to learned orthodoxy—even converting heretics!—to the most dire heresy.

Origen's heresy is marked at its core by the baleful influences of "the world" (*ho kosmos*): Roman power, evident in persecution, and Greek knowledge, evident in overly intellectualized biblical interpretation. Yet Epiphanius himself is deeply embedded in both *imperium* and *paideia* as a learned bishop riding comfortably in the eddies of imperial Christian power. But perhaps this reflection is not accidental: Epiphanius succeeds where (according to him) Origen fails. The outside forces that Epiphanius sees as responsible for Origen's conversion to heresy are now contained safely within Epiphanius's own orthodox Christianity. Of course the projection of worldly power into the realm of heresy even as it remains within the orbit of orthodoxy places Epiphanius's imperial Christianity in a problematic situation, one that certainly haunted post-Constantinian Christianity: what is the relationship between Christianity and "the world"? Epiphanius's life of Origen—converter of heretics, convert to heresy—does not resolve this ambiguity, but merely embodies and contains it.

If Origen's conversion problematizes the secular foundations of Epiphanius's Greco-Roman Christian empire, Arius's tale bears witness to the power of empire to squeeze out evil and defend its own

---

heresy. In this detail, as many others in his long account of Origen's life, Epiphanius provides more (and probably less reliable) detail than the positive account of Origen in Eusebius's *Historia ecclesiastica*; see Dechow, *Dogma and Mysticism*, 125–38.

74. Epiphanius, *Panarion* 64.3.2–4 (GCS 31:405–7).

boundaries. Epiphanius prefaces his account of Arius with just such an image of masterful expulsion: "[Alexander] removed him and cast him out from the church and the city, as a great evil proliferating among the living."[75] Epiphanius (impossibly) aligns the beginning of Arius's life with Christian empire, as the heresiarch was "born in the time of the great and blessed emperor Constantine."[76] Arius even functions as an inverse Constantine: whereas the first Christian emperor "was godlike in his Christianity (*ektheiazomenon en Christianismōi*) and the faith of the fathers," Arius "came to detach a great number [from it]."[77] Like most of the heretical conversions in the *Panarion*, Arius's does not follow some intellectual or psychological encounter with a new truth or belief. Indeed, Epiphanius at one point portrays the origin of all of Arius's false beliefs as the result of a persistent misreading of a single verse of Scripture.[78]

Arius's religious transformation comes from the outside: through the inspiration of the devil. Arius's conversion to heresy begins when "a spirit of Satan ... entered" him,[79] and ends when his body "bursts" (*lakēsas*), and he "expires."[80] Obviously modeled on Judas, the false disciple, Arius also represents the vulnerability of the Christian body politic to outside influence. Inspired by Satan, filled to bursting with wickedness, he succeeds in seducing others to his evil heresy: clergy, monks,

---

75. Epiphanius, *Panarion* 69.1.1 (GCS 37:152).

76. Epiphanius, *Panarion* 69.1.3 (GCS 37:153). Possibly Epiphanius means to say that Arius "emerged" at this time, but the Greek seems fairly clear: ἐγένετο δὲ οὗτος ὁ Ἄρειος ἐν χρόνοις Κωνσταντίνου τοῦ μεγάλου καὶ μακαρίτου βασιλέως, υἱοῦ Κωνσταντίου. Such dating would make Arius in Epiphanius's account in his teens and twenties at the height of his heretical mischief (especially since Epiphanius also antedates Arius's death by at least a decade; see further discussion below).

77. Epiphanius, *Panarion* 69.1.4 (GCS 37:153).

78. Epiphanius, *Panarion* 69.12.1–3 (GCS 37:162). The verse is Proverbs 8:22.

79. Epiphanius, *Panarion* 69.2.1 (GCS 37:153); cf. Luke 22:3.

80. Epiphanius, *Panarion* 69.10.3 (GCS 37:160); cf. Acts 1:18. The comparison with Judas is explicit in *Panarion* 68.6.9 (GCS 37:146–47): "At night Arius entered the toilet to attend to his needs, he burst (ἐλάκησε), just like Judas at one time. And thus his end came about in a stinking and unclean place."

virgins, even bishops. Arius is "inspired by diabolic power"[81] and "taken away by his swelled head."[82] Even after Arius is expelled from Alexandria, he flits around the eastern Mediterranean like a heretical tse-tse fly, carrying his contagion across provincial boundaries and within other city walls. To stop Arius's evil, it takes the full force of the bishops of the East and the threat of imperial sanction, and especially the efforts of Bishop Alexander of Constantinople, who prayed for the humiliating death that came to Arius while he sat on the toilet.[83]

On Epiphanius's quirky timeline, Arius's death is followed immediately by the Council of Nicaea, the very watershed of Christian empire: the juxtaposition of the obliterated boundaries of Arius's body and the newly constituted boundaries of the Christian Roman Empire is striking. So striking, indeed, that it must help explain Epiphanius's curious—and impossible—chronology of Arius's life. Supposedly born "during the time of Constantine," Arius was somehow also "an old man" (*gerōn*) when "he departed from the prescribed path" and entered into heresy sometime in the second decade of the fourth century.[84] So too we know (and imagine Epiphanius knew) that Arius outlived the Council of Nicaea by a decade or more.[85] Strict chronology is not Epiphanius's concern here: rather, as in the heretical slide of Origen, Epiphanius gazes upon the conversion of heretics and contemplates in them the force, or failure, of empire.

---

81. Epiphanius, *Panarion* 69.12.1 (GCS 37:162).

82. Epiphanius, *Panarion* 69.3.1 (GCS 37:154).

83. Epiphanius, *Panarion* 69.10.2–3 (GCS 37:160). Arius's humiliating death became embedded in the (literary, at least) landscape of Constantinople, where the event supposedly occurred; see Ellen Muehlberger, "The Legend of Arius' Death: Imagination, Space, and Filth in Late Ancient Historiography," *Past & Present* 227 (2015): 3–29.

84. Epiphanius, *Panarion* 69.3.1 (GCS 37:154). Indeed, Epiphanius's testimony about Arius's advanced age in the second decade of the fourth century is often cited as evidence for dating Arius's birth to the 250s; see Rowan Williams, *Arius: Heresy and Tradition* (London: SCM Press, 2001), 30. Kim, *Epiphanius*, 113: "Epiphanius's narrative ... is a jumbled mess of confused details and conflated events."

85. In the previous chapter on the Melitians, Epiphanius correctly notes that Arius lived for some time after the Council of Nicaea, which anathematized him: *Panarion* 68.4.4–6, 6.7–9 (GCS 37:144–46).

BECOMING A CHRISTIAN

Conversion within Christian hierarchy speaks to the instability of episcopal control; conversion to Christian heresy problematizes the foundations of Christian empire; conversion to Christianity itself both materializes and dissolves the absolute frontiers of Christian identity, ultimately closing the religious frontier zone and folding "the other side" within. As a bishop, Epiphanius surely presided over many individual and communal conversions from non-Christian to Christian life. Unlike other contemporary bishops, however, he had little interest in preserving any catechetical instruction or advice for the *illuminandi*.[86] He did, however, preserve several telling narratives of conversion to Christianity that cohere with his larger interests in religious transformations as illuminating moments of Christian discourse. Several of his lengthier accounts of conversion to Christianity involve conversion from Judaism. As Daniel Boyarin has convincingly argued, Epiphanius lingers on the Jewish-Christian border so long precisely in order to create a meaningful ideological divide between two messily interpenetrated religious categories.[87] But the manner in which Epiphanius asserts control over the Jewish-Christian frontier zone leads him ultimately to embed the Jewish "other" within his own Christian territory.[88]

In a "digression" in *Panarion* 30, his chapter against the Jewish-Christian "Ebionites," Epiphanius tells the story of Count Joseph of Tiberias, a Christian aristocrat whom Epiphanius met in the 350s or early 360s in Scythopolis.[89] Joseph's conversion narrative is long and convoluted;

---

86. Calogero Riggi, "La catéchèse adaptée aux temps chez Epiphane," *SP* 17.1 (1982): 160–68, argues that we can derive major aspects of Epiphanius's catechetical instruction from the *Ancoratus* and *Panarion*.

87. Boyarin, *Border Lines*, 206–8. See also Jacobs, *Christ Circumcised*, 100–118.

88. Epiphanius's hagiographers would claim that he had himself been raised Jewish until the age of sixteen (*Vita Epiphanii* 3–10 [Rapp, "*Vita* of Epiphanius," 2:51–60]), a claim that medieval and some modern scholars took at face value. I discuss this tradition in more detail in chapter 6.

89. D. A. Washburn, "Tormenting the Tormentors: A Reinterpretation of Eusebius of Vercelli's Letter from Scythopolis," *CH* 78 (2009): 731–55, gives the historical context

indeed, its length and complication seem to be something of the point, as we shall see. When Epiphanius meets Joseph, Joseph is an orthodox Christian living in Scythopolis, a Palestinian town full of Arians.[90] Previously, however, Joseph had been a Jew and assistant to the Jewish patriarch Hillel. Upon Hillel's death, Joseph was charged with keeping Hillel's unruly child in line until he could assume the patriarchate. A series of events before and after Hillel's death led Joseph toward Christianity—slowly, and haltingly—until, once baptized as an orthodox Christian, he befriended Constantine and was given a high rank and the thankless task of building churches in Galilee. Multiple conversions to Christianity from Judaism pervade this story, further echoing and complicating Joseph's own conversion narrative: from the secret, deathbed conversion of Patriarch Hillel to an anonymous young ex-Jew living a closeted orthodox life in Scythopolis.[91]

Joseph's own story is one of several not-quite conversions. After watching, incredulous, as the Jewish patriarch received deathbed catechism and baptism, Joseph discovers a secret cache of Hebrew translations of New Testament texts.[92] Neither of these fortuitous events convinces Joseph to embrace Christianity; nor does his wonder at the prophylactic force of Christ's name and cross, which protect a Christian maiden from the wicked magic of the patriarch's nefarious orphan son.[93]

---

for Epiphanius's presence in Scythopolis in the early 360s; see also Stephen Goranson, "The Joseph of Tiberias Episode in Epiphanius: Studies in Jewish and Christian Relations" (PhD diss., Duke University, 1990); Goranson, "Joseph of Tiberias Revisited: Orthodoxies and Heresies in Fourth-Century Galilee," in *Galilee through the Centuries: A Confluence of Cultures,* ed. Eric M. Meyers, Duke Judaic Studies 1 (Winona Lake, IN: Eisenbrauns, 1999), 335–43; and Kim, *Epiphanius,* 85–90.

90. Epiphanius, *Panarion* 30.3.5–6 (GCS n.F. 10.1:337).

91. Epiphanius, *Panarion* 30.4.5–7, 6.1–5 (Hillel) (GCS n.F. 10.1:339, 340–41); *Panarion* 30.5.7 (anonymous Scythopolitan convert) (GCS n.F. 10.1:340).

92. Epiphanius, *Panarion* 30.6.7–9 (GCS n.F. 10.1:341). The memory of these texts, and Joseph's discovery of them, are the hook for Epiphanius's digression, after mentioning Ebionite use of Hebrew translations of the New Testament (*Panarion* 30.3.8–4.1 [GCS n.F. 10.1:338]).

93. Epiphanius, *Panarion* 30.7.6–8.10 (GCS n.F. 10.1:342–44). The son, whose name Epiphanius thinks might be Judas (*Panarion* 30.7.2 [GCS n.F. 10.1:342]) had seen the

Miracles follow: Joseph rises from his sickbed after receiving a vision of "the Lord" and himself cures a "naked madman (μαινόμενος)" by invoking Jesus's name.[94] When his final conversion does come, it is almost an accident: unhappy provincial Jews discover Joseph reading borrowed copies of the Gospels, and throw him in a river to drown. Rescued from drowning, Epiphanius announces, Joseph was now "deemed worthy of holy baptism."[95] It is unclear whether Epiphanius means that the attempted murder of Joseph by his coreligionists proved him (to himself? to other Christians?) worthy of baptism, or whether the near drowning itself was deemed ritually sufficient. Either way, the Jew has at last become a Christian, and an orthodox one: he receives a title and a commission from Constantine to build Christian churches in Galilee.[96]

The stuttering nature of Joseph's conversion demonstrates the force required in Epiphanius's narrative to bring closure to the frontier zone of Judaism and Christianity, and the yawning distance established between the two religious territories. Conversion requires masterful force to yank the recalcitrant convert to the other side (force emblematized, at the end of Joseph's conversion, by the imperial figure of Constantine). Yet other characters within the text curiously minimize this discursive distance, partially retangling the painstakingly separated religious threads. I refer here not to the heretical "Ebionites," the Jewish-Christian heretics the refutation of whom has been interrupted by Joseph's tale. Rather I refer to other Jews who precede Joseph in conversion from Judaism to Christianity. The first, and most surprising (to Joseph and the reader), is the patriarch, Hillel: out of nowhere, it seems, Hillel calls for a bishop to come and baptize him. The rest of the house-

---

Christian woman in a bath; he and a friend attempted to cast spells on her, but she was protected by the "seal and faith of Christ," teaching Joseph that "where Christ's name was, and the seal of his cross, the power of witchcraft (φαρμακείας) had no strength" (*Panarion* 30.8.10 [GCS n.F. 10.1:344]).

94. Epiphanius, *Panarion* 30.10.1 (vision of the Lord) (GCS n.F. 10.1:345); *Panarion* 30.10.3–7 (invocation of Jesus's name) (GCS n.F. 10.1:345).

95. Epiphanius, *Panarion* 30.11.3–7 (GCS n.F. 10.1:346–47).

96. Epiphanius, *Panarion* 30.11.7–10 (GCS n.F. 10.1:347).

hold is tricked into the thinking the bishop is a doctor and the water is medicinal: only Joseph, "peeping through the joints of the doors," knows the truth.[97] Later, when Joseph himself falls ill, he is visited by "a man of those learned in the law, a certain elder," who also reveals himself as a crypto-Christian: he "whispers" to Joseph, encouraging him to accept Jesus as Lord.[98] That such instances of secret conversion and proselytism are not outliers is made clear by Epiphanius, who indicates that they are apparently common: "I have heard this sort of thing from someone else," yet another Jew who "honored and loved Christians" apparently because someone (we don't know who) "in a whisper in his ear" when he was sick told him that he would be judged by "Jesus Christ, the crucified Son of God."[99]

Hillel and two sickbed whisperers: what purpose does this trio of crypto-Christian Jewish converts serve, especially when juxtaposed with Joseph, the almost comically reluctant convert? In a discourse on conversion that emphasizes individuality, interiority, and introspection, these four converts might speak to the difficult nature of internal reorientation: like Augustine crying out for "chastity, but not yet," these Jews crave Christ, but cannot wholeheartedly give themselves to him. But Epiphanius does not structure his conversion stories through the internal mechanics of the soul. Instead he frames his tale with bishops and emperors, with patriarchs and aristocrats, with orthodoxy and heresy. Viswanathan writes that, in the colonial context, "converts function as strategic displacements of religious and ethnic groups, allowing writers to probe questions of selective incorporation and exclusion not easily approached by more direct means."[100] When addressing the "heresy" of the Ebionites, the question of incorporation and exclusion is paramount: What part of Judaism remains in Christianity? Where

---

97. Epiphanius, *Panarion* 30.4.5–7, 6.2 (GCS n.F. 10.1:339, 340).
98. Epiphanius, *Panarion* 30.9.2–3 (GCS n.F. 10.1:344). He literally "announces in his ear" (εἰς τὸ οὖς αὐτοῦ ἀπήγγειλε).
99. Epiphanius, *Panarion* 30.9.4–5 (GCS n.F. 10.1:344).
100. Viswanathan, *Outside the Fold*, 26.

does the authoritative bishop establish his closed frontier? The long-deferred, but always imminent, conversion of Joseph, resonating and rebounding off of these ancillary characters, allows Epiphanius to portray a Christianity that has always already contained the remains of Judaism, whispering secretively even in the bedchamber of the most prestigious Jews in Palestine. In the end, the frontier does not so much close as dissolve while the true Jews morph, in slow motion before our eyes, into orthodox Christians.[101]

Epiphanius indicates this absorption of Judaism by Christianity when he briefly mentions another conversion narrative in the same chapter of the *Panarion*. It seems the Ebionites themselves claim that the apostle Paul was originally a pagan (*phaskousin auton einai Hellēna*) who

> set his heart (*epitethumēkenai*) on the daughter of the high priest, to marry her, and for this reason he became a proselyte and was circumcised; but still not receiving that type of maiden he grew angry and wrote against circumcision and against the Sabbath and the legislation.[102]

That is, Paul had been a pagan, and then a Jew, and then (more or less) a Christian. The progression across these borders into Christianity makes sense in Epiphanius's larger scheme of religious transformation, eliciting the fluidity and dynamism of identity and community, but it works exactly against Epiphanius's particular concern in his chapter on Jewish-Christians. Paul must be *authentically* Jewish before becoming truly Christian—just like Joseph of Tiberias, Joseph's patriarchal employer, and the other Jews-made-Christians in the *Panarion*. The question, after all, revolves around the ability of Christianity to absorb true and authentic Judaism, at its core. For Paul to be an ersatz Jew would defeat the purpose of recounting these conversion stories at all.

---

101. As Boyarin, *Border Lines*, 213, notes, "All of the formerly orthodox Jews have now become orthodox Christians, a conversion portrayed as without remainder."

102. Epiphanius, *Panarion* 30.16.9 (GCS n.F. 10.1:355).

Epiphanius in fact returns to the apostle Paul's religious transformation, from Jew to Christian, in one of his later works: his treatise *De XII gemmis*, in which he provides intertextual interpretations of the twelve gemstones in the breastplate of the Israelite high priest (Exod 28:15–20).[103] Epiphanius ascribes the last stone, onyx, to the tribe of Benjamin: the mention of this youngest son of Israel allows Epiphanius to link the gem also to Paul, "of the tribe of Benjamin" (Phil 3:5; Rom 11:1), the "last of the apostles."[104] (In the Coptic version the "lastness" of Paul is further reflected in his name change from "Saul" to "Paul, which in the Roman language [*nrhōmikon*] means 'least' [*elachistos*]."[105]) This section of the treatise (like many other sections) is a dazzling intertextual display; here much of it is in the voice of Paul, stitched together out of passages from Paul's letters and verses of Psalms. Old and New Testament recombine, even dance together, as focus shifts back and forth from Benjamin (the Old) to Paul (the New). The goblet of Benjamin covered in onyx (combining Gen 44 and Exod 28) becomes the cup from which Paul serves the "draft of the knowledge of God";[106] Benjamin, the "ravening wolf" of Genesis 49, becomes Paul, who, "in his youth, like a wolf, ravened and champed the bones and the flesh of many."[107]

Paul's transformation from ravening wolf and persecutor of the church into most beloved apostle is the main theme of Epiphanius's spiritual interpretation of the onyx. Twice Epiphanius places us, with Paul, on the imperial road to Damascus,[108] hearing the chastising voice of God and becoming the "chosen vessel" of God's word. The layers of

---

103. On the origins and date of this treatise, see my discussion in the introduction. I explore this treatise in more depth in chapter 4.

104. Blake and Vis, *Epiphanius*, 166 (Coptic: 312–13). This portion of the treatise also survives (in fragmentary form) in the early Coptic translation, which I cite parenthetically from the Blake/Vis edition.

105. Blake and Vis, *Epiphanius*, 316–17.

106. Blake and Vis, *Epiphanius*, 169.

107. Blake and Vis, *Epiphanius*, 169 (Coptic: 318–19).

108. Blake and Vis, *Epiphanius*, 167–68, 170 (Coptic: 314–15, 320–21; the extant Coptic ends at this point).

transformation are thick: from Benjamin (whom Epiphanius also associates with Damascus, the site where he was called, like Paul, "out of his mind"[109]) to Paul, from "wolf" to apostle, from Old Testament into New. Here the value of revisioning conversion with Epiphanius becomes most evident. For Augustine, Paul's transformation on the road to Damascus became the index by which to understand God's inscrutable correction of the individual, fallen soul.[110] Here, at the climax of Epiphanius's spiritual interpretation of Aaron's bejeweled breastplate, that same conversion condenses the outwardly visible power and majesty of the total transformation of "old" into "new," the absorption of Judaism into Christianity, of the past into present. The frontier zone between Judaism and Christianity closes, but we discover that Judaism remains *within* that frontier, enfolded within a totalizing Christian vision of religious truth.

BECOMING/UNBECOMING

When we peel back the genealogical layers of conversion—past A. D. Nock's "reorientation of the soul"[111] and William James's unification of "a self hitherto divided,"[112] past what modern interpreters still at times privilege as Augustine's overpowering introspective, retrospective gaze—sharpened at the geographic and historical limits of empire, we arrive at a discourse that is at once more expansive and, upon reflection, less stable than we once believed. Exteriorized, conversion becomes a social process no longer safeguarded invisibly within the psyche but rather subject to the structuring power of discourse. Fur-

---

109. Blake and Vis, *Epiphanius*, 318–19 and 320–21, citing Psalms 67:28. I cite from the Coptic version here, rather than the Georgian, which Blake translates as "he was marvelous in his youth" (Blake and Vis, *Epiphanius*, 170). Not only is the Coptic closer to the original Greek Septuagint, but the invocation of Benjamin "in ecstasy" (*hn tekstasis*) creates a clearer parallel with Paul on the road to Damascus.
110. See Fredriksen, "Paul and Augustine."
111. Nock, *Conversion*, 7.
112. James, *Varieties*, 189.

thermore, conversion, on my reading, indicates any religious transformation in which borders are acknowledged, crossed, and carefully (although never with total success) managed. The movement from layperson to monk or cleric, of orthodox Christian to heretic, of Jew to Christian, is imagined along the same terrain of socially embedded becoming.

Narratives about change in religious status articulate moments at which the borders of religious identity become visible; and because visible, they are subject to control. So Epiphanius, whose writings are replete with boundaries and borders crossed and defended, also relishes the narrative of border crossing because, in those moments in which the religious transformation is inscribed on the page, he displays control. The Roman Empire similarly demonstrated its imperial mastery through the control of frontiers and boundaries, which, as recent studies have shown, operated not as high walls that kept the "other" outside, but rather as porous membranes that sought to control how others entered into the space of Roman management.[113] Roman historian David Cheery has remarked: "We would do better to define the Roman frontiers in the same way that historians of the western United States have long described the American frontier, that is, as a *cultural process*."[114] Of course, the Roman Empire's frontier mastery eventually became a site for the disintegration and reformation of new European identities. We must be careful, however, not to project a future not yet realized into the fabric of Epiphanius's—and his contemporaries'—understanding of

---

113. A good summary of such work, incorporating theoretical work on "frontiers," may be found in David Cherry, *Frontier and Society in Roman North Africa* (Oxford: Oxford University Press, 2002), 24–74.

114. Cherry, *Frontier and Society*, 27 (emphasis original). Cherry's model is primarily economic (the Romans' "only identifiable policy in the [North African] frontier-zone is one of 'exploitation'" [74]), but he also signals his openness to cultural models. In this he follows the important work of C. R. Whittaker, much of which is condensed in his "Frontiers," in *The Cambridge Ancient History*, vol. II, *The High Empire, A.D. 70–192*, ed. Alan Bowman, Peter Garnsey, and Dominic Rathbone (Cambridge: Cambridge University Press, 2000), 293–319.

conversion and religious status. In the late fourth century, at the height of the bishop's prestige, he imagined for his coreligionists a dizzying perspective from which to survey the myriad crossings and double-crossings, becomings and unbecomings, at work in the Christian empire. It is only from our perspective (postcolonial and postmodern) that we can look upon Epiphanius's masterful constructions of Christian becoming and see, in those very same moments, the anxiety of change: of un-becoming. The loss of containment, the failure to adequately police the borders of Christianity, from our vantage point necessarily haunt Epiphanius's imperial narratives from the frontier zone of Christian becoming.

CHAPTER THREE

Discipline

IMPROVISATIONAL STYLE

In one of the more notorious scenes of the *Panarion*, Epiphanius recounts how, as a young man, perhaps while living in Egypt,[1] he helped to expose and disperse a nest of gnostic Christians preying upon the unsuspecting orthodox.[2] Drawn to them possibly by their many curious

---

1. Historians often assume this incident took place in Egypt, based on Epiphanius's age and inexperience and the proliferation of various "gnostic" sects there. Epiphanius perhaps also hints at his Egyptian period when he compares the women attempting to seduce him to Potiphar's wife, "that murderous and adulterous Egyptian wife of the chief cook" (*Panarion* 26.17.4 [GCS n.F. 10.1:297]). Elsewhere, Epiphanius describes meeting a gnostic group (the Sethians) and notes: "I think perhaps I came across this heresy also in the land of the Egyptians, but I can't remember precisely the land in which I came across them" (*Panarion* 39.1.2 [GCS 31:72]).

2. Epiphanius, *Panarion* 26.17.4–8 (GCS n.F. 10.1:297–98). Epiphanius explains that the women "desired me in my youthful age" (τῇ νέᾳ ἡμῶν ἡλικίᾳ ὀρεχθεῖσαι) (*Panarion* 26.17.4 [GCS n.F. 10.1:297]). Epiphanius himself labels this group "Gnostics" (Γνωστικοί), but notes they are also called Borborians, Koddians, Zaccheans, Barbelites, and (in Egypt) Stratiotics and Phibionites (*Pan* 26.3.5–7 [GCS n.F. 10.1:279]). David Brakke, *The Gnostics: Myth, Ritual, and Diversity in Early Christianity* (Cambridge, MA: Harvard University Press, 2010), has argued that of the many, diverse groups that scholars routinely lump together under the umbrella "Gnosticism," one school of early Christian thought likely did identify themselves as *gnōstikoi*, although he is leery of using Epiphanius's chapter against them as evidence (see pp. 45–46).

books,³ and almost certainly by the deliberate seductiveness of their women initiates,⁴ Epiphanius eventually sussed out their "true intention" (*ton noun tēi alētheiai*). He recalls:

> Running away and not being caught on their bait, in that hour I hastened to report them to the bishops who were in that place and to ferret out the individuals (*onomata*) who were hiding in the church. And they were driven out of the city (*tous autous apelathēnai tēs poleōs*), around eighty individuals (*onomata*), and the city was purified of their weedy and thorny thicket.⁵

I begin with this well-known story because of what it says—and does not say—about the way Epiphanius portrays the exercise of religious discipline. Certainly, on first glance, we see the triumph of institutional authority, represented by the local bishops, over the insidious and shadowy heretics. What began as an infested ecclesiastical body ends as a purified one. Orthodox structure prevails over heretical chaos, symbolized by the weeds. The purification of heresy from the church stands in miniature for the entire project of the *Panarion*, which ostensibly instructs its readers how to weed out the impure from the faithful.

Yet I want to point out also what we do not see: the actual process by which this purification is effected. What exactly occurs between the moment when Epiphanius wriggles off the hook of the seductive gnostic women and when eighty named individuals (*onomata*) are expelled from the city? What process did the bishops employ to ferret out the eighty or so heretics, and how were they expelled? And why is Epiphanius so casual about identifying the institutional agents? He refers to "the bishops who were in that place" (*tois episkopois tois en tōi topōi*), but fails to explain

---

3. Epiphanius escapes their clutches "after reading their books" (*Panarion* 26.17.8 [GCS n.F. 10.1:298]) and had earlier noted of them (admiringly?) that "they have lots of books" (τὰ μὲν βιβλία αὐτῶν πολλά) (*Panarion* 26.8.1 [GCS n.F. 10.1:284]). On this incident, see Young Richard Kim, *Epiphanius of Cyprus: Imagining an Orthodox World* (Ann Arbor: University of Michigan Press, 2015), 35–43.

4. Epiphanius explains the honey-pot stratagem of this sect and admits of the women of the group that "their visible form was very easy on the eyes (εὐπροσωπόταται)" (*Panarion* 26.17.6–8 [GCS n.F. 10.1:298]).

5. Epiphanius, *Panarion* 26.17.8 (GCS n.F. 10.1:298).

how these multiple bishops exercised authority over a single "city" (*poleōs*). For the author of an anecdote (and of a text) so concerned with correcting institutional error, Epiphanius is notably vague about how discipline is deployed in the course of that correction.

It is possible that Epiphanius doesn't remember the details of the incident, how many bishops there were—although his recollection of "about eighty individuals" suggests a fairly clear memory—or even where the incident took place. Yet Epiphanius does not hesitate to provide ample, even excessive, detail elsewhere in the *Panarion*—regardless of its reliability—when it suits his purposes.[6] The lack of procedural detail, combined with the certainty of procedural results, is conspicuous and, I argue, tells us something significant about Epiphanius's broader representation of church discipline and, in turn, gives us new insight into discipline in late fourth-century Christianity. The vague nature of Epiphanius's recitation of events surrounding the expulsion of the gnostics speaks to the bishop's larger style of discipline and authority, a style characterized, I suggest, by improvisation. I do not mean by this term to suggest that Epiphanius lived his life in a carefree and inconsistent manner, imposing discipline on himself and others without regard for institutional norms and strictures. Indeed, as we see in the incident of the gnostics, Epiphanius is very careful to represent his church as orderly, institutional, and orthodox. I speak, rather, of a particular *style* by which Epiphanius imposes his disciplinary boundaries.

In musical and theatrical parlance, improvisation indicates a peformative mode that has the appearance of spontaneity and composition in the moment.[7] Distinct from scripted or precomposed works,

---

6. Indeed, *Panarion* 26 for some historians represents the height of Epiphanian mendacity; see, for example, Bart D. Ehrman, *Forgery and Counterforgery: The Use of Literary Deceit in Early Christian Polemics* (New York: Oxford University Press, 2013), 19–24; Michael Williams, *Rethinking "Gnosticism": An Argument for Dismantling a Dubious Category* (Princeton, NJ: Princeton University Press, 1996), 179–84.

7. Bruno Nettl, "Thoughts in Improvisation: A Comparative Approach," *Musical Quarterly* 60 (1974): 1–19; Philip Alperson, "On Musical Improvisation," *Journal of Aesthetics and Art Criticism* 42 (1984): 17–29; R. Keith Sawyer, "Improvisation and the Creative

improvisations combine the creativity of an author with the virtuosity of a performer.[8] At the same time, for an improvisational performance to be legible to an audience, it must follow certain predetermined rules, or models.[9] That is, somewhat paradoxically, every improvisation is at once entirely unique and utterly dependent on previous creative productions. Improvisation evokes spontaneity, but does so through preexisting structures. What distinguishes improvisation from other performative acts, therefore, is not its lack of structure or rules but rather its deliberate emphasis on its own performativity: it is not merely an interpretation of a previously existing cultural production, but an entirely new experience for audience and performer alike. This deliberate and ostentatious performativity, the *style* of improvisation, is what gives an improvised performance its air of virtuosity.

Of course, modern notions of improvisation in music, theater, or dance are historically contingent and dependent upon complicated layers of cultural value in specific contexts.[10] Nonetheless, we can speak of

---

Process: Dewey, Collingwood, and the Aesthetics of Spontaneity," *Journal of Aesthetics and Art Criticism* 58 (2000): 149–61; Curtis L. Carter, "Improvisation in Dance," *Journal of Aesthetics and Art Criticism* 58 (2000): 181–90.

8. Carol S. Gould and Kenneth Keaton, "The Essential Role of Improvisation in Musical Performance," *Journal of Aesthetics and Art Criticism* 58 (2000): 143–48, argue that all musical performances (and *mutatis mutandis*, all artistic performances) are improvisational because both so-called improvisation and performance of precomposed pieces "involve intentional acts that are performed according to rules, but have an element of fluency and immediacy about them" (146). While true, Gould and Keaton's maximalist notion of improvisation ignores the reception by an audience who perceives one performance to be scripted and another spontaneous.

9. Nettl, "Thoughts," 11: "The improviser, let us hypothesize, always has something given to work from—certain things that are at the base of the performance, that he uses as the ground on which he builds. We may call it his model." See also Sawyer, "Improvisation," 157: "All improvisers know that improvisation does not mean that anything goes—improvisation always occurs within a structure, and all improvisers draw on *ready-mades*—short motifs or clichés—as they create their novel performance" (emphasis in original).

10. See, for example, Anna G. Piotrowska, "Expressing the Inexpressible: The Issue of Improvisation and the European Fascination with Gypsy Music in the 19th Century," *International Review of Aesthetics and Sociology of Music* 43 (2012): 325–41.

analogous styles of improvisation in Epiphanius's late ancient context as well. After briefly surveying this improvisational style in ancient public discourse, I turn to examine Epiphanius's own improvisational style in multiple Christian disciplinary contexts. By attending to Epiphanius's own improvisational style—which ultimately serves to create an even tighter sense of control over Christian discipline—we can rethink some of our narratives of the "development" of early Christian institutions in the post-Constantinian era.

ANCIENT IMPROVISATION

Ancient Roman society in the imperial period was shot through with a style of improvisation. The very educational curriculum that formed young men into literate leaders relied upon improvisational exercises, precisely in order to instill in them the moral and technical components of *paideia*. These gentlemen-in-training, once they had proceeded past the elementary stages of grammatical schooling, were drilled in declamations, which rehearsed rhetorical *topoi* and techniques in hypothetical situations of persuasion or argumentation.[11] Historians of ancient education have compared these improvisational exercises to "hot jazz": "a performance that at its best combines inventive improvisation with structural discipline and technical virtuosity."[12] In this formative educational context, improvisation was a form of *mimēsis*, an assumption of an improvised and contingent persona, in which the visibility of the underlying structure of oratory was as important as the

---

11. Robert Kaster, "Controlling Reason: Declamation in Rhetorical Education at Rome," in *Education in Greek and Roman Antiquity*, ed. Yun Lee Too (Leiden: Brill, 2001), 317–18. Seneca the Elder compiled the *Controversiae*, ten books of notes on various declamation topics (presumably) familiar to his highly literate readers; similar notebooks survive from the high empire.

12. Kaster, "Controlling Reason," 322, citing H.-I. Marrou, *A History of Education in Antiquity*, trans. G. Lamb (Madison: University of Wisconsin Press, 1956), 200 (original: "Ne le constatons-nous pas dans la pratique de la technique *hot* de notre musique de jazz?"; *Histoire de l'éducation dans l'antiquité* [Paris: Éditions du Seuil, 1948], 275).

student's ability to sift and arrange these structural elements in a creative and original manner.[13]

While the improvisational exercises of *paideia* were restricted to and formative of a particular social class, various modes of public performance translated this improvisational style into popular demonstrations of individual virtuosity.[14] Classical Latin forensic rhetoric theory debated the value of improvisation versus memorized speeches;[15] popular public speakers (sophists) throughout the imperial period, however, relished demonstrating their technical expertise and panache through improvisational performance.[16] The transformation of impromptu themes into

---

13. On the role of assumed personas and the fashioning of identities in the declamations, see W. Martin Bloomer, "Schooling in Persona: Imagination and Subordination in Roman Education," *CA* 16 (1997): 57–78; Erik Gunderson, *Declamation, Paternity, and Roman Identity: Authority and the Rhetorical Self* (Cambridge: Cambridge University Press, 2003).

14. The rather racy topics routinely treated in school declamations suggest that the performative line between professional rhetoric and more widely accessible theater was not terribly wide; see Kaster, "Controlling Reason," 317–18.

15. Cicero bears witness to debates over the effectiveness of prepared and memorized speeches over against speaking *ex tempore* (*De oratore* 1.23); Quintilian, decades later, praised skilled improvisation as the mark of the most skilled orator. Glyn P. Norton, "Improvisation and Inspiration in Quintilian: The Extemporalizing of Technique in the *Institutio Oratoria*," in *Inspiration and Technique: Ancient to Modern Views on Beauty and Art*, ed. John Roe and Michele Stanco (Bern: Peter Lang, 2007), 83–104; Chris Holcomb, "'The Crown of All Our Study': Improvisation in Quintilian's *Institutio Oratoria*," *Rhetoric Society Quarterly* 31.3 (2001): 53–72

16. Tim Whitmarsh, *The Second Sophistic* (Cambridge: Cambridge University Press, 2005), 25: "In general, however, it was indeed in improvisation that the real cachet lay; it was only by extemporizing that these ambassadors of the elite could present themselves as naturally, effortlessly superior." Philostratus, *Vitae sophistarum* 1.prol (482) begins his treatise on the "Second Sophistic" (σοφιστική ... δευτέρα) by exploring the roots of the "wells of impromptu speech" (σχεδίων δὲ πηγὰς λόγων) in the Attic period that began to flow anew in the Roman era, and later notes: "Improvisation is the triumph of the fluent tongue" (αὐτοσχέδιος γὰρ γλώττης εὐροούσης ἀγώνισμα) (*Vitae sophistarum* 2.9 [583]). He refers throughout his treatise to the impressive feat of extemporaneous speech on topics given by audiences: *Vitae sophistarum* 1.18, 21, 23, 24, 25; 2.1, 3, 4, 5, 6, 7, 10, 13, 15, 17, 24, 33 (509, 515, 521, 527–29, 535, 565, 567, 570, 571, 574, 576–77, 588–89, 594, 595, 598, 607, 628). Philostratus also remarks that Aristides notably lacked a talent for improvisation (ἐπὶ δὲ τὸ σχεδιάζειν μὴ ἑπομένης αὐτῷ τῆς φύσεως) (*Vitae sophistarum* 2.9 [581]).

polished rhetoric on the spot showcased the sophist's intellectual superiority, while also creating an audience appreciative of technical dazzle and display.[17] Audiences were similarly conditioned to appreciate on-the-spot improvisation in the imperial theater: classical tragedy and comedy had, by the Roman imperial period, given way to looser performances of broad comedy and masked dance, mime and pantomime.[18] The actors in mime, particularly, were noted for their improvisational comedy, even though, like improvising orators, these actors relied heavily on tradition, convention, and previous performances.[19] Ruth Webb has argued that the appearance of improvisation on the stage may have resonated in profound ways with audience members: "The very fact that the mimes improvise (or are thought to improvise) their roles, often with a minimum of material resources, makes them an emblem of the ordinary citizen, doing the best he or she can."[20] Both sophistic oratory and theatrical performance trained audiences to respond to and admire improvisation.[21]

17. Martin Korenjak, *Publikum und Redner: Ihre Interaktion in der sophistischen Rhetorik der Kaiserzeit*, Zetemata 104 (Munich: C. H. Beck, 2000). Heinrich von Staden, "Galen and the 'Second Sophistic,'" in "Aristotle and After," ed. Richard Sorabji, special issue, *Bulletin of the Institute of Classical Studies* 41 (1997): 33–54, details the ways in which medical practitioners also participated in this culture of public, extemporaneous performance before audiences in the high empire.

18. Blake Leyerle, *Theatrical Shows and Ascetic Lives: John Chrysostom's Attack on Spiritual Marriage* (Berkeley: University of California Press, 2001), 12–41, provides an excellent overview of late ancient theater in its social historical context. From the performative side, see Ruth Webb, *Demons and Dancers: Performance in Late Antiquity* (Cambridge, MA: Harvard University Press, 2008).

19. On mime and improvisation, see Webb, *Demons and Dancers*, 112–14, 132–35. On the popular perception of ancient mime as improvised, Webb cites Cicero, *Pro Caelio* 65 and Macrobius, *Saturnalia* 2.7.6–7 (*Demons and Dancers*, 96 and 114). Presumably the reputation of mime as improvised must also depend on audience recollection of seeing the same play performed in different ways.

20. Webb, *Dancers and Demons*, 133.

21. Oratory and theater often occupied the same physical, as well as conceptual, space; see Webb, *Dancers and Demons*, 27–28; and now Christine Shepardson, *Controlling Contested Places: Late Antique Antioch and the Spatial Politics of Religious Controversy* (Berkeley: University of California Press, 2014), 32–50.

This admiration of audiences for improvisation opens up three key elements of this Roman performative style that are important for understanding Epiphanius and fourth-century church discipline more broadly. First, there is the significance of the *perception* of improvisation by an audience, even if a speaker or actor was reciting prepared words from memory.[22] Improvisation does not need to describe the truth of a performance, only the manner in which an audience has perceived an act of spontaneous creativity.[23] When Lucian tells the story of an orator who tried (and failed) to fake an improvised speech on Pythagoras, he reports that the ruse failed as much because of faulty style as the recognizably plagiarized content.[24] Presumably, a speech that could "mimic improvisation" would impress its audience regardless of its actual spontaneity.[25] Second, we see the degree to which relations of *power* were evoked through this improvisational style. Both the speaker (or performer) and the audience were inculturated into a broadly hierarchical—even imperial—worldview in which performance disciplined organized populations into actors and the acted-upon.[26] At the same time, the role of the audience as connoisseurs of improvisation,

---

22. Webb, *Dancers and Demons*, 112–13, describes evidence for varied levels of scripting in late ancient mime.

23. Von Staden, "Galen," 40: "The sophists delighted their audiences by improvising in public—or at least by pretending to speak extemporaneously."

24. Lucian, *Pseudologista* 5–8.

25. Demetrius, *De elocutione* 224 notes that it is appropriate for spoken dialogues to "mimic improvisation" (ὁ μὲν γὰρ μιμεῖται αὐτοσχεδιάζοντα), whereas written letters (one half of a dialogue, as it were) should be "more prepared" (ὑποκατεσκυάσαι πως μᾶλλον) (text in *Demetrius, On Style: The Greek Text of Demetrius "De Elocutione" Edited after the Paris Manuscript*, ed. and trans. W. Rhys Roberts [Cambridge: Cambridge University Press, 1902], 172). See Tim Whitmarsh, *Beyond the Second Sophistic: Adventures in Greek Postclassicism* (Berkeley: University of California Press, 2013), 87.

26. Bloomer, "Schooling in Persona," 59: "Roman education developed to a training in persona—the acculturation and socialization of the schoolboy, from whatever province or status (nearly), into a Roman imperial culture." See also Thomas Schmitz, *Bildung und Macht: Zur sozialen und politischen Funktion der zweiten Sophistik in der griechischen Welt der Kaiserzeit*, Zetemata 97 (Munich: C.H. Beck, 1997), 159: "So kann man eine gelungene Improvisation als Synekdoche begreifen: Dieser Augenblick bündelte in sich die Überlegenheit, die das gesamte Wesen des Sprechers auszeichnete."

and of the performer as gazed-upon spectacle, could reverse the "natural" flow of hierarchical authority. Improvisation did not just open up a space for the exercise of power through performance, but for the negotiation and possibly even subversion of power.[27]

Finally, improvisation draws attention, in a somewhat sideways manner, to the role of *institutions* in the production of culture. By *institution* I mean the set of structures and models that lie behind a performative act, in both its material and theoretical sense (think of the multiple meanings of the term *theater* in English or, perhaps more aptly, *church*). On the one hand, what impresses about improvisation is its spontaneity and extemporaneity, the audience's knowledge that it is witness to something totally original: it is a product of novel creativity, not institutional predictability. On the other hand, the audience's ability to understand and evaluate this new cultural production must be grounded in familiarity with existing models, tropes, and traditions, familiarity with the institution in which it is performed. Improvisation both highlights and obscures the role of institution in cultural production.

These three elements—perception, power, and institution—extend beyond the explicitly performative corners of Roman culture in late antiquity.[28] In a broad sense, most locations where institutionalized power was present became open to the intervention of improvisation. The household, for instance, was the site in which the *paterfamilias*

---

27. Webb, *Demons and Dancers*, 133, has suggested that Augustus's purported final words to his friends (according to Suetonius, *Divus Augustus* 99, "He asked them whether he had accomplished the *mimus vitae* appropriately") may refer not only to playing a social role, generally, but specifically to "successful adaptation to circumstance and effective improvisation in the face of overwhelming odds." I would add these words also convey the unstable power dynamics of being "on the public stage" as both a display of superiority and an object of others' scrutiny and gaze.

28. Thomas Habinek, *The Politics of Latin Literature: Writing, Identity, and Empire in Ancient Rome* (Princeton, NJ: Princeton University Press, 2001), 54; Erik Gunderson, *Cambridge Companion to Ancient Rhetoric* (Cambridge: Cambridge University Press, 2009), 18: "If we attend to the drama of the Roman self we are able to see the whole of life as an earnest improvisational game filled with rhetorical competitions."

regulated relations of power among the members of the household. While household manuals exist stretching back to the Hellenistic period,[29] the actual execution of paternal authority had to be relatively fluid and improvised and the "success" of a *dominus* might be gauged by his ability to handle unexpected household situations with aplomb. Other sites of (predominantly) male power, from economy to politics to religion, likewise could be open to an improvisational style. Even the exercise of imperial power, from the time of Augustus onward, can be said to be broadly characterized by this improvisational style, bound by certain conventions and expectations but also impressive for its ability to revise and adapt itself based on circumstance.[30] When Christian leaders begin to assume leadership roles modeled on Roman forms, particularly the episcopacy, we should not be surprised, then, to see them assuming an improvisational, performative style that adapted and echoed the wider cultural systems they inhabited.[31]

29. On literature *de oeconomia*, see Kristina Sessa, *The Formation of Papal Authority in Late Antique Italy: Roman Bishops and the Domestic Sphere* (Cambridge: Cambridge University Press, 2011), 4–8. I would suggest reading this literature as analogous to rhetorical handbooks: guides for the improvisational display of topical mastery.

30. Greg Woolf's recent broad survey of Roman imperial history emphasizes throughout the essentially improvisatory fashion in which the empire was constituted and maintained: *Rome: An Empire's Story* (Cambridge: Cambridge University Press, 2012), 71–73, 149–50, and passim. Frank Kolb, *Diokletian und die erste Tetrarchie: Improvisation oder Experiment in die Organisation monarchischer Herrschaft?* (Berlin: De Gruyter, 1987), argues that Diocletian's "invention" of the tetrarchy was not an ad hoc or spontaneous arrangement, but rather relied on previous models (especially the shared governance of the Severans). Of course, improvisation in a more technical sense is never totally ad hoc but relies in various ways on preexisting models and structures, carefully rearranged.

31. Unsurprisingly—since many educated Christian preachers passed through the same general rhetorical curriculum as their non-Christian neighbors—scholars have noted the improvisational style of early Christian homiletics: Alistair Stewart-Sykes, *From Prophecy to Preaching: A Search for the Origins of the Christian Homily* (Leiden: Brill, 1995), 5, 29–31; William Harmless, *Augustine and the Catechumenate* (Collegeville, MN: Liturgical Press, 1995), 174. More broadly, Ivor Davidson, "Staging the Church? Theology as Theater," *JECS* 8 (2000): 413–51, has outlined the theatrical, performative construction of Christian leadership by Ambrose of Milan, even characterizing his *De officiis* (modeled, of course, on Cicero's example) not as a "script" for Christian leaders

Yet when we think of the development of religious discipline in early Christianity, we do not tend to think in terms of improvisational performance; rather, we tell a story of increasing rigidity and of an institutionalization that forecloses the possibility of flexibility and spontaneity. Our histories of early Christianity, for all of their recent emphasis on diversity and "Christianities," take hardening institutions as their primary developmental milestones. We trace the development of creeds and the circulation of canons (both biblical and ecclesiastical); we chart the narrowing of orthodoxy, and the increasing marginalization and exclusion of diverse beliefs and practices. (Of course, we might single out a text like Epiphanius's *Panarion* as partially responsible for our focus on increasing intolerance and rigidity.) We portray late antiquity, and the Christian Roman Empire, as a "totalizing discourse,"[32] or a calcifying culture (imaged, often, by the static face of a Byzantine icon on a dust jacket),[33] present to us in a series of highly scripted texts: monastic rules, church orders, law codes, synodical decrees, and heresiologies. The teleological temptation that haunts all history writing leads us, perhaps too easily, to emphasize limit and constraint over fluidity and flexibility.

---

but rather as a set of "stage directions" (421, 427, 448), evoking, once more, the fluid yet institutional style of improvisation recommended by rhetorical handbooks.

32. Often cited is Averil Cameron, *Christianity and the Rhetoric of Empire: The Development of Christian Discourse,* Sather Classical Lectures 55 (Berkeley: University of California Press, 1994); see, drawing on Cameron, my own *Remains of the Jews: The Holy Land and Christian Empire in Late Antiquity,* Divinations (Stanford, CA: Stanford University Press, 2004), 23. Cameron likewise detailed the foreclosing of cultural horizons in her essay "Ascetic Closure and the End of Antiquity," in *Asceticism,* ed. Vincent Wimbush and Richard Valantasis (New York: Oxford University Press, 2002), 147–61. But see now her comments in *Dialoguing in Late Antiquity,* Hellenic Studies Series 65 (Washington, DC: Center for Hellenic Studies, 2014), 9.

33. Several recent covers (of both popular and scholarly works): Charles Freeman, *A New History of Early Christianity* (New Haven, CT: Yale University Press, 2009); Everett Ferguson et al., *Encyclopedia of Early Christianity* (London: Taylor & Francis, 1998); Joseph Lynch, *Early Christianity: A Brief History* (New York: Oxford University Press, 2010); G.W. Bowersock, Peter Brown, and Oleg Grabar, *Late Antiquity: A Guide to the Postclassical World* (Cambridge: Belknap Press of Harvard University Press, 1999); Susan Ashbrook Harvey and David G. Hunter, *The Oxford Handbook of Early Christian Studies* (Oxford: Oxford University Press, 2008).

Of course, it is true that Christians over the course of the late fourth and fifth centuries produced a culture of exclusion, hierarchy, and constraint. What Epiphanius can help us reimagine, however, is how they managed it: how certain Christians (primarily an episcopal class) succeeded in producing this conservative culture through a performative style that emphasized its own ad hoc, improvisational nature. That Epiphanius was familiar with, and even comfortably conversant in, the rhetorical and theatrical venues of improvisational performance is clear from his writings.[34] Moreover, we can see him adopting a self-consciously improvisational style of discipline in his own writings about the church. Here I focus on two interrelated modes: discipline over the individual body and discipline over the communal body.

BODY AND DISCIPLINE

Like many monk-bishops in the fourth and fifth centuries, Epiphanius brought his monastic sensibilities to the Christian population in general.[35] Epiphanius avers that virginity is the most admirable sexual

---

34. Although he strikes a self-consciously oppositional pose to *paideia* in his broadsides against Origen (see my discussions in chapters 1 and 4), Epiphanius elsewhere unproblematically shows off his own familiarity with systems of *paideia* and with theatrical conventions: he compares heretical myths (negatively) to "Greek education" (τῶν Ἑλλήνων παιδείαν) and "drama" (τραγῳδία) (*Panarion* 31.2–3, 8.1; 36.1.3 [GCS n.F. 10.1:383–87, 398; 31:44]), bemoans both "excess" and paucity of education (*Panarion* 32.3.8; 76.2.1–2 [GCS n.F. 10.1:442; 37:341]), compares heretical deception to "the theater" (δραματουργία) (*Panarion* 73.1.2 [GCS 37:267]), and in an almost pedantic flourish facetiously addresses the arch-heretic Mani: "Raise your mask, Menander, you comic-writer!" (ἔπαρόν σου τὸν προσωπεῖον, ὦ κωμῳκοποιὲ Μένανδρε) (*Panarion* 66.46.11 [GCS 37:84]).

35. See my discussion in chapter 5. Claudia Rapp, *Holy Bishops in Late Antiquity: The Nature of Christian Leadership in an Age of Transition*, TCH 37 (Berkeley: University of California Press, 2005), details the ways that the ascetic authority of bishops combined with their apostolic and spiritual authority. Peter Brown, *The Body and Society: Men, Women, and Sexual Renunciation in Early Christianity*, Lectures on the History of Religions n.s. 13 (New York: Columbia University Press, 1988), particularly in his chapter on John Chrysostom (305–22), deftly shows how ascetic logic could reshape the Christian city; Brown is followed by Leyerle, *Theatrical Shows*.

state for all Christians, and he routinely (and, as in the case of the "gnostic" heresy with which I began, sometimes graphically) objects to the sexual libertinism of various heretical groups in the *Panarion*.[36] He is also supportive of ascetic rigor wherever it may appear, even among the Pharisees or the heretical followers of Hieracas. Notably, in both cases, Epiphanius is critical not of the ascetic intentions of these heretics, but of their extremism. While it is presumably laudable that the Pharisees enter into extended periods of sexual abstinence, the "ordeals" (*agōna*) they undergo to avoid sleep (and nocturnal emissions) are presented as comical.[37] Likewise, while Hieracas was "astounding in his asceticism" (*ekplēktos tēi autou askēsei*), he goes too far in his total rejection of marriage, claiming that Christ came "to preach abstinence (*tēn enkrateian*) in the world and to gather up purity and abstinence for himself; for without this no one will be able to have life."[38] Epiphanius can admire Hieracas's personal asceticism, but not its inflexibility: even Christ, Epiphanius points out, attended a wedding early in his ministry precisely "to honor holy matrimony."[39]

Indeed, Epiphanius, particularly in the *Panarion*, was more frequently critical of extreme asceticism than of moral laxity. The Severians, we

---

36. Epiphanius, *Panarion* 23.2.5; 26.4–5, 9; 32.4.2; 63.1.4–6; 76.4.8 (GCS n.F. 10.1:251, 280–82, 285–86, 443; 31:399; 37:345).

37. Epiphanius, *Panarion* 16.1.2–4 (GCS n.F. 10.1:210–11): Epiphanius reports that they sleep on narrow benches, put stones in their bedclothes, and have thorny mattresses to avoid "shameful bodily discharge through dreams" (δι' ὀνειράτων ἀηδῆ ῥύσιν σώματος).

38. Epiphanius, *Panarion* 67.1.6, 9 (GCS 37:133–34).

39. Epiphanius, *Panarion* 67.6.6 (GCS 37:138), referring to John 2:1–12. More than a decade later the western monk Jovinian deployed the wedding at Cana in a similar manner, and was refuted harshly by Epiphanius's theological ally, Jerome, *Adversus Iovinianum* 1.40 (PL 23:269). While Epiphanius concedes in this same passage that Christ was born of a virgin "to honor virginity" (παρθενίαν τιμήσῃ), he suggests elsewhere, in defending Christ's true humanity and divinity against Apollinarians, that Christ's resistance to hunger (and his abstinence in general) should be credited to his divinity, not "abstaining philosophically, like we do" (ὡς φιλοσοφικῶς καθ' ἡμᾶς ἐγκρατευόμενος) (*Panarion* 77.18.9 [GCS 37:432]). That is, Christ was not in his incarnation an ascetic model for humans.

learn, reject both wine drinking and sexual intercourse, since the former "disturbs the human mind," while the latter "is the work of Satan."[40] Nonsense, Epiphanius replies: every bodily desire has been placed in the body by God: "Even that yearning according to bodily desire is not unseemly," he asserts.[41] And how could these heretics believe that the God who declared "I am the true vine" (John 15:1) forbids drinking wine?[42] Epiphanius continues his argument against such rigid teetotaling in response to the Encratites, who claim the apostle Paul must have been a "drunkard" (*methustēn*) to approve of marriage as honorable.[43] Epiphanius objects that "all immoderation (*ametron*) is entirely harmful (*luperon*), and abides beyond the established pale. For not only about wine would I say this, but also about all insatiability (*aplēstia*)."[44] Epiphanius certainly agrees that overindulgence is harmful, but suggests that these heretics are just as "insatiable" in their "immoderate" inflexibility. Epiphanius dismisses these "immoderate" ascetics as impelled not by piety but rather by "boasting,"[45] much like other heretical ascetics whose extraordinary excesses in the name of abstinence paradoxically prove their impiety.[46]

I am not suggesting that Epiphanius was a "middle-of-the-road" ascetic, advocating a more tepid form of bodily discipline than some of his contemporaries. Rather, I argue that Epiphanius's objections to

---

40. Epiphanius, *Panarion* 45.1.8, 2.1 (GCS 31:200).
41. Epiphanius, *Panarion* 45.3.2–3 (GCS 31:201).
42. Epiphanius, *Panarion* 45.4.4 (GCS 31:201–2).
43. Epiphanius, *Panarion* 47.2.2–3 (GCS 31:217). The "apostolic" passage in question is Heb 13:4: "Honorable is marriage and undefiled the marriage-bed."
44. Epiphanius, *Panarion* 47.2.5–6 (GCS 31:217).
45. Epiphanius, *Panarion* 47.3.1 (GCS 31:218): "They boast about their seeming abstinence" (Σεμνύνονται δὲ δῆθεν ἐγκράτειαν).
46. Epiphanius routinely condemns "showy" asceticism: *Panarion* 23.2.5 (GCS 25:251), on Satornilus's "so-called ascetic life" (δῆθεν πολιτείας); 40.2.4 (GCS 31:82), on the Archontics, who "claim to fast" and "boast in the guise (προσχήματι) of monastic renunciation"; 46.2.2 (GCS 31:205), on Tatian's "guise of abstinence" (προσχήαμτι τῆς ἐγκρατείας); 52.2.3 (GCS 31:313), on the Adamites, who "claim abstinence" and pray completely naked; and 58.1.5–6 (GCS 31:358), on the Valesians, who undergo voluntary and forced castration for (presumably) ascetic reasons.

these ascetic overachievers have more to do with their inflexibility than their actual bodily practices. We see this argument clearly in Epiphanius's refutation of the "Apostolics," another group of ascetics who "actually do not allow marriage."[47] What Epiphanius explicitly finds objectionable about these Apostolics is their "one-size-fits-all" approach to Christian bodily discipline. Not all Christians are fit for the same level of bodily discipline, he explains: "For you see one harmony, one hope and one faith in the church, bestowed to each according to his own ability and according to his own toil and struggle."[48] Some can renounce all sex, others are chaste within marriage; some renounce all wealth and goods, others "abide in righteous ownership."[49]

"God's holy chuch is like a ship," Epiphanius elaborates.[50] Just as the individual parts of a ship—the keel, the anchor, the "beams, planks and ribs, its frame-timbers, the stern, sides and cross-rods, the mast and the steering paddles, the seats and the oar-handles, the tillers and all the rest"—are made of "different kinds of wood," so too does the church comprise different members with different abilities and constitutions. Only heresies, Epiphanius concludes, are "made of just one kind of wood."[51] Epiphanius's colorful elaboration of Paul's metaphor of the body and its members likely relies on the antiquarian literature of which he was so fond: sources such as Theophrastus note that different woods have different properties (of hardness, durability, resistance to

---

47. Epiphanius, *Panarion* 41.1.2 (GCS 31:380). Epiphanius reports they also call themselves the "apotactics."

48. Epiphanius, *Panarion* 41.3.3 (GCS 31:383).

49. Epiphanius, *Panarion* 41.3.1 (GCS 31:382).

50. Epiphanius, *Panarion* 41.3.4 (GCS 31:383). The idea of the church as a "ship" has a long tradition (and even contributes to Epiphanius's central metaphor in the *Ancoratus*, the "well-anchored discourse"); Everett Ferguson, "Community and Worship," in *The Routledge Companion to Early Christian Thought*, ed. D. Jeffrey Bingham (London: Routledge, 2010), 319–20, surveys several examples, many of which draw on the image of Noah's ark (cf. 1 Pet 3:20–22); Robin Jensen, *Understanding Early Christian Art* (London: Routledge, 2000), 138–41, points out the links between ship metaphors in art and the cross/anchor motif. Most of these visual and textual examples portray the church (both the institution and, at times, the building) as the locus of salvation.

51. Epiphanius, *Panarion* 41.3.4–5 (GCS 31:383).

moisture, and so forth) that make them suitable to different parts of the boat.[52] Epiphanius's orthodox ship, therefore, is not only accommodating of different abilities but practical in its use of them. A "single-wood" (*monoxulos*) ship (that is, a heresy) lacks the flexibility of the orthodox church.

Epiphanius's approach to bodily discipline is rigorous but flexible, as we see in those few instances when he speaks prescriptively about bodily discipline. One section of his chapter against the Montanists serves as a kind of minitreatise "on virginity." He rails against the Montanist preaching against marriage, insisting that the orthodox church makes room for "virginity, singleness (*monotēta*), purity, widowhood, and marriage."[53] Unlike the inflexible heretics, the orthodox "make allowances for human form (*plasei*) and its weakness."[54] Epiphanius endorses Paul's advice (1 Cor 7:6–7) as a matter of practical necessity and a mark of orthodox flexibility: "As for us, we do not impose a requirement (*hēmeis de ouk anankēn epititheamen*). Exhorting with good counsel, we advise the one who is able, but do not impose a requirement on the one who is unable."[55]

We see Epiphanius's ascetic flexibility at work in an encounter with his ascetic protégée Paula. According to Jerome, in his eulogy at Paula's death, she had once lain ill and refused to relax her ascetic regimen in order to regain her health. (I discussed this scene in chapter 1 as well.) Jerome calls upon Epiphanius to intervene:

---

52. Theophrastus, *Historia plantarum* 5.7.1–3. Pliny, *Historia naturalis* 13.9, 16.13, 16.64, 16.76, 16.80 notes various kinds of plants and trees useful for different parts of shipbuilding as well. That ships were built of diverse materials seems clear from recovered remains of ships; for one survey, see G. Giacchi et al., "The Wood of 'C' and 'F' Roman Ships Found in the Ancient Harbour of Pisa (Tuscany, Italy): The Utilisation of Different Timbers and the Probable Geographical Area Which Supplied Them," *Journal of Cultural Heritage* 4 (2003): 269–83.

53. Epiphanius, *Panarion* 48.9.1 (GCS 31:230).

54. Epiphanius, *Panarion* 48.9.4 (GCS 31:231); see also 48.9.8: "The holy Word everywhere called upon us to bear up the weakness of the weak" (GCS 31:232).

55. Epiphanius, *Panarion* 48.9.8 (GCS 31:231–32).

And I myself, in secret, beseeched *papa* Epiphanius that he might admonish her, even compel her to drink wine; but she, as she was prudent and of skillful genius, right away sensed the trap; and smiling, intimated that what he was saying was mine. What more? When the blessed *pontifex*, after many exhortations, came out, he answered (when I asked him how it went): "Only that I got to the point that she almost persuaded me, as an old man, that I shouldn't drink wine!"[56]

Besides a rare glimpse into the lighter side of the bishop of Constantia, this story also attests to Epiphanius's ascetic flexibility as well as the improvisational manner in which he imposed his bodily discipline. As we have seen, Epiphanius has no principled objection to wine and believes asceticism must respond to given circumstance. We can imagine (as Jerome asks us to) the interchange with Paula, as she craftily points out that Epiphanius himself was old and perhaps unable to maintain his ascetic regimen as he had in his youth. That Epiphanius considered relaxing his discipline—even in jest, to Jerome—shows that his flexible ascetic style was familiar enough to his friends. What we glean from this story is a style of flexibility and improvisation, not tepidity or lack of rigor; certainly Paula and Jerome, notably rigorous in their ascetic teaching, would not continue to reverence a monastic lightweight. Indeed, the logic of Jerome's anecdote requires that Epiphanius be a man of notable ascetic rigor, or else his advice to Paula would be unconvincing. What we mark here is not laxity but flexibility.

In this jocular moment, as in Epiphanius's broader discussions in the *Panarion*, we can see how an improvisational style of bodily discipline might play out among ascetically minded Christians. We recall that the perception of improvisation can call into question relations of power and evoke (although in a sideways manner) institutional norms. That Epiphanius's disciplinary style was flexible and improvisational—in a way that, say, Jerome's was not—is implicit in Jerome's "secret" request that Epiphanius be the one to persuade Paula to take some wine. Paula would

---

56. Jerome, *Ep.* 108.21.2–3 (CSEL 55:337).

find Epiphanius's on-the-spot relaxation of ascetic rules more believable than if it came from the notoriously rigid monk Jerome. This perception of ascetic improvisation, in turn, allows Paula to respond without offense and thereby maintain the lines of hierarchical, master-disciple relations that had existed since their first meeting in Rome in the early 380s. At the same time, Paula could turn the tables on her old ascetic maestro, proposing that while *he* might need to drink wine, she did not. At the end of the episode, Paula's own rigid ascetic norms have been reinforced for all the parties involved. Improvisation, in this case, does not degrade the discipline of Christian elites but rather affirms their superior bodily way of life. At the same time, the lines of ascetic authority and mastery have—if ever so briefly—been (even jokingly) called into question.

CHURCH AND DISCIPLINE

Throughout the *Panarion* the discipline of an individual Christian's body is directly related to the discipline of the whole church body. Epiphanius recounts how Audius, in the early fourth century, was well known in his homeland of Mesopotamia "on account of his inviolate way of life and zeal for God and faith."[57] Emboldened by his own purity, Audius felt free to publicly criticize the bishops of the churches when they failed to live morally rigorous lives. The result of Audius's ascetic inflexibility was ecclesiastical schism: "for he separated himself from the church, and many bucked the reins (*aphēniazousi*) with him and in this way he effected a division (*diairesin eirgasato*)."[58] The lesson, for Epiphanius, is clear: inflexible personal discipline could fracture the body politic as well.[59]

57. Epiphanius, *Panarion* 70.1.2 (GCS 37:233).
58. Epiphanius, *Panarion* 70.1.5 (GCS 37:233).
59. According to Epiphanius, the stringent standards of Melitius of Egypt and his followers in denying restoration of lapsed clerics to their station ultimately led to the rise of Arianism in the eastern Roman Empire: "Oh, but rather if those Melitians, who had received the most righteous truth, had held communion (ἐκοινώνησαν) with the fallen after penance, instead of with Arius and those with him" (*Panarion* 68.6.4 [GCS 37:146]).

The "Catharites" (that is, "purists" or Novatianists) likewise combine a strict asceticism with a rigid and inflexible idea of church discipline, evident in their refusal to take communion with remarried Christians.[60] Like the "one-size-fits-all" Apostolics, the Catharites insist that all Christians must be like priests: "blameless, the husband of one wife, abstinent" (cf. 1 Tim 3:2).[61] In his response, Epiphanius at first sounds like he might agree with the stringent Catharites. He proudly declares that the church not only insists on priests being married only once, but enforces celibacy on those priests who are still married to a first wife. "Steadfastly does God's holy church closely preserve this with strictness (*meta akribeias*)," he boasts.[62] As he elaborates, however, he also begins to hedge, noting that the rule on clerical celibacy is in place for all ordained clergy "*especially* where the churchmen are 'strictly by the book'" (*malista hopou akribeis kanones hoi ekklēsiastikoi*).[63] This "especially" signals that Epiphanius's high theoretical standards might be more flexible on the ground. Indeed, he quickly admits that "in some places ... priests, deacons, and subdeacons are still fathering children. This is not 'by the book' (*touto de para ton kanona ginetai*), but on occasion human intention is neglectful and" (he admits more frankly) "staff (*huperēsia*) can't be found for the multitudes."[64] Epiphanius's clerical

60. Epiphanius, *Panarion* 59.3.1 (GCS 31:366). They likewise insist that "after baptism, no one can ever receive mercy once they have fallen" (*Panarion* 59.1.2 [GCS 31:364]).

61. Epiphanius, *Panarion* 59.4.1 (GCS 31:367). Epiphanius's citation of 1 Tim 3:2 here substitutes ἐγκρατῆ (abstinent) for the more common σώφρονα (chaste or temperate), possibly mixing the verse with Tit 1:8. It doesn't seem that he is citing the Catharites, but rather reproducing his own stricter understanding of the verse as referring to priestly celibacy. Contemporary Latin versions of the New Testament understood σώφρων in a stricter sense to refer to chastity (see Elizabeth A. Clark, *Reading Renunciation: Asceticism and Scripture in Early Christianity* [Princeton, NJ: Princeton University Press, 1999], 114–15).

62. Epiphanius, *Panarion* 59.4.2 (GCS 31:367).

63. Epiphanius, *Panarion* 59.4.3 (GCS 31:367) (emphasis added). Alternately, we might translate this caveat "especially where the church rules are strict." The gist is much the same.

64. Epiphanius, *Panarion* 59.4.4 (GCS 31:367–68).

concession—that, sometimes, "strictness" must give way in the face of practical concerns—in turn informs his flexibility surrounding lay sexual activity. Not only does he admit that widows may remarry, but even that in certain cases the church will sanction divorce and remarriage.[65] Epiphanius counsels flexibility with respect to bodily and church discipline.

This is not to say that Epiphanius endorses lax disciplinary standards for the members of the church and (especially) Christian clergy. He holds strict standards for church discipline, generally. He insists, for instance, that only men can be ordained[66] and he is a firm proponent of the authority of apostolic succession.[67] Nonetheless, his desire to keep strictly to church rules (*kanones*) is moderated time and again by an ostensibly realistic and flexible approach to the maintenance of discipline within the church. We can see this elucidated in the final section of the conclusion to the *Panarion*, at the end of a long and rambling recitation of belief entitled (presumably by Epiphanius) "A Summary and True Account of the Catholic and Apostolic Faith of the Church" (*suntomos alēthēs logos pisteōs katholikēs kai apostolikēs ekklēsias*). Embedded into this tract "on faith" (*peri pisteōs*) is a brief church manual "on rules" (*peri thesmōn*) that may have been a separate treatise of Epiphanius's now incorporated into his concluding chapter.[68] Epiphanius proposes to

---

65. Epiphanius, *Panarion* 59.4.10 (GCS 31:369). See Calogero Riggi, "Nouvelle lecture du *Panarion* LIX, 4 (Épiphane et le divorce)," *SP* 12.1 (1975): 129–34, who (even after amending the critical text to make it somewhat stricter) admires this "précieux témoignage d'indulgence" on Epiphanius's part (134). On the precise translation of these difficult lines of *Panarion* 59.4, see Pierre Nautin, "Divorce et remariage chez Saint Épiphane," *VC* 37 (1983): 157–73, with a less "indulgent" interpretation by Henri Crouzel, "Encore sur divorce et remarriage selon Épiphane," *VC* 38 (1984): 271–80.

66. Epiphanius, *Panarion* 42.4.5; 49.2.2; 79.2–3 (GCS 31:100, 244–43; 37:476–78), against the ordination of women.

67. Epiphanius, *Panarion* 27.6.2–8 (GCS 25:308–10).

68. Epiphanius, *De fide* 21–24 (GCS 37:521–25). The previous paragraph, which concludes a long (and somewhat digressive) discussion of Christian faith, ends with a summary of the entire *Panarion* and a doxology (*De fide* 20.5 [GCS 37:521]). Epiphanius then abruptly transitions from his discussion περὶ πίστεως to a discussion περὶ θεσμῶν (*De fide* 21.2 [GCS 37:521]) and, in his (actual) concluding paragraph, describes the entire

survey "as many [rules] as have actually been observed in [the church] and are observed, whether from command (*ek prostagmatos*) or according to voluntary acceptance (*kata apodochēn proaireseōs*)."[69] What follows is a whirlwind tour of Christian disciplinary life, including regulations on virginity, clergy, fasts, vigils, memorials, monastic habits (such as food and clothing), hospitality, forbidden activities, and prayers.

Compared to other church manuals of the fourth and fifth centuries, Epiphanius's foray is brief and notably elastic.[70] When Epiphanius discusses the requirements for the priesthood, "the crown" of church offices, he explains that the priesthood "is drawn for the most part from virgins, but if not from virgins, from solitaries (*monazontōn*).[71] If there aren't sufficient solitaries for staffing needs (*hupēresian*), then from those abstaining from their own wives or those widowed from a single marriage."[72] Epiphanius advises even more flexibility with regard to the suborders, from which a bishop may draw "even men who have been joined to a second wife after the death of the first."[73] The sliding scale of sexual requirements for clergy recalls Epiphanius's earlier hedging against the Catharites: there are certain standards and strictures, but

---

concluding section as a discourse "on the faith of the church, and the rules which are reported in her" (*De fide* 25.1 [GCS 37:525]). That Epiphanius's περὶ θεσμῶν might have been a preexisting treatise or pamphlet I infer from the transition here and Epiphanius's penchant for incorporating previously written texts (his own or others') into the *Panarion*.

69. Epiphanius, *De fide* 21.2 (GCS 37:521).

70. Epiphanius is aware of these church manuals, and notes that the Audians cite the *Didascalia apostolorum* (called here τὴν τῶν ἀποστόλων διάταξιν), which Epiphanius admits "to many is doubtful (ἀμφιλέκτῳ), but is not discredited (οὐκ ἀδόκιμον)" (*Panarion* 70.10.1 [GCS 37:242]).

71. Frank Williams, in his revised translation of the *Panarion*, translates μοναζόντων as "once-married men" (replacing his earlier "single men") (*The Panarion of Epiphanius of Salamis*, vol. 2, *Books II and III, De fide,* trans. Frank Williams, 2nd rev. ed., NHMS 79 [Leiden: Brill, 2013], 678), which makes a certain sense in context, but I can't find any evidence that a fourth-century author would use μονάζω in this way (particularly since Epiphanius elsewhere in the *Panarion* uses the word to mean "monastic").

72. Epiphanius, *De fide* 21.7–8 (GCS 37:522). On this passage, see also Nautin, "Divorce et remariage," 168–71.

73. Epiphanius, *De fide* 21.9 (GCS 37:522).

the bishops who make these appointments must make do with what they have. Liturgical and moral customs are similarly adaptable: "In some places also they prescribe church services on the Sabbaths, but not everywhere. But among the elites they guard against swearing altogether, and reproaching, and cursing, from the commandment of the Savior, and indeed from lying, as much as they can (*hoson kata to dunaton*). And most people sell what they have and give to the poor."[74] "Not everywhere," "as much as they can," and "most people" indicate Epiphanius's seeming willingness to countenance a degree of variability in response to circumstances. He speaks in similarly variable tones about Lenten fasts, dietary restrictions, and monastic habitations.[75] All of these topics are subjects to "rules" (*thesmoi*), which are, in turn, irregularly enforced if not altogether ignored.[76] I think any reader who has progressed through the three volumes of the *Panarion* preceding the treatise *De fide* will not mistake Epiphanius for a casual, open-minded bishop accepting and welcoming of diversity and difference. Yet in this minitreatise, as throughout the *Panarion*, Epiphanius goes out of his way to portray his Christian rules as flexible and subject to extemporaneous relaxation. How then do we account for Epiphanius's portrayal of a body of ecclesiastical "rules" that are as often overlooked as enforced?[77]

It may help us to explore a few of his own direct interventions in church discipline, as these accounts appear in his own writings. What

---

74. Epiphanius, *De fide* 24.7 (GCS 37:525).

75. Epiphanius, *De fide* 22.10–14, 23.2–5 (GCS 37:523–24).

76. Epiphanius, *De fide* 23.3 (GCS 37:524) notes with surprising calm: "It has pleased some to have long hair, on account of so-called ascetic practice (δῆθεν πολιτείας), from their own idea, although the Gospel doesn't command it and the apostles do not allow it: for the holy apostle Paul has proscribed this fashion (τὸ σχῆμα)." On long-haired monks in a western context, see now Maria Doerfler, "'Hair!' Remnants of Ascetic Exegesis in Augustine of Hippo's *De Opere Monachorum*," *JECS* 22 (2014): 79–111.

77. Calogero Riggi, "La figura di Epifanio nel IV secolo," *SP* 8.2 (1966): 99, notes: "Egli che fu così intransigente e polemico per quanto riguardava i fondamenti della fede, sembra però sia stato straordinariamente comprensivo ed elastico in quello che riguardava le questioni pratiche della tradizione ecclesiastica"; see pp. 102–3 on Epiphanius's flexible ascetic attitudes as well.

comes into focus—and helps explain his display of disciplinary flexibility in the *Panarion* and *De fide*—is how Epiphanius's improvisational style affirms institutional norms and expands the potential scope of episcopal power. We have already seen how Epiphanius recalls his rooting out of gnostics from a community in his youth, with clear references to institutions (bishops, orthodoxy, the "church"). What is less clear is the manner in which Epiphanius or the bishops exercised their authority: by appeal to local magistrates or formal anathematization or local council or even mob action. We see a similar combination of institutional surety and improvisational style as Epiphanius recalls his intervention in the episcopal tangle in the city of Antioch.

The episcopacy of Antioch had been hotly contested for some decades, not merely between Nicene and homoian Christians, but even among ostensible allies.[78] By the mid-370s, three claimants to the episcopal see, Paulinus, Vitalius, and Meletius, all proclaimed allegiance to the Nicene Creed. With Meletius in exile,[79] Paulinus and Vitalius argued over the rightful (Nicene) holder of the bishop's throne. Each accused the other of theological irregularities: Paulinus was a follower of Eustathius of Antioch who, like Eustathius, stood accused of "Sabellianism";[80] and Vitalius had been ordained by Apollinarius of

---

78. Adam Schor, *Theodoret's People: Social Networks and Religious Conflict in Late Roman Syria*, TCH 48 (Berkeley: University of California Press, 2011), 61 and 63, provides two excellent charts (derived mainly from Theodoret's *Historia ecclesiastica*) detailing the timelines of the various ordinations and counterordinations, as well as the theological leanings of the various claimants to the Antiochene see. See now also Shepardson's lucid summary in *Controlling Contested Places*, 16–18.

79. Meletius was exiled multiple times by emperors antipathetic to Nicene Trinitarianism, this last time by Valens from around 369 to 378 (at Valens's death), and was in exile at the time Epiphanius wrote the *Panarion* (see *Panarion* 73.34.2 [GCS 37:309]).

80. Epiphanius, *Panarion* 77.20.7 (GCS 37:434): "For Vitalius charged Paulinus with the label of a follower of Sabellius." Paulinus had been ordained Eustathius's successor by Lucifer of Cagliari in 362, but rarely spent time on the episcopal throne of Antioch. Like many Nicene Christians (including Epiphanius in the early 370s, and like the original Nicene Creed), Paulinus rejected three-*hypostasis* language.

Laodicea,[81] whose disciples had already alarmed Epiphanius with their unorthodox teachings about the nature of Christ.[82] Somehow, Epiphanius became involved in their conflict.[83] I say "somehow" because the roots of his intervention are unclear; at least, they are unclear in the way that Epiphanius recounts events. "While among the Antiochenes (*epi tēs Antiocheōn gar genomenoi*)," he writes in the *Panarion*, "I met with their leaders (*tois akraimosin*)."[84] Was he in Antioch in order to meet with their leaders? Had he come *because* of the episcopal struggles between the Nicene factions? If anything, his tone makes it sound as if he happened to be "on the spot" and decided—on a whim!—to attempt to settle their conflict.

If Epiphanius's initial presence is unexplained, so too is his course of action. Because he "wished to reunite both of them in peace,"[85] he holds interviews with each of the claimants. He is satisfied with Paulinus's orthodoxy when Paulinus provides a sworn statement affirming his agreement with the theology of the late Athanasius of Alexandria.[86]

---

81. Specifically, Paulinus accused Vitalius of saying "that Christ did not become a perfect human (τέλειον... ἄνθρωπον)" (*Panarion* 77.22.2 [GCS 37:435]).

82. Epiphanius, *Panarion* 77.2.2–4 (GCS 37:417). It is unclear why "students" (παῖδας) of Apollinarius visited (ἀφικομένους, ἐρχομένοις) Epiphanius, presumably in Cyprus, and presumably in the late 360s or very early 370s. Some read Epiphanius's account in this chapter against the Apollinarians to mean that Epiphanius himself convened a council, the minutes of which he sent to Athanasius, who then wrote a letter to Epictetus of Corinth (preserved as *Panarion* 77.3–13 [GSC 37:417–27]) (see, for instance, Jon Dechow, *Dogma and Mysticism in Early Christianity: Epiphanius of Cyprus and the Legacy of Origen*, PMS 13 [Macon, GA: Mercer University Press, 1988], 60–61; Young Richard Kim, *Saint Epiphanius of Cyprus, Ancoratus*, FC 128 [Washington, DC: Catholic University of America Press, 2014], 36). All of the verbs in this passage, however, are frustratingly passive: "it was necessary for a synod to be assembled" (ἀνάγκη γέγονε σύνοδον συγκροτηθῆναι); "minutes were taken (ὑπομνήματα πέπρακται])... they were sent to Athanasius (Ἀθανασίῳ ἀπεστάλη)" (*Panarion* 77.2.5–6 [GCS 37:417]).

83. See Kim, *Epiphanius*, 165–72.

84. Epiphanius, *Panarion* 77.20.3 (GCS 37:434).

85. Epiphanius, *Panarion* 77.20.6 (GCS 37:434).

86. Epiphanius, *Panarion* 77.20.7–8 (GCS 37:434). Epiphanius reproduces the brief statement (*Panarion* 77.21 [GCS 37:434–35]), which was presented at the Council of Alexandria in 362 and was appended to Athanasius's *Tomus ad Antiochenos*. Had

Epiphanius then questions Vitalius directly on his orthodoxy, specifically his views of Christ's humanity.[87] The dialogue, as Epiphanius reports it, has the feel of an interrogation: even while hoping to discover that his interlocutor is orthodox, Epiphanius also feels the need to keep pressing with more and more detailed questions, "since I know the intention of those who appropriate their own brothers' opinion through pretenses."[88] Ultimately Vitalius admits that he does not believe Christ "took a mind" when he was incarnate, and Epiphanius realizes the depth of his heresy.[89] Epiphanius discusses the matter with Vitalius and his followers ("we held a long dialogue about this"[90]) but is ultimately "unable to persuade them in their contentiousness (*autous... philoneikountas*)."[91] There is no resolution, other than Epiphanius's communion with Paulinus and rejection of Vitalius. "My life's condition was greatly aggrieved, then," Epiphanius reports, before transitioning into the rest of his refutation of the "Dimoirites," the theologically deficient disciples of Apollinarius represented by Vitalius.[92]

The first question we can ask about this series of meetings, interrrogations, affiliations, and condemnations is, what exactly *was* it?[93] We might be tempted to describe it as a synod or council, although such

---

Epiphanius requested this documentation ahead of time? Did Paulinus produce it upon request? We are not told.

87. Epiphanius, *Panarion* 77.22.2 (GCS 37:435). Was this at the same meeting at which Paulinus produced his sworn affidavit? Did Epiphanius interview the claimants separately? Where? Under what auspices? We are not told.

88. Epiphanius, *Panarion* 77.22.3 (GCS 37:435).

89. Epiphanius, *Panarion* 77.23.1 (GCS 37:436): νοῦν ἔλαβεν ἐλθών ὁ Χριστός; ὁ δὲ εὐθὺς ἠρνήσατο λέγων, οὐχί.

90. Epiphanius, *Panarion* 77.23.3 (GCS 37:436).

91. Epiphanius, *Panarion* 77.23.6 (GCS 37:436); see also 77.23.3 (GCS 37:436): "I quit, since both parties had not been persuaded because of evident contentiousness (διὰ τὴν προκειμήνην φιλονεικίαν)."

92. Epiphanius, *Panarion* 77.24.3 (GCS 37:437).

93. Kim, *Epiphanius*, 171, notes that Epiphanius narrates the incident with "a certain degree of literary flair and suspicious construction."

language is conspicuously absent from the account.[94] Indeed, Epiphanius rarely (if ever) mentions his own attendance at church councils or synods, although we might reasonably assume (given his strict adherence to the Nicene Creed and canons) that, as metropolitan bishop of Cyprus, he did preside over formal meetings of his episcopal colleagues.[95] Epiphanius makes no mention, in his later writings, of attendance at the Council of Constantinople in 381, and is not found on the surviving lists of signatories.[96] Whether or not we can plausibly argue Epiphanius's attendance at, or absence from, this major council, Epiphanius himself never makes mention of conciliar attendance, at Constantinople or elsewhere.[97] When he does mention ecclesiatical meetings—as in his meeting(s) with Paulinus and Vitalius in Antioch—they do not have the formal quality of a synod or council. Epiphanius happens to be in Antioch; Epiphanius meets with, and interrogates, two claimants for the episocopal throne; he sides with one, rebukes the other, and fails to bring them together peaceably. He

94. Compare, for instance, Epiphanius's description of the first time Arius's heresy came to light, which results in a more formal process: "Alexander summoned (συγκαλεῖται) then the presbytery and certain other bishops who were present, and performed an interrogation (ἀνέτασιν) and examination (ἀνάκρισιν) of him" (*Panarion* 69.3.7 [GCS 37:155]).
95. The fifth canon of the Council of Nicaea (325) called for twice-yearly provincial councils of bishops. Socrates and Sozomen describe Epiphanius holding a synod in Cyprus to condemn Origenism (at the prompting of Theophilus of Alexandria), but Epiphanius does not mention it; Socrates, *Historia ecclesiastica* 6.10.4–6 (GCS n.F. 1:328).
96. Indeed, some scholars have argued that because the Council of Constantinople was initially presided over by Meletius of Antioch, and Epiphanius had by then endorsed Paulinus for the Antiochene see, he refused to attend the council; see Pierre Nautin, "Épiphane (saint) de Salamine," *Dictionnaire d'histoire et de géographie ecclésiastique* 15 (1963): 622; and Dechow, *Dogma and Mysticism*, 87. Claudia Rapp, "Epiphanius of Salamis: The Church Father as Saint," in *"The Sweet Land of Cyprus": Papers Given at the Twenty-First Jubilee Spring Symposium of Byzantine Studies,* ed. A.A.M. Bryer and G.S. Georghallides (Nicosia: Cyprus Research Center, 1993), 172, remarks: "There is reason to believe that Epiphanius attended the Second Ecumenical Council held in 381 in Constantinople," based partly on events recounted in his later *vita*.
97. Dechow, *Dogma and Mysticism*, 88, remarks that "Epiphanius' authority in some circles transcended conciliar attendance," citing *Apophthegmata Patrum* 334, which I discuss in chapter 1.

(presumably) departs, and the Antiochene see remains a tangle for the next four decades.[98]

Of course, there may have been some more formal structure in place (why else, we might wonder, did Paulinus bring a signed theological affadavit to his meeting with Epiphanius?). My point is that, in his own self-representation, Epiphanius eschews formal structure in favor of an ad hoc "dialogue." Church discipline, executed by the visiting bishop, retains an improvisational quality. So, too, does Epiphanius's own ambiguous role in the proceedings. He casually mentions that he "summoned" Vitalius for their theological conversation,[99] but doesn't explain his authority to do so. Likewise, Paulinus immediately provides Epiphanius with his affidavit of *bona fides,* but Epiphanius does not tell us why. Epiphanius's representation of these events, I think, draws on the three elements of improvisation I outlined above: perception, power, and institution. Whatever the series of events that led Epiphanius to question the two contenders for Antioch's episcopacy, he frames them in terms of improvisation: we perceive his ad hoc manner, his "dialogue" with Vitalius, his attempts to forge peaceful cooperation before throwing up his hands and giving up.

Once we perceive Epiphanius's improvisational style, we also appreciate the way he engages with the power and the institutional structures of the church. Epiphanius styles himself as a sort of elder statesmen, routinely receiving and evaluating younger disciples (in his account of Vitalius's interrogation he refers, again, to the followers of Apollinarius as "children," *paidōn*).[100] Epiphanius's theological authority operates outside of the episcopal hierarchy, according to which in

---

98. At the death of the Meletius, the assembled bishops at Constantinople appointed Flavian, who received recognition from most of the Christian empire, and two bishops succeeded him, while the disciples of Paulinus (who was succeeded by Evagrius) remained in schism until 415. Vitalius seems to disappear from the historical record; presumably Apollinarius's condemnation at the Council of Constantinople made his party's position in Antioch less tenable.

99. Epiphanius, *Panarion* 77.20.5 (GCS 37:434): Βιτάλιον, ὑφ' ἡμῶν μετακληθέντα.

100. Epiphanius, *Panarion* 77.22.5 (GCS 37:435).

this period the bishop of Antioch could plausibly claim jurisdiction over the archbishop of Cyprus.[101] At the same time, of course, we cannot forget that the entire debate into which Epiphanius has inserted himself has to do with the rightful, singular holder of the episcopacy of Antioch: a question that, by its very premises, affirms the institutional structures of the church. By portraying his intervention as fundamentally improvisational, Epiphanius in one stroke both upholds the institutional structures of the church and creates a means to intervene from outside those formal structures.

We have only Epiphanius's account of the impromptu Antioch meeting, and therefore no sense of how his intervention was received.[102] Similar improvisational interventions from near the end of Epiphanius's life drew more volatile reaction.[103] In 394, Epiphanius was visiting

---

101. The Council of Ephesus (431) affirmed (or, possibly, instituted) Cypriot independence from the patriarch of Antioch; see *Acta conciliorum oecumernicorum, Concilium universal Ephesenum*, vol. 1.1, pt. 7, ed. E. Schwartz (Berlin: De Gruyter, 1929), 118–22, and discussion with sources in Claudia Rapp, "The *Vita* of Epiphanius of Salamis: An Historical and Literary Study" (PhD diss., Oxford University, 1991), 1:142–48. Benedict Englezakis, "Epiphanius of Salamis, the Father of Cypriot Autocephaly," in *Studies on the History of the Church of Cyprus, 4th-20th Centuries*, trans. Normal Russell (Aldershot, UK: Ashgate, 1995), 29–40, lays out the historical and textual contexts for Cypriot independence from the Antiochene patriarchate before and after the Council of Ephesus. As Englezakis notes (38–39), the rise of veneration of Barnabas (as in the *Acta Barnabae* and *Laudatio Barnabae*) as the "founding apostle" of Cyprus is no doubt linked to fifth-century claims of autocephaly; see also Bernd Kollman, *Joseph Barnabas: His Life and Legacy* (Collegeville, MN: Liturgical Press, 2004), 56–59; Joseph P. Huffman, "The Donation of Zeno: St. Barnabas and the Origins of the Cypriot Archbishops' Regalia Privileges," *JEH* 66 (2015): 235–60.

102. Since Vitalius more or less disappears from historical view soon after Epiphanius's visit, it may be that Epiphanius's siding with Paulinus was effective in transforming the church structure in Antioch. The end of Meletius's exile at the death of Valens, however, shifted the terrain once more. According to Jerome, Epiphanius and Paulinus went to Rome in 382 to try to secure Paulinus's right to the episcopacy against Meletius's successor, Flavian (*Ep.* 108.6.1–2 and 127.7.1 [CSEL 55:310 and 56:150]).

103. An issue that relates to the earlier conflict in Antioch as well, prompted, as it was, by Apollinarius's irregular ordination of Vitalius as bishop of Antioch. On this event in the larger context of the Origenist controversy, see Young Richard Kim, "Epiphanius of Cyprus vs. John of Jerusalem: An Improper Ordination and the Escalation of the Origenist Controversy," in *Episcopal Elections in Late Antiquity*, ed. Johan Leemans,

his former monastery in Palestine and received visitors from the nearby monastery supervised by Jerome. The monks, among them Jerome's brother Paulinian,[104] had come to make peace with Epiphanius over some "grudge or other I had against them" (*nescio quid adversum eos habebam tristitiae*).[105] Knowing that Paulinian had been targeted for ordination, since the priests in Jerome's monastery refused their clerical service,[106] Epiphanius had him seized and ordained when they all went to celebrate communion.[107] According to Epiphanius, everything about this ordination is improvised, from the very moment Paulinian appears before him: "I was sufficiently amazed (*satis miratus*) when, at the arrangement of God, he came to me."[108] According to Epiphanius, such opportunistic ordinations outside of one's proper episcopal jurisdiction are commonplace in Cyprus.[109] He is therefore "amazed" (*admiratus*) to hear that he had supposedly promised not to perform any ordinations in Palestine, and that he had protested: "Am I a child? Don't I know the rules (*Numquid iuuenis sum aut canones ignoro*)?"[110] Epiphanius responds that, like any human being, he may have forgotten things he has said, but writes: "I do not recall having heard this, nor having myself used this kind of language."[111] Of course, Epiphanius does

---

Peter Van Nuffelen, Shawn Keough, and Carla Nicolaye, Arbeiten zur Kirchengeschichte 119 (Berlin: De Gruyter, 2011), 411–22. I discuss this incident in chapter 2.

104. We know very little about Paulinian, and what little we know comes almost entirely from Jerome and almost entirely in the context of the Origenist controversy; see Young Richard Kim, "Jerome and Paulinian, Brothers," *VC* 67 (2013): 517–30.

105. Epiphanius, *Ep. ad Ioannem* (= Jerome, *Ep.* 51) 1.5 (CSEL 54:397).

106. Epiphanius, *Ep. ad Ioannem* (= Jerome, *Ep.* 51) 1.5 (CSEL 54:396).

107. Epiphanius, *Ep. ad Ioannem* (= Jerome, *Ep.* 51) 1.5–6 (CSEL 54:397).

108. Epiphanius, *Ep. ad Ioannem* (= Jerome, *Ep.* 51) 1.5 (CSEL 54:397).

109. Epiphanius, *Ep. ad Ioannem* (= Jerome, *Ep.* 51) 2.1–2 (CSEL 54:398). Epiphanius was (of course) aware that extrajurisdictional ordination was a provocative and potentially schismatic maneuver, as he discusses in terms of Melitius of Egypt: *Panarion* 68.3.6 (GCS 37:143).

110. Epiphanius, *Ep. ad Ioannem* (= Jerome, *Ep.* 51) 2.3 (CSEL 54:398).

111. Epiphanius, *Ep. ad Ioannem* (= Jerome, *Ep.* 51) 2.4 (CSEL 54:398). Epiphanius also reports, more seriously, that he has witnesses to the supposed conversation (with Rufinus) who recall his silence in this exchange. It is notable that Epiphanius does not deny

know the rules; he is also adept at bending or ignoring them when the situation requires it.

Epiphanius's explanations are unlikely to satisfy his letter's recipient, John, the bishop of Jerusalem in whose jurisdiction Jerome's monastery lay. Jerome and his monastic brothers had already been turned against John by Epiphanius's "letters,"[112] and most of Epiphanius's letter to John—after this halfhearted apology—comprises a series of theological accusations against John's Origenism.[113] According to Jerome's own treatise against John, written a few years later, antipathy between the two bishops had not decreased in the intervening time.[114] Indeed, if Jerome is to be believed, the ordination of Paulinian was one move in a much longer struggle between Epiphanius and John, inaugurated a year earlier when the two bishops had publicly accused each other of heresy.[115] Of course, as with the intervention in Antioch, what we

---

that Rufinus indeed asked: "Do you think that the holy bishop will be ordaining others?" (Epiphanius, *Ep. ad Ioannem* [= Jerome, *Ep. 51*] 2.5 [CSEL 54:399]). In other words, discussion of Epiphanius ordaining priests in Palestine was already "in the air" before his "chance" encounter with Paulinian.

112. Epiphanius, *Ep. ad Ioannem* (= Jerome, *Ep. 51*) 1.3 (CSEL 54:396): "in monasterio fratrum—et fratrum peregrinorum, qui prouinciae tuae nihil debuere et propter nostrum paruitatem et litteras, quas ad eos crebro direximus, communionis quoque tuae coeperunt habere discordiam."

113. Elizabeth A. Clark, *The Origenist Controversy: The Cultural Construction of an Early Christian Debate* (Princeton, NJ: Princeton University Press, 1992), 94–102, surveys Epiphanius's more fully developed anti-Origenism in this letter; see also Dechow, *Dogma and Mysticism*, 416–33. Jerome himself remarks to John that "*papa* Epiphanius ... openly calls you a heretic (*aperte ... haereticum vocat*) in the letter he sent" (*Contra Ioannem Hierosolymitanum* 4 [PL 23:358]). Kim, *Epiphanius*, 211, aptly refers to Epiphanius's attacks against John as "passive-aggressive verbal confrontations." I discuss Epiphanius's attacks on John from a theological perspective in chapter 5.

114. Jerome, *Contra Ioannem Hierosolymitanum* 10, 41, 44 (PL 23:363, 392–94); John still referred to the ordination of Paulinian as the root of ongoing disputes with Jerome's monastery, not Epiphanius's accusations of heresy. Much of Jerome's treatise reads like a commentary and reiteration of Epiphanius's letter to John, incorporating, near the end, some of John's responses.

115. Jerome, *Contra Ioannem Hierosolymitanum* 11 (PL 23:364). Dechow, *Dogma and Mysticism*, 397–401, reconstructs the totality (if not the exact order) of events in the slow-burn confrontation between the two bishops. Kim, "Epiphanius vs. John," 418, argues

should attend to here is not a hypothetical reconstruction of events, but rather Epiphanius's representation of his mode of church discipline: as an ad hoc act of masterful improvisation.[116] When Epiphanius chides John for his warrantless overreactions, he chooses language that emphasizes his own flexibility over John's rigidity: "We should not dwell on what was done, but rather on what occasion, and in what way, and where, and why it was done."[117] In this way Epiphanius focuses John's, and a wider readership's, attention on questions of style over substance.

What does Epiphanius gain in this debate by highlighting his improvisational style over against John's narrow and (he hints) rather precious approach to church discipline?[118] As we have seen above, this perceived improvisational style allows Epiphanius to circumvent the operations of power (here, the ecclesiastical hierarchy of the Jerusalem see) while still ultimately affirming the established institutions of the church. After all, the goal of these extracurricular ordinations is to build up and support those institutions, not undermine them.[119] Epiphanius also, of course,

---

that "this improper ordination was in fact a calculated move" that cornered John and forced Jerome to declare his anti-Origenist allegiances (see also Kim, "Jerome and Paulinian," 527: "Epiphanius disregarded this [i.e., John's jurisdiction over Paulinian's monastery] and deliberately violated ecclesiastical custom in order to provoke a response"). Kim's reconstruction of events is almost certainly accurate; my focus, however, is on Epiphanius's self-representation.

116. Riggi, "Figura di Epifanio," 100, cites Epiphanius's description of "open" ordination on Cyprus as part of his flexible pastoral governing style.

117. Epiphanius, *Ep. ad Ioannem* (= Jerome, *Ep.* 51) 1.4: "nec considerandum, quid factum est, sed quo tempore et quo modo et in quibus et quare factum sit."

118. Epiphanius, *Ep. at Ioannem* (= Jerome, *Ep.* 51) 2.1 (CSEL 54:398) sarcastically notes: "O blessed gentleness and goodness of the bishops of Cyprus (what to your feeling and judgment is our boorishness [*nostra rusticitas*]) which is worthy of God's mercy!" Federico Fatti, "*Pontifex tantus:* Giovanni, Epifanio e le origini della prima contrversia origenista," *Adamantius* 19 (2013): 30–49, explains Epiphanius's provocative conduct as part of a longer effort to ensure Cypriot dominance among eastern bishops.

119. Although we have no account from Epiphanius, Socrates, *Historia ecclesiastica* 6.12, 14 (GCS n.F. 1:333–34, 335–36) describes him executing a similar extracanonical ordination in Constantinople during his visit there in 403 as part of his power struggle with John Chrysostom.

shows his own mastery by adapting to circumstances: recognizing unexpected opportunity, acting quickly, and achieving his goals even if feathers will be ruffled. Epiphanius emerges from his tussle with John (at least according to his own narrative self-representation) more authoritative, more pious, and even more masculine than the bishop of Jerusalem.

IMPROVISATION, INSTITUTION, AND EMPIRE

Epiphanius's improvisational style is important in our rethinking of the Theodosian-era church precisely because it does not eschew institutions in its flexible approach to power relations. Epiphanius's seemingly ad hoc style of Christian discipline creates room outside the normal bounds of institutions to correct and administer those institutions. This extracanonical authority was not, however, without its perils. We get a sense of the dangers of improvisation in the final chapter of the *Panarion*, in Epiphanius's refutation of the Massalians.[120] Their penchant for plein-air worship,[121] with which Epiphanius begins, signals religious lives lived totally without structure, literal or metaphorical: "The Massalians have no beginning (*oute archē*), no end, no head, no root, but everything about them is wobbly and lawless and deluded (*astēriktoi kai anarchoi kai ēpatēmenoi*), wholly lacking the fixedness of a name (*stērigmon onomatos*) or rule or position or legislation."[122] Absolute lack of bodily discipline ("they are uninhibited" [*akōlutoi de eisi*]) leads to communal anarchy: men and women not only pray together, but "when it is summertime, all willy-nilly (*anamix*), men with women and women with

---

120. For an analysis of Epiphanius's chapter against the Massalians, see Daniel Caner, *Wandering, Begging Monks: Spiritual Authority and the Promotion of Monasticism in Late Antiquity*, TCH 33 (Berkeley: University of California Press, 2002), 86–89.

121. Epiphanius, *Panarion* 80.3.2 (GCS 37:487). Their outdoor worship styles associate them (as Epiphanius reports) with pagan, Jewish, and Samaritan heretics (called, variously, Euphemites, Satanians, and Martyrians): *Panarion* 80.1.1–2.4 (GCS 37:485–86).

122. Epiphanius, *Panarion* 80.3.3 (GCS 37:487).

men, they sleep together in the same place, in the open streets."[123] Literally homeless, these ersatz ascetics have *no* discipline, in contrast to the real "servants of God, truly established on the firm rock of truth and securely building their house."[124] Epiphanius's own improvisational style operates in service of, and in connection with, "rules, positions, and legislation," and avoids heretical anarchy.[125]

My basic argument is not that Epiphanius is unique or even necessarily innovative in his deployment of an improvisational style of church discipline; rather, he reveals a crucial strategy for the development of orthodox Christian institutionalism in the last decades of the fourth century. In the wake of the incredibly divisive debates over the Trinity,[126] compounded by the shock of the reign of Julian the Apostate, Christians in the Theodosian age devised new ways to couple the perceived need for institutional rigor with a public style of leadership that could naturalize institutional power. The *Panarion* itself enacts this improvisational performance of institutional power in miniature: a rigorously detailed set of books, insistent on the singularity of orthodox truth, published in a style of Greek that cannot help but highlight the performative aspects of its own composition. As anyone who has read Epiphanius's Greek can attest, his preferred method of composition was to dictate, often with supporting texts at hand to read out, and have his dictation taken down in shorthand by an amanuensis who would

---

123. Epiphanius, *Panarion* 80.3.4 (GCS 37:487).
124. Epiphanius, *Panarion* 80.4.6 (GCS 37:489).
125. See also Epiphanius, *Panarion* 75.8.2 (GCS 37:340), against the followers of Aerius, who reject clerical hierarchy, fasts, and festivals: "But our mother the church had rules (θεσμούς) in her, established as unbreakable (αλύτους), which cannot be abolished."
126. Carlos R. Galvão-Sobrinho, *Doctrine and Power: Theological Controversy and Christian Leadership in the Later Roman Empire*, TCH 51 (Berkeley: University of California Press, 2013), has traced the dramatic shift in episcopal debate and controversy in the wake of the Alexandrian crisis over Arius, and the inauguration of a new "aggressive" (7) and "combative" (33) style of episcopal confrontation.

then transcribe the entirety.[127] Epiphanius then sent the final transcription out without further editing. The resulting text is a pastiche of rigorous, moralizing orthodoxy in loose, spontaneous language.

In his discussions of Christian discipline, and his own disciplinary activities, Epiphanius embodies this rhetorical approach to orthodox rigor in a spontaneous style. The result is a carefully crafted persona able to intervene into monastic, ecclesiastic, or even political situations in the guise of a well-meaning "problem-solver," a fixer making do with the tools at hand, all the while reinforcing and strengthening the underlying institutions. Such a persona was useful not only in the fraught and contentious setting of ecclesiastical controversy, but also for an orthodoxy increasingly entangled with the political operations of the Roman Empire.

More than thirty years ago, Stephen Greenblatt characterized the "psychic mobility" of improvisation as a mode of power embedded in our "Western consciousness."[128] He placed this style of improvisation in the context of nascent Western imperial power, as a tool that could enable that power. Greenblatt defined improvisation as

> the ability both to capitalize on the unforeseen and to transform given materials into one's own scenario. The spur-of-the-moment quality of improvisation is not as critical here as the opportunistic grasp of that which

---

127. Epiphanius, *De fide* 25.3–4 (GCS 37:526): "All the brothers with me greet Your Honor, especially Anatolius, who taking notes and drafting (σημείων καὶ σχεδαρίων) the matters of these heresies (I mean the eighty) with a lot of trouble and affection, has been deemed worthy to transcribe and correct them, along with Hypatius, his most-honored fellow deacon, who made the transcription from the drafts into quires." See also Epiphanius, *Ancoratus* 119.16 (GCS n.F. 10.1:149): "All the servants of the Lord greet you, especially myself, Anatolius, who writes this book which is entitled 'the Well-Anchored Discourse' and I pray that you are strengthened in the Lord."

128. Stephen Greenblatt, "The Improvisation of Power," in *Renaissance Self-Fashioning: From More to Shakespeare* (Chicago: University of Chicago Press, 1980), 224. The characterization of "Western consciousness" sounds a bit outmoded in our present critical context. Greenblatt's assertion is placed in a more careful context by Talal Asad, *Genealogies of Religion: Discipline and Reasons of Power in Christianity and Islam* (Baltimore: Johns Hopkins University Press, 1993), 11–12.

seems fixed and established. Indeed, as Castiglione and others in the Renaissance well understood, the impromptu character of an improvisation is itself often a calculated mask, the product of careful preparation.[129]

Improvisation, as Greenblatt argues, is a tool of domination that operates precisely by masking its dominating goals: "The heart of a successful improvisation lies in concealment, not exposure; and besides, as we have seen, even a hostile improvisation reproduces the relations of power that it hopes to displace and absorb."[130] As Greenblatt notes, this improvisational mask of power—concealing as it operates—reaches back from the Renaissance into the classical period, and is a rhetorical mode of contesting, reshaping, and enforcing institutional authority that persisted throughout the Roman imperial period in multiple cultural forms.[131] Epiphanius's improvisational framing of his Christian imperial power can also explain his lapses into ambiguity and vagueness when recounting his own ecclesiastical interventions, whether among the Egyptian gnostics, Antiochene bishops, or Palestinian monks.[132] What we begin to glimpse in the Theodosian age, exemplified by Epiphanius, is the adaptation of a rhetorical tool to the contingencies of a new Christian imperial culture, one that will, ultimately, become totalizing in its hierarchical scope and reach; in the service of an imperializing church, Epiphanius deployed the "opportunistic grasp" of a bishop attuned enough to the currents of religious and political power to swim against them when it suited his larger goals.

---

129. Greenblatt, "Improvisation of Power," 227.
130. Greenblatt, "Improvisation of Power," 253.
131. Greenblatt, "Improvisation of Power," 227: "present to varying degrees in the classical and medieval world and greatly strengthened from the Renaissance onward."
132. Asad, *Genealogies of Religion*, 17: "And ambiguity—as we saw in Greenblatt's example—is precisely one of the things that gives 'Western power' its improvisational quality."

CHAPTER FOUR

Scripture

EPIPHANIUS AND HIS BIBLE

Of all the reasons modern scholars tend to dislike Epiphanius, the bishop's opposition to the brilliance of Origen seems to rank high. Reciting a list of Epiphanius's off-putting qualities, modern translator Frank Williams concludes: "Above all he vehemently opposed the teachings of the great commentator Origen, the first Christian systematic theologian and as a thinker far superior to Epiphanius."[1] Indeed, modern scholarship often turned to study Epiphanius primarily through his opposition to Origen,[2] not least because of what the contrast between the two fathers seems to convey: intellect versus ignorance, spirituality versus earthliness, enlightenment versus demagoguery. All of these contrasts are visible in their respective Bibles: whereas Origen's use of

---

1. *The Panarion of Epiphanius*, vol. 1, *Book I (Sects 1–46)*, ed. Frank Williams, 2nd rev. ed., NHMS 63 (Leiden: Brill, 2009), xxxi.

2. Jon Dechow, *Dogma and Mysticism in Early Christianity: Epiphanius of Cyprus and the Legacy of Origen*, PMS 13 (Macon, GA: Mercer University Press, 1988); Elizabeth A. Clark, *The Origenist Controversy: The Cultural Construction of an Early Christian Debate* (Princeton, NJ: Princeton University Press, 1992), 86–104; J. Rebecca Lyman, "Ascetics and Bishops: Epiphanius on Orthodoxy," in *Orthodoxie, Christianisme, Histoire/Orthodoxy, Christianity, and History*, ed. Susanna Elm, Éric Rebillard, and Antonella Romano, Collections de l'École Française de Rome 270 (Paris: de Boccard, 2000), 149–61.

the Bible is sophisticated, philosophical, and allegorical, Epiphanius's, it is claimed, is "literal," uneducated, and flat.[3]

For instance, in the *Ancoratus,* Epiphanius criticizes Origen's allegorical interpretation of the garden of Eden.[4] Epiphanius's fulminations seem almost comical: how can Origen claim that the rivers flowing out of paradise are an allegory when Epiphanius has "seen" the rivers "real (*aisthēton*) and not allegorical"?[5] If the rivers are not "real," Epiphanius worries, but mere fantasy, then none of Genesis is real!

> If Paradise is not real (*aisthētos*), there is no source; if there is no source, there is no river; if there is no river, the four headwaters do not exist: if there is no Pishon, there is no Gihon, there is no Tigris; if there is no Tigris, there is no Euphrates. If there is no Euphrates, there is no fig tree, there are no leaves, there is no Adam, there is no eating, there is no Eve: if there is no Eve, she did not eat from the tree; if she did not eat from the tree, neither did Adam; if Adam didn't, there are no humans, but finally the truth is a myth and everything is allegorical (*alla muthos loipon hē alētheia kai allēgoreitai ta panta*).[6]

For Epiphanius, the narrative of Genesis is like a carefully laid-out chain of dominoes: if one falls, the rest must fall as well, and salvation itself is lost.[7] Epiphanius must have found this argument rather

---

3. So Josef Lössl, "'Apocalypse? No.'—The Power of Millennialism and Its Transformation in Late Antique Christianity," in *The Power of Religion in Late Antiquity,* ed. Andrew Cain and Noel Lenski (Burlington, VT: Ashgate, 2009), 39, describes Epiphanius as an "anti-Origenist literalist." Mark Elliott describes Epiphanius's *De XII gemmis* as "hyperbaric in its literalism" (*The Song of Songs and Christology in the Early Church, 381–451,* Studies and Texts in Antiquity and Christianity 7 [Tübingen: Mohr-Siebeck, 2000], 27).

4. On the dating and origin of the *Ancoratus,* see my discussion in the introduction and chapter 5.

5. Epiphanius, *Ancoratus* 58.3 (GCS n.F. 10.1:68), speaking of the river Gihon (Gen 2:13).

6. Epiphanius, *Ancoratus* 58.6–8 (GCS n.F. 10.1:68–69); he repeats this fear in *Ancoratus* 55.1–2 and 61.1–2 (GCS n.F. 10.1:64, 73).

7. Dechow, *Dogma and Mysticism,* 336, also refers to this (somewhat impatiently) as a "domino theory," further characterizing Epiphanius's insistence on earthly paradise as indulging in "absurdity."

compelling, as it reappears in the *Panarion*,[8] and is found yet again decades later in his polemical anti-Origenist letter to Bishop John of Jerusalem. In that letter, his antiallegorical argument has taken on even more sensory urgency:

> I, I myself have seen (*ego ego vidi*) the waters of Gihon, I have laid eyes of flesh upon them! ... I have also drunk from the great Euphrates River, actual waters (*aquas simpliciter*), which I could touch with my hand and drink with my mouth, not spiritual waters (*aquas spiritales*). Where there are rivers and waters which are seen and drunk, there, it follows, is the fig tree and other trees.... Moreover if the water which is perceived (*cernitur*) is true water, it is necessary that the fig tree is real and the other trees.[9]

As modern scholars point out, it is highly unlikely that Origen denied the existence of the Euphrates River in all its tangible potability, or the existence of trees or sin or even bodily salvation.[10] We are left with the impression that Epiphanius just doesn't *get* allegory, or figurative interpretation, but remains trapped in a simplistic and even rather embarrassing biblical literalism.[11] Taking Epiphanius's biblical interpretation seriously, however, may give us insight into alternative ways of reading the Bible that his contemporaries found compelling.

On a closer look, Epiphanius's chain of dominoes in the *Ancoratus* reveals more than just inept, literalist Bible thumping. Origen's false allegory appears in the midst of a discussion of different biblical idioms for "seeing" God;[12] right away Epiphanius's chain of theological dominoes becomes like a fun-house of cards, with theological propositions piled precariously upon geographic assertions folded into doctrinal polemic. I

---

8. Epiphanius, *Panarion* 64.4.11 (GCS 31:413): "The rest he allegorizes, whatever he is able: paradise and the waters over the heavens and the water under the earth."

9. Epiphanius, *Ep. ad Iohannem* (= Jerome, *Ep. 51*) 5.6 (CSEL 54:404–5).

10. See particularly Dechow, *Dogma and Mysticism*, 342: "Epiphanius does not appreciate the richness of Origen's thought on paradise."

11. Clark, *Origenist Controversy*, 88, ascribes Epiphanius's antiallegorism as much to rhetorical strategy as to intellectual simplicity.

12. Epiphanius, *Ancoratus* 54.1–7 (GCS n.F. 10.1:63–64); Epiphanius repeats this argument in *Panarion* 70.7.6–8.4 (GCS 37:239–40).

summarize as briefly as I can: the reference to "allegory" recalls, for Epiphanius, Origen's "fantasy" that paradise does not exist on earth. Consideration of paradise leads to discussion of "the image" in which Adam was created (as both body and soul), which leads to assertion of Christ's uniqueness, which leads to discussion of paradise and its rivers, which flows into a list of Adam's descendants (who may be called "souls," but certainly also had bodies!), generation by generation, all the way down to Joseph the "old widower" who cast lots to become Mary's guardian before she gave birth to Christ in the fortieth (or forty-second) year of Augustus's reign. This dating leads to a recitation of the number of years of the reign of every Roman emperor from Augustus down to the present day, "the ninetieth year after Diocletian, ten since Valentinian and Valens, six years of Gratian, in the third consulship of Gratian Augustus and the illustrious Equitius, in the second indiction."[13] The argument then twists back: Christ's incarnation is affirmed, as is Adam's creation as body-and-soul (here Epiphanius rejects Origen's understanding of the "tunics of skin" as allegory for the bodies granted to Adam and Eve after their fall). Origen's theology is condemned, along with that of other heretics: gnostics, Valentinians, Manichaeans, Marcionites, Arians, Anomoians, Sabellians, Pneumatomachoi, and Dimoirites. From here, Epiphanius launches into an extended discussion of his own Trinitarian faith. All of this—from the first discussion of "seeing God" to the condemnation of heresy—Epiphanius has squeezed into ten chapters of the *Ancoratus*.[14] We might summarize this meandering section of the *Ancoratus* as being, more or less, a defense of God's unity and humanity's dual nature. But how do we account for the list of emperors, the geographic details on the rivers of Eden, the list of Adam's descendants from Seth through Christ, and the not quite coherent collection of heresiarchs? As clear and concise forensic argumentation, these ten chapters fall sadly short. Instead, I suggest, they resonate with the aesthetics of antiquarian writing.

---

13. Epiphanius, *Ancoratus* 60.5 (GCS n.F. 10.1:72–73). The year is 374.
14. Epiphanius, *Ancoratus* 55–63 (GCS n.F. 10.1:64–76).

From Pliny the Elder down to John Lydus and Isidore of Seville we possess antiquarian treatises that implicitly supported Roman claims to totalized mastery of the world's knowledge.[15] The particular desires that lay behind antiquarianism, of course, precede the Roman Empire: the literary collections of the Hellenistic period, the posthumous conjuring of "schools" of philosophy, early attempts to provide ethnographic histories of particular peoples.[16] These threads all twine together in the particular political and cultural matrix of the late Roman Republic and early Roman Empire. Arnaldo Momigliano—the great historian of antiquity and antiquarianism—described one such project in these terms: "a systematic survey of Roman life according to the evidence provided by language, literature, and custom."[17] Antiquarians—like Varro, Pliny, Plutarch, Athenaeus, Aulus Gellius, a host of erudite gentlemen in Greek and Latin Roman contexts—took the disconnected raw materials of culture and reassembled them in a format that conveyed an image of that culture. That it was a "survey" conveys its potential vastness and scope; that it was "systematic" meant that we are always made aware of the directive hand of an

---

15. Trevor Murphy, *Pliny the Elder's "Natural History": The Empire in the Encyclopedia* (Oxford: Oxford University Press, 2004), 13–14, notes the "Roman-ness" of the encyclopedic tradition that emerges in the late Republic/early empire, a tradition that appropriates the Greek concept of *enkyklios paideia*.

16. Jason König and Tim Whitmarsh, "Introduction: Ordering Knowledge," in *Ordering Knowledge in the Roman Empire*, ed. König and Whitmarsh (Cambridge: Cambridge University Press, 2007), 8–10; Rebecca Flemming, "Empires of Knowledge: Medicine and Health in the Hellenistic World," in *A Companion to the Hellenistic World*, ed. Andrew Erskine (Malden, MA: Blackwell, 2003), 449–63; and Andrew Erskine, "Culture and Power in Ptolematic Egypt: The Museum and Library of Alexandria," *Greece & Rome* 62 (1995): 38–48.

17. Arnaldo Momigliano, "Ancient History and the Antiquarian," *Journal of the Warburg and Courtauld Institutes* 13 (1950): 288; see pp. 286–89 for Momigliano's survey of premodern antecedents of European antiquarianism. He returns to many of the same themes in his Sather lecture of 1962, "The Rise of Antiquarian Research," in *The Classical Foundations of Modern Historiography*, Sather Lectures 54 (Berkeley: University of California Press, 1990), 54–79. On both of these texts, see Peter N. Miller, *Momigliano and Antiquarianism: Foundations of the Modern Cultural Sciences* (Toronto: University of Toronto Press, 2007), 8–25.

author guiding a reader through the minutiae and trivia that he has assembled.[18]

This antiquarian impulse permeated the diverse strata of the intellectual elite of Roman antiquity, resulting in what one study has dubbed an age of "compilatory texts."[19] Authoritative passages were excised from their original context, collated with other texts, and woven together to form a new whole. Typically the antiquarian made visible his work as collector, so that the final product was at once a new text and a newly organized library of prior texts. Such encyclopedic texts collected knowledge—sometimes on a specific subject, like aqueducts; sometimes on the totality of "natural history"[20]—and laid it out in orderly fashion on the page. Like the early modern museum or curio,[21] the assemblage of previous texts into a new collection gave shape to Roman culture: conjuring a "past" (eventually, even, a "classical past") that could speak authoritatively—or even subversively—to the present.[22]

Some antiquarian texts are sprawling and lack any obvious organizing principle, like Aulus Gellius's *Noctes Atticae*. Indeed, it is their lack of a central argument—their lack of thesis—that often creates friction with modern readers.[23] It is incorrect, however, to say such texts lack

18. Momigliano, "Rise of Antiquarian Research," 61–62.
19. König and Whitmarsh, "Introduction," 3–4 (they also refer to a "habit of compilation").
20. Alice König, "Knowledge and Power in Frontinus' *On Aqueducts*," in König and Whitmarsh, *Ordering Knowledge*, 177–205; Murphy, *Pliny*.
21. See Marjorie Swann, *Curiosities and Texts: The Culture of Collecting in Early Modern England*, Material Texts (Philadelphia: University of Pennsylvania Press, 2001); Tony Bennett, *The Birth of the Museum: History, Theory, Politics* (London: Routledge, 1995); and Jeffrey Abt, "The Origins of the Public Museum," in *A Companion to Museum Studies*, ed. Sharon MacDonald, Companions to Cultural Studies 12 (Malden, MA: Wiley-Blackwell, 2006), 115–34.
22. G. Maslakov, "The Roman Antiquarian Tradition in Late Antiquity," in *History and Historians in Late Antiquity*, ed. Brian Croke and Alanna M. Emmett (Sydney: Pergamon Press, 1983), 100–106; and Catherine M. Chin, *Grammar and Christianity in the Late Roman World*, Divinations (Philadelphia: University of Pennsylvania Press, 2008).
23. William Stenhouse, "Antiquarianism," in *The Classical Tradition*, ed. Anthony Grafton, Glenn W. Most, and Salvatore Settis (Cambridge: Belknap Press of Harvard

order, as they are very clearly ordered by their authors.[24] Indeed, it is this ability to bring even incoherent order to a mass of otherwise unconnected bits of knowledge that reveals the political edge of Roman antiquarianism. As Jason König and Tim Whitmarsh remark, "This was not a secondary culture held in thrall to its originating predecessors (as older scholars, preoccupied with the romantic ideal of creative originality, sometimes assumed): it was rather an imperial power mapping and colonising the enormous expanse of pre-existing knowledge."[25] To say that this power of disassemblage and collation is *imperial* is not, of course, to say that all antiquarian texts were produced in the service of the Roman Empire.[26] But such texts nonetheless participated in an imperial way of knowing, made visible in their vastness and totalization.

Scholars of late antiquity have not given due attention to this kind of antiquarian impulse in early Christian reading of the Bible. The Bibles we are drawn to are, to coin a phrase, theorized Bibles: Bibles that are made to transcend their immediate material and mundane circumstances, Bibles that may be disassembled and reconstituted, but always (ideally) in service of a central *skopos* or principle (Trinity, Christology, asceticism, politics, and so forth).[27] Antiquarianism is messier than

---

University Press, 2010), 51: antiquarianism "often has negative connotations." So too König and Whitmarsh, "Introduction," 3: antiquarian texts "may look unwieldy or purely functional to modern eyes."

24. Erik Gunderson, *Nox philologiae: Aulus Gellius and the Fantasy of the Roman Library*, Wisconsin Studies in Classics (Madison: University of Wisconsin Press, 2009), offers a bracing and creative investigation of the "antiquarian logic" that undergirds texts like Aulus Gellius's, and refuses, throughout, to see the text as a simple miscellany.

25. König and Whitmarsh, "Introduction," 29.

26. Michael Maas, *John Lydus and the Roman Past: Antiquarianism and Politics in the Age of Justinian* (London: Routledge, 1992), has argued that John Lydus's early Byzantine antiquarian texts were produced precisely as a form of resistance to Justinian's Christian Roman Empire. König and Whitmarsh, "Introduction," 38, also note that "'imperial,' of course, does not necessarily mean 'pro-imperial.'"

27. Two recent examples of this tendency, operating from very different perspectives, are Frances M. Young, *Biblical Exegesis and the Formation of Christian Culture* (Cambridge: Cambridge University Press, 1997), and Elizabeth A. Clark, *Reading Renunciation: Asceticism and Scripture in Early Christianity* (Princeton, NJ: Princeton University Press, 1999).

philosophy, as Seneca the Younger scornfully noted,[28] and we have internalized such prejudices.[29] Yet what if the ancient experience of the Christian Bible was not always philosophical and theoretical? What if the ancient Bible was also, for many Christians, an antiquarian Bible: a source of (seemingly) disconnected pieces of knowledge, taken apart and reconstituted without any central argument, ordered but not orderly?

Indeed, once we adjust our lens, Epiphanius's mode of biblical interpretation resonates strongly with antiquarian writing, which "prizes metaphor and associative drift, variety of content and arrangement."[30] Antiquarian compositions bring an ostentatiously fragmented order to knowledge. They are not clearly structured (in the sense of Origen's philosophically organized Bible), but they are comprehensive and totalizing. Erik Gunderson writes that antiquarians

> sift and arrange the past. But they do so less as critics of power than as gay scientists luxuriating within it. The archive animates them. The radical possibility of reassembling different orders of things, different *mots et choses*, is for them only the radical possibility of being shot through with word-power and wielding the same among and against one's peers.[31]

Later Gunderson adds that, for an antiquarian, "the distinction between raw material and result can be indistinct."[32] That is to say, the effect of Epiphanius's rhetoric is in the display of all the bits and pieces (*les mots et choses*), not in their careful arrangement according to rhetorical or philosophical principles.[33]

---

28. Seneca, *Epistulae morales* 88.36–39, cited (along with *Epistulae morales* 108.23) by Gunderson, *Nox philologiae*, 17, who notes: "Moral philosophy scoffs at pedantry."

29. Although we do not mind, it seems, producing our own antiquarian fare out of Roman antiquarianism; see J. C. McKeown, *A Cabinet of Roman Curiosities: Strange Tales and Surprising Facts from the World's Greatest Empire* (New York: Oxford University Press, 2010).

30. Murphy, *Pliny the Elder*, 24–45; see also pp. 37–38.

31. Gunderson, *Nox philologiae*, 16.

32. Gunderson, *Nox philologiae*, 119.

33. On Epiphanius's antiquarianism generally, see Hervé Inglebert, *Interpretatio Christiana: Les mutations des savoirs (cosmographie, géographie, ethnographie, histoire) dans l'Antiquité chrétienne, 30–630 après J.-C.*, Collection des Études Augustiniennes, Série

When we look at Epiphanius through the lens of rhetoric and philosophy, we find bizarre appeals to literalism ("I have tasted the waters of the Euphrates!") and unexpected digressions, lists, numbers, and logical gaps. Yet we are also astounded at the sheer number of *things* Epiphanius can invoke in the course of an argument: geography, history, politics, doctrine, dates, names, citations, assertions, predictions. The *Panarion*, of course, has long been mined by modern scholars for its bits and pieces of information: from lost gnostic treatises to the evolution of doctrinal politics in the later fourth century. To look upon the whole of it is a dizzying experience indeed. But that kaleidoscopic effect is, surely, part of its point. Epiphanius's intent is not to persuade or philosophize; it is to catalogue and know.[34] This aesthetic pattern of compilation and assemblage persists throughout Epiphanius's oeuvre and, I suggest, provides a means for understanding his approach to the Bible.

THE BIBLE IN THE *ANCORATUS* AND *PANARION*

Epiphanius, as we might expect, remains supremely confident in his own use of the Bible and is not afraid to deploy a variety of interpretive tools, including figurative and allegorical interpretation, when it suits him.[35] In the *Ancoratus*, Epiphanius is particularly fond of stringing together long chains of proof-texts to make any number of theological points: the

---

Antiquité 166 (Paris: Institut d'Études Augustiniennes, 2001), 438 and 448, in a section (443–49) on "encyclopedism" in early Christian heresiology.

34. So asserts Averil Cameron, "How to Read Heresiology," in *The Cultural Turn in Late Ancient Studies: Gender, Asceticism, and Historiography*, ed. Dale B. Martin and Patricia Cox Miller (Durham, NC: Duke University Press, 2005), 198–200. See now also Todd S. Berzon, *Classifying Christians: Ethnography, Heresiology, and the Limits of Knowledge in Late Antiquity* (Oakland: University of California Press, 2016).

35. A few examples of Epiphanius's figurative and allegorical interpretation: *Ancoratus* 45.4–46.2, 48.1–5, 102.2–3; *Panarion* 51.32.5–6, 59.9.1–10, 77.36.6; *De fide* 3.4, 7.5 (GCS n.F. 10.1:55–56, 57–58, 122–23; 31:305–6, 373; 37:449, 499, 503). Of course, Epiphanius also rails against allegory at times in a way that is almost comically literalist: in *Panarion* 66.38/39.1–4 (GCS 37:77) Epiphanius insists that the "gnashing of teeth" in the afterlife must be literal, so there must be some kind of food for the resurrection body.

difference between "spirits" and the "Holy Spirit"; examples of resurrection, particularly involving whole bodies (and not merely parts); places where God seemingly professes ignorance; biblical figures who are described as "good," and so forth.[36] To be sure, this tendency to disaggregate and reassemble the Bible into chains of theological proof-texts is not unique to Epiphanius.[37] Indeed, in the *Panarion* he complains of Origen's tendency to "slather on proof-texts (*marturias*)."[38] My point is not that Epiphanius has innovated new ways of reading the Bible, but rather that he gives us an opportunity to appreciate from a new vantage point the ways in which the early Christian Bible cohered with a particular Roman literary aesthetics. Whatever social and religious contexts may have engendered "proof-texting" as a mode of theological argumentation in the early Christian period, we may also understand it as part and parcel of antiquarian reading and writing practices.[39]

The Bible also provides Epiphanius the occasion for antiquarian digressions on matters historical, geographic, and ethnographic. In some instance, the Bible provides the antiquarian information; in other cases, Epiphanius supplies his own tidbits to make sense of a biblical text. Toward the end of the *Ancoratus,* Epiphanius defends God's benevolence: why should some fools say God is not good because he allowed the Egyptians to be despoiled by the Israelites (Exod 12:35–36)?[40] "What were the

---

36. Epiphanius, *Ancoratus* 18.3–5, 72.1–9, 94.3–97.8, 98.3–99.5, 108.1–109.6 (GCS n.F. 10.1:26–27, 89–91, 115–20, 132–33).

37. The Trinitarian controversies seemed to open up rival proof-texting as a vibrant mode of theological argumentation throughout the fourth century; see James D. Ernest, *The Bible in Athanasius of Alexandria* (Leiden: Brill, 2004); Sara Parvis, "'Τὰ τίνων ἄρα ῥήματα θεολογεῖ?' The Exegetical Relationship between Athanasius' *Orationes Contra Arianos I-III* and Marcellus of Ancyra's *Contra Asterium*," in *The Reception and Interpretation of the Bible in Late Antiquity,* ed. Lorenzo DiTommaso and Lucian Turcescu, Bible in Ancient Christianity 6 (Leiden: Brill, 2008), 337–67.

38. Epiphanius, *Panarion* 64.4.7 (GCS 31:412).

39. On the polemical context of proof-texts as *testimonia*, see Martin C. Albl, *"And Scripture Cannot Be Broken": The Form and Function of the Early Christian* Testimonia *Collections*, Supplements to *Novum Testamentum* 96 (Leiden: Brill, 1999).

40. Epiphanius, *Ancoratus* 109 (GCS n.F. 10.1:133). The "spoiling of the Egyptians" had been an exegetical concern of many previous Christian exegetes, including Origen,

Egyptians thinking," Epiphanius fulminates, "that they sought to make the Jews do these things without pay, and not just for some years, but for 215 years, plus the fifteen years of Joseph?"[41] Obligingly, Epiphanius then counts out the years from Abraham to Moses—215 years in Canaan and 215 years in Egypt—concluding: "After the Jews worked so many years without a wage, was it not just before God and humanity that they were given this wage even if it was at the end? So God is not unjust, leading his own people from there with spoils!"[42] Neither the 430 years nor the calculation (based on the reproductive ages of the Old Testament patriarchs) is original to Epiphanius, but of course the point of antiquarian digression is not originality but collation.

At this point, Epiphanius is on an antiquarian roll. He wonders if these (unnamed) opponents of God's benevolence will accuse the "God of the Law of defrauding (ἐπλεονέκτησε) the Canaanites so that the Israelites might take their Land." Nonsense, Epiphanius retorts, he was merely pursuing the justice of "many generations."[43] Epiphanius returns the reader to the time of Noah, after the flood, as his sons divided up the world. He lists all the descendants of Noah and every land over which he came to hold sway after the "scattering of tribes and kingdoms," from the Elymians to the Spanish: 137 distinct lands (some under multiple names), along with 39 islands, all listed in order so that Epiphanius can, eventually, explain how descendants of Canaan treacherously stole land from descendants of Shem and, ultimately, were punished by God for their oath breaking.[44] Then, for good measure,

---

who (naturally) allegorized this incident; see the discussion of Peter Martens, *Origen and Scripture: The Contours of the Exegetical Life*, OECS (Oxford: Oxford University Press, 2012), 30–32.

41. Epiphanius, *Ancoratus* 110.1–2 (GCS n.F. 10.1:133–34).
42. Epiphanius, *Ancoratus* 110.3–111.1 (GCS n.F. 10.1:134–35).
43. Epiphanius, *Ancoratus* 111.4–5 (GCS n.F. 10.1:135–36).
44. Epiphanius, *Ancoratus* 113–14 (GCS n.F. 10.1:139–42); see also *Panarion* 9.1.4 (GCS n.F. 10.1:198). The "oath taking" of the sons of Noah is not found in Genesis, but probably derives from Jubilees 9:14. I address Epiphanius's use of Jubilees briefly below. On the descendants of Noah in the context of early Christian ethnography, see Inglebert, *Interpretatio Christiana*, 168–76.

Epiphanius lists the nineteen descendants of Shem from the time of the flood to Salmon, son of Nashon, who married Rahab the harlot and in whose generation Canaan's crime against Shem was punished.[45] From a rhetorical perspective, the pages of lists of names of people and characters are weak, and even distracting; yet as a performance of arcane knowledge, extracted and collected for display, they are exemplary.[46]

The Bible provides an opportunity to pile on not just historical but geographic and ethnographic knowledge as well. Against the Jewish sect of the Nasareans, who honor the patriarchs but not the Scriptures that speak of them, Epiphanius exclaims, "Not only are the events recorded in Scripture famous to this day, but even the sites of the wonders are preserved," and then lists several sites from the life of Abraham. In addition, the customs recounted in Exodus are preserved among Epiphanius's Egyptian contemporaries who still "smear their lambs" with "red lead," although they have forgotten why. Finally, the very remains of Noah's ark can still be seen in Cardyaei and presumably (were one to search diligently) one could even find the remains of Noah's altar![47] The move from text to material remains is also a common trope of antiquarian literature, linking the imperial acquisitions of knowledge and territory more tightly together.[48]

Epiphanius's geographic arcana do not always clearly serve his immediate heresiological agenda. Against Tatian, who claims that "Adam was not saved,"[49] Epiphanius feels compelled to introduce a bit of geographic knowledge. Doesn't Tatian know that the site of the crucifixion,

---

45. Epiphanius, *Ancoratus* 114.6–7 (GCS n.F. 10.1:142). But in *Panarion* 66.84.5 (GCS 37:127), Epiphanius places the "righteous judgment" (presumably for Canaan's oath breaking) in the time of Nashon, not Salmon.

46. Chin, *Grammar and Christianity*, 34–35 and 73, explains how lists function to suggest unity, completeness, community, and control.

47. Epiphanius, *Panarion* 18.2.4–3.4 (GCS n.F. 10.1:216–17).

48. Murphy, *Pliny*, 154–64, evokes the parallel of the triumphal procession, which also integrates land, *spolia*, and knowledge in a procession before the viewer: "The world is summoned up and sent on a slow procession, name by name, under the scrutiny of its ruler" (164).

49. Epiphanius, *Panarion* 46.2.1 (GCS 31:205).

Golgotha, is also Adam's burial site? The "Place of the Skull" must be named for a real skeleton, Epiphanius assures us, because "the contour of the site bears no resemblance to a skull. Nor is it on some peak so that this can be interpreted as a skull, as we say of the head's position on a body." For good measure, Epiphanius informs us that two nearby hills—the Mount of Olives, directly opposite Golgotha, and Gibeon, "eight milestones off," are much higher, not to mention Mount Zion itself.[50] In this chapter, it is less clear how this biblically inspired geographic detail supports his heresiological point (that Adam was saved). The point seems rather the effect of the Bible as a site of antiquarian display.

The *Panarion* as a whole is prone to antiquarian digression,[51] so it should not surprise that the Bible offers Epiphanius one more source from which to extract authoritative knowledge.[52] Once we are sensitive to them, Epiphanius's antiquarian flourishes are conspicuous. After noting that the heresiarch Basilides immigrated to Egypt, to "the nome of Saites," Epiphanius interjects:

> For the Egyptians call the neighborhood or environs of each city a "nome." You may find even this of use to you, scholarly reader (*philologe*), for love of learning and clarity (*pros philomatheian kai saphēneian*), as a pious confirma-

---

50. Epiphanius, *Panarion* 46.5.1–5 (GCS 31:208–9).

51. Some examples among many: Epiphanius, *Panarion* 27.6.1–7 (GCS n.F. 10.1:308–9; mention of "the time of Anicetus" leads to a listing of the first bishops of Rome); 51.22.24 (GCS 31:290–91; list of the consulships during Jesus's lifetime); 66.13.3–5 (GCS 37:35; on the different Syriac alphabets and dialects in Persia); 66.20.1–5 (GCS 37:45–48; the bishops of Jerusalem until the time of Mani, and then until the present, and a list of emperors from the time of Mani to the present); 75.1.1 (GCS 37:333; a list of seven "vices" that inspire heresies); 77.12.1–7 (GCS 37:426–27; that lionesses cannot have more than one child); *De fide* 9 (GCS 37:504–9; list of forty-four philosophies), 10 (GCS 37:509–11; references to non-Greek philosophers and Greek mysteries), 11–13 (GCS 37:511–14; Egyptian, Babylonian, and Persian mysteries).

52. Of course, the *Panarion* is explicitly modeled on naturalist antiquarian literature (books on "beasts and reptiles" and "roots and plants"): Epiphanius, *Panarion* proem II.3 (GCS n.F. 10.1:171–72). See Joseph Verheyden, "Epiphanius of Salamis on Beasts and Heretics: Some Introductory Comments," in *Heretics and Heresies in the Ancient Church and Eastern Christianity: Studies in Honor of Adelbert Davids*, ed. Joseph Verheyden and Herman Teule, Eastern Christian Studies 10 (Leuven: Peeters, 2011), 143–73.

tion and explanation of the points of sacred Scripture that cast some into confusion on account of inexperience. Whenever in the holy prophet Isaiah you find it written about the "nomes" of Egyptian cities,[53] like Tanis or Memphis, or the "nome" of Bubastis, it signifies the perimeter of the city in question. And there, let it be translated for you for the sake of the love of learning (*philomatheias heneken*)![54]

Epiphanius's tone is both educational and condescending, but it is also the tone of the polymathic antiquarian, for whom every bit of knowledge is relevant and in need of explanation. Even Epiphanius's archheretic, Origen, is to be admired for his antiquarian displays:

> Now for what he said in his sermons and prefaces on customs and the natures of animals and other things a modest report is given about him: he recounted agreeable things quite often (*pollakis charienta diēgēsato*); but for the doctrines he made, about faith and higher interpretation, he is found to be the weirdest (*atopōtatos*) of all those who came before and after him![55]

From a philosophical viewpoint, Epiphanius sounds lowbrow and hidebound, preferring the mundane to the metaphysical. From an antiquarian perspective, however, Epiphanius is merely evaluating the uses to which Origen has put his biblical knowledge. Extracting useful knowledge from the Bible—which includes animals as well as ethics—is fine, but speculative doctrine is "weird" (literally, "most out of place").

Epiphanius's antiquarianism also informs the way the Bible is itself portrayed in his theological works. Above all, for Epiphanius, the Bible is a consistent and coherent whole. Because heretics do not respect the integrity of the Bible, they fail to understand the sense of the text in front of their face: Noetus "chops up the Scriptures, explicates ambiguities, cites the verses out of sequence and does not quote them consistently or

---

53. The Greek word νομός appears only once in Isaiah (Isa 19:2), and only one other time in the Septuagint (3 Macc 4:3).

54. Epiphanius, *Panarion* 24.1.2–3 (GCS n.F. 10.1:256). Momigliano, "Rise of Antiquarian Research," 60, notes φιλόλογος as one of several Greek and Latin terms used to approach the semantic field of our "antiquarian."

55. Epiphanius, *Panarion* 64.5.5 (GCS 31:414).

exactly ... or expound them in order."⁵⁶ Similarly Marcion "amputates" the limbs of Scripture into "myriad bits and pieces" (*muriōs ... kata lepton*).⁵⁷ Yet even as Epiphanius attacks others for disregarding the integrity of the Bible, he is more than willing, on occasion, to disrupt its coherent wholeness in the name of antiquarian research.

Although Epiphanius insists upon the integrity of the closed canon against some heretics,⁵⁸ in practice he often strays beyond the canon in his theological treatises. In his long account of biblical history that structures the first several chapters of the *Panarion*, Epiphanius draws on the pseudepigraphic book of Jubilees, without clearly differentiating his canonical and noncanonical sources.⁵⁹ He quotes one of the beatitudes from the *Acts of Thecla* as "Scripture,"⁶⁰ and draws heavily on the *Protoevangelium of James* in his two chapters on Marian heresy.⁶¹ He explicitly cites a parable from an *Apocryphon of Ezekiel*, and in fact provides the largest extant fragment of this otherwise little-attested apocryphon.⁶²

Epiphanius's antiquarianism reconciles his clear awareness of and respect for canon and his willingness—indeed, eagerness—to incorpo-

---

56. Epiphanius, *Panarion* 57.6.2 (GCS 31:351).

57. Epiphanius, *Panarion* 42.13.7–8 (GCS 31:183).

58. Epiphanius reiterates the significance of the canon for correct theology: *Panarion* 8.6.1–4; 76.22.5 (GCS n.F. 10.1:191–92; 37:369).

59. Epiphanius often fails to cite his sources, and his use of sources—not just Jubilees, but the world chronicles of Eusebius, Julius Africanus, and others—is quite tangled. See William Adler, "The Origins of the Proto-Heresies: Fragments from a Chronicle in the First Book of Epiphanius' *Panarion*," *JTS* n.s. 41 (1990): 472–501; and Young Richard Kim, *Epiphanius of Cyprus: Imagining an Orthodox World* (Ann Arbor: University of Michigan Press, 2015), 51. Epiphanius does refer explicitly to Jubilees ("which is also called 'The Little Genesis'") in his chapter on the Sethians, providing the names and numbers of all of Adam's sons and daughters (*Panarion* 39.6.1–5 [GCS 31:76–77]); see Kim, *Epiphanius*, 46–48.

60. Epiphanius, *Panarion* 77.27.7 (GCS 37:440); he refers to Thecla again in 78.16.7 (GCS 37:467), but doesn't quote from the *Acts of Thecla* there.

61. Epiphanius, *Panarion* 78–79 (GCS 37:452–84); he doesn't cite the *Protoevanglium Iacobi* directly, or refer to it by title, in these sections but refers multiple times to its narrative.

62. Epiphanius, *Panarion* 64.70.5–15 (GCS 31:515–17). I discuss this fragment, and its parable of the blind man and the lame man, in chapter 5.

rate extracanonical works. Epiphanius views the canon as itself an antiquarian device, another authoritative list he can rattle off in the service of his knowledgeable display.[63] So we learn about the Hebrew numbering of the Old Testament and, in another place, the Hebrew names of the books of the Pentateuch.[64] The same antiquarian disposition will allow Epiphanius to refer as unproblematically to pseudepigraphic texts as to Scripture: What was the name of Seth's wife? When did idolatry begin? Where is Noah's ark? If these answers can't be found in Genesis, they may be found in Jubilees.

Epiphanius also evinces an antiquarian interest in the multiple linguistic layers of the Christian Bible. The heresiologist celebrated as *pentaglossus* by his admirer Jerome refers to the Hebrew as well as multiple Greek versions, even as he insists on the primacy of the Septuagint.[65] He mocks both the Nicolaitans and gnostics for mistaking Hebrew phrases for proper names, and then worshipping them as gods.[66] In typical antiquarian fashion, one such notice—the Archontics "suppose that

---

63. Epiphanius will, at times, note that heretics use noncanonical texts: so the gnostics "have lots of books" (καὶ τὰ μὲν βιβλία αὐτῶν πολλα) (*Panarion* 26.8.1 [GCS n.F. 10.1:284]), and the Encratites use "principally the so-called Acts of Andrew, John, Thomas, and certain apocrypha" as Scriptures (*Panarion* 47.1.5 [GCS 31:216]). Presumably he means to chastise them for their noncanonical Scriptures, but he is much more interested in (and angered by) their misuse of canonical texts: so the gnostics "use both Old and New Testaments" but "twist it into their own desire" (τοῦτον μετασκευάζοντες εἰς τὴν ἑαυτῶν ἐπιθυμίαν) (*Panarion* 26.6.1–2 [GCS n.F. 10.1:282–83]), and the Encratites pick and choose texts that support their excessive asceticism (*Panarion* 47.2.3–4 [GCS 31:217]).

64. Epiphanius, *Panarion* 9.2.1. (GCS n.F. 10.1:198).

65. Jerome, *Adversus Rufinum* 2.22, 3.6 (SC 303:164, 230). Jürgen Dummer, "Die Sprachskenntnisse des Epiphanius," in *Die Araber in der alten Welt*, ed. F. Altheim and R. Stiehl (Berlin: De Gruyter, 1968), 392–435 (repr. in *Philologia sacra et profana: Ausgewählte Beiträge zur Antike und zu ihrer Wirkungsgeschichte*, ed. Meinolf Vielberg, Altertumswissenschaft Kolloquium 16 [Stuttgart: Franz Steiner Verlag, 2006], 29–72), lays out the skeptical case that Jerome exaggerated Epiphanius's linguistic prowess. Our modern critical evaluation does not detract from the obvious *display* of linguistic prowess that Epiphanius achieves in his writings.

66. Epiphanius, *Panarion* 25.4.3–5 (GCS n.F. 10.1:270–71): the Nicolaitans mistake the Hebrew phrase *qav l'qav* ("hope upon hope": Isa 28:10) for an archon named Kaulakau; *Panarion* 26.10.11–13 (GCS n.f. 10.1:288): the gnostics think Sabaoth is a proper name, when it is a title ("Lord of Hosts").

Sabaoth is a name for some god"—leads Epiphanius to list and translate ten different Hebrew names for God used in the Old Testament.[67] Many of these translations are incorrect, but this is to be expected in antiquarian etymology, which was more interested in the "force" (*dunamis*) of a word than its precise linguistic origins.[68]

When Epiphanius puts this linguistic knowledge to theological use, his linguistic expertise may be more disorienting than corrective. He assails the Arian interpretation of Proverbs 8:22 that the Son was a "creature." Not so fast, Epiphanius warns: these heretics "have not tackled the Hebrew phrases (*tas lexeis tas Hebraikas oute psēlaphēsantes*) or learned about them or what their meaning (*dunamis*) is!"[69] Epiphanius points out that Aquila, the post-Septuagintal translator from the Greek, does not translate "created" (*ektise*) here but rather "acquired" (*ektēsato*), which is used more typically of parents and children.[70] Does this linguistic insight refute the Arians? No, Epiphanius continues, that's not quite right either. He introduces the Hebrew word (*kanani*) in order to suggest an entirely different—and, to be sure, bizarre—translation: "The Lord *hatched* (*enosseuse*) me." This image, Epiphanius claims, leaves no doubt as to the consubstantiality of the Father and the Son.[71] Also, of course, it makes little sense in its scriptural context.[72]

In his refutation of the Anomoians, Epiphanius first cites Isaiah 26:2–3 in transliterated Hebrew, then in the translation of Aquila, and

---

67. Epiphanius, *Panarion* 40.5.8–11 (GCS 31:86): El, Elohim, Eli, Shaddai, Rabboni, Jah, Adonai, Jahweh, Elyon, Sabaoth.

68. Helen Peraki-Kyriakido, "Aspects of Ancient Etymologizing," *CQ* n.s. 52 (2002): 478–93. See also Gunderson, *Nox philologiae*, 115 n. 33.

69. Epiphanius, *Panarion* 69.25.1 (GCS 37:174).

70. Epiphanius, *Panarion* 69.25.1–2 (GCS 37:175).

71. Epiphanius, *Panarion* 69.25.6–7, 26.1–2 (GCS 37:175–76). It's not clear what Hebrew verb Epiphanius is thinking of here; Williams (*Panarion*, 2:345 n. 78) plausibly suggests the Hebrew *qn* (to nest), which is similar to the roots "to create" and "to acquire" (both *qnh*). Epiphanius introduced this translation of Prov 8:22 already in *Ancoratus* 44.1–2 (GCS n.F. 10.1:54), but without any discussion.

72. On this linguistic point in its larger theological context, see Mark DelCogliano, "Basil of Caesarea on Proverbs 8:22 and the Sources of Pro-Nicene Theology," *JTS* n.s. 59 (2008): 183–90.

finally in the Septuagint version. (The verse is supposed to demonstrate that "the Son ... is no different from the Father.") The reason for citing the Hebrew and the version of Aquila seems to be the single phrase "in the Lord is the Lord" (more correctly translated into the Septuagint simply as "the Lord God"), but Epiphanius does not trouble himself to explain any detail: "How much is there to say about this?" he comments, before making one of his standard disclaimers about "burdensome length."[73] For Epiphanius, the authoritative point is made as soon as he has laid out his three versions, in two languages: the *performance* of knowledge is as decisive as its content.

As the citations of Aquila in these examples show, Epiphanius was familiar with the three post-Septuagintal translators (Aquila, Symmachus, and Theodotion).[74] When insisting on the true begottenness of the Son against Paul of Samosata, Epiphanius provides multiple version of Psalms 109:3 ("Before the morning star I have begotten thee from the womb"), beginning with the Septuagint, followed by the "other versions" (*alloi ekdotai*) of Aquila, Symmachus, and Theodotion. He then gives the Hebrew in transliteration, and translates it word for word in order to show that "from this phrase you will know that the independently real God-Word (*ho enupostatos theos logos*)[75] was begotten out of the nature of the Father, without beginning and without temporality before anything was."[76] Once more, the purpose of this multilingual citation is unclear, since the direct translation from the Hebrew matches the original citation from the Septuagint almost exactly (the order of the words is merely changed). So what rhetorical purpose does this

---

73. It should be noted this disclaimer comes in the middle of the seventh section of this chapter, which contains fifty-four sections.

74. Epiphanius, *Ancoratus* 97.2 (GCS n.F. 10.1:118) refers to the "translators" (ἑρμηνευταί) as a group; see my discussion of *Ancoratus* 41–44 above for a more extensive citation of Aquila and the original Hebrew. He discusses the three translators Aquila, Symmachus, and Theodotion in more detail in *De mensuris et pondibus* (see my discussion in chapter 2).

75. On Epiphanius's use of the term ἐνυπόστατος, see my discussion in chapter 5.

76. Epiphanius, *Panarion* 65.4.4–7 (GCS 37:6–7).

reference to these multiple versions serve? Perhaps no rhetorical purpose, but a clear antiquarian one: Epiphanius's theological authority is established through collation and citation, not rhetoric and argumentation.

As Frank Williams notes in his translation of the *Panarion*, it is likely that Epiphanius relies in this chapter directly on Origen's Hexapla (or, at least, someone else's citation of it).[77] In the *Panarion*, and in more detail in his later exegetical treatise *On Weights and Measures*, Epiphanius positively describes Origen's massively complex text-critical project.[78] Indeed, he suggests early on in his quite lengthy chapter against Origen in the *Panarion* that had Origen merely stopped at the "toilsome" (*meta kamatou*) work of the Hexapla, his fame might have lasted "untarnished (*asbeston*) until the end."[79] Yet just a few paragraphs later, while dissecting Origen's commentary on the first Psalm, Epiphanius balks at a citation of the three Greek translators: "Then—since it is his custom to amaze with the translators (*hōs ethos estin autōi apo tōn ekdoseōn phantazein*)!—he says, 'Just so Theodotion, Aquila, and Symmachus.'"[80] It is a curious statement from Epiphanius, who praised Origen's textual prowess and is himself fond of citing multiple versions of a biblical passage. From the antiquarian perspective, Epiphanius plays a common card: the offended accusation of pedantry leveled even in the middle of the most pedantic of texts.[81]

Even as his own antiquarian interventions disrupted the surface of the biblical text, Epiphanius remained above all committed to the absolute continuity of scriptural truth. The Bible must signify consistently

---

77. Williams, *Panarion*, 2:212 nn. 26–27.

78. Anthony Grafton and Megan H. Williams, *Christianity and the Transformation of the Book: Origen, Eusebius, and the Library of Caesarea* (Cambridge, MA: Harvard University Press, 2006), 92–94, are skeptical that Epiphanius had firsthand experience of the Hexapla.

79. Epiphanius, *Panarion* 64.3.5–8 (GCS 31:407–9).

80. Epiphanius, *Panarion* 64.10.1 (GCS 31:419).

81. Gunderson, *Nox philologiae*, 17: "Gellius too rails against pedantry. This text can argue against itself while nevertheless remaining distinctly itself. Antiquarianism scoffs at logic where it does not feel inclined to merely archive it."

and coherently across the entire sacred canon. Yet, ironically, Epiphanius's own antiquarian sensibilities often serve to disrupt a sense of biblical flow and continuity even as he argues for it. Against the Manichaeans he insists, time and again, "The Old Testament is no different from the New, or the New from the Old."[82] Epiphanius cites from the New Testament to demonstrate its affinity with the Old Testament in moral tone and theological significance. When Mani claims the New Testament abrogates the Sabbath of the Old Testament, Epiphanius scoffs: "What ignorance!" He recounts the story of Joshua and the fall of Jericho: obviously, if Joshua and his men marched for a full week, they more than transgressed the laws of Sabbath travel![83] When Mani accuses the God of Israel of being evil for ordering the spoiling of the Egyptians and displacement of the Canaanites, Epiphanius brings forward his old argument from the *Ancoratus* on the curse of Canaan and here—as there—offers an account of the division of the world by Noah's sons (although much abbreviated).[84] His genealogy ends with Nashon, in the time of Joshua, son of Nun, which allows Epiphanius—some chapters later—to circle back to the fall of Jericho, "when the Sabbath was violated so that righteousness would be fulfilled."[85] It is easy to read a section like this and assume that Epiphanius has merely lost his train of thought, and gotten tangled in his recitation of biblical refutations.[86] Yet such repetitive, digressive textuality is characteristic of an antiquarian mind-set, encouraging a style more recursive than linear.[87]

82. Epiphanius, *Panarion* 66.74.1–85.11 (GCS 37:114–28); the quotation is from 66.85.10 (GCS 37:128).
83. Epiphanius, *Panarion* 66.82.2–6 (GCS 37:123–24).
84. Epiphanius, *Panarion* 66.83.2–84.6 (GCS 37:124–27).
85. Epiphanius, *Panarion* 66.84.7 (GCS 37:127).
86. Particularly given Epiphanius's oral dictation style of composition (see my discussion in the introduction and chapter 3).
87. For other places where Epiphanius defends the unity of Old and New Testaments, see *Panarion* 23.6.3–5 and 70.7.6–8.4 (which uses the same prophetic verses as *Ancoratus* 53 [GCS n.F. 10.1:61–63] but for the purpose of harmonizing the Gospels and prophets) (GCS n.F. 10.1:254–55; 37:239–40).

Digression similarly disrupts biblical coherence in Epiphanius's attempts to reconcile and harmonize the Gospel accounts of Jesus's life, particularly in his chapter against the so-called Alogi.[88] These heretics reject the writings of John—the Gospel and Revelation—"because his books do not agree with the other apostles."[89] Epiphanius launches into an exhaustive discussion of the agreement between the four Gospels, particularly the historical circumstances under which each evangelist operated. In this way, he can explain why some Gospels contain information not found in others (why should Luke repeat what Matthew has already recounted?). To be sure, Epiphanius must, at times, infer some points not immediately clear from the texts. For instance, in harmonizing Luke's and Matthew's nativity narratives, Epiphanius explains that Joseph, Mary, and Jesus must have returned to Bethlehem two years after Christ's birth—"as a sort of memorial (*mnēmēs*)"—at which point they met up with the magi (in a house, he points out, not a manger in a cave, as in Luke) and received the angel's warning sending them to Egypt.[90] Through such creative reading between the lines, Epiphanius handily reconciles the nativity accounts.

Epiphanius explains other points of seeming difference: the baptismal accounts, the order of Christ's miracles (when did he come to Cana?), the timeline of the passion, and so forth. None of Epiphanius's harmonizing efforts are especially novel, although he certainly scores some points for thoroughness: his chapter on the Alogi (a "heresy" constituted almost entirely by a single canonical quirk) is one of the longer

---

88. Epiphanius, *Panarion* 51.3.1–3 (GCS 31:250) coins the name himself, both because these heretics reject John's account of the "Word" and because they are stupid (ἄλογοι). See Timothy Scott Manor, "Epiphanius' *Alogi* and the Question of Early Ecclesiastical Opposition to the Johannine Corpus" (PhD diss., University of Edinburgh, 2012); and Manor, "Epiphanius' Account of the *Alogi*: Historical Fact or Heretical Fiction?" *SP* 52 (2012): 161–70. Epiphanius had already given a harmonized recitation of Christ's life in his excursus *De incarnatione*, between the twenty chapters on pre-Christian heresy and the remaining sixty chapters of the *Panarion*.

89. Epiphanius, *Panarion* 51.4.5 (GCS 31:251–52).

90. Epiphanius, *Panarion* 51.9.9–13 (GCS 31:260–61).

in the *Panarion*, taking up more than sixty pages in the critical edition. Part of the length is due to the numerous digressions and interruptions. When Epiphanius notes that "the Savior was born during the forty-second year of the Roman emperor Augustus," a veritable minitreatise on calendars, dates, and Christian festivals ensues. First we learn what a "solstice" (τροπή) is, as Epiphanius assures us Christ was born thirteen days after the winter solstice, "eight days before the ides of January."[91] We then learn how pagans unwittingly mimic the nativity by celebrating Kore's "virgin birth" (and the difference between the pagan rites in Alexandria and Petra).[92] Next comes a summary of Augustus's political dealings with Judea followed by a list of Roman consulships during Christ's life.[93] An assertion that Christ lived thirty-three years (not thirty, as the Valentinians claim) leads Epiphanius to give the day of Christ's birth according to ten different calendars (Roman, Egyptian, Syrian, Cypriot, Paphian, Arabian, Macedonian, Cappadocian, Athenian, and Hebrew).[94] We might ask which is foreground and which is background: is the invocation of biblical harmony merely an excuse to discuss arcane calendars and pagan festivals, or do the antiquarian details function as footnotes or cross-references in support of the larger biblical argument? Antiquarian literature resists this kind of textual hierarchalization. Biblical passages, lists of consuls, calendrical trivia, theological argument, are all flattened into a potentially endless display of totalizing knowledge.

The interruption of biblical narrative by antiquarian arcana is frequent in this chapter, as we move rapidly between scriptural events and minute ethnographic and historical details drawn from the diversity of the Roman Empire. Such rhetorical discontinuity in the midst of an argument about biblical harmony is, we might say, ironic, if not contradictory. Yet when we step back and look at the ways Epiphanius invokes,

---

91. Epiphanius, *Panarion* 51.22.3–7 (GCS 31:284–85).
92. Epiphanius, *Panarion* 51.22.8–11 (GCS 31:285–86).
93. Epiphanius, *Panarion* 51.22.19–24 (GCS 31:288–91).
94. Epiphanius, *Panarion* 51.23.5–24.1 (GCS 31:292–93).

defines, explains, and even disrupts the Christian Bible in his theological treatises, we see a consistent pattern. Not only is the Bible a source of antiquarian knowledge (lists of names, histories, peoples, and places), it is also an object of antiquarian thinking: disaggregated and supplemented and reassembled with bits of historical, linguistic, and ethnographic knowledge. The result (biblical coherence, Christian orthodoxy) and the process (antiquarian exegesis) cannot be separated out, but together form the nexus of Epiphanius's imperial Christian culture.

THE BIBLE IN *DE MENSURIS ET PONDERIBUS* AND *DE XII GEMMIS*

We can gain an even clearer sense of Epiphanius's antiquarian use of the Bible in his two surviving biblical treatises, probably both written toward the end of his life: a treatise traditionally titled *On Weights and Measures* and another *On Twelve Gems*.[95] Neither of these texts constitutes a biblical commentary in the traditional sense: that is, Epiphanius does not move, verse by verse, through a book of the Bible, providing commentary as he proceeds. Even the treatise *On Twelve Gems*, which has as its ostensible point of departure a specific biblical passage from the book of Exodus, ranges far beyond its narrow scriptural context. Both texts bear the obvious mark of antiquarianism: comprehensive lists, definitions and etymologies, historical and ethnographic trivia, tangential anecdotes, and folklore. Nonetheless, both texts are very much *about* the Bible. In the first treatise, *On Weight and Measures*, the Bible is configured as a source of antiquarian knowledge, supplementing and even, in some sense, displacing classical knowledge; in the second treatise, *On Twelve Gems*, the Bible becomes a receptacle for, and a reconfiguration of, classical antiquarian knowledge. When

---

95. *De mensuris et ponderibus* was written in 392 (see *De mensuris et ponderibus* 20 [Dean, *Weights and Measures*, 39 [Eng.] and 58d [Syr.]). On the dates and origins of *De mensuris et ponderibus* and *De XII gemmis*, see my discussion in the introduction.

these two treatises are taken together, we can see the Bible becoming the complex surface upon which an antiquarian bishop might reimagine the contours of Christian culture in the fourth-century Roman Empire.

According to a preface appended to the Syriac translation of *On Weights and Measures,* Epiphanius composed the treatise at the request of a Persian priest he met at the court in Constantinople: "He devoted himself to the task of collecting (information) from all the divine Scriptures and a multitude of histories."[96] Whether this story is authentic is unknowable, but the image of a Christian bishop importing and exporting biblical knowledge (supplemented with "histories") in the imperial capital is, nonetheless, evocative. On the one hand, the use of the Bible as a primary source of historical authority—on all manner of natural and cultural phenomena, as we shall see—calls into question the naturalized authority of the Roman Empire. On the other hand, the ability of Epiphanius—a learned bishop firmly speaking from the discourses of imperial and orthodox authority—to manipulate and re-present this ancient wisdom creates a new, Christianized empire.

While the treatise is preserved as *On Weights and Measures,* perhaps a better title might be *On the Parts of the Bible.* The commentary not only explains the weights and measures mentioned in the Bible, but also surveys the structure and contents of the Bible and includes a brief discussion of biblical place-names. The treatise actually begins on the surface of Epiphanius's biblical text, in a discussion of punctuation and diacritical marks. After listing the marks of Greek punctuation (indicating lengths of vowels, smooth and rough breathing, and elision), Epiphanius explains the text-critical marks in his manuscript.[97] The asterisk, obelus, lemniscus, and hypolemniscus all indicate places where the Septuagint differs from other Hebrew and Greek versions. He gives not

---

96. Epiphanius, *De mensuris et ponderibus* 1 (Dean, *Weights and Measures,* 11 [Eng.] and 45a [Syr.]).

97. Epiphanius, *De mensuris et ponderibus* 2 (Dean, *Weights and Measures,* 16 [Eng.] and 47b-c [Syr.]; Moutsoulas, "Περὶ μέτρων," ll. 12–15).

only examples of the use of each, but even history and etymology.[98] Epiphanius's discussion of the obelus is especially detailed.

Epiphanius notes that the obelus indicates words included in the Septuagint but not found in the other Greek versions. This observation leads him to explain how the Seventy-Two translators of the Septuagint worked: in pairs, in thirty-six cells, each pair receiving one book at a time. How many books were there? Twenty-seven, "but twenty-two when counted according to the letters of the alphabet of the Hebrews."[99] How can there be twenty-seven and twenty-two? Just as five of the twenty-two Hebrew letters have two forms (medial and final), so five books are joined to companion volumes in the canon. What are the books of that canon? There are "four pentateuchs" and two leftover books, which Epiphanius lists in order, followed by the two books of Wisdom. But the book of Psalms is also a Pentateuch, since it is divided into five sections (Epiphanius precisely notes where the breaks take place). And these are the books the Seventy-Two translated, while the king of Egypt supervised, and their translations were in perfect accord. To conclude his discussion of the asterisk and obelus, Epiphanius introduces Origen's construction of the Hexapla—"if only other things he had done as well! (*eithe oun kai ta alla outō kalōs epoise*)"[100]—and, finally, moves on to the third diacritical mark, the lemniscus.[101]

The obelus contains multitudes: information historical, geographic, linguistic, numerological, literary, and ethnographic. The rest of this section on the marks of punctuation—indeed, the rest of the treatise as a whole—is similarly expansive, marked by the antiquarian's "associa-

---

98. Epiphanius, *De mensuris et ponderibus* 2–8 (Dean, *Weights and Measures*, 16–23 [Eng.] and 47b-51c [Syr.]; Moutsoulas, "Περὶ μέτρων," ll. 12–227).

99. Epiphanius, *De mensuris et ponderibus* 3 (Dean, *Weights and Measures*, 18 [Eng.] and 49a [Syr.]; Moutsoulas, "Περὶ μέτρων," ll. 92–95).

100. Epiphanius, *De mensuris et ponderibus* 7 (Dean, *Weights and Measures*, 21 [Eng.] and 50c [Syr.]; Moutsoulas, "Περὶ μέτρων," ll. 175–76).

101. The section covers five chapters of the treatise: Epiphanius, *De mensuris et ponderibus* 3–7 (Dean, *Weights and Measures*, 17–22 [Eng.] and 48b-50d [Syr.]; Moutsoulas, "Περὶ μέτρων," ll. 63–192).

tive drift."[102] It is not accurate to say it is unorganized or disorderly: everything returns, eventually, to the main topic at hand (the parts of the Bible). Yet we note from the outside how the text of the Bible has been disrupted. Shadows of other versions, missing words, extra phrases, alternate translations, now hover over Epiphanius's Bible, rendering that unitary Bible visible also in its aggregate parts.[103]

The unity of the Bible is also shadowed and interrupted by the flow of history. As Epiphanius moves on to describe the history of the major translations of the Old Testament—from the Septuagint to the later Greek versions—he also provides a running chronology of the monarchs in whose reigns the translations took place. First, he lists the Ptolemaic dynasts from Ptolemy I Soter to Cleopatra.[104] Next follows a list of the Roman emperors, interrupted by accounts of the translations of Aquila under Hadrian, and Symmachus and Theodotion around the time of Severus and Caracalla.[105] Biblical activity and imperial chronology become hopelessly entangled: the discovery of the *quintus* and *sextus*, two additional anonymous Greek translations of the Old Testament, is recounted with the reigns of Antoninus and the Severans; the flourishing of Origen, his production of the Hexapla (expanded with the two additional translations into the Octapla), and the rise of Mani all flow in and out of the emperors of the later third century; finally, as if impelled by antiquarian momentum, Epiphanius recites the reigns of all of the Roman emperors from Aurelian up to the present day, in the "second consulship of Arcadius Augustus" (392 CE), the time in which

---

102. So Epiphanius explains in some detail the medical origins of the lemniscus before explaining its text-critical significance (marking a variant translation): *De mensuris et ponderibus* 8 (Dean, *Weights and Measures*, 22–23 [Eng.] and 50d-51c [Syr.]; Moutsoulas, "Περὶ μέτρων," ll. 193–227).

103. See Chin, *Grammar and Christianity*, 93–96, for a similar discussion of Origen's Hexapla.

104. Epiphanius, *De mensuris et ponderibus* 12 (Dean, *Weights and Measures*, 28 [Eng.] and 53c-d [Syr.]; Moutsoulas, "Περὶ μέτρων," ll. 330–45).

105. Epiphanius, *De mensuris et ponderibus* 13, 16 (Dean, *Weights and Measures*, 28–29, 32 [Eng.] and 53d-54a, 55b-c [Syr.]; Moutsoulas, "Περὶ μέτρων," ll. 346–56, 424–29).

Epiphanius's own biblical work takes place.[106] The careful listing of *all* Greek and Roman rulers, from Ptolemy I to Arcadius and Honorius, is surely more than a simple biblical chronology requires. It is, in fact, not particularly useful as a historical device: after Aquila and Symmachus, the translations are no longer clearly pegged to particular imperial regimes, and we are left with loosely intertwined histories, of Bible and empire. In one sense, the historical flow of empire seems to be subordinated to the traditions of the Bible: emperors (indeed, empires) pass in between the work of biblical translators, collators, and interpreters. Yet the work of biblical transmission is, at every step, supported and enabled by empire, from Ptolemy I to "Arcadius Augustus." Ultimately, in this first section, empire and Bible are flattened into each other—even as both remain, of course, controlled by the hand of the bishop.

These preliminary discussions of the biblical text out of the way, Epiphanius then proceeds to list and describe all manner of measurements found in the entire Bible.[107] This longest section of the treatises is divided into clear sections: first, the dry measures, followed by liquid measures;[108] next, weights and monetary amounts;[109] a list of "local measures" that are not found in Scripture, but which Epiphanius has mentioned in passing already;[110] and finally biblical land area measures.[111] Some descriptions are brief and occasion little commentary: the

---

106. Epiphanius, *De mensuris et ponderibus* 18–20 (Dean, *Weights and Measures*, 34–39 [Eng.] and 56c-58d [Syr.]; Moutsoulas, "Περὶ μέτρων," ll. 483–589).

107. On modern historians' use of Epiphanius's comparative measures, see Kim, *Epiphanius*, 208–9 and notes.

108. Epiphanius, *De mensuris et ponderibus* 21–31, 32–43 (Dean, *Weights and Measures*, 40–56 [Eng.] and 59b-67a [Syr.]; Moutsoulas, "Περὶ μέτρων," ll. 606–770; the Greek grows much sparser throughout this section).

109. Epiphanius, *De mensuris et ponderibus* 45–53 (Dean, *Weights and Measures*, 56–63 [Eng.] and 67a-70a [Syr.]; Moutsoulas, "Περὶ μέτρων," ll. 771–810).

110. Epiphanius, *De mensuris et ponderibus* 54–56 (Dean, *Weights and Measures*, 63–66 [Eng.] and 70a-71d [Syr.]; Moutsoulas, "Περὶ μέτρων," ll. 811–23; the Greek ends at this point). Epiphanius defends his description of these nonbiblical measures at *De mensuris et ponderibus* 57 (Dean, *Weights and Measures*, 66 [Eng.] and 71d [Syr.]).

111. Epiphanius, *De mensuris et ponderibus* 58–60 (Dean, *Weights and Measures*, 67–70 [Eng.] and 71d-73b [Syr.]).

"handful" of 1 Kings 17:12, Epiphanius remarks, is "simple and known to all."[112] More often Epiphanius provides some basic etymology and equivalencies, where available, as in his explanation of the *bath*:

> The *bath* (Gk.: *badon*; Syr.: *ba'da'*), so called, is also from the Hebrew language, the oil press being synonymously called *bith*, for *bath* means "oil press." It consists of 50 *xestai*, and is the measure of the craft of the oil press. The *mnasis* and *medimnos* are taken, I think, from the language of the Romans, for in that language *medium* is interpreted "middle." The *mnasis*, however, is used as a measure among the Cyprians and other people; and it is 10 *modii* of wheat or barley by the *modius* of 17 *xestai* among the Cyprians. But the *medimnos* varies among the Cyprians; for the people of Salamis, that is to say, of Constantia, have a *medimnos* of five *modii*, while those of Paphos and the Sicilians measure it as 4 1/2 *modii*.[113]

Multiple forms of measurement overlap here, in multiple languages. The *bath* is mentioned in only two prophetic passages (Isa 5:10 and Ezek 45:10–14), but seems to be equated here (or merely compared?) by Epiphanius with the contemporary dry measurements of *mnasis* and *medimnos*, which he then explains in their particular linguistic and geographic contexts. Various systems of measurement (including "Roman") are thereby subordinated to an esoteric biblical term.

In his discussion of the *modius*, which follows soon after, we see most clearly how Epiphanius corrals arcane expertise to place imperial power and biblical knowledge in a tensile relationship. First, he asserts throughout that the term *modius*, as well as its true measurement, originates from the Hebrew language. *Modius*, he explains, comes from the Hebrew for "confession,"[114] because the sacred measurement of the *modius* stands for the benevolent acts of God in creation and throughout

---

112. Epiphanius, *De mensuris et ponderibus* 27 (Dean, *Weights and Measures*, 47 [Eng.] and 62c [Syr.]; Moutsoulas, "Περὶ μέτρων," l. 733).

113. Epiphanius, *De mensuris et ponderibus* 21 (Dean, *Weights and Measures*, 40–41 [Eng.] and 59c-d [Syr.]; Moutsoulas, "Περὶ μέτρων," ll. 616–26).

114. Epiphanius, *De mensuris et ponderibus* 21, 23, 24 (Dean, *Weights and Measures*, 41, 45 [Eng.] and 59d, 61c-d [Syr.]; Moutsoulas, "Περὶ μέτρων," ll. 632–36, 701–6). Epiphanius seems to be thinking of the Hebrew/Aramaic root *ydh*.

sacred history. Epiphanius knows this because the "just" *modius*—that is, the correct *modius* indicated by the Old Testament—contains exactly twenty-two *xestai*, which figuratively indicates the twenty-two acts of God during the seven days of creation, the twenty-two "heads of the people" from Adam to Jacob, the twenty-two letters of the Hebrew alphabet, and the twenty-two books of the Old Testament. Each of these sets of twenty-two is listed in turn, and the books of the Bible (a fitting culmination for this series of lists) are recorded with their Greek and Hebrew names.[115] Epiphanius has concocted a numerical and figurative interpretation of the *modius* that connects sacred history, divine order, and the form of the Hebrew Bible.[116] His figurative exegesis is also thoroughly antiquarian, thick with historical, textual, and linguistic detail.

What's more, as Epiphanius makes clear in his discussion, he has also subordinated imperial order to his antiquarian parade:

> Also among the Romans, it happens that the measure is called by a similar name, *modium* (Gk.: *modioum;* Syr.: *modiom*); just as among the Hebrews a child is admonished to "learn *aleph*" and among the Greeks it happens to be called "to seek to make alpha" (*to alphein zētein*). Whence it has come to be known that from the Hebrew it has been transferred to other languages.[117]

Most readers (ancient and modern), especially those who know Latin, would likely find Epiphanius's etymology suspicious. Yet as I noted above, specious etymology is par for the course in antiquarian writing (and also in ancient biblical interpretation), indicating not so much a

---

115. Epiphanius, *De mensuris et ponderibus* 22–24 (Dean, *Weights and Measures*, 41–45 [Eng.] and 59d-61d [Syr.]; Moutsoulas, "Περὶ μέτρων," ll. 632–715).

116. See also Epiphanius, *De mensuris et ponderibus* 30 (Dean, *Weights and Measures*, 49 [Eng.] and 63c [Syr.]), where the "three measures of fine flour" of Gen 18:6 represent the Trinity; and *De mensuris et ponderibus* 35 (Dean, *Weights and Measures*, 52–53 [Eng.] and 64c-65d [Syr.]), where the "four *xestai*" of the *stamnos* lead from a recitation of "fours" (four books in the ark, rivers of Eden, quarters of the world, seasons, night watches, times for prayer, creatures representing the Gospels) to an interpretation of the *stamnos* (which contained the manna) as the Virgin Mary (also an ark containing God's word).

117. Epiphanius, *De mensuris et ponderibus* 24 (Dean, *Weights and Measures*, 46 [Eng.] and 62a [Syr.]; Moutsoulas, "Περὶ μέτρων," ll. 718–22).

lack of scientific linguistic rigor but rather the cultural priorities of the etymologist.[118] The effect of this etymological sleight of hand here seems to be to displace Greece and Rome in favor of "ancient" Hebrew wisdom. Yet, at the same time, this ancient Hebrew *modius*, and the deeper biblical wisdom it symbolizes, belong to Greece and Rome, just as the Hebrew aleph has been transformed into the Greek alpha, the base unit of literary knowledge. Epiphanius, the Greco-Roman bishop learned in Hebrew, embodies and masters this cultural and historical tension.

The ensuing discussion of weights (which is, mostly, a discussion of currencies) provides, as we might imagine, endless opportunities for antiquarian display, as Epiphanius converts talents into lepta into staters into shekels. He can also introduce his own eyewitness experience, as when once—on a stroll—he came upon an "ancient castle" with piles of arrows left in a heap, "which were fashioned by early man for use as money."[119] (Again, Epiphanius himself triumphantly bears witness to the fall of empires.) From weights and land measures Epiphanius moves, somewhat inexplicably, to a discussion of biblical places, many drawn from Eusebius's *Onomastikon*.[120] Place-names are translated, and some

---

118. Davide Del Bello, *Forgotten Paths: Etymology and the Allegorical Mindset* (Washington, DC: Catholic University of America Press, 2007), suggests that premodern etymology aimed for metaphysical truth in a manner analogous to allegorical interpretation. A clear example of such etymological allegorism is the Philonic understanding of "Israel" as "one who sees God," picked up by Christians. See Graham Harvey, *The True Israel: Uses of the Names Jew, Hebrew, and Israel in Ancient Jewish and Early Christian Literature* (Leiden: Brill, 1996), 219–24, 254–55; Columba Stewart, *Cassian the Monk* (Oxford: Oxford University Press, 2002), 48, 71; and David Brakke, *Demons and the Making of the Monk: Spiritual Combat in Early Christianity* (Cambridge, MA: Harvard University Press, 2006), 18–19, 45.

119. Epiphanius, *De mensuris et ponderibus* 49 (Dean, *Weights and Measures*, 59–60 [Eng.] and 68c-d [Syr.]). Epiphanius reports that in ancient times "the life of man before the coming of Christ was hemmed in by wars," such that people were so well-armed that they used arrows for money, leading to the term for an *obolus*.

120. See my discussion of the *Onomastikon* in *Remains of the Jews: The Holy Land and Christian Empire in Late Antiquity*, Divinations (Stanford, CA: Stanford University Press, 2003), 34–36.

interesting local tidbits shared: apparently, ever since Christ's visit (see John 11:54), the village of Ephraim was free of all "vipers or other noxious reptiles."[121] Tired of place-names (apparently), Epiphanius suddenly begins to zoom outward: he describes "the four quarters of the world," that is, the origins of the terms for the cardinal directions (although he imagines his reader expressing surprise: "You have told us something superfluous in speaking of east and west and north and south!").[122] The final chapters become increasingly disjointed: from the four winds to the borders of Palestine to the major constellations to the types of mountains, hills, and ridges, until finally Epiphanius peters out: "Here we arrive at the end of our writing for you."[123] Has the elderly bishop lost his train of thought, and begun merely piling on bits of wisdom connected—even at some remove—to the pages of Scripture? Is the transmitter or translator of the treatise at fault, inserting pages out of order, forgetting to copy out segues, losing track of the original text? Any of these explanations is possible, of course, but all derive from the simple fact that the text itself is only ever loosely held together by Epiphanius's antiquarian disposition. There is no argument, thesis, or even scriptural order structuring these bits and pieces, only the mind of the author. Antiquarian literature is, by nature, a constellation of fragments loosely and contingently united: here, at the deteriorating end of Epiphanius's biblical treatise, we sense how truly fragile the masterful collection of knowledge can be.

Epiphanius's final extant work, his treatise *On Twelve Gems,* is at once his most antiquarian and his most thoroughly scriptural; indeed, we see how fully the two impulses are intertwined in Epiphanius's interpretive process. This treatise, like all of his other extant writings, was

---

121. Epiphanius, *De mensuris et ponderibus* 67 (Dean, *Weights and Measures,* 73 [Eng.] and 74a-b [Syr.]).

122. Epiphanius, *De mensuris et ponderibus* 80 (Dean, *Weights and Measures,* 78 [Eng.] and 76a [Syr.]).

123. Epiphanius, *De mensuris et ponderibus* 84 (Dean, *Weights and Measures,* 83 [Eng.] and 78a [Syr.]).

composed at the request of a fellow ecclesiastic, to explain the meanings of the twelve gems set into the high priest's breastplate (Exod 28:15–21).[124] The image of the breastplate inset with shining gems, with names then etched into those gems, provides an apposite image for the treatise itself. Like the breastplate, the treatise becomes a framework into which Epiphanius can insert an array of bits of knowledge, inscribed with biblical information.

Drawing on the classical tradition of lapidarian literature,[125] Epiphanius begins in full antiquarian mode by explaining the origins and properties of the twelve stones found on the high priest's breastplate. He describes each stone's color and then usually compares it to and distinguishes it from other similar stones (whose properties he also catalogues). Usually Epiphanius also provides some description of the stone's medicinal or alchemical uses. Sardion has "healing power";[126] topaz "has a beneficial working in disorders of the eyes";[127] sapphire "heals scabs, swellings, and tumors";[128] those who look upon amethyst "become drunk and are cognizant beforehand of winter and rain."[129] Other bits of esoteric knowledge appear: we hear of the time Nero painted a mountainside green and how ligure is harvested from an

---

124. This treatise also has a complicated transmission history; see my discussion in the introduction of the various translations and versions, as well as the date and addressee.

125. Blake and Vis, *Epiphanius*, xc-xcvii, traces the classical tradition of lapidary and gemmological treatises in the Greek-speaking world. They assume that Epiphanius had recourse to a variety of treatises, based (in part) on his citation of multiple treatises on "roots and plants" and "poisons and antidotes" in his second proem of the *Panarion*; possibly his lapidarian knowledge has been mediated through handbooks or other digests (see Jürgen Dummer, "Ein naturwissenschaftliches Handbuch als Quelle für Epiphanius von Constantia," *Klio* 55 [1973]: 289–99, repr. in *Philologia sacra*, 82–95). On gemmological treatises in antiquity through to the modern period, see Christel Meier, *Gemma spiritalis: Methode und Gebrauch der Edelsteinallegorese vom frühen Christentum bis ins 18. Jahrhundert*, vol. 1, Münstersche Mittelalter-Schriften 34.1 (Munich: Fink, 1977), 56–67 (on classical lithologies) and 99–111 (on Epiphanius).

126. Blake and Vis, *Epiphanius*, 103.

127. Blake and Vis, *Epiphanius*, 105.

128. Blake and Vis, *Epiphanius*, 112.

129. Blake and Vis, *Epiphanius*, 120.

inaccessible abyss by eagles devouring carrion.[130] Biblical knowledge piles on as well, even in this more strictly "naturalist" section of the treatise: Aquila does not translate "emerald" the same as the Septuagint;[131] the river Pishon, which flows from Eden, is the source of the marvelous stone chalcedony.[132]

In a separate section of the treatise, Epiphanius provides spiritual interpretations of the stones, based (in part) on the names etched onto the stones.[133] Epiphanius goes by birth order, assigning each son in turn to a stone based on his age (Reuben first, Benjamin last).[134] These associations between stones and biblical figures allow for deeper ruminations and associations. Sometimes the properties of the stone are related (even tangentially) to qualities of a son of Jacob. For instance, sardion, the first stone, comes from Babylon; the tower built at Babylon led to the "first division" of the family of humanity; Reuben, on account of his "passions," had a "divided mind," and was cursed by his father. Sardion also heals with its dust; likewise, Reuben "healed" his sins when he intervened to save Joseph from death at his brothers' hands.[135] The tribe of Asher "was acquainted with work and labor on the land," and the color of agate is yellow and tawny, "the color of the earth." Of course, "tawny" is also the color of a lion, a royal animal, befitting the son of Jacob, whose name means "riches."[136] Even the tribal allotments of the sons are relevant: Zebulon's allotment is

---

130. Blake and Vis, *Epiphanius*, 106, 118.

131. Blake and Vis, *Epiphanius*, 107–8.

132. Blake and Vis, *Epiphanius*, 107.

133. This section survives complete only in the Old Georgian version. In some versions of the treatise this section comes last (note the doxology at Blake and Vis, *Epiphanius*, 172); in others, it follows immediately upon the naturalist discussion of the stones; see my discussion below.

134. Josephus also made this assumption (*Antiquitates* 3.162–67), but the Targum Ps.-Jonathan places the sons in a different order (sons of Leah, the sons of the handmaids, and the sons of Rachel). See Josiah Derby, "Rashi's Conjectures," *Jewish Bible Quarterly* 32 (2004): 125–29, for brief discussion. Given the final section of *De XII gemmis*, Epiphanius was clearly aware that there were many options for ordering the names on the stones.

135. Blake and Vis, *Epiphanius*, 123.

136. Blake and Vis, *Epiphanius*, 148–49.

"near the sea" and "there come to him all the riches of the sea," including the bloodstone, which comes "on ships" from "remote districts."[137]

While Epiphanius frequently returns to certain passages having to do with Jacob's sons—the blessing of Jacob (Gen 49), the allotment of tribal lands (Num 2, Josh 13–19), Moses's farewell speech (Deut 33)—he also ranges far and wide across the biblical canon, creating connections between passages based on his own antiquarian expertise. Zebulon's seaside allotment, it turns out, is "near Nazareth of Galilee," the home of Mary, who gave birth to Jesus, who (like the gold-colored bloodstone) gives light to the world. Having likened Christ to the golden bloodstone, Epiphanius remarks that it is found "in Babylon of the Achaemenids." "Let no one think it is called 'of the Achaemenids' in vain," he adds, forestalling (it seems) an accusation of pedantic overdescription. For it is common to distinguish people and places that share a name. He provides an appropriately biblical example: four "Jesuses," from the Old and New Testaments (Joshua son of Nun; Joshua son of Jehozadak [Hag 1:1], Jesus ben Sira, and "Jesus our Lord"). So, too, he means to distinguish this Mesopotamian Babylon from another one in Egypt.[138] After recalling the natural properties of the bloodstone (including its healing properties), he reflects once more on the stone's intertextuality:

> Let us now look at Zebulon, who is inscribed upon the gem bloodstone. The lot of the heritage of Zebulon was Nazareth, where there was graciously given to the Virgin the conception of our Lord Jesus Christ, like to whom is the gem bloodstone. On it is inscribed the name of Zebulon, who had many riches from the sea. Truly, gifts were offered from all the quarters of heaven to our Lord Jesus Christ [cf. Matt 2], who himself is the precious cornerstone and heals all wounds and ailments.[139]

From the Old Testament tribal allotments to the annunciation, from the "riches" of Zebulon to the gifts of the magi, from the rejected

---

137. Blake and Vis, *Epiphanius*, 153.
138. Blake and Vis, *Epiphanius*, 153–55.
139. Blake and Vis, *Epiphanius*, 155.

cornerstone to the stone that heals wounds, visible and invisible, Epiphanius intertwines threads of natural and biblical wisdom into a great knot of learning.

Several of Epiphanius's spiritual interpretations of the stones permit him to reflect upon biblical intertextuality. The jacinth "glows like a glowing coal," calling to mind Isaiah 54:11, "I shall change your stones to glowing coals and lay your foundations on sapphire." "Jacinth" and "sapphire," in turn, recall the dual natures of Christ and his kingdom, the colors of fire and blood, of redemption and judgment. Immediately, Epiphanius bounces back to Isaiah, as the "glowing coal" reminds him also of Isaiah 6:6–7, and the seraph who pulled a "glowing coal" from the heavenly altar with which to purify Isaiah's prophetic lips recalling (once more) Christ's "ransom and purification."[140] Epiphanius remembers that jacinth is found in the biblical river Pishon, "which means 'face of fire,'"[141] recalling at once the "heat of the spirit" that came from Christ as well as the prophet Nahum, who mentions Pishon as well.[142] The glowing coal also suggests illumination, shining in the face of God's chosen "saints": Moses, Elijah, and Stephen.[143] The stone reflects multiple moments and characters from the Bible simultaneously.[144]

The stone ligure similarly conjures up a bewildering host of biblical characters, connected to each other by multiple associations.[145] First, geographic: because ligure is assigned the name of Gad on the priestly

---

140. Blake and Vis, *Epiphanius*, 129–30.

141. Pishon does not, of course, mean "face of fire," although it seems vaguely reasonable—from the perspective of antiquarian etymology—that Epiphanius is thinking of the root *pn-* (which appears in place-names like Penuel [Gen 32:32]) in some combination with *'š* (fire).

142. Blake and Vis, *Epiphanius*, 131: "This also the prophet Nahum has said: 'P'ison came down and spread itself abroad on thy face.'" Epiphanius seems to be thinking of Nahum 2:2, which, in the Septuagint, has the word ἐμφυσῶν, which Epiphanius is remembering as *Pison;* see Blake and Vis, *Epiphanius*, cxii.

143. Blake and Vis, *Epiphanius*, 131–32.

144. See the brief discussion of Meier, *Gemma spiritalis*, 104–6.

145. On Epiphanius's reliance on multiple lithographic associations to produce his allegories, see Meier, *Gemma spiritalis*, 106–7.

breastplate, Epiphanius calls to mind the territory of Gilead (near the tribal lands of Gad), and so naturally thinks of Elijah, as well as other priestly figures associated with the area: Abiathar, Samuel, and Eli.[146] Next, mineralogical: because the stone is resistant to fire, it once more evokes Elijah, who rode to heaven in a fiery chariot and, before that, called down fire upon the altar on Mount Carmel.[147] Now we are thinking of holy biblical figures resistant to fire: we must then also speak of the "three youths" in the book of Daniel who survived the furnace, and, for good measure, Thecla, who also survived her own fiery punishment.[148] After getting briefly lost in a digression on the story of Susanna and the elders,[149] Epiphanius returns to the medical properties of the ligure: this greenish, glowing stone eases conception and birth. How fitting it should be attached to Gad, who was born from Leah's maidservant Zilpah but raised up with the other sons of Jacob. Now we are thinking of the blessing of children, which has been secured by other prophets: Elijah (a third time), who restored the widow's son to her (1 Kings 17:17–23), as did Elisha (2 Kings 4:18–37), who additionally blessed the waters of Jericho with "fruitfulness" (2 Kings 2:19–23). The life-giving power of the ligure is brought forward into the time of the New Testament as well, for the apostles "give birth" to the pagans who convert to Christianity.[150]

This figurative linkage of Old and New Testament figures continues in other places as well. Topaz, the stone of Simeon, was upon its early discovery an object of commercial trickery and royal celebration. The stonecutters who discovered it were cheated by the merchants who bought it from them for a meager price and sold it for a hefty markup to

---

146. Blake and Vis, *Epiphanius*, 139–40.

147. Blake and Vis, *Epiphanius*, 140.

148. Blake and Vis, *Epiphanius*, 140–41. We have already seen, above, Epiphanius's willingness to push canonical boundaries in the service of biblical antiquarianism.

149. Blake and Vis, *Epiphanius*, 143–45. The exegetical chain of thought is a bit confusing here, but seems to begin with Rom 5:14, and the overlap of sin, punishment, death, and Babylon.

150. Blake and Vis, *Epiphanius*, 147–48.

the citizens of Thebes. The Thebans gave it to their king, who placed it on a crown on his forehead.[151] These elements together—Simeon, money, treachery, kingship, betrayal—lead Epiphanius to see an allegory of Judas Iscariot. Judas "possessed the stone," which was fellowship with Christ, but sold it to the scribes and Pharisees, "who are of the race of Simeon,"[152] for a price far below its worth. Christ is given over to Pontius Pilate, just as the Thebans gave the topaz to their king. But the "king" is also the church, which receives the seal of Christ on its forehead just like the Theban king who put the topaz in his crown.[153] The style of allegory on display is markedly associative: suggestive elements are juxtaposed, but never quite brought into perfect alignment.[154]

If the topaz evokes Judas, the emerald—bright, shining, priestly (as the stone of Levi)—evokes John the Baptist, who served his priestly duties with "toil" and "expelled the passions." The emerald also illuminates, bringing true knowledge to the one who prophetically proclaimed: "This is the Lamb of God who will take away the sins of the world" (John 1:29).[155] The onyx, the stone of Benjamin, conjures up Paul, "of the tribe of Benjamin," who—like the onyx stone—was fashioned into a spiritual "vessel."[156] Kings and brides both delight in cups made

---

151. Blake and Vis, *Epiphanius*, 104 and 124. This story about the origins of topaz may go back to the classic (but lost) *Lithognomion* of Xenocrates (first century CE). Whether Epiphanius knew the text of Xenocrates or learned this story through an intermediary source (for instance, Origen; see Alan Scott, "Origen's Use of Xenocrates of Ephesus," *VC* 45 [1991]: 278–85) remains unclear (see Meier, *Gemma spiritalis*, 101 n. 239).

152. Perhaps Epiphanius is thinking of Simon the Pharisee (Luke 7:36–50)? Simeon, the son of Jacob, is also associated with treachery because of his massacre of the Shechemites (Gen 34:25–31, 49:5–7).

153. Blake and Vis, *Epiphanius*, 124–25.

154. Does the stone represent Christ, or fellowship with Christ? How can Pilate and "the church" both be symbolized by the king?

155. Blake and Vis, *Epiphanius*, 127–28. The first reference to John—the priest, prophet, and virgin—is certainly John the Baptist; the second reference could be to the Baptist (who speaks the quoted verse) or the evangelist, in whose Gospel it appears.

156. Blake and Vis, *Epiphanius*, 166. Epiphanius also notes that Esther and Mordecai were of the tribe of Benjamin (165).

from onyx, Epiphanius explains.[157] Brides, kings, Paul, the church, knowledge, and redemption all flow together in this intertextual play.[158] The idea of a cup made of onyx also, naturally, evokes the story of Benjamin and Joseph's cup from Genesis 44.[159] Multiple associations between Benjamin and Paul bounce through the text: Paul was a "wolf" like Benjamin (see Gen 49:27), before being called by God; Paul saw the Lord on the road to Damascus, where Benjamin was also described as "out of his mind" (Ps 68:27);[160] just as Benjamin was Jacob's youngest son, so Paul was the last of the apostles called to serve.[161]

One function of this thick intertextuality is, of course, to emphasize the harmony and unity of the Bible. We have seen already in his theological treatises how important scriptural unity was to Epiphanius. The particular mode of intertextuality at play in Epiphanius's commentary, however—knotty with interruptions, associations, and digressions—has a flip side, as well. To see these passages knitted together through the interpretation of the stones, to watch Epiphanius juxtapose Simeon and Judas, Benjamin and Paul, the prophets with the apostles of Christ, is also to become aware of the ways in which the Scriptures are also variegated, multiple, and disjoined. The antiquarian Bible is harmonious and unitary only insofar as the antiquarian himself holds it together, and therefore is also liable to dissolution in the wrong hands.

A third section of the treatise is itself a meditation on the multiple ways the Bible is prone to reconfiguration and reordering. In determining which names of Jacob's sons are inscribed on which stones, Epiphanius proposes to examine fourteen places where the sons of Jacob are listed (thirteen in the Hebrew Bible, one in Revelation) and to consider

---

157. Blake and Vis, *Epiphanius*, 166.
158. Blake and Vis, *Epiphanius*, 169.
159. Blake and Vis, *Epiphanius*, 166.
160. Blake and Vis, *Epiphanius*, 318–19 and 320–21, citing Ps 67:28. (I cite from the Coptic version here; see my discussion in chapter 2, n. 105.) Ps 67:22 mentions Bashan, which is near Damascus; it's unclear if Epiphanius is consciously or unconsciously equating the two.
161. Blake and Vis, *Epiphanius*, 166–70.

whether any of these orderings suit the stones better than the ordering he has chosen. His procedure in this section is much like that in the interpretations of the stones themselves: first he goes over the facts about each ordering and then returns to consider their deeper significance, particularly in light of the properties of the stones of the priestly breastplate. Naturally, Epiphanius finds all of the other orderings lacking for a variety of reasons: this one is missing Simeon, that one joins two sons together, this one lists Joseph's sons instead of Joseph, that one leaves no place for Levi at all.[162]

This ordered meditation on ordering is supremely antiquarian: it adds nothing substantive to Epiphanius's discussion of the stones and the sons of Jacob (in the end, there is no question but that he will stick with the birth order); it exists purely for edification, that is, as a display of Epiphanius's bounty of knowledge. It demonstrates the multifarious ways in which the Bible can be approached, dissected, categorized, and reindexed. It also gives Epiphanius an opportunity for one more learned digression, which comes in his discussion of the eleventh ordering of the sons of Israel. Moses had commanded the tribes of Israel to divide themselves upon entering into the Land, with six tribes on Mount Gerizim and six tribes on Mount Ebal (Deut 27:12–13).[163] Epiphanius describes the location of these two mountains ("over against Jericho on the eastern side near Gilgal"[164]) and then remarks that "certain people ... think that

---

162. Blake and Vis, *Epiphanius*, 179, 181–82. Epiphanius does briefly consider the order by which the sons of Israel departed Egypt (Exod 1:1–5), which lists Joseph last, only because he has seen a Hebrew version of the breastplate stones that places the beryl (the eleventh stone in the Greek text, and the one associated by Epiphanius with Joseph) in the twelfth position (Blake and Vis, *Epiphanius*, 180).

163. Blake and Vis, *Epiphanius*, 177 and 183–84. Even though the tenth ordering comes from Deut 33, Epiphanius lists the division of Deut 27 in eleventh place, presumably because the actual division of the tribes took place later (see Josh 8:30–35, which does not include the list of the tribes).

164. Blake and Vis, *Epiphanius*, 184, citing Deut 11:29–30. In locating "Gerizim and Ebal" near Jericho, and not near Shechem in Samaria, Epiphanius is probably following Eusebius (*Onomastikon* [GCS 11.3:64]), who may, in turn, be drawing on local rabbinic interpretation (which may, in turn, like Epiphanius's account, have a distinctly anti-Samaritan tone); see Reinhard Pummer, *Early Christian Authors on Samaritans and*

Mount Gerizim is elsewhere."[165] These "certain people," he goes on to explain, are the Samaritans, who believe that Mount Gerizim is located near Shechem ("now called Neapolis").

Suddenly, we find ourselves in the midst of a history and ethnography of the Samaritans, stitched together out of bits and pieces of the *Panarion*.[166] Epiphanius recounts their origins, their discovery of the Jewish Law (which they keep imperfectly), what idols they have concealed in their ersatz Temple, only then circling back to his point of departure: their mistaken identification of their holy mountain with the Mount Gerizim mentioned in Deuteronomy.[167] From ethnography we move to geography: Epiphanius describes *their* Mount Gerizim, its enormity, and the 1,500 steps incised in its slope that rises a mile or more. He returns again to the Deuteronomy passage under consideration: with such a high mountain, Epiphanius asks, how could the assembled Israelites have possibly heard the "curses and blessings" pronounced from Gerizim and Ebal, as Moses commanded? "By all this," he concludes, "the error of the Samaritans is disproved, for these are not the mountains on which the sons of Israel spoke the blessings and the curses!"[168] After explaining (once more!) the distance between the Gerizim of the Pentateuch and the "mighty Gerizim" of the Samaritans, Epiphanius suddenly, and abruptly, ends his digression.

In the Old Georgian version of *De XII gemmis,* this abrupt ending actually concludes the entire treatise: "Let this be sufficient for the relation and understanding of all this."[169] We might express a bit of dismay at the abrupt conclusion: What of the other "orderings" of the sons of Israel, not yet explained? Has Epiphanius simply lost steam? Or is

---

Samaritanism, Texts and Studies in Ancient Judaism 92 (Tübingen: Mohr-Siebeck, 2002), 86.

165. Blake and Vis, *Epiphanius,* 185.
166. Epiphanius, *Panarion* 8.8.5–10 and 9.1.2–2.6 (GCS n.F. 10.1:195–96, 198–99); and Pummer, *Early Christian Authors,* 121–83 (on all of Epiphanius's writings on Samaria).
167. Blake and Vis, *Epiphanius,* 185–91.
168. Blake and Vis, *Epiphanius,* 192–93.
169. Blake and Vis, *Epiphanius,* 193.

this a question of faulty transmission, copying, or translation? Other, less complete versions of the treatise place this survey of the "orderings" before the allegorical section.[170] The highly fragmentary Coptic version breaks off in the midst of the anti-Samaritan digression and picks up again with a brief consideration of the twelfth and thirteenth orderings before another manuscript lacuna.[171] This early witness suggests that originally Epiphanius did complete his survey of the twelve tribes before turning, in the final section of the treatise, to his allegorical interpretation.[172] Yet at some point in the manuscript transmission process, it made just as much sense to a copyist or translator to read the end of the Samaritan digression and take it for the end of the treatise. Indeed, this breaking off from a digression into an abrupt conclusion, similar to the end of the treatise *On Weights and Measures,* makes sense in light of Epiphanius's commentarial style:[173] he twists around and around his subject, spinning out facts and information, bits of knowledge scriptural, historical, ethnographic, mineralogical, weaving it all together until he has exhausted the material, the reader, and himself.[174] We remember that, for the antiquarian, "the distinction between raw material and result can be indistinct."

170. The newly published Armenian version places the beginning of this section between the naturalist and allegorical interpretations of the stones, but only a small piece of it (Albrecht and Manukyan, *Über die zwölf Steine,* 17–19 [Arm.], 65–67 [Ger.]). The Latin version places the "orderings" discussion immediately following the initial naturalist discussion of the stones, and provides a segue: "Hic iam nunc quaeritur, quibus modis eum ordinem consequentiae, qui est certissimus et congruens, approbemus" (CSEL 35:756). The Latin version also ends abruptly near the end of the anti-Samaritan section, just a few lines shy of the Old Georgian version, and does not contain the allegorical section (CSEL 35:773).

171. Vis, *Epiphanius,* 284–85. The Coptic version has fragments of all of the sections of the treatise, except for the cover letter to Diodorus of Tyre.

172. As posited already in a review of Blake and Vis, *Epiphanius,* by W. Hengstenberg in *BZ* 37.2 (1937): 400–408.

173. It is also how the extant Latin version ends (CSEL 35:773); on the "abrupt" ending, see Meier, *Gemma spiritalis,* 109 n. 361.

174. Meier, *Gemma spiritalis,* 109, remarks that, even considering the possibility of problems in transmission, "das Werk ist ... gekennzeichnet durch einen hohen Schwierigkeitsgrad und mangelnde Zugänglichkeit."

However it was originally structured, in *De XII gemmis* we see clearly how the antiquarian elements—stones, mountains, emperors, histories, languages, medicinal properties—are indistinguishable from the religious elements—Scriptures, theology, orthodoxy. As in *De mensuris et ponderibus*, we might initially suspect Epiphanius of performing a kind of baptism on classical knowledge, taking a classical body of knowledge "on stones" and subordinating it to biblical truth. But antiquarian composition resists such stratification: "classical" and "Christian" are now totally intertwined and reinforcing. Christian culture is built out of individual bits of knowledge, harnessed and brought together in totalized order. The location of Mount Gerizim, the properties of the emerald, the nature of the resurrection body, the Greek text of Aquila, all line up together like items in an index, creating by their sheer juxtaposition a snapshot of "Christianity" that encompasses all aspects of life but still remains atomized and prone to rearrangement.[175]

THE JEWELED BIBLE

When classicist Michael Roberts wrote about the "jeweled style" in late antiquity, he too began with a late ancient contemplation of the jeweled breastplate of Aaron, included in a Latin verse rendering of the first seven books of the Old Testament.[176] For Roberts, the poet's inclusion of these few verses signaled a particular poetic sensibility in late antiquity, one that (like Aaron's breastplate) emphasized variation, arrangement, and pattern over simple artistic sense and meaning. The effect, Roberts argues, was to emphasize the process of poetic construction

---

175. F. Allan Hanson, *The Trouble with Culture: How Computers Are Calming the Culture Wars* (Albany: SUNY Press, 2007), 83–87, proposes that indexing ("an analytic procedure that divides information into particles and treats them independently" [83]) leaves culture more open to creativity and change than the static (and imperializing) forms of classification.

176. Michael Roberts, *The Jeweled Style: Poetry and Poetics in Late Antiquity* (Ithaca, NY: Cornell University Press, 1989), 9–13; the text under consideration is Cyprianus Gallus's *Heptateuchos*.

above (or, at least, coterminous with) the poetic product. The work of the poet, visible in the dazzling juxtaposition of elements, comes ostentatiously into view, for it is only the poet's art that holds these diverse "jewels" together.

Such poetry, Roberts notes ruefully, has been condemned by modern readers, but its variegated and discontinuous aesthetic must have spoken more vibrantly to the ancient readers who valued these poets and their art.[177] Roberts's insight into this "aesthetics of discontinuity" has been drawn productively in the study of late ancient Christianity by Patricia Cox Miller and Catherine Chin.[178] I, too, find many significant resonances with the antiquarian aesthetic I have been investigating here: the highly visible assemblage, the privileging of learned display over rhetorical or philosophical theory, the way these variegated parts—without losing their "partness"—create a new and unitary cultural entity ("Christianity").[179]

The Bible that emerges from Epiphanius's interpretation partakes in this discontinuous-yet-unifying aesthetic, drawing on the imperial Roman tradition of antiquarian erudition. It is full of lists, dates, highly tangential (if not, indeed, irrelevant) data and assertions, and it doesn't seem to lead us anywhere concrete. It is not how we imagine the intellectual, philosophical Bible of the great minds of early Christianity: smooth, untangled, heavy with meaning, certainly, but clear, bright, and continuous. That is, perhaps, how we imagine Origen's Bible. Of course, even Origen was not immune to the lure of antiquarian display: lists, proof-texts, ethnographic and historiographic digressions. Nor are Epiphanius's interpretive maneuvers unique to the Cypriot bishop: other biblical commentaries have their antiquarian moments, where

177. Even in the wake of Roberts's own study; see J. B. Hall, "Review of *The Jeweled Style: Poetry and Poetics in Late Antiquity*," *Classical Review* n.s. 41 (1991): 359–61.
178. Patricia Cox Miller, "1997 NAPS Presidential Address; 'Differential Networks': Relics and Other Fragments of Late Antiquity," *JECS* 6 (1998): 113–38; Chin, *Grammar and Christianity*.
179. Chin, *Grammar and Christianity*, 170, on "subjective disassembly and reconstitution."

unexpected associations and digressions interrupt the commentarial flow.[180]

My point is that Epiphanius is not unique, and not performing a new or unusual biblical literary act. I do think, when we read Epiphanius, the marks of antiquarian sensibility are more pronounced. In the *Ancoratus* and *Panarion*, the Bible functions as both a source of knowledge and an object of antiquarian speculation. In the treatises *On Weights and Measures* and *On Twelve Gems*, the Bible confronts and absorbs the "classical" systems of knowledge that seemed (to other Christians, at least) so problematic. The result, for Epiphanius, is a Bible that (I would argue) is eminently suited to his late fourth-century context: as Christianity and empire came to become increasingly identified, as Christian religion signaled Roman power. To be sure, intellectual titans of the time were constructing complex theological edifices out of the sacred Scriptures. Equally appealing, it seems, was a bishop who could demonstrate the power of Christian culture to perfectly contain and display, in tiny bits and morsels, all the knowledge of the world.

---

180. See the comments of John O'Keefe and R. R. Reno, *Sanctified Vision: An Introduction to Early Christian Interpretations of the Bible* (Baltimore: Johns Hopkins University Press, 2005), 1–3.

CHAPTER FIVE

Salvation

MORALITY

Epiphanius loiters in the footnotes of modern studies of post-Nicene Trinitarian theology. Although he will, on rare occasion, make it into the body of a scholarly text, more often we find him at the bottom of the page (or, more frequently, at the back of the book). There, he rarely provides new insight into the twists and turns that took institutional Trinitarian theology from Nicaea to Constantinople. He plays, rather, a supporting role, like something of a pro-Nicene recording secretary. Scholars mine the *Panarion* for otherwise incomplete or missing documents by more important players (such as Athanasius of Alexandria) or supporting characters (such as George of Alexandria) or to fill in gaps in our theological chronology: who met where, with whom, and when? As a creative thinker and intellectual contributor to the construction of a persuasive theology based on the Nicene Trinitarian concept of *homoousios* (divine "consubstantiality"), Epiphanius simply does not rate attention. Modern scholarship views him as a flamboyant controversialist—the "hatchet man" of the "Nicene right"[1]—an incoherent rambler, a rhetorical bomb-thrower,

---

1. The memorable description of Jon Dechow, *Dogma and Mysticism in Early Christianity: Epiphanius of Cyprus and the Legacy of Origen*, PMS 13 (Macon, GA: Mercer University Press, 1988), 13.

an inveterate liar (although apparently an accurate transmitter of other people's documents), but not a theologian of the significance of Athanasius, the Cappadocians, or Augustine.

Yet in the early 370s, less than a decade after his move from the monastic life to the episcopacy, we find him writing a lengthy treatise on Trinitarian theology at the request of a group of monks and priests from Asia Minor. Throughout the 360s and 370s, he seems to be consulting frequently and fruitfully with the "big names" of pro-Nicene theology: the *Panarion* not only preserves their letters and movements throughout this period, but records Epiphanius's own conversations and contributions to this growing theological movement.[2] At one point, Epiphanius recalls a (private?) conversation with Athanasius, in which the two discussed the orthodoxy of Marcellus of Ancyra:

> I myself, on some occasion (*chronōi tini*), asked the blessed *papa* Athanasius about this Marcellus, how he felt about him. He did not defend him nor again did he bear any hostility against him, only, with a smile on his face (*monon de dia tou prosōpou meidiasas*), he hinted that he had not been far from depravity, but he had acquitted himself.[3]

The casual recollection—"on some occasion"—reinforces the impression that Epiphanius frequently held close conversations with the leaders of the Nicene vanguard (he can't be bothered to remember at *which* meeting with Athanasius this conversation took place).[4] Even before his move from the monastic life in Palestine to the episcopacy in

---

2. In addition Basil of Caesarea, *Ep.* 258 (PG 32:948–53) replies (courteously, but firmly) to a (nonextant) letter of Epiphanius on several topics: disputes among Palestinian monks, presumably pertaining to Origen; Epiphanius's (or others'?) suggested additions to the Nicene Creed; the divided episcopacy at Antioch; and a query about "Maguseans," a Persian sect Epiphanius mentions in the *Ancoratus* and *De fide* but does not include in the *Panarion* (*Ancoratus* 113.2 [GCS 10.1:139]; *De fide* 12, 13 [GCS 37:512]).

3. Epiphanius, *Panarion* 72.4.5 (GCS 37:259).

4. Although the order of events is somewhat difficult to reconstruct, Epiphanius must also have consulted with Athanasius on disputes over the disciples of Apollinarius, as Epiphanius possesses a letter written by Athanasius to the bishop of Corinth following a meeting to condemn various Apollinarian Christologies; see *Panarion* 77.2.1–7 (GCS 37:416–17); and Dechow, *Dogma and Mysticism*, 49.

Cyprus, Epiphanius seems to have become part of a cross-empire network of Nicene partisans in and out of exile under non-Nicene emperors.[5] In the 370s, as we saw in chapter 3, Epiphanius inserted himself as a kind of Nicene *éminence grise* into the mixed-up episcopal situation of Antioch,[6] afterward pursuing his advocacy of Paulinus all the way to the doorstep of the bishop of Rome in the 380s.[7] In the 390s, he had enough theological influence to launch a crusade against the Origenist heresy in Palestine and Egypt;[8] in the last decade of his life, he set his sights on deposing the "heretical" bishops of Jerusalem and Constantinople.[9] Most modern theological histories of the fourth and fifth centuries have little use for Epiphanius. R.P.C. Hanson memorably wrote: "In Epiphanius we meet another second-rate theologian standing in the

---

5. He recounts a time (probably in the late 350s) when he went to visit Eusebius of Vercelli, a Nicene bishop in exile in Scythopolis (*Panarion* 30.5.2 [GCS 10.1:339]), on which see Daniel Washburn, "Tormenting the Tormentors: A Reinterpretation of Eusebius of Vercelli's Letter from Scythopolis," *CH* 78 (2009): 748–49; and Young Richard Kim, *Epiphanius of Cyprus: Imagining an Orthodox World* (Ann Arbor: University of Michigan Press, 2015), 85–88.

6. Epiphanius, *Panarion* 77.20–24 (GCS 37:434–37); see my discussion in chapter 3.

7. According to Jerome, *Ep.* 108.6.1–2 and 127.7.1 (CSEL 55:310 and 56:150).

8. The initial instigator of the anti-Origenist movement in Palestine was a certain Atarbius who demanded that Jerome and Rufinus renounce Origen's teachings: Jerome, *Adversus Rufinum* 3.33 (SC 303:300–302); several scholars (following J.N.D. Kelly, *Jerome: His Life, Writings, Controversies* [London: Duckworth, 1975], 198) have inferred from Jerome's vague description of events in this passage that Atarbius was acting as Epiphanius's agent; see Pierre Lardet, *L'apologie de Jérôme contre Rufin: Un commentaire*, Supplements to *Vigiliae Christianae* 15 (Leiden: Brill, 1993), 364–66. Epiphanius's stirring up of trouble in Palestine in the mid-390s provided cover for Theophilus to launch his anti-Origenist strike against the monks of Nitria; see Elizabeth A. Clark, *The Origenist Controversy: The Cultural Construction of an Early Christian Debate* (Princeton, NJ: Princeton University Press, 1992), 37–50, 105–6. Theophilus had been asked to mediate between John of Jerusalem and Jerome in 396–97 (see Jerome, *Ep.* 63 [CSEL 54:585–86]), and seemed to side with John against the anti-Origenists. Two years later, he had condemned the Origenists of the Egyptian desert, and sent copies of his condemnation to Palestine and Cyprus (preserved by Jerome, *Ep.* 92 [CSEL 55:147–55]; see below).

9. The sources for Epiphanius's disastrous confrontations with John Chrysostom come some decades later, in the historians Socrates (*Historia ecclesiastica* 6.12, 14 [GCS n.F. 1:333–34, 335–36]) and Sozomen (*Historia ecclesiastica* 8.14–15 [GCS n.F. 4:367–70]). Theodoret, the other fifth-century historian, does not mention Epiphanius.

tradition of Athanasius."[10] Hanson's relegation of Epiphanius to a lower theological rung persists, if in milder forms, in contemporary historical theology.[11] Epiphanius's fourth-century contemporaries, on the other hand, found something about his theological thinking not only compelling but authoritative.

In this chapter I argue that we can gain a fresh, if not necessarily transformative, perspective on the theological concerns and desires of late fourth-century Christians by taking seriously the cantankerous metropolitan bishop of Cyprus. The theology of Epiphanius does not, to be sure, reach the metaphysical heights of the Cappadocians or of his friend Athanasius. Indeed, Epiphanius at times emphasizes the lowliness and simplicity of his own theological comprehension. In the *Panarion*'s chapter against Marcellus of Ancyra (in the course of which he evokes a smiling Athanasius), Epiphanius cites a "written statement of faith of Marcellus," which he prefaces by saying: "Now orthodox people, and our brothers and confessors, say that they have received from some of Marcellus's disciples, whom he left behind, a confessional defense of his faith, whose meandering points, which I myself fail to grasp (*ta leptologēmata, autos mē kateilēphōs autēn*), I insert here."[12] After reproducing this defense of faith, Epiphanius all but shrugs as he announces: "If then it can be understood by intelligent people (*dunatai para sunetōn noeisthai*) to be correct, then let it be established as such. But

---

10. R.P.C. Hanson, *The Search for the Christian Doctrine of God: The Arian Controversy, 318–381* (Edinburgh: T. & T. Clark, 1998), 658.

11. For instance, Lewis Ayres, *Nicaea and Its Legacy: An Approach to Fourth-Century Trinitarian Theology* (Oxford: Oxford University Press, 2004), 5, lists Epiphanius among "a number of figures who most certainly deserve treatment [but] have not been accorded individual treatment in the interests of space."

12. Epiphanius, *Panarion* 72.10.4 (GCS 37:265). The term λεπτολογήματα seems to be unique to Epiphanius; it appears also in *Ancoratus* 9.8 (GCS n.F. 10.1:16) to mean something similar, a broad range of theological "finer points." Frank Williams (*The Panarion of Epiphanius of Salamis*, vol. 2, *Books II and III, De fide*, 2nd rev. ed., NHMS 79 [Leiden: Brill, 2013], 441) and Young Richard Kim (*Saint Epiphanius of Cyprus, Ancoratus*, FC 128 [Washington, DC: Catholic University of America Press, 2014], 76) both translate the term as "subtleties."

if, there again, through the argument in that very defense, some certain things fail to be orthodox, again let it be established in this way by the scholars (*tois philomathesi*)."[13] The "intelligent" and "the scholars" dabble in "meandering points" of theological niceties; Epiphanius separates himself from their number. Doubtless, given Marcellus's uncertain legacy in the late 370s, it behooves Epiphanius to feign ignorance rather than to side with a heretic.[14] Furthermore, the posture of simplicity over against the complications of heresy is, by this period, a well-worn trope Epiphanius is happy to adopt when it suits him.[15]

We can also understand Epiphanius's eschewal of metaphysically complex theology as part of an alternative theological discourse. Epiphanius's theology is structured fundamentally as a discourse of morality, rather than one of metaphysics. He will rely on complex terminology when it suits his purpose, although he will also change his terminological bearings in order to make his central moral concepts clearer to his audience.[16] Epiphanius is often understood as producing a reactionary theology, a perception no doubt enhanced by his fame as a heresiologist. Two of his most insistent theological themes are his strict, even rigid devotion to a theology of Trinitarian consubstantiality and his obsessive emphasis on the unity of the body and soul, in this life and

---

13. Epiphanius, *Panarion* 72.12.6 (GCS 37:267).

14. Epiphanius, probably influenced by Athanasius's continuing respect for Marcellus up to his death, resists condemning the late bishop despite his poor reputation in the late fourth century. On the two older bishops, see Kelley McCarthy Spoerl, "Athanasius and the Anti-Marcellian Controversy," *ZAC* 10 (2006): 34–55.

15. Basil, *Ep.* 258.2 (PG 32:949) uses the same rhetorical strategy in response to Epiphanius himself. The bishop of Cyprus had recommended some anti-Apollinarian additions to the Nicene Creed, to which Basil responded: "The teachings woven into that Faith, concerning the Incarnation of the Lord, I have neither examined nor accepted, since they are deeper than my comprehension (ὡς βαθύτερα τῆς ἡμετέρας καταλήψεως)."

16. Most famously, between the publication of the *Ancoratus* and the *Panarion*, Epiphanius moves from a one-*hypostasis* to a three-*hypostasis* confession of the Trinity; see Kim, *Epiphanus of Cyprus*, 35–37; and Oliver Kösters, *Die Trinitätslehre des Epiphanius von Salamis: Ein Kommentar zum "Ancoratus,"* Forschungen zur Kirchen- und Dogmengeschichte 86 (Göttingen: Vandenhoeck & Ruprecht, 2003), 371–73.

especially in the resurrection. Frequently these Epiphanian touchstones are read as primarily reactive: Epiphanius's Trinitarianism is "anti-Arian," and his resurrection theology is "anti-Origenist."[17] That is, Epiphanius's theological claims are preceded by an inchoate (and, it is suggested, unreasoned) objection to opposing Christian camps: polemics precede any constructive theology.

I would like to suggest, however, that these two theological touchstones, the resurrection and the *homoousion,* are, in fact, mutually reinforcing planks of a coherent fourth-century theology.[18] Epiphanius's beliefs are structured by an insistence on the moral unity of both human and divine being. That is, the moral unity of the human person both informs and reflects the united being of the threefold Godhead, and vice versa. I begin by exploring Epiphanius's constructive (although still certainly polemical) theology as he outlines it in the *Ancoratus* and the *Panarion.* In both of these treatises—but especially the *Ancoratus*—we see Epiphanius's articulation of a theology of moral unity that encompasses human identity, salvation, and the special particularity of Christ. The composite human person—the body/soul—acts both as a reflection of divine unity (the three persons of the Trinity) and as the location of the saved image of that divine unity in humans. I then explore the explicitly polemical (although still theologically constructive) arguments of the *Panarion,* in which the moral unity extends from the individual to the corporate, a precarious moral unity of all of humanity.

I then turn to reexamine Epiphanius's crusade against the teachings of Origen, which began in the 370s but was renewed with vigor in the 390s. Here we see the power and force of Epiphanius's theology of moral unity as well as its greatest rival: the teachings of another

---

17. So Dechow, *Dogma and Mysticism,* 95 n. 9, remarks (of the *Panarion,* but also of Epiphanius in general): "Epiphanius' basic viewpoint is a staunch anti-Arianism and anti-Origenism, a rigorous and non-reflective adherence to the *homoousion,* according to which all past human and Christian expressions are evaluated."

18. In addition to Kösters, *Trinitätslehre,* see now also Kim, *Epiphanius,* 130–37.

theologian who linked moral responsibility to the human person (body and soul) but with an emphasis on transformation rather than continuity (refracted, *mutatis mutandis*, through a slippery description of divine unity). I conclude by suggesting that, at the beginning and end of Epiphanius's theology of moral unity, we discover an essentially monastic understanding of the work, and reward, of the human body. I would go so far as to argue that the human body stands at the productive center of Epiphanius's Nicene theology, and that this theologized body found a receptive audience in the late fourth century.

UNITY

A clear theology of moral unity informs and undergirds both the *Ancoratus* and the *Panarion*. The treatises, composed in such close proximity, approach Epiphanius's theological concerns from distinct but complementary angles.[19] It's not quite accurate to say one is "constructive" (*Ancoratus*) and the other is "polemical" (*Panarion*). As scholars have pointed out, much of the *Ancoratus* is directed against those Christians Epiphanius perceives as theologically deficient;[20] likewise, the *Panarion* is as interested in producing notions of Christian culture and history as it is in refuting heretics.[21] Together, they provide a window into Epiphanius's mature theology in the 370s.

---

19. On the dates and circumstances of the composition of these treatises, see my discussion in the introduction; and Kösters, *Trinitätslehre*, 42–43. On their theological complementarity, see Gabriella Aragione, "Una 'storia' universale dell'eresia: Il *Panarion* di Epifanio," in *Epifanio di Salamina: Panarion, Libro primo*, ed. Giovanni Pini, Letteratura Cristiana Antica, nuova serie 21 (Brescia: Morcelliana, 2010), 5.

20. When Epiphanius later cites from the *Ancoratus* in his chapter against the "Pneumatomachoi," he prefaces it by describing the earlier work as (in part, at least) "things already said by me in the great discourse concerning faith ... in response to those blaspheming against the Holy Spirit" (*Panarion* 74.1.5 [GCS 37:314]).

21. Several recent studies have noted the culturally productive aspects of the *Panarion:* Jeremy Schott, "Heresiology as Universal History in Epiphanius' *Panarion*," *ZAC* 10 (2007): 546–63; Young Richard Kim, "Reading the *Panarion* as Collective Biography: The Heresiarch as Unholy Man," *VC* 64 (2010): 382–413.

We can discern the theological contexts of Epiphanius's thinking during this period from the prefatory materials appended to his *Ancoratus*. Epiphanius dictated the *Ancoratus* after he was approached by separate groups of Christians in Syedra, across the Mediterranean in Asia Minor; their community had been destabilized by "heretics" who did not believe in the full divinity of the Holy Spirit.[22] Epiphanius includes the two letters from this community as proems to the *Ancoratus:* the first from a group of presbyters and the second from (apparently) a monk named Palladius.[23] Epiphanius also mentions concerns from Egypt he has received from Hypatius (perhaps a monk from Epiphanius's old monastery in Palestine) and Konops (perhaps a fellow priest or bishop).[24] The Syedrans are familiar with Athanasius's writings in defense of the Holy Spirit: the first group to write to Epiphanius remarks that many erring brothers had been corrected "through the writings of Bishop Athanasius, of worthy and blessed memory."[25] Indeed, they seem to view Epiphanius as a reasonable substitute for the recently deceased Alexandrian bishop. They evince some passing, and approving, familiarity with Epiphanius's own teachings, and now request

> that Your Reverence deem it worthy to focus your letter for our church and, through a broader account (*dia platuterou diēgēmatos*), expound the correct and healthy faith so that even the more simple and those wavering about their faith might be able to be shored up through your holy writings.[26]

---

22. On this varied cast of characters, see Kösters, *Trinitätslehre*, 90–106 and 110; on the Pneumatomachoi, see Kim, *Epiphanius*, 104–6.

23. Epiphanius, *Ancoratus* proem 1–2 (GCS n.F. 10.1:2–4).

24. Epiphanius, *Ancoratus* 1.3–4 (GCS n.F. 10.1:6).

25. Epiphanius, *Ancoratus* proem 1.3 (GCS n.F. 10.1:2). Along with Athanasius the Syedrans here credit "your coworker, the most pious Proclianus," an otherwise unknown Christian (presumably a regionally known bishop). Kösters, *Trinitätslehre*, 90–91 and 94–95, proposes that the community in Syedra may have received copies of Athanasius's letters to Serapion on the Holy Spirit (on which more below), written in the previous decade, and also Basil of Caesarea's *Contra Eunomium*. On Epiphanius as Athanasius's "successor," see Kim, *Epiphanius*, 104–37.

26. Epiphanius, *Ancoratus* proem 1.4 (GCS n.F. 10.1:2).

Palladius, in the second letter of request, likewise asks Epiphanius to "expound the faith of the holy Trinity through very broad and very clear account (*dia platuterou kai saphesterou diēgēmatos*)."[27]

Epiphanius replies (modestly: "I, the least of the bishops"[28]) in a manner that picks up and even expands their request for something "very broad":

> You and our brothers inquire from us about the matters of salvation from the divine and holy Scriptures, the firm foundation of the faith concerning the Father and Son and Holy Spirit and everything else about salvation in Christ: I mean the resurrection of the dead and the coming in the flesh of the only-begotten, and about the holy testament [covenant], the old and the new, and all of the other general proofs of complete salvation.[29]

The Syedrans had not really asked about "everything else about salvation in Christ," but Epiphanius—as the treatise makes clear—cannot discuss Trinitarian theology without discussing salvation more broadly. Oliver Kösters reiterates in his commentary on the *Ancoratus* that Epiphanius's theological perspective is, from beginning to end, soteriological: to teach about God is to teach about salvation, that is, divine and human actions and postures that redeem the human condition.[30] Fourth-century debates about the Trinitarian nature of God were concerned, almost from the beginning, with human salvation.[31] When, in the 360s, pro-Nicene advocates began to elaborate a theology of the

---

27. Epiphanius, *Ancoratus* proem 2.5 (GCS n.F. 10.1:4).
28. Epiphanius, *Ancoratus* prol. (GCS n.F. 10.1:5) and *Ancoratus* 1.1 (GCS n.F. 10.1:5): "because I am not sufficient" (μὴ ὄντες ἡμεῖς ἱκανοί).
29. Epiphanius, *Ancoratus* 1.3 (GCS n.F. 10.1:6).
30. Kösters, *Trinitätslehre*, 47, 54, 58, 62, 75, 113, 372: "Seine Motivation ist soteriologisch, die Logik tritt dahinter zurück."
31. Already outlined by Dennis Groh and Robert Gregg, *Early Arianism: A View to Salvation* (Philadelphia: Fortress Press, 1981). Ayres, *Nicaea and Its Legacy*, 56, objects that "there is also something very modern about explaining a cosmology as *really* about the practicalities of soteriology"; but see also pp. 77–78 and 302–12 on the soteriological and christological roots and implications of Nicene theology as it developed across the fourth century.

Holy Spirit,[32] they did not limit their concerns to questions about God's multiplicity and unity but also attended to salvation. Athanasius wrote a series of letters to the Egyptian bishop Serapion in the late 350s, which were probably familiar to the Syedrans who wrote to Epiphanius. In the first letter, refuting those Christians who consider the Spirit a creature like the angels, Athanasius insists that, without a fully divine Holy Spirit, humans have no hope of salvation: "With this disposition, what kind of hope do you have? Or who will join you to God, if you don't have the spirit of God, but that of the creation?"[33] Athanasius's immediate context is baptism: how can the waters of regeneration be effective if the three names invoked are not all those of God? Baptism is, however, the seal of the saved Christian: in short, a lack of fully divine Spirit means a lack of human salvation.[34]

For Epiphanius, the promise of human salvation is most visible in the human body, envisioned here in two states: resurrection and incarnation.[35] Indeed, his discussions of the body and the Trinity flow into each other: "Then if he [Christ] bore a soul and a body, just as it has been demonstrated, then (*ara*) the Godhood was not diminished from the Father's essence (*tēs tou patros ousias*)."[36] Epiphanius's main opponents in the *Ancoratus* are as deficient in their understanding of the role

---

32. According to ardent Nicene proponents like Athanasius and Basil, opponents of the Council of Nicaea rejected the full consubstantiality of the Holy Spirit. It may be, however, that moderate Nicenes (who proposed, for instance, theologies of "similarity" rather than "dissimilarity") also resisted granting full, substantial divinity to the Spirit; see Ayres, *Nicaea and Its Legacy*, 214–15.

33. Athanasius, *Ep. ad Serapionem* 1.29.2; text in *Athanasius Werke*, vol. 1.1: *Die dogmatischen Schriften*, pt. 4, *Epistulae I-IV ad Serapionem*, ed. Kyriakos Savvidis (Berlin: De Gruyter, 2010), 522. See also *Ep. ad Serapionem* 1.25.5 and 1.30.3 (Savvidis, *Athanasius*, 514–15, 524).

34. So Ayres, *Nicaea and Its Legacy*, 212: "Athanasius's concern here is a fundamentally soteriological one: just as he insists on God's immediate work in Christ, the Spirit too must be part of that immediate divine activity."

35. Dechow, *Dogma and Mysticism*, 15: "Both *Ancoratus* and *Panarion* have as their central axis an integral incarnation/resurrection concern."

36. Epiphanius, *Ancoratus* 36.1 (GCS n.F. 10.1:45), following a five-chapter defense of the Son's full humanity; see also *Ancoratus* 44.1–6 (GCS n.F. 10.1:54–55).

of the body in redemption as they are in their understanding of the Trinity. Epiphanius chastises those who do not concede full humanity to the incarnate Word, who propose that "he took only flesh, but not a soul."[37] (In the *Panarion*, Epiphanius associates this error with the heretical students of Apollinarius, although in the *Ancoratus* he is more circumspect.[38]) Epiphanius also refutes those "faithless who deny the whole resurrection (*to pan anastaseōs*)" of the human, body and soul.[39] Epiphanius associates this position with the followers of Origen as well as with those of the Egyptian monk Hieracas.[40]

At the center of all of these theological topics—resurrection, incarnation, and Trinity—lies Epiphanius's deep concern for unified moral agency. In the *Panarion*, toward the end of his long chapter against the Origenists, Epiphanius recounts a parable drawn from the "secret book" of Ezekiel in order to provide a "riddling" (*ainigmatōdōs*) story "concerning the just judgment in which the body and soul share (*ei koinōnei psuchē kai sōma*)."[41] Two disgruntled subjects of a king, one blind, one lame, decide to destroy the king's garden out of spite. They can only accomplish the affront working together: the blind man carrying the lame man telling the blind man where to go. When the king has them arrested and tried separately, each man insists he cannot be guilty

---

37. Epiphanius, *Ancoratus* 76.1 (GCS n.F. 10.1:95).

38. Epiphanius does mention "Apollinarians" (Ἀπολλινάριοι) in his digressive list of heresies (*Ancoratus* 13.8 [GCS n.F. 10.1:22]), but not in the portions of the treatise (*Ancoratus* 76–81 [GCS n.F. 10.1:95–102]) against Christians who believe that the divinity of the Son took the place of a human mind in the incarnation; much of this argument, however, is elaborated and reproduced in *Panarion* 77, his chapter against the Apollinarians.

39. Epiphanius, *Ancoratus* 83.1 (GCS n.F. 10.1:103).

40. Origen: *Ancoratus* 87.2 (GCS n.F. 10.1:107–8); Hieracas: *Ancoratus* 82.3 (GCS n.F. 10.1:102–3).

41. Epiphanius, *Panarion* 64.70.6 (GCS 31:515–16). Epiphanius is one of our main sources for the *Apocryphon of Ezekiel*; see James Mueller, *The Five Fragments of the Apocryphon of Ezekiel: A Critical Study*, Journal for the Study of the Pseudepigrapha 5 (Sheffield: JSOT Press, 1994); and Richard Bauckham, "The Parable of the Royal Wedding Feast (Matthew 22:1–14) and the Parable of the Lame Man and the Blind Man (*Apocryphon of Ezekiel*)," *JBL* 115 (1996): 471–88.

because he could not alone accomplish the act of vandalism.[42] The wise judge then has the two men tortured together until they admit joint guilt for the crime. Epiphanius understands this tale as a parable of the sinful body and soul: "So the body is joined to the soul, and the soul to the body, in the proof of their deed, and the final judgment is of both the body and the soul, for their works, both good and petty."[43] Each element of the human person is distinct, but their moral responsibility before God, "the king," is unified.

This lesson of embodied moral unity came out just as forcefully, if less colorfully, in the *Ancoratus:*

> How also can a soul be judged alone (according to the logic of the heresies) without the body which sinned with it being present? For such a soul would speak against God's judgment, saying that the sins were committed by the body.... For it can say: I have not sinned, but the body! For from the time I left out of the body, I have not fornicated nor committed adultery, nor stolen nor killed nor worshipped idols nor have I done anything evil or ruinous. And its defense will be found to be well spoken! What shall we say when it defends itself so well?[44]

Of course, as Epiphanius points out, the body can mount the same defense: "Sin came from that soul; I was not its cause! For since I was released and that one [i.e., the soul] stood apart from me, I have not committed adultery, I have not fornicated, I have not stolen, I have not worshipped idols, nor have I committed any such offenses!"[45] The moral calculus for Epiphanius is clear: those discrete elements that *together* sinned against God must face punishment together: "On this account, as the body and the soul became one united person (*sunthetos heis anthrōpos*) out of God, again the righteous Judge will raise the body

---

42. Epiphanius, *Panarion* 64.70.6–16 (GCS 31:516–17).

43. Epiphanius, *Panarion* 64.70.17 (GCS 31:517). See also Epiphanius, *Panarion* 64.63.9 (GCS 31:502): "The same commonality of the body and soul is one, and one activity" (μία γὰρ καὶ ἡ αὐτὴ κοινωνία τοῦ τε σώματος καὶ τῆς ψυχῆς καὶ μία ἐργασία).

44. Epiphanius, *Ancoratus* 87.4–6 (GCS n.F. 10.1:108). Epiphanius repeats this argument in *Panarion* 64.71.9 (GCS 31:519).

45. Epiphanius, *Ancoratus* 88.7 (GCS n.F. 10.1:109).

and he give his soul to him. And in this way, God's judgment will be righteous, with both sharing in either the punishment through sin or virtue through piety and the recompense that is going to be given to the saints."[46] That body and soul are discrete elements of the human—separable even—is clear to Epiphanius. It is not *impossible*, he says, for God to raise the body alone for judgment: unsouled bodies rise in the Old Testament to demonstrate precisely this power of God's.[47] But the question is one of moral justice: like the lame man and the blind man, the body and soul together acted against God, and so they must face judgment or reward together in the resurrection. What's more, the *same* flesh and the *same* soul that sinned (or, to be sure, that fasted and kept vigils) must appear before God in judgment, and not, as the heretics claim, "another body instead of the one that fell."[48] The moral unity of the human person also requires a moral *continuity* of that person, in this life and the next.[49]

This moral unity and continuity of the human person patterns and models Epiphanius's Trinitarian theology as well. Epiphanius replicates this precise pattern of discrete elements active in a single, continuous unity of being in his discussion of the three members of the Trinity. Father, Son, and Holy Spirit, he insists throughout the *Ancoratus* and in the chapters of the *Panarion* written against Trinitarian heretics, are unquestionably *homoousios*, consubstantial. What Scripture ascribes to one member of the Trinity—light, goodness, wisdom, and so on—must also be ascribed to the other two members of the Trinity.

---

46. Epiphanius, *Ancoratus* 88.8 (GCS n.F. 10.1:109–10). Clark, *Origenist Controversy*, 89, clearly identifies these moral stakes in Epiphanius's refutation of Origen in the *Ancoratus*.

47. Epiphanius, *Ancoratus* 88.1–5 (GCS n.F. 10.1:108–9); Epiphanius repeats and expands this argument in *Panarion* 64.71.9–13 (GCS 31:519–20).

48. Epiphanius, *Ancoratus* 89.1 (GCS n.F. 10.1:110).

49. On the composite nature of humans in the resurrection in an earlier period, see Taylor G. Petrey, *Resurrecting Parts: Early Christians on Desire, Reproduction, and Sexual Difference*, Routledge Studies in the Early Christian World (London: Routledge, 2016), esp. 52–69 (on Athenagoras).

Yet, at the same time, they can only be understood as discrete and fully autonomous agents united *into* one. Early in the *Ancoratus* he writes:

> Saying "of the same substance" (*homoousion*) is the common link of faith. For if you say "of the same substance" (*to homoousion*) you have broken Sabellius's power:[50] for wherever there is "of the same substance" (*homoousion*) it is indicative of a single reality (*mias hupostaseōs*). But also it means that the Father is independently real (*enupostaton*) and the Son is independently real (*enupostatos*) and the Holy Spirit is independently real (*enupostaton*).[51]

In the *Ancoratus* Epiphanius does not clearly distinguish between *ousia* and *hypostasis* (as he will a few years later in the *Panarion,* and as will become standard Nicene orthodoxy following the Council of Constantinople). From the perspective of metaphysical theology, crafted into terminological precision by the Cappadocians, Epiphanius lacks clarity. When we recall Epiphanius's discussion of the human agent—a moral unity crafted out of discrete elements (body/soul)—his Trinitarian logic makes a different kind of sense.

The members of the Trinity must form a united whole, they must come together out of one substance (*ousia*) into a single "reality" (*hypostasis*). At the same time, they are each "independently real" (*enhypostatos*), and cannot be "elided" into each other.[52] This particular theological term—*enhypostatos*—is rare in fourth-century theology, but is a

---

50. "Sabellianism" had become a code word by the mid-300s for an overly exuberant form of Nicene Trinitarianism that overemphasized the identity of Father, Son, and Holy Spirit (as in the writings of Marcellus of Ancrya).

51. Epiphanius, *Ancoratus* 6.4 (GCS n.F. 10.1:12).

52. Epiphanius, *Ancoratus* 7.3 (GCS n.F. 10.1:13–14): "The Trinity is not an elision (οὐ συναλοιφὴ ἡ τριάς), nor does anything stand apart from this self-same unity (τῆς ἰδίας αὐτῆς μονάδος), in the reality (ἐν ὑποστάσει) of perfection the Father is perfect, the Son is perfect, the Holy Spirit is perfect: Father and Son and Holy Spirit." Kim renders συναλοιφή as "coalescence" in his translation of the *Ancoratus*. See also *Ancoratus* 5.6, 6.3, 6.10, 10.7 (GCS n.F. 10.1:11–13, 18); and *Panarion* 76.6.4 (GCS 37:346): "And this is the one Godhead, one God, one Lord, Father and Son and Holy Spirit, and no elision (οὐ συναλοιφή τις) of the Son into the Father, nor the Holy Spirit, but the Father is Father, and the Son Son and the Holy Spirit Holy Spirit, three Perfects, one Godhead, one God, one Lord."

favorite term of art for Epiphanius precisely because of how it articulates the dynamic oneness and threeness of the Trinity.[53] Like body and soul—independently real but "united" (*sunthetoi*) by God—the Father, Son, and Holy Spirit are at the same time one *hypostasis* and *enhypostatoi*. This term allows Epiphanius to navigate between the "Sabellians," who do not distinguish enough between the members of the Trinity, and the "Arians," who distinguish too much:

> The father is independently real (*enupostatos*), the Son is independently real (*enupostatos*), the Holy Spirit is independently real (*enupostatos*), and there is no elision (*ou sunaloiphē*) in the Trinity, as Sabellius thought, nor is it alienated (*ēlloiōmenē*) from its own eternity and glory, as chatterbox Arius taught, but the Trinity is eternally Trinity and the Trinity never takes any addition.[54]

Like the human being who always exists as the total unity of his discrete parts, the Trinity suffers neither "elision" nor "addition," remaining a total unity comprising three independently real persons in one being.[55]

In the *Ancoratus* Epiphanius plays with the language of conjoining that makes sense of his Trinitarian theology and his anthropology

---

53. Benjamin Gleede, *The Development of the Term ἐνυπόστατος from Origen to John of Damascus*, Supplements to *Vigiliae Christianae* 113 (Leiden: Brill, 2012), who suggests (15) that the term may have been coined by Origen, notes that it appears sporadically in the early fourth century; he then remarks (35) that "Epiphanius of Salamis was really fond of the term: In his two most important works, *Ancoratus* and *Panarion*, written between 374 and 377, ἐνυπόστατος occurs 74 times, of which only four references belong [in] a non-trinitarian context." To compare the use of the term in these works of Epiphanius with a slightly later author's corpus (who, Gleede notes, was "again really fond of our term"), in all of Cyril of Alexandria's much more expansive corpus, it occurs fifty-one times (38). See Kim, *Epiphanius*, 131 n. 132.

54. Epiphanius, *Panarion* 62.3.5 (GCS 31:392). As Epiphanius continues in this passage, he also asserts the three *hypostaseis* of the Trinity, but we can see how theologically there is little difference from his stance in the *Ancoratus*. See similarly his use of *enhypostatos* against the "patripassionist" Noetians (*Panarion* 57.4.1–2 [GCS 31:348]).

55. Gleede, *Development*, 41, notes that fourth-century Trinitarian theologians used the term quite differently from later, christologically minded controversialists in the wake of the Council of Chalcedon.

(my awkward translation deliberately replicates Epiphanius's rhythm here):

> The Trinity is holy, the Trinity is co-holy (*sunagia*); the Trinity is existent, the Trinity is coexistent (*sunuparkta*); the Trinity is uniform (*emmorpha*), the Trinity is conform (*summorpha*); the Trinity is active, the Trinity is coactive (*sunerga*); the Trinity is independently real (*enupostata*) and commonly real (*sunupostata*), in common being with each other (*allēllois sunonta*); the Trinity itself is called holy, the Trinity being one (*onta*), a single common voice (*mia sumphōnia*), a single Godhead of the same substance (*tēs autēs ousias*) of the same Godhead of the same independent reality (*tēs autēs hupostaseōs*).[56]

Besides spinning a melodious, almost hymnic description of the Trinity, Epiphanius marks in clear, if repetitive, terms the simultaneous distinctiveness and unity of the persons of the Godhood. His goal is not terminological precision, but his repetition of *sun-* (with) compounds throughout this passage highlights how the three persons are united without losing their threeness, and the common operations of the Godhead.[57]

Epiphanius relates this logic of unified divine difference back to his understanding of human embodied difference through discussions of the incarnate humanity of Christ and discussion of the "image of God" in humans. For much of the middle sections of the *Ancoratus*, Epiphanius zigzags between discussion of the absolute consubstantiality of the Father and Son and the true humanity of Christ incarnate. He insists that the Son was not made, but begotten, which leads to a discussion of Christ's human birth from Mary;[58] from a detailed discussion (to which I return in a moment) of the necessity of Christ possessing both

---

56. Epiphanius, *Ancoratus* 67.4 (GCS n.F. 10.1:82).

57. Indeed, the doubled insistence on unity and differentiation in the *Ancoratus* makes it easy enough for Epiphanius to shift from one-*hypostasis* to three-*hypostasis* language in the *Panarion*, as at *Panarion* 73.36.4 (GCS 37:310): "For 'homo' signifies that they are two with respect to *hypostasis*, but not different in nature" (τὸ γὰρ ὁμο δύο μὲν ὑποστάσεών ἐστι σημαντικόν, οὐκ ἀλλοτρίων <δὲ> τῇ φύσει). See Kösters, *Trinitätslehre*, 371–73; and Kim, *Epiphanius*, 121–25.

58. Epiphanius, *Ancoratus* 29–33 (GCS n.F. 10.1:37–43).

body and soul, Epiphanius returns to his argument that the Son was always fully God.[59] He returns eventually to the "begotten not made" argument (in which he digresses into the rather specious "hatching" etymology of Proverbs 8:22 that I discussed in chapter 4) and then suddenly asks in the voice of a "quarrelsome" opponent: "Why do you talk about 'the body'?"[60] allowing him to turn, once again, to the incarnation. About two-thirds of the way through the treatise he breaks into the ostensible topic of his text—the divinity of the Holy Spirit[61]—before returning once more to Christ's incarnate body. The incarnate body keeps irrupting into the Trinitarian discussion not merely as a digression, but as an important elucidation.

Epiphanius insists that incarnate Christ was a "complete human" (*anthrōpos teleios*),[62] and by this phrase Epiphanius means Christ possessed all the requisite parts of a human: "So the Word became flesh not apart from a soul, not apart from the whole system (*ouk ektos pasēs pragmateias*)."[63] Just as the human being is a "composite" (*suntheton*) of parts working in unison, so is the incarnate Word.[64] Those who claim that Christ was merely the Word wrapped in flesh, without a soul or a mind, are denying that Christ was a real human being: "So what is a human being? Soul, body, mind, and whatever else there is. So what did the Lord come to save? The complete human being (*anthrōpon teleion*), certainly! So then he took upon himself all those things (*panta*)

---

59. Epiphanius, *Ancoratus* 34–37 (GCS n.F. 10.1:43–47).

60. Epiphanius, *Ancoratus* 51.1 (GCS n.F. 10.1:60).

61. Epiphanius, *Ancoratus* 65–73 (GCS n.F. 10.1:77–93), most of which is reproduced as the bulk of *Panarion* 74, his chapter against the Pneumatomachoi.

62. Epiphanius, *Ancoratus* 75.8 (twice) (GCS n.F. 10.1:95).

63. Epiphanius, *Ancoratus* 78.2 (GCS n.F. 10.1:97). See also Epiphanius, *De mensuris et ponderibus* 35 (Dean, *Weights and Measures*, 51–54 [Eng.] and 64c-66a [Syr.]), in an extended series of allegories of the "ark of the covenant," including an understanding of the ark as "his perfect human nature" (*methbarnshanutha' dileh mshamlaitha'*), which presumably translates the Greek ἄνθρωπος τέλειος (Dean, *Weights and Measures*, 65d); and *De XII gemmis* (Blake and Vis, *Epiphanius*, 126) likewise describes Christ as "perfect in every respect as to this our human nature" (see also Blake and Vis, *Epiphanius*, 146).

64. Epiphanius, *Ancoratus* 78.4 (GCS n.F. 10.1:98).

completely."⁶⁵ Epiphanius makes fun of heretics who worried that if too many elements are present in Christ, God will end up becoming more than a Trinity, loaded up with too many parts. Even if these misguided heretics replace the "mind" with the spirit of God, they must still contend with Christ's composite reality:

> If the mind is the Spirit and the Spirit the mind, as even they suppose, but the soul is a different reality (*hupostasis*) from the mind and from the spirit, no longer are two realities (*hupostaseis*) in a human being collected into a single reality (*miai sunagomenai hupostasei*), no longer one independently real soul and one independently real body (*ouketi enupostatos monē psuchē kai enupostaton to sōma*) but then we find four: real mind, real soul, real spirit, real body.⁶⁶

There may even be more than four, Epiphanius continues:⁶⁷ the important thing is that whatever parts a human has, Christ has them too. In fact, his unified composition is what Epiphanius finds crucial. How do all of these "realities" (*hupostaseis*) create one single reality (*hypostasis*)? Epiphanius can't say: "It is not necessary to be overly inquisitive," he scolds.⁶⁸ Interestingly, here is one of the few places in Epiphanius's corpus where he uses the term *enhypostatos* to speak of the independent reality of the human body and soul.⁶⁹ The overlap with his Trinitarian language, I'm suggesting, is not accidental. Christ, in his incarnate

---

65. Epiphanius, *Ancoratus* 78.5 (GCS n.F. 10.1:98).
66. Epiphanius, *Ancoratus* 77.5 (GCS n.F. 10.1:96–97); see also Epiphanius, *Panarion* 69.66.6 (GCS 37:214) (against the Arians), speaking of Christ's body in the resurrection: "And again he fulfilled the complete resurrection in the same Godhead, in the same soul, in the same holy body, finally unifying the entire dispensation into one spiritual unity, into one unified Godhead, into one dispensation, into one perfection."
67. Epiphanius, *Ancoratus* 77.6 (GCS n.F. 10.1:97): Epiphanius (probably, at this point, a bit facetiously) cites the "interior human" of Romans 7:22 and the "exterior person" of 2 Corinthians 4:16 as two more possible *hypostaseis*.
68. Epiphanius, *Ancoratus* 77.6 (GCS n.F. 10.1:97): οὐ χρὴ δὲ καὶ πολυπραγμονεῖν.
69. In only one place does Epiphanius use *enhypostatos* apart from his discussions of Trinity and incarnation: he characterizes the Syrian Basilides as claiming that "there never was 'evil,' nor has there been a root of evil, nor is 'evil' independently real (οὔτε ἐνυπόστατον τὸ κακόν ἐστιν)" (*Panarion* 24.6.1 [GCS n.F. 10.1:263]).

form, embodies both the unified reality of the Trinity and the unified reality of the human person:[70] the same logic undergirds both, a logic of composite parts united into a whole operating with one will and one morality.

Humanity's creation "in the image" also irrupts into the text of the *Ancoratus*, breaking apart discussions of the Trinity, and receives more elaboration in the *Panarion*. While discussing the divinity of the Spirit in the opening chapters of the *Ancoratus*, and the difference between the Creator and creation, Epiphanius cites Genesis 1:26 and notes that "every human has the image [of God] as a gift (*charismati*), but no one will be made like his own master."[71] Later, when discussing the plural and unified nature of the Trinity, Epiphanius again invokes Genesis 1:26. The particular form of the locution—"Let us make the human being in our image and likeness"—shows both the plurality of the Godhead ("us") but also its unity (the three members share a single "image and likeness").[72]

Later in the treatise, Epiphanius is drawn once more to the image of God in humans. Here, following a discussion of the true unity of Father and Son, and the truth of the prophets, Epiphanius discusses the reality and specificity of the "image of God" in humans. He denounces, first, those Christians who claim that the "image" is located in any particular part of the human: the soul, the body, the mind, the virtue, even in baptism.[73] Epiphanius refuses to locate the image of God, and will do no more than insist that the image is *in* the human person and—what's more—it cannot be taken away once given by God.[74] Mark

---

70. So Kösters, *Trinitätslehre*, 111, notes that "die Inkarnation für [Epiphanius] das Zentrum des Heilsgeschehens darstellt."

71. Epiphanius, *Ancoratus* 11.7 (GCS n.F. 10.1:20).

72. Epiphanius, *Ancoratus* 28.1–3 (GCS n.F. 10.1:36–37).

73. Epiphanius, *Ancoratus* 55.5–6, 56.1–5 (GCS n.F. 10.1:64–66).

74. Epiphanius, *Ancoratus* 57.2 (GCS n.F. 10.1:66). Here (in *Ancoratus* 57.1–2 [GCS n.F. 10.1:66]) Epiphanius also distinguishes between the "image," which humans possess, and the "nature," which God possesses. Much of this argument is taken up again in *Panarion* 70, Epiphanius's chapter against the "Audians," or those who claim that if

DelCogliano places Epiphanius's "image" arguments in a larger theological context and concludes that Epiphanius ascribed "the image of God to the whole human being, not a particular part."[75] Indeed, I would extend this analysis even further and suggest that the "image of God" humans have received lies precisely in the combinatory logic of parts—body, soul, mind, virtue, and so forth—that operate as a moral unit.

When I say that Epiphanius locates the divine image in the composite moral unity of the human being, I do not mean to suggest that he speaks in an ontological sense, but rather a moral or even epistemological one. That is, he does not seek to understand the metaphysical truth of God's Trinitarian *being* in this combinatory logic of parts that he also sees operative in the human being. After all, each member of the Trinity is self-sufficiently divine (*enhypostatos*) in a way that the parts of a human being (body, soul, mind, and so on) are not. Epiphanius explicitly disavows this ontological identification of divine and human "parts" in the *Ancoratus*.[76] He decries the believer who wrongly "models the divine on us (*aph' hēmōn to theion apeikasas*), saying to himself that as I have body, soul, and human spirit, so also is the divinity. The Father is so to speak the form (*eidos*), the Son is like the soul in the person, and the Spirit just like the breath (*empneon*) through the person."[77] Epiphanius objects to the strict identification of parts—Father/form, Son/soul, Spirit/breath—precisely because this patterning misinterprets the way in which the

---

humans are embodied and made in God's image, then God too must possess some kind of body. There, too, he refuses to say *where* the image is located, only that it cannot be isolated in the human person and cannot be lost once given by God. See Ayres, *Nicaea and Its Legacy*, 326.

75. Mark DelCogliano, "Situating Sarapion's Sorrow: The Anthropomorphite Controversy as the Historical and Theological Context of Cassian's Tenth Conference on Pure Prayer," *Cistercian Studies Quarterly* 38.4 (2003): 407 (and 401).

76. In order to try to come to terms with how humans can possess God's "image" but be of a different "nature," Epiphanius tries to explain the analogical relationship of God to humanity. Just as Christ could gesture to a round loaf of bread—which, obviously, was entirely dissimilar to him—and say, "This is my body," so (he suggests) humans should understand "the image": Epiphanius, *Ancoratus* 57.1–6 (GCS n.F. 10.1:66–67).

77. Epiphanius, *Ancoratus* 81.5–6 (GCS n.F. 10.1:102).

human is modeled on the divine. Humans in their composite nature are not modeled directly on the divine *being*, but rather the divine *activity*. Just as the body and soul together must stand in judgment for how they have behaved in their composite activity, so too the *enhypostatoi hypostasis* of the Trinity is not a composite being but a united activity: "a single divinity and one will and a single lordship" (*mia theotēs kai hen thelēma kai mia kuriotēs*).[78] The logic of partness, for Epiphanius, is thus a moral logic, a way of understanding how unified, discrete elements should act in concert. The human being (body and soul) should ideally reflect and enact the unified will (*thelēma*) of the members of the Trinity.

DIVERSITY

In the *Ancoratus* and *Panarion*, Epiphanius's concern for moral unity links his understanding of the human person—a composite being (body/soul) morally continuous from its creation through its resurrection—to his understanding of the Trinity—a composite reality (Father/Son/Holy Spirit) totally united in its operations and "essence" but comprising distinctive (*enhypostatoi*) persons. This theory of moral continuity and the union of discrete elements ties together Epiphanius's multiple theological concerns, from the image of God in humans to the incarnate nature of Christ to the resurrection state of the human being. Moreover, this overarching theological logic of moral unity and composite being can help explain the heresiological logic at work in the production of the *Panarion* (at least in part).

We often do not pause, in our considerations of Epiphanius, to ask why he should produce such a singular text. We inscribe him into a heresiographic lineage, from Justin Martyr to Irenaeus to Hippolytus and so on;[79] but upon closer examination his text is formally similar but

---

78. Epiphanius, *Panarion* 57.4.9 (GCS 31:349). I am extraordinarily grateful to Mark DelCogliano for pressing me to clarify this distinction.

79. So Aline Pourkier, *L'hérésiologie chez Épiphane de Salamine*, Christianisme Antique 4 (Paris: Beauchesne, 1992).

ideologically rather different from these earlier writings against heresies.[80] It is true that, even in the second century, we hear of texts written "against all of the heresies which have come to be" (*suntagma kata pasōn tōn gegenēmenōn haireseōn*).[81] Yet "all" the heresies in the second and early third centuries seem to comprise a specific list of contemporary theological "others" (with roots, to be sure, in the apostolic and subapostolic past).[82] In the third century, Hippolytus's massive *Elenchos* greatly expanded the scope of this enterprise, reaching back to catalogue the errors of Greek philosophy as well historical and contemporary heresies. Even if we grant Hippolytus totalizing pretensions similar to (and influential upon) Epiphanius, his rhetorical strategy is markedly different. Hippolytus seeks to protect and isolate the tradition of orthodoxy by casting heretics as totally beyond the Christian pale: they are not Christians at all, but rather twisted philosophers and crypto-pagans.[83] Epiphanius, on the other hand, incorporates all of

---

80. Young Richard Kim, "The Imagined Worlds of Epiphanius of Cyprus" (PhD diss., University of Michigan, 2006), 8–21, discusses the *Panarion* in light of earlier heresiography; see also Kim, "The Transformation of Heresiology in the *Panarion* of Epiphanius of Cyprus," in *Shifting Frontiers in Late Antiquity*, ed. Hugh Elton and Geoffrey Greatrex (Burlington, VT: Ashgate, 2015), 53–65. See also Hervé Inglebert, *Interpretatio Christiana: Les mutations des savoirs (cosmographie, géographie, ethnographie, histoire) dans l'Antiquité chrétienne, 30–630 après J.-C.*, Collection des Études Augustiniennes, Série Antiquité 166 (Paris: Institut d'Études Augustiniennes, 2001), 393–461; and Averil Cameron, "How to Read Heresiology," in *The Cultural Turn in Late Ancient Studies: Gender, Asceticism, and Historiography*, ed. Dale B. Martin and Patricia Cox Miller (Durham, NC: Duke University Press, 2005), 193–211.

81. Justin Martyr, *Apologia* 1.26.8; text in *Iustini Martyris Apologiae pro Christianis*, ed. Miroslav Marcovich, Patristische Texte und Studien 38 (Berlin: De Gruyter, 1999), 71. Most historians understand Justin to be referring here to a (lost) text of his own, although Geoffrey S. Smith, *Guilt by Association: Heresy Catalogues in Early Christianity* (Oxford: Oxford University Press, 2014), 49–86, suggests Justin merely possesses a text that he is "advertising" to the philosophical emperors.

82. On the invention of the "technology" of the heresy catalogue among early Christians, see now Smith, *Guilt by Association*.

83. See Clemens Scholten, "Die Funktion der Häresienabwehr in der Alten Kirche," *VC* 66 (2012): 229–68; and Todd S. Berzon, *Classifying Christians: Ethnography, Heresiology, and the Limits of Knowledge in Late Antiquity* (Oakland: University of California Press, 2016).

heresy into his capacious Christian history (including, at multiple points, Greek philosophy). From Adam onward, truth and error have existed side by side, mirror images of each other, mutually productive and destructive.

Given its vast scope, and its deliberate inclusion of both extinct and only partially verified heresies, the *Panarion* can hardly claim to be a functional text, a handbook used to identify or even refute real-life erring Christians.[84] It is rather a statement on human history, morality, and divisibility, a story of how humans have moved away, and continue to move away, from unity with each other and with God, viewed through the lens of "heresies and infamous human ideas (*kakadoxou gnomes anthrōpeias*) sown by erring men (*andrōn*) into the world from the time when humanity was formed on the earth until our own day."[85] Thematically, the *Panarion* more closely resembles Augustine's *City of God* than Irenaeus's *Against Heresies* inasmuch as the *Panarion* is an account that connects individual human action and belief to the origins and ultimate destiny of all of humanity. Indeed, the treatise *De fide*, which Epiphanius attached to the *Panarion* as an epilogue, begins with an image of the pious Christians who have learned truth from error arriving, weary and grateful, at "the holy Jerusalem,"[86] the singular bride of Christ who is also "this holy city of God."[87]

Epiphanius's view of humanity, as articulated in the *Panarion*, operates according to the same theological and moral logic as his accounts of human and divine unity outlined above. That is, human beings should ideally comprise an aggregate moral unit made up of discrete

---

84. The desire for more functional heresiography led to the anonymous epitomization of the *Panarion* into the *Anakephalaioses* and later especially Latin "handbooks"; see Judith McClure, "Handbooks against Heresy in the West, from the Late Fourth to the Late Seventh Centuries," *JTS* n.s. 30 (1979): 186–97.

85. Epiphanius, *Panarion* proem II 2.3 (GCS n.F. 10.1:170). See Kim, *Epiphanius*, 80: "The *Panarion*, a quintessential heresiology, was also a work of history."

86. Epiphanius, *De fide* 1.6 (GCS 37:497).

87. Epiphanius, *De fide* 2.9 (GCS 37:498): τῆς ἁγίας πόλεως θεοῦ, a phrase he draws from Ps 86:3.

agents ("orthodox Christians"). The entire *Panarion*, as Epiphanius describes it near the end, is about how the "gaps, cleavages, fissures, and divisions which have arisen in the world" have disrupted this ideal.[88] As in his articulation of individual human moral unity, Epiphanius invokes the unity of God in the Trinity and of Christ in the incarnation to model the ideal corporate unity of humans in the church:

> In Godhead therefore the Father and Son are one; in humanity the Son and the disciples are one, led (on account of the honor of the disciples' call to the indescribability of his love of humanity) into the single unity of adoption (*eis mian henotēta huiothesias*), through the goodwill of the Father and the Son and the Holy Spirit.[89]

These layers of composite unity—Trinity, incarnation, church ("the disciples")—work vertically to connect morality on earth to the transcendent salvation of divinity.

The narrative of heresy in the *Panarion* illustrates this composite/unitary model of human morality: individual agents (heretics) are responsible for breaking the composite unity of the faithful. Not surprisingly, given the logical relationship he has articulated between the Trinity and the church, we see this breaking of the faith of the unified church most starkly depicted in Epiphanius's chapters against Trinitarian heretics. Already in the *Ancoratus*, Epiphanius had sketched the general relationship between the divine unity of the Trinity and the unity (or disunity) of human believers: "For those who have not received the Holy Spirit have not learned the depths of God and they have been torn off into these heresies and into the quarrels of schisms on account of a pretext. For having abandoned truth they have marched down many paths, here and there imagining one thing after another."[90] Even though the *Panarion* attacks a diverse range of "wrong" beliefs and

---

88. Epiphanius, *Panarion* 70.15.6 (GCS 37:249). See Elias Moutsoulas, "Der Begriff 'Häresie' bei Epiphanius von Salamis," *SP* 7 (1966): 368: "Wie das Christentum von Anfang an in der Weltgeschichte war, so auch wie Häresien."
89. Epiphanius, *Panarion* 69.69.10 (GCS 37:318).
90. Epiphanius, *Ancoratus* 14.4 (GCS n.F. 10.1:24).

practices, the consubstantial Trinity, according to Epiphanius, always stands at its center as a model of correct human unity:

> Just so also in all places, while making my treatise against all heresies (*kata pasōn tōn haireseōn poioumenos ton logon*), I have shown that God is one, who made and created everything, the Father of our Lord Jesus Christ; and his Only-Begotten Son is one, our Lord and Savior and God; and his Holy Spirit is one, a single, holy, and consubstantial Trinity (*mia trias hagia kai homoousios*), from which all things have been well created.[91]

The moral unity of individual Christians, as well as the corporate moral unity of the church, should rightfully embody that divine goodness and oneness.

Trinitarian heretics, on Epiphanius's account, bear a particular responsibility for disrupting the moral unity of the one church. One of the longest chapters in the *Panarion* is against Arius and the "Ariomaniacs," and a great deal of this chapter is given over to the precise ways that Arius both misunderstood the consubstantial Trinity and how his misunderstanding spread and fractured the communal church.[92] Arius's breaking apart of the unified, consubstantial Trinity leads directly into his breaking apart of the unified, catholic church:

> Then, from this single passage [Prov 8:22], he drove his own wickedly inclined mind onto many wicked paths; he and his successors put their hand to making ten thousand blasphemies—and more!—against the Son of God and against the Holy Spirit. They broke the front line (so to speak) (*parelusan de hōs eipein to stiphos*) and the unity (*homonian*) of the holy and orthodox faith and church.[93]

The term *stiphos* here can have military connotations (a unified front line of troops) or a more metaphorical sense of a "mass"; either way, the

---

91. Epiphanius, *Panarion* 36.4.3–4 (GCS 31:49).

92. Epiphanius actually begins his account of Arius's perfidy in the previous chapter, against the Melitians: *Panarion* 68.4.1 (GCS 37:143).

93. Epiphanius, *Panarion* 69.12.4 (GCS 37:162). The translation of παρέλυσαν τὸ στῖφος follows Frank Williams's translation.

image is vivid: a unified body of Christians blasted apart by the heretical blasphemies of a single man. The model of a single bad actor wreaking havoc and disrupting the unified body of Christ does not, of course, originate with Epiphanius. Its roots reach back into the letters of Paul, where the spirit of God that unites all the faithful in Christ can be corrupted by any one of its members (1 Corinthians).[94] The *Panarion* depicts this moral panic on the broadest possible canvas, berating those who willfully blaspheme the Trinity from creation to the present day.

In another chapter Epiphanius rails against the "Anomoians," those radical anti-Nicene Christians (according to Epiphanius) who preach that the persons of the Trinity are "dissimilar" (*anomoios*). Epiphanius proclaims that it is the Anomoian heretic who makes himself "other" (*anomoios*) from the body of pious Christians through his heterodoxy:

> How much will my middling mind have to strengthen itself to speak to you, O "Other" (*ō Anomoie*)? How fittingly you happen to be "Other" (*Anomoios*), you who deviate from the manners and opinion of people who have acquired union with God (*tēn sunesin tou theou kektēmenōn*) and who have true faith. For you haven't become "other" (*anomoios*) from humans by progressing toward good, but you became other from the sons of the church of God (*anomoios egenou tōn huiōn tēs tou theou ekklēsias*) by turning aside from the way of truth: taking as a pretext the Son of God who is actually like his Father and saying that he is "other" from the Father you become "other," inheriting this label (*touto to onoma*), no longer like (*homoios*) those who remain saved.[95]

Just as the individual human bears the image of God in the moral unity of his body and soul, so too the "sons of the church of God" likewise bear that image in their composite moral unity (on analogy with God, the "sons of the church of God" are *homoousioi*). The Anomoian rejects God's Trinitarian unity and thereby becomes alien to the moral

---

94. Dale B. Martin, *The Corinthian Body* (New Haven, CT: Yale University Press, 1995).

95. Epiphanius, *Panarion* 76.10.1–2 (GCS 37:351).

community of Christians formed and united in God's unified Trinitarian image.

If heretical Trinitarian beliefs potentially fracture and disrupt the unified moral community of Christians, then orthodox belief, enacted in ritual and creed, creates the moral unity of Christian believers. In his refutation of the Audians, Epiphanius notes how important it is that all Christians celebrate Easter on the same day, recalling earlier times when observance varied across the Christian world:

> But under Constantine, through the bishops' zeal, the division was united into a single harmony (*sunēnōthē ... to schisma eis mian homonoian*); what, therefore, is more important and most graceful than to rescue a people for God from the corners of the earth on a single day, to be of one voice and keep vigils and to conduct the same days equally, in vigils and entreaties and harmony and service, with fasting and xerophagy and purity and all the other good things pleasing to God on this all-holy day?[96]

Multiple moral unities are enacted in the observance of Easter on the correct date: the proper balance of body and soul (in the strict Lenten renunciations); the unity of the church in "all corners of the earth" in proper worship; even the unity of empire, brought together under one pious ruler (Constantine). And, above all of these bodies unified in prayerful worship, the unitary God, the three-in-one.

The most striking enactment of the formation of multiple elements into a composite unity—of God, church, even empire—for Epiphanius is the recitation of the proper creed confessing the Trinity. At the end of his refutation of the "Pneumatomachoi," Epiphanius produces the Nicene Creed as the final "antidote" to their heretical poison:

> But see from the confession itself (*ap' autēs tēs homologias*) that not anything will be found in it that they are saying, those who blaspheme against the Spirit, those "Spirit-Fighters" and strangers to its gift and sanctification. For straightaway the creed confesses (*hē ekthesis homologei*) and does not deny: "For we believe in one God the Father, Almighty." But "we believe"

---

96. Epiphanius, *Panarion* 70.14.3–4 (GCS 37:247).

is not said by itself (*haplōs*), but the faith is in God "and in one Lord Jesus Christ." And this is not said by itself, but the faith is in God "and in the Holy Spirit." And this is not said by itself, but in a single glorification (*eis mian doxologian*) and in a single unity of Godhead (*mian henōsin theotētos*) and a single consubstantiality (*mian homoousiotēta*), in three perfects, but a single Godhead, a single essence, a single glorification, a single Lordship from "we believe" and "we believe" and "we believe." And here their argument has collapsed.[97]

The creed itself performs the same moral unity that it defends in God: composite parts (particular words) united together into a single confession of correct faith. By reciting these morally unifying words, the communion of the church of God is formed. Those heretics who do not recognize the moral unity of the creed are excluded from the moral unity of the church, since they fail to recognize in that creed the moral unity of the Godhead.

Recognizing the creed as a rhetorical performance of the very same theology of moral unity it professes, we understand Epiphanius's repeated insistence on creedal precision. In the decades prior to the composition of the *Ancoratus*, diverse councils of bishops had met to debate how best to interpret the faith promulgated at Nicaea. The multiplicity of creeds out of these various synods not only attests to the multiplicity of theological positions in the mid-fourth century, but also to a growing fluidity of theological positions that allowed individual communities to move away from a rigid insistence on one specific recitation of words.[98]

Epiphanius, however, sought to strengthen and enforce the Nicene Creed. We no longer possess his letter to Basil of Caesarea, but apparently (among other issues) he proposed making specific additions to the Nicene Creed to incorporate language about the Holy Spirit and the incarnation, the two theological issues at the center of the *Ancoratus*.[99]

---

97. Epiphanius, *Panarion* 74.14.6–8 (GCS 37:332).
98. Ayres, *Nicaea and Its Legacy*, 162–63.
99. Basil, *Ep.* 258.2 (PG 32:949); see my discussion above, n. 15.

The *Ancoratus* itself concludes with a recitation of two creeds, which Epiphanius frames as a patrimony passed down from "the holy fathers," that is, the apostles, to present-day bishops, who must also "hand this teaching over to your own children."[100] The first creed in our extant copies of the *Ancoratus* bears a striking similarity to the revised Nicene Creed that would be promulgated at the Council of Constantinople a few years later; most scholars assume it has been interpolated into manuscripts that originally contained the Nicene Creed of 325.[101] Then, in the closing chapter, Epiphanius includes an expanded version of the creed, presented because, "in our generation, some other heresies have reared their head in succession."[102] The recitation and passing on of this creed (which includes stronger language about Christ's incarnation and the divinity of the Holy Spirit) explicitly enact and reproduce the moral unity of the orthodox church:

> Because of this you and I and all the orthodox bishops and the entire collective holy catholic church, in response to heresies subsequently rising up, in this manner, in the faith established by those holy fathers, we say (especially to those approaching the holy laver), in order that they might profess and speak in this way.[103]

The creedal formation of a unified moral body of Christians, united in their faith in the full incarnation of Christ and the consubstantiality of the Trinity—indeed, reflecting those unified entities—stands as a bul-

---

100. Epiphanius, *Ancoratus* 118.5–6 (GCS n.F. 10.1:146). On the framing of theological filiation as reproductive, in reflection of the gendered filiation of the Trinity, see Virginia Burrus, *"Begotten Not Made": Conceiving Manhood in Late Antiquity*, Figurae (Stanford, CA: Stanford University Press, 2000).

101. So Kim, *Epiphanius of Cyprus*, 222–23 n. 4; and Kösters, *Trinitätslehre*, 322–23, following Bernd Weischer, "Die urpsrüngliche nikänische Form des ersten Glaubenssymbols im Ankyrōtos des Epiphanios von Salamis: Ein Beitrag um die Enstehung des konstantinopolitanischen Glaubenssymbols im Lichte neuester äthiopistischer Forschungen," *Theologie und Philosophie* 53.3 (1978): 407–14.

102. Epiphanius, *Ancoratus* 119.1 (GCS n.F. 10.1:147).

103. Epiphanius, *Ancoratus* 119.2 (GCS n.F. 10.1:147–48).

wark against the surge of heretical division, reproducing itself endlessly across time and space.

Another monastic theologian in the late fourth and early fifth centuries pondered the creed recited by Christians in communion as a means of understanding divine perfection and its relation to human salvation. As Catherine Chin has demonstrated, Rufinus of Aquileia in his *Commentary on the Apostles' Creed* emphasized the rhetorical fluidity of the reception of this (ostensibly) primeval creed based on its geographical location.[104] For Rufinus, this fluid recitation of faith mirrors the fluidity of human identity reflective of a particular, transformative relationship between God (in his Trinity) and the human (in his saved state). Whereas Epiphanius saw the creed as rhetorically enacting the moral continuity of the eternal church and the human being in their composite parts, Rufinus saw something very different: a theology of moral transformation characteristic of fourth-century interpreters of Origen. It is to this opposition between continuity and transformation, and Epiphanius's Origenist controversy, that I now turn.

HERESY

Many readers of Epiphanius view him as primarily a reactive polemicist with an inability to grasp complex concepts: that is, he is a controversialist rather than a theologian. Elizabeth Clark, in her remarkable book on the fourth-century Origenist controversy, notes that throughout his twenty years of opposition to Origen, Epiphanius consistently refuses to specify his understanding of "the image of God"; she concludes that "his adamance on this point appears simply as a reflex of his Biblical literalism."[105] When Epiphanius argues against Origenist interpretations of the body, Clark similarly notes: "Epiphanius is clearly

---

104. Catherine M. Chin, "Short Words on Earth: Theological Geography in Rufinus's *Commentary on the Apostles' Creed*," *JECS* 21 (2013): 391–412.

105. Clark, *Origenist Controversy*, 100–102 and 104.

more interested in pressing a literal reading of the Bible than in engaging in philosophical debate about the status of materiality."[106] Jon Dechow (probably one of Epiphanius's closest readers) chalks up Epiphanius's resistance to Origen's theology of the human body, soul, and image of God to his lack of "philosophical capacity,"[107] positing that Epiphanius was pandering to the "anti-philosophical and anti-speculative attitude of many of his fellow monks."[108] This objection to Epiphanius's theological writings, that they are not "philosophical," is fair if we understand the philosophical underpinnings of fourth-century theology to be primarily metaphysical: that is, concerned with articulating the connection between divine and human in language derived from the speculative or mystical traditions of Plato or Aristotle.

From another perspective, however, it is not quite accurate to tar Epiphanius's theology as "anti-philosophical," since it is shaped by a consistent and abiding concern for the moral life of humans. (As Clark also acknowledges, "One of Epiphanius's main objections to an anthropology that separates soul and body, either here or in the hereafter, is moral."[109]) The cultivation of a moral self was central to the philosophical life in antiquity,[110] a cultivation that was eagerly taken up and theologized by Christian monks in the fourth and fifth centuries.[111] For Epiphanius, this moral cultivation was driven by a coherent theological logic linking Epiphanius's thinking about the Godhead, the human person, and the communal church. For Epiphanius, the human person has been constituted out of diverse parts (body and soul, most basically)

---

106. Clark, *Origenist Controversy*, 88.
107. Dechow, *Dogma and Mysticism*, 254.
108. Dechow, *Dogma and Mysticism*, 311.
109. Clark, *Origenist Controversy*, 89.
110. See the still classic work of Pierre Hadot, *Philosophy as a Way of Life: Spiritual Exercises from Socrates to Foucault*, trans. Arnold Davidson (Oxford: Blackwell, 1995).
111. The letters of the monk Antony demonstrate clearly the dual "philosophical" nature of some quarters of Egyptian monasticism, both metaphysical and moral; see Samuel Rubenson, *The Letters of St. Antony: Monasticism and the Making of a Saint*, Studies in Antiquity and Christianity (Minneapolis: Fortress Press, 1995).

into a continuous moral agent, whose actions before God will determine judgment in the resurrection, and whose moral unity and continuity reflect the image of a similarly composite-yet-unified Godhead. This idea of incorporated parts also drives Epiphanius's understanding of human history in the *Panarion,* and his understanding of "heresy" as deviation from the unified moral whole of the human race. Any movement to chip away at any element of this theology of moral unity would, therefore, be anathema to Epiphanius. Epiphanius's ferocity with respect to Origen can be explained not simply as literalist and reactionary ignorance versus sophisticated philosophy.

Epiphanius's list of accusations against Origen remains fairly consistent, from the first broadside in the *Ancoratus* in the early 370s to his letter to John of Jerusalem some twenty years later.[112] Despite changes in wording and specific arguments, Epiphanius's charges remain clustered around the two central poles of Epiphanius's theology: the equality and unity of the members of the Trinity, and the unity and continuity of the human person (especially in the resurrection).[113] In the *Ancoratus,* Origen appears as a purveyor of various "frenzied," "mythical," "sophistic," and "maddening" theological errors: that the "paradise" of Genesis was not a physical, but a spiritual, place;[114] that the "coats of skin" in Genesis 3:21 were likewise allegorical;[115] that the Son was "different" from the Father;[116] and that the resurrection body differed from the body in which humans live

---

112. Much of the core of Dechow, *Dogma and Mysticism,* 243–433, is devoted to tracing Epiphanius's accusations from the *Ancoratus* through his *Letter to John of Jerusalem;* see also Clark, *Origenist Controversy,* 86–104.

113. Clark, *Origenist Controversy,* 90, notes the persistence of the "charges" against Origen between the *Ancoratus* and the *Panarion:* "Trinitarian issues" and "notions of the body." Dechow, *Dogma and Mysticism,* 433, further notes that *Panarion* 64 structures the list of "charges" against Origen in Epiphanius's *Letter to John.*

114. Epiphanius, *Ancoratus* 54.2 (GCS n.F. 10.1:63).

115. Epiphanius, *Ancoratus* 64 (GCS n.F. 10.1:76–77).

116. See, for example, Epiphanius, *Ancoratus* 63.2 (GCS n.F. 10.1:75–76): "Let those certain ones read Origen's *On First Principles,* and let those who seem to be sons of the universal church learn, and let them not dare to separate the Son from the Godhood of the Father."

their mortal lives.[117] The "reality" of Genesis (which inspires Epiphanius's first two accusations) must relate directly to the "reality" of the resurrection body: the physical grounds of human creation and redemption must not be separated, or else "nothing that follows is true."[118] Origen's teachings are dangerous, according to the *Ancoratus*, precisely because of how they dissolve the multiple moral unities that structure the logic of human salvation: divine, human, individual, communal, historical.

While the extended refutation of Origenism in the *Panarion* rehearses the accusations in the *Ancoratus*, by far the majority of the long chapter explains how Origen "renders the resurrection of the dead deficient."[119] Epiphanius cites from Origen's commentary on the first Psalm, which tut-tuts at the overly simplistic belief that the "whole substance" (*tēs ousias holēs*) of a human will be resurrected, a belief promulgated by those "green ones who do not understand that being is in flux (*rheustēn einai tēn ousian*)."[120] Origen mocks: Do these simpletons think all the blood they ever lost, or all the hair they ever grew, will be restored to them for final judgment?[121] Epiphanius dismisses Origen's "niggling little phrases" and "sophistical conjecture" as poor attempts to overthrow "the confession in our true hope of the actual resurrection."[122] As we have already seen, Epiphanius must insist on the full continuity of the human person—body and soul—in order to ensure moral justice.

---

117. Epiphanius, *Ancoratus* 87.2 (GCS n.F. 10.1:107–8).

118. Epiphanius, *Ancoratus* 55.1 (GCS n.F. 10.1:64). Epiphanius emphasizes Genesis to highlight the unity of the Trinitarian God as well: heretics should not misunderstand from Genesis 1:26 that only the Father was creating "in the beginning"; "the beginning is one and the divinity itself is one" (μία δέ ἐστιν ἀρχὴ καὶ ἡ αὐτὴ μία θεότης) (*Ancoratus* 29.2 [GCS n.F. 10.1:37]).

119. Epiphanius, *Panarion* 64.4.10 (GCS 31:412). Dechow, *Dogma and Mysticism*, 349: "The main thrust of *Panarion* 64, and that for which the other charges are preparatory, is against Origen's doctrine of the resurrection."

120. Epiphanius, *Panarion* 64.10.4–5 (GCS 31:419). Epiphanius also critiques what he sees as Origen's subordinationist theology in this excerpt (a supposed reference to the Son as γενητός, "created"): *Panarion* 64.7.4, 8.1–8 (GCS 31:416–18).

121. Epiphanius, *Panarion* 64.10.5 (GCS 31:419).

122. Epiphanius, *Panarion* 64.11.1–3 (GCS 31:420).

So diabolical does he find Origen's attack on faith in the resurrection that he introduces a lengthy excerpt from Methodius's anti-Origenist tract *De resurrectione* to rebut Origen's "sophistry."[123] As Clark and others have pointed out, Methodius's rebuttal of Origen does not seem to have clearly understood Origen's own position on body and materiality,[124] nor is Epiphanius's own attack on Origen's resurrection body in "flux" logically consistent. On the one hand, Epiphanius insists that the resurrection must be of "the whole body" (*holou tou sōmatos*);[125] on the other hand, he concedes that the body that rises will be "purified" (*katharōtaton*) of excess material (like blood that was shed, hair that was cut, and so forth), much like a freshly woven garment.[126] Epiphanius's defense of the full resurrection against Origen disappoints modern scholars, who find it wanting from an analytic perspective. Yet analytic consistency is not Epiphanius's theological goal; it is, rather, *moral* consistency. We have already seen, at the beginning of this chapter, Epiphanius's recitation against Origenists of the parable of the blind man and the lame man from the *Apocryphon of Ezekiel*, the point of which is clear:

> God, in his wisdom, brings our bodies which have died and our souls to rebirth (*palingenesian*), in his promise of goodwill, so that the one who has toiled in holiness will receive the entire good repayment from God and those who have done profane things will likewise be judged, body with soul and soul with body.[127]

---

123. Epiphanius, *Panarion* 64.12–62 (GCS 31:421–99). The excerpts from Methodius make up more than half of the long chapter against Origen. See now also Jon Dechow, "From Methodius to Epiphanius in Anti-Origenist Polemic," *Adamantius* 19 (2013): 10–29.

124. Clark, *Origenist Controversy*, 93–94; Dechow, *Dogma and Mysticism*, 359–66.

125. Epiphanius, *Panarion* 64.67.4 (GCS 31:509). That Epiphanius has paraphrased Origen's phrase "the whole substance" (ἡ οὐσία ὅλη), which Methodius also quotes (*Panarion* 64.12.3 [GCS 31:421]), as "the whole body" suggests that he is interested in the composite human being and not more abstruse questions of essence and substance.

126. Epiphanius, *Panarion* 64.67.6–7 (GCS 31:510).

127. Epiphanius, *Panarion* 64.71.13 (GCS 31:520).

Epiphanius does not strive for logical argumentation; he is impelled, rather, by a desire to preserve at all costs the moral unity and continuity of the human person. Those Christians who toiled (presumably ascetics) and those who did not must meet their final reward with the body and soul that earned it.

By the time Epiphanius wrote his letter to John of Jerusalem in the 390s, complaining about the Palestinian bishop's dangerous sympathies for the theology of Origen, new issues had been added to Epiphanius's list of complaints.[128] Nonetheless, the first two charges—and the two that remain central to Epiphanius's theology—are about the Trinity and the human person. Everything else flows from this initial insistence upon moral unity in heaven and on earth. First (according to Epiphanius), Origen claims in his treatise *On First Principles* that "the Son cannot see the Father, nor can the Holy Spirit see the Son," positing their essential inequality.[129] Next, he denies that the soul and body of a human are naturally conjoined, but that preexistent souls became trapped in bodies like "tombs."[130] For Epiphanius, the theological consequences of breaking apart these two moral unities is dire: "If this is true, where is our faith? Where is the preaching of the resurrection?"[131] Without the composite unity of God and the composite unity of humanity, there is no hope for salvation.

Next, Epiphanius introduces a new charge against Origen: he taught that "the devil will be in the future what he once was, and restored to his former dignity he will rise again to the Kingdom of Heaven. O horror (*proh nefas*)!" Epiphanius declares it "foolish" and "inane" to think that

---

128. Both Clark, *Origenist Controversy*, 99–101, and Dechow, *Dogma and Mysticism*, 421–23, attribute the change in Epiphanius's attacks on Origen to the rise of particular Origenist theologies propounded by Evagrius Ponticus in the monastic communities of Egypt. On Epiphanius's skirmishes with John, see Kim, *Epiphanius*, 211–17.

129. Epiphanius, *Ep. ad Ioannem* (= Jerome, *Ep. 51*) 4.1 (CSEL 54:400–401). On the origins and transmission of this letter, see my discussion in the introduction.

130. Epiphanius, *Ep. ad Ioannem* (= Jerome, *Ep. 51*) 4.3–4 (CSEL 54:401–2).

131. Epiphanius, *Ep. ad Ioannem* (= Jerome, *Ep. 51*) 4.4 (CSEL 54:402).

such saintly luminaries as "John the Baptist and Peter and John the Apostle and Evangelist, even Isaiah and Jeremiah and the rest of the prophets, will be made co-heirs with the devil in the Kingdom of Heaven."[132] In light of the larger theological argument of the *Panarion*, regarding the moral unity of the human race as a reflection of divine unity, the grounds for Epiphanius's "horror" are clear: how can a theology of moral unity and continuity accommodate those who work against that unity? As Clark notes, "Epiphanius's objection... is moral," grounded in a desire to preserve "the hope of reward for righteous living."[133] That "reward" only makes sense if there is a moral continuity not just of the human person (which Epiphanius addresses next) but of the community of human persons reflecting God's moral goodness and unity.

Epiphanius turns immediately from this defense of corporate Christian moral unity to a renewed defense of individual moral unity, in the body/soul creation of Adam and Eve. Epiphanius rejects Origen's allegorical reading of the "tunics of skin" provided by God as the human body produced only after the fall of primeval minds. He links this assertion immediately to the truth of the "resurrection of the flesh" and then an extended disquisition on the physical, earthly reality of paradise.[134] Modern readers sympathetic to Origen tend to dismiss much of this discussion as Epiphanius's knee-jerk anti-intellectual opposition to allegory.[135] But, as Patricia Cox Miller notes, "there is more to this clash than a disagreement about scriptural interpretation." Building on an observation by Peter Brown,[136] Miller writes: "Epiphanius's tangible imagination of place signaled a shift in the role that 'the real' might play

---

132. Epiphanius, *Ep. ad Ioannem* (= Jerome, *Ep. 51*) 5.1 (CSEL 54:403).
133. Clark, *Origenist Controversy*, 99.
134. Epiphanius, *Ep. ad Ioannem* (= Jerome, *Ep. 51*) 5.2–7 (CSEL 54:403–5).
135. So, notably, Dechow, *Dogma and Mysticism*, 334–47.
136. Peter Brown, *The Body and Society: Men, Women, and Sexual Renunciation in Early Christianity*, Lectures on the History of Religions n.s. 13 (New York: Columbia University Press, 1988), 381–82, emphasizes the monastic immediacy of Epiphanius's materialist preaching, on which more below.

in formulating human possibility."[137] Epiphanius locates the possibilities of human salvation squarely in a material *and* spiritual reality that must remain continuous throughout our human existence in order to make moral sense. This continuous moral unity leads Epiphanius, once more, to contemplate the image of God in humans, which (he asserts) Origen erroneously claims humans have lost.[138] He continues to refuse to locate that image squarely in any one *part* of the human;[139] as we have seen above, for Epiphanius the image resides, in some sense, in the composite nature of the human. Therefore his defense of Adam's creation as body-and-soul is linked directly to the persistence of the image of God in humans.[140]

Epiphanius's decades-long resistance to Origenist theology does not stem from its strangeness and complexity, but rather from similar theological concerns articulated in radically different modes. Both Origen and Epiphanius seek to link moral responsibility to the human person (constituted in this life as a body and soul), and to understand that moral agent in relation to a particular conception of the divine. Morality and free will stand at the center of their theological inquiry. For Epiphanius, the human being in God's image possesses moral unity and continuity from creation through redemption. For Origen, and his fourth-century monastic followers, the physical body of this life was an instrument for the salvation of the person, who would—when perfected—inhabit a different kind of body. Origen's was a theology of personal transformation, not personal continuity.

Both Origen and Epiphanius are also deeply engaged with the body. For Epiphanius, the body united to a soul bears the image of God so that the body/soul unity acts as a continuous moral agent. For Origen,

---

137. Patricia Cox Miller, *The Corporeal Imagination: Signifying the Holy in Late Antiquity*, Divinations (Philadelphia: University of Pennsylvania Press, 2009), 23.

138. On this point, Epiphanius may be eliding Origen and his later monastic interpreters; see Clark, *Origenist Controversy*, 101–2.

139. Epiphanius, *Ep. ad Ioannem* (= Jerome, *Ep.* 51) 7.2 (CSEL 54:409).

140. Epiphanius, *Ep. ad Ioannem* (= Jerome, *Ep.* 51) 6 (CSEL 54:405–9).

the body is the workhouse by means of which the soul makes moral choices to recover God's image and reunite with the divine. Epiphanius's body *cannot* be transformed if it is to remain part of a continuous, unified moral agent. For Origenists, bodies are continuously moving on an ontological scale toward and away from God, changing states as they change moral status. Only God remains fixed and unchanging. For Epiphanius, the continuity of the human person is the only way to understand its moral agency, and its relation to God's image. Time and again in the *Ancoratus,* Epiphanius tells his correspondents that "the resurrection of our flesh ... is the hope of every good work,"[141] that the resurrection is "our salvation."[142] The resurrection signals more than just redemption in a Pauline (and, perhaps, Origenist) sense, the transformation of what was corruptible into the incorruptible, salvation as change. Resurrection of this composite person, comprising body and soul, into immortality constitutes the just reward of that human person, and thus represents the entire moral logic of Epiphanius's theology.

BODY

So if we begin to understand Epiphanius not merely as a reactionary crank but as a bishop seeking to craft a persuasive theological description of human redemption and divine unity, we also begin to understand the depth of his resistance to Origen. Origenism was not simply too fancy or fanciful for Epiphanius. The problem was that it asked the same questions as Epiphanius—about moral agency, human redemption, God, and the body—but provided answers that struck against the core of Epiphanius's own theological viewpoint: the moral unity and continuity of the human being, received as a reflection and image of God's own composite unity. If the same body and soul are not raised—

---

141. Epiphanius, *Ancoratus* 89.2 (GCS n.F. 10.1:110).
142. Epiphanius, *Ancoratus* 91.3, 99.6 (GCS n.F. 10.1:112, 120).

united—for judgment before God, then there is no clear link between human salvation, divine justice, and our moral selves.

I suggested above that Epiphanius's theology begins with the body: that is, his theology emerges from a particular set of desires and imperatives around the human body and eventually comes to explain not only individual human redemption but human history and divine unity as well. We recall his rhetorical opponent in the *Ancoratus* asking him peevishly: "Why do you talk about 'the body'?"[143] To talk about the body, for Epiphanius, was to talk about the link between human personhood, divine intervention, and ultimate salvation. In this final section I would like to reflect on how Epiphanius's bodily theology connects to the monastic desert that provided his early Christian formation.[144] What Epiphanius has produced in the late fourth century was a monastic, bodily theology configured for all Christians.[145] Although we know little about Epiphanius's very early life, we know that he became a monk (first in Egypt, then in Palestine) at a young age; his view of Christian salvation is monastic, that is, grounded in bodily practices and spiritual exercises. The hope of salvation lay in the body, *this* body, the body that toiled and sweated.[146] The monks influenced by Origen also placed their hope in the ascetic body, but their hopeful body was transitory and practical, a schoolhouse designed for human progress but ultimately abandoned for spiritual perfection. The Origenist monks anticipated that this body, which suffered in heat and fasting and vigils, which embodied the imperfect incorruptibility of humanity, would dissolve away and leave a perfect image and likeness of God in its place.[147]

---

143. Epiphanius, *Ancoratus* 51.1 (GCS n.F. 10.1:60).

144. Dechow, *Dogma and Mysticism*, 74: Epiphanius's "basic outlook appears determined primarily by Egyptian-Palestinian monastic conservatism." See also Dechow, "From Methodius," 22.

145. Kim, *Epiphanius*, 26–28.

146. Dechow, *Dogma and Mysticism*, 270: "In the latter half of the fourth century, the problem of corporeality was especially urgent among the monks, whose lives were devoted to the disciplining and salvation of body and soul."

147. For a sympathetic account of fourth-century Origenism, see Clark, *Origenist Controversy*, 43–84 and 159–93.

Because Epiphanius's bodily hope emphasized moral unity and continuity of the human person, body and soul, the resurrection body always hovered nearby like a tangible and familiar reflection. The resurrection body emblematized the hope for redemption that was being realized in the labor of the monastic life. We can hear not-too-distant echoes of Epiphanius's monastic endeavors in the *Ancoratus:*

> For first if another [flesh] in its place will be raised according to their reasoning, the judgment of God is not just; according to their myth, it judges another flesh instead of the one that sinned and carries another body into the glory of the inheritance of the Kingdom of Heaven, instead of the body which grew weaker in fasting and vigils and mortifications (*diōgmois*) on behalf of God's name.[148]

The hard work of this life should bear fruit, the body that toils should receive its reward along with the soul. Nonmonastic Christians found Epiphanius's bodily theology persuasive, it seems, and were willing, and eager, to imagine the image of God fully active, even in their occasionally sinful, but ultimately redeemable, human bodies.[149]

After Epiphanius's death, we see his bodily theology returning to the deserts of its origins. Epiphanius's ally in his attacks against Origen, Bishop Theophilus of Alexandria, transmitted versions of Epiphanius's anti-Origenism back into the desert in the early fifth century through his festal letters.[150] In these letters (most of which survive only in Jerome's Latin translations, or in Greek and Coptic fragments), we hear

---

148. Epiphanius, *Ancoratus* 87.3 (GCS n.F. 10.1:108).

149. Epiphanius's link between human embodiment and the image of God no doubt led his contemporaries, and later Christians, to impute "anthropomorphite" ideas about God to him: so Socrates, *Historia ecclesiastica* 6.10 (GCS n.F. 1:327). See Paul A. Patterson, *Visions of Christ: The Anthropomorphite Controversy of 399 C.E.*, Studien und Texte zu Antike und Christentum 68 (Tübingen: Mohr-Siebeck, 2012).

150. Clark, *Origenist Controversy*, 105–21, outlines Theophilus's charges against Origenism. Dechow, *Dogma and Mysticism*, 218–20, discusses an early Sahidic translation of the *Ancoratus* and its possible influence on fifth-century Egyptian monasticism. See also Enzo Lucchesi, "Un corpus épiphanien en copte," *Analecta Bollandiana* 99 (1981): 95–99, on the possibility of a greater body of Coptic Epiphaniana; and my discussion of *De XII gemmis* in the introduction.

echoes of Epiphanius's theology of moral unity, originating and returning to the human body.[151] The early part of Theophilus's *Festal Letter* of 401 evokes familiar themes: defense of Christ's assumption of full humanity, which did not "divide the soul and the flesh";[152] an affirmation of the coequal Trinity;[153] and a condemnation of Origen, who "among other things also in this way ... corrupts and violates the resurrection of the dead, which is the hope of our salvation."[154] Epiphanius, too, had affirmed resurrection as "the hope of our salvation," signaling a profound link between the redemption of the body—*this* body—and the moral continuity of the self. Whatever Theophilus's personal theological views,[155] he clearly found Epiphanius's emphasis on bodily morality a persuasive way to frame his attacks on his Origenist opponents.[156]

Theophilus's mediation of Epiphanius's theology back into the monastic desert bore fruit even after the Alexandrian bishop's death, as we can see from the writings of the fifth-century archimandrite Shenoute.[157] In his analysis of Shenoute's Christology, Stephen Davis notes

---

151. For a translation of the various anti-Origenist documents of Theophilus, see Norman Russell, *Theophilus of Alexandria*, The Early Church Fathers (London: Routledge, 2007), 91–174. For a recent rhetorical reevaluation of Theophilus and his monastic context, see Krastu Banev, *Theophilus of Alexandria and the First Origenist Controversy: Rhetoric and Power*, OECS (Oxford: Oxford University Press, 2015).

152. Theophilus, *Ep. fest.* 16 (= Jerome, *Ep.* 96) 3.3 (CSEL 55:161). See also Theophilus's defense of the incarnation against Apollinarius in *Ep. fest.* 17 (= Jerome, *Ep.* 98) 4–8, esp. 8.1 (CSEL 55:192): "showing the perfect likeness of our condition."

153. Theophilus, *Ep. fest.* 16 (= Jerome, *Ep.* 96) 5.1–2 (CSEL 55:162–63).

154. Theophilus, *Ep. fest.* 16 (= Jerome, *Ep.* 96) 13.1 (CSEL 55:159–81).

155. His contemporaries and Christians in the fifth century generally described Theophilus's motives as more personal and political than theological; see Russell, *Theophilus*, 18–35.

156. Clark, *Origenist Controversy*, 121: "As with Epiphanius, so with Theophilus: issues pertaining to the body have upstaged earlier concerns, and the villain's role has been assigned to Origenists rather than Origen alone."

157. The study of Shenoute has undergone a renaissance in the past decade, following the collation of surviving fragments of the abbot's work by Stephen Emmel, *Shenoute's Literary Corpus*, 2 vols., CSCO Subsidia 111–12 (Leuven: Peeters, 2004). I thank Caroline Schroeder for drawing my attention to the links between Shenoute and Epiphanius, and for helping me navigate the world of Shenoute studies.

the abbot's emphases on the "union of body and soul" and his theology of the incarnation and redemption. Davis ascribes these emphases, in part, to the theological influence of Shenoute's contemporary, Cyril of Alexandria.[158] Yet we can also detect the lingering influence of Epiphanius as well.[159] As Davis points out, Shenoute links the moral union of the body and soul in the human to "the union of divinity and humanity in the Incarnation."[160] The constructive logics of the human and divine are intertwined. In one of his theological treatises, conventionally titled *I Am Amazed*,[161] Shenoute insists on those two familiar planks of Epiphanius's theological works: the union of body and soul, in this life and the resurrection, and the consubstantiality of the Trinity. What's more, Shenoute defends these positions against heretics also familiar from Epiphanius: Origenists and Apollinarians (as well as gnostics and Nestorians).[162]

---

158. Stephen J. Davis, *Coptic Christology in Practice: Incarnation and Divine Participation in Late Antique and Medieval Egypt*, OECS (Oxford: Oxford University Press, 2008), 74–76.

159. Much of Epiphanius's influence may be mediated through the writings of Theophilus; see Dechow, *Dogma and Mysticism*, 233; Clark, *Origenist Controversy*, 153.

160. Davis, *Coptic Christology*, 74.

161. Emmel, *Shenoute's Literary Corpus*, 2:646, 794, has assigned this title based on a Coptic manuscript page listing "incipits" for many of Shenoute's works (see *Shenoute's Literary Corpus*, 1:71–75, 236–42). I cite the text according to the chapter numbers provided in the translation of Hans-Joachim Cristea, *Schenute von Atripe: Contra Origenistas*, Studien und Texte zu Antike und Christentum 60 (Tübingen: Mohr-Siebeck, 2011), and the paragraph divisions of Tito Orlandi, *Shenute, Contra Origenistas, testo con introduzione e traduzione* (Rome: C.I.M., 1985), with reference to Cristea's textual edition in parentheses. I have consulted the Italian translation of Tito Orlandi; the partial English translation of Davis, *Coptic Christology*, 279–86; the English translation of Michael Foat, "I Myself Have Seen: The Representation of Humanity in the Writings of Apa Shenoute of Atripe" (PhD diss., Brown University, 1996), 114–40; and that of Andrew Crislip in *Selected Discourses of Shenoute the Great: Community, Theology, and Social Conflict in Late Antique Egypt*, ed. David Brakke and Andrew Crislip (Cambridge: Cambridge University Press, 2015), 54–82.

162. So significant is the anti-Origenist material in the treatise that Tito Orlandi titled his edition and Italian translation *Contra Origenistas* (see above, n. 161), a title retained (for its familiarity) in the more recent edition of Hans-Joachim Cristea (see above, n. 161). On the anti-Apollinarian material, see Shenoute, *I Am Amazed* 29 (490–96) (Cristea, *Contra Origenistas*, 200–202).

Some of Shenoute's arguments speak to his specific monastic context,[163] while others recall Epiphanius's broader theology of the body quite closely. A spirited defense of the true unity of the Father, Son, and Spirit as "of one substance" (*teiousia nouōt*) leads directly to a defense of the moral unity of the body and soul.[164] Against (presumably) Origen's teaching that souls existed before being implanted as a punishment into bodies, Shenoute protests: "So can a soul sin (*nobe*) without a body, or a body without a soul?"[165] Just as Epiphanius had argued with his parable of the blind and lame thieves, Shenoute asserts that bodies and souls operate together, distinct elements brought together into a moral unity:[166] "No human being (*rōme*) is without a soul, and no soul is apart from a human being; for the soul and the body exist together in the womb."[167] Shenoute weaves through multiple arguments in this treatise: about the incarnation, the Eucharist, the redemption of the body, the unity of the Trinity, and the truth of Scriptures. We could read this treatise as primarily reactive, a refutation of Shenoute's various theological opponents; but we can also read Shenoute's constructive theological topics as united by a general concern for moral unity: of God, of Christ incarnate, of the individual human, and of the community of Christians united in prayer and the Eucharist, and divided from heresy.

163. Especially Shenoute's discussion of the monastic "Jesus prayer" as reflective of homoousian Trinitarian theology: Shenoute, *I Am Amazed* 32–33 (650–56; 800–808) (Cristea, *Contra Origenistas*, 205–9). Note there are roughly eight pages missing in the middle of this section (Cristea, *Contra Origenistas*, 206), so Shenoute's discussion of the "Jesus prayer" is rather extensive. See Aloys Grillmeier, *Christ in the Christian Tradition*, trans. O.C. Dean, vol. 2, pt. 4 (Louisville, KY: Westminster/John Knox Press, 1996), 184–89; and Clark, *Origenist Controversy*, 154.

164. Shenoute, *I Am Amazed* 6 (332) (Cristea, *Contra Origenistas*, 147); see also *I Am Amazed* 33 (803, 806) (Cristea, *Contra Origenistas*, 208), where Shenoute affirms the *homoousion*, that is, multiple *hypostases* and single *ousia* of the Trinity, as well as the "unity of [God's] nature" (*ntmntoua ntefphusis*).

165. Shenoute, *I Am Amazed* 8 (335) (Cristea, *Contra Origenistas*, 148).

166. Like Epiphanius, Shenoute is clear on the separability of body and soul: *I Am Amazed* 19 (411) (Cristea, *Contra Origenistas*, 172–73).

167. Shenoute, *I Am Amazed* 8 (340) (Cristea, *Contra Origenistas*, 150).

As Caroline Schroeder argued in her monograph on Shenoute's ascetic discipline, the monastic body stood at the productive center of the Egyptian abbot's thinking about God and humanity: "For Shenoute," she writes, "the body is the site of redemptive transformation. It is also the site for theological development, social control, and the construction of Christian identity."[168] Schroeder outlines Shentoue's ascetic theology, one that begins with and returns to the body: as both a moral subject and an object of God's redemptive action.[169] Through language of purity and pollution, Shenoute crafts a disciplinary discourse of both individual accountability (the monk preserving his or her bodily integrity) and communal participation (the monk preserving the integrity of the monastic community). Materially and metaphorically, the monk's body delimits the space within which a self is conceived of in relation to divine perfection and human totality, morally continuous from its creation to its resurrection. Because of this need for moral continuity at the individual and communal level, the future resurrection of the body looms large in Shenoute's theological thinking, to be held up and defended against the onslaught of heretics.[170]

The links between Shenoute's fifth-century theology and Epiphanius's several decades earlier should be clear. Yet my point is not merely to suggest how the bishop of Cyprus influenced the abbot of the White Monastery, but rather to use Shenoute as a mirror to reflect back on the significance of Epiphanius's own theological work. As I suggested earlier, Epiphanius's theology of human salvation and divine perfection very likely had its roots in a monastic theology grounded in the body. Certainly the full flower of Egyptian theology under Shenoute demonstrates how such a theology might further develop. Yet when Epiphanius

168. Caroline T. Schroeder, *Monastic Bodies: Discipline and Salvation in Shenoute of Atripe*, Divinations (Philadelphia: University of Pennsylvania Press, 2007), 5.

169. Schroeder, *Monastic Bodies*, 126–57.

170. As David Brakke, "The Egyptian Afterlife of Origenism: Conflicts over Embodiment in Coptic Sermons," *Orientalia Christiana Periodica* 66 (2000): 277–93, points out, this monastic theology of the body was, like Epiphanius's, also disseminated among nonmonastic Christian populations.

produced his mature theology in the 370s, he was no longer writing solely for a monastic audience.[171] By the time he inserted himself (or was invited to do so) into the major theological disputes of the later fourth century, he had extended this monastic theology to a broader pastoral audience.[172] This audience, moreover, seemed to find a theology of moral unity as compelling as did an audience of monks decades later. For all of the scholarly attention paid to Origen and his followers, and for all of their evident popularity throughout late antiquity, it is important to remember that Epiphanius's particular theological view "won" the day. No doubt a variety of reasons led to the triumph of Epiphanius over the memory of Origen: political, cultural, personal, but also theological. We consign Epiphanius to the margins of theological history, a bizarre and intolerant figure too wedded to "literalism" to appreciate the sophisticated metaphysics of Origen. Yet his monastic theology, grounded in the experience of and hope for the body—*this* human body—must have spoken as clearly and persuasively (if not more so) to the theological concerns of much of fourth-century Christian culture.

---

171. Although, according to Jerome, Epiphanius still acted as a leader to various monastic communities in Cyprus; Jerome, *Ep.* 108.7.3 (CSEL 55:312–13) describes the many monasteries on Cyprus filled with "brothers whom love of the holy man [i.e., Epiphanius] drew from all over the world." Epiphanius in the 390s also describes his continuing leadership over his monastery in Palestine: *Ep. ad Ioannem* (= Jerome, *Ep.* 51) 1.5–7 (CSEL 54:396–97).

172. Calogero Riggi, "La catéchèse adaptée aux temps chez Epiphane," *SP* 17 (1982): 160–68, even suggests that the *Ancoratus* reflects Epiphanius's prebaptismal teaching on morality, doctrine, and creed. See now also Young Richard Kim, "The Pastoral Care of Epiphanius of Salamis," *SP* 67 (2013): 247–56.

CHAPTER SIX

After Lives

SAINT AS CULTURAL SIGNIFIER

The historical figure of Epiphanius has given us new insight into the formation of a particular Christian culture in the late fourth century, one that inhabited and transformed late Roman culture. As we saw in chapter 1, however, the historical Epiphanius could not contain the cultural force of the *celebrity* he became during his life and after his death. It is even possible that the memory of Epiphanius could work to undermine or even subvert the cultural formation of Epiphanius the man.

In this final chapter, I turn away from Epiphanius the historical figure to think about Epiphanius the *saint* through two hagiographic texts. My goal is not to excavate these texts to arrive at Epiphanius the *holy man*, à la Peter Brown:[1] Brown's holy man emerged murkily from the lives of saints, articulating the fuzzy boundary between social history and literary analysis that has characterized the study of late antiquity

---

1. Peter Brown, "The Rise and Function of the Holy Man in Late Antiquity," *JRS* 61 (1971): 80–101; see Brown's retrospective piece, "The Rise and Function of the Holy Man in Late Antiquity, 1971–1997," *JECS* 6 (1998): 353–76, with the accompanying introductory piece to that special issue by Susanna Elm, "Introduction," *JECS* 6 (1998): 343–51.

since the 1970s.[2] My interest in this chapter is to consider how Epiphanius the *saint* became a cultural signifier, whose written life clarifies but also disrupts the production of cultural values.

The life of a saint is, in most cases, a compelling but often contradictory story of virtue.[3] The saint is at once exemplary, modeling the values that constitute a particular religious culture, and impossible, performing acts and inhabiting spaces that are not only challenging but often expressly forbidden to the marveling audience.[4] The saint models admirable holiness, but also dangerous excess: the saint's world, as Françoise Meltzer and Jaś Elsner write, "is a world of transgressions: transvestism, death by torture, possession and exorcism, astral projection, talking to animals, supranormal visions and voices, leprosy cured and leprosy attained."[5] (Some of these transgressive elements find their way into the lives of Epiphanius.) As figures of imitation and transgression, saints provide an opportunity for audiences to interrogate their cultural values. To quote Meltzer and Elsner once more: "The holy man or woman provides a space in which to think differently, to think against and outside socially normative patterns, and this in a variety of religions. Saints queer stable

---

2. The extraction of social history from the often flamboyant literature of saints' lives precedes Brown's sociological interventions; see Evelyne Patlagean, "Ancienne hagiographie byzantine et histoire sociale," *Annales ESC* 23 (1968): 106–26. On the larger move toward social scientific historical studies of early Christian texts, see Elizabeth A. Clark, *History, Theory, Text: Historians and the Linguistic Turn* (Cambridge, MA: Harvard University Press, 2004).

3. Michel de Certeau, "A Variant: Hagio-Graphical Edification," in *The Writing of History*, trans. Tom Conley (New York: Columbia University Press, 1988), 277: "Generally speaking, hagiography is a discourse of virtues."

4. Edith Wyschogrod, *Saints and Postmodernism: Revisioning Moral Philosophy* (Chicago: University of Chicago Press, 1990), 11: "It is crucial to notice that institutional norms often thwart saintly intention and, conversely, that saintly acts frequently impinge on entrenched custom and explicitly articulated practice"; Virginia Burrus, "A Saint of One's Own: Emmanuel Levinas, Eliezer ben Hyrcanus, and Eulalia of Mérida," *L'Esprit Créateur* 50 (2010): 6: "The saint's life queers custom, perverts nature, and transgresses limits, including the limits of selfhood."

5. Françoise Meltzer and Jaś Elsner, eds., *Saints: Faith without Borders* (Chicago: University of Chicago Press, 2011), xii.

binary structures."⁶ Unlike the Brownian holy man, who gives us access to the concrete workings of society, the flamboyant saint embodies and performs the uncertainties of culture, its questions and ambiguities. Consideration of hagiographies of Epiphanius extend my discussion of his celebrity in chapter 1 to a broader cultural and chronological canvas.

I approach the saintly Epiphanius through two hagiographies written roughly 1,400 years apart. The first is a Greek *Vita Epiphanii* from the late fifth or early sixth century; the second is an Anglo-Catholic novella written in 1874. These obviously disparate historical contexts share illuminating similarities: we are dealing with two imperial cultures struggling to articulate the role of political power in the production of religious community, and to come to terms with the problem of religious otherness in the past and the present. Their affinities are, of course, not merely accidental but highly reflective: the Victorians thought long and hard about the Roman Empire as both model and caution.⁷ Their common questions about empire, religion, and difference come to life at these two parallel moments through a very particular Saint Epiphanius. This Epiphanius, unlike his historical counterpart, was born a Jew, was converted by miracles, and became a wonder-worker and monastic paragon. This saintly ex-Jewish monastic hero opens up a space—in both the Roman and Victorian eras—for interrogating the relationship between power, piety, and the problem of religious difference.

VITA EPIPHANII: "THE GLORY OF THE ROMANS"

"The Life and Conduct of Our Holy Father Epiphanius" was likely written in the mid- to late fifth century, perhaps even drawing on writings from the bishop's own followers.⁸ The *vita*, like most saints' lives of

---

6. Meltzer and Elsner, *Saints,* ix.

7. Norman Vance, "Anxieties of Empire and the Moral Tradition: Rome and Britain," *International Journal of the Classical Tradition* 18 (2011): 264–61.

8. This dating has been argued by Claudia Rapp, "The *Vita* of Epiphanius of Salamis: An Historical and Literary Study" (D.Phil. thesis, Oxford University, 1991),

the time, circulated its image of the saint in primarily religious contexts, such as liturgical celebrations and monastic gatherings. Yet these *vitae* also addressed the larger political contexts that, by the later fifth century, pervaded the religious realm. Much of the fifth and sixth centuries saw the growing, yet contested, interpenetration of Roman and Christian identity, particularly in the eastern half of the Roman Empire.[9] Political and religious ideologies and operations overlapped and reinforced each other, but also (at times) clashed and conflicted.[10] Inevitably, then, the literature of holy Christians also reflected, and refracted, questions about political and cultural identity.

Incidents from Epiphanius's actual life structure the main events of the *vita*;[11] however, the saint we meet in this early Byzantine hagiogra-

---

1:99–103; the *terminus ante quem* is well established by sixth-century Coptic and Syriac translations (100); see also Sebastian Brock, "Two Syriac Translations of the Life of Epiphanios," in *Mosaic: Festschrift for A.H.S. Megaw*, ed. Judith Herrin, Margaret Mullett, and Catherine Otten-Froux, British School at Athens Studies 8 (London: British School at Athens, 2001), 19–25. Rapp brings the compilation further down into the "mid-fifth century" (102) based on circumstantial evidence. See also Rapp, "Epiphanius of Salamis: The Church Father as Saint," in *"The Sweet Land of Cyprus": Papers Given at the Twenty-fifth Jubilee Spring Symposium of Byzantine Studies*, ed. A.A.M. Bryer and G.S. Georghallides (Nicosia: Cyprus Research Center, 1993), 169–87, esp. 178–83. I am extremely grateful to Claudia Rapp for sharing with me her dissertation, including her critical edition of the *Vita Epiphanii*, which comprises volume 2 (from which I cite below).

9. Anthony Kaldellis, *Hellenism in Byzantium: The Transformations of Greek Identity and the Reception of the Classical Tradition*, Greek Culture in the Roman World (Cambridge: Cambridge University Press, 2007); Claudia Rapp, "Hellenic Identity, *Romanitas*, and Christianity in Byzantium," in *Hellenisms: Culture, Identity, and Ethnicity from Antiquity to Modernity*, ed. Katerina Zacharia (Aldershot, UK: Ashgate, 2008), 144: "For the Byzantines, the Roman Imperial tradition was inextricably linked to their Christian religion. The fusion of *romanitas* and *christianitas* became a strong and persistent marker of identity in the Byzantine Empire and later."

10. Particularly true at the tail end of the Theodosian dynasty and in its aftermath; see, among many studies, Kathryn Chew, "Virgins and Eunuchs: Pulcheria, Politics, and the Death of Emperor Theodosius II," *Historia* 55 (2006): 207–27.

11. Epiphanius the saint (like his historical counterpart) has a monastic stint in Egypt; he travels to Rome and Constantinople (at least twice); he eradicates heresy in Cyprus; he confronts the bishops of Jerusalem and Constantinople; and he dies on a return voyage from the capital to Cyprus. Most of these events are, however, jumbled

phy is a strikingly different character.[12] Instead of a fierce defender of orthodoxy, tearing back and forth across the Mediterranean to battle the baleful influence of heretics, we meet in the *Vita Epiphanii* a wonder-working monk. While much of the early chapters of the *vita* is indebted to the famous *Life of Antony*, there is little in the way of temptation or demonic struggle. The tone of this later life resembles more closely such miraculous lives as the Latin *Life of Martin of Tours*, which had probably been translated into Greek by the time our life was written.[13] Virginia Burrus has described the Martin of the Latin *vita* as "above all a worker of miracles, a flamboyant performer of the impossible," a description that suits the Epiphanius of the Greek *vita* as well.[14] In the course of the *vita* Epiphanius brings people to life and condemns them to death;[15] he casts out demons and heals medical

in order and given vastly different motivations. Young Richard Kim, *Epiphanius of Cyprus: Imagining an Orthodox World* (Ann Arbor: University of Michigan Press, 2015), 157–59, tentatively uses the *vita* to reconstruct Epiphanius's early episcopacy.

12. Rapp, "Epiphanius the Saint," gives a thorough comparison of the historical and hagiographic accounts.

13. While I can't show direct influence of Sulpicius Severus's *Vita Martini* on the author of the *Vita Epiphanii*, its general tenor of a miraculous monk-turned-bishop could easily have influenced the hagiographic style of the fifth and sixth centuries. On translation of the *vita Martini* into Greek by the mid-400s, see E. Dekkers, "Les traductions grecques des écrits patristiques latins," *Sacris Erudiri* 5 (1953): 202–3; on hagiographic transmission between the East and West more generally, see Claudia Rapp, "Hagiography and Monastic Literature between Greek East and Latin West in Late Antiquity," in *Cristianità d'occidente e cristianità d'oriente (secoli vi-xi)*, Settimane di Studio della Fondazione Centro Italiano di Studi sull'Alto Medioevo 51 (Spoleto: Presso La Sede della Fondazione, 2004), 1221–80. See now Todd Edison French, "Just *Deserts:* Losing Origen and Gaining Retributive Judgment in the Hagiographical Literature of the Early Byzantine World" (PhD diss., Columbia University, 2013), who traces the rise of a hagiographic style eschewing Origenist universalism in a Christian imperial context.

14. Virginia Burrus, *The Sex Lives of Saints*, Divinations (Philadelphia: University of Pennsylvania Press, 2004), 92; she further remarks: "Sulpicius writes Martin's Life as science fiction. Like much (although by no means all) science fiction, these texts are austerely masculine, covertly homoerotic, and finally strangely sexed—eminently queerable" (93). Arguably, this description suits the *Vita Epiphanii* as well.

15. Resurrections: *Vita Epiphanii* 28, 83, 88 (Rapp, "*Vita* of Epiphanius," 2:87–88, 156, 161–62). Condemnations to death: *Vita Epiphanii* 66, 81, 98, 105 (Rapp, "*Vita* of Epiphanius," 2:134, 153–55, 175–76, 185).

afflictions;[16] he has divine visions and speaks to animals;[17] he turns wine into water and causes rain to fall;[18] he silences heretics with a glance and blinds a greedy bishop with a harsh word.[19] He leads an austere and ascetic life, but his force emanates from his divine power. At one point, the saint engages in a days'-long debate with a Syrian philosopher (also named Epiphanius), comparing philosophical and sacred texts on creation. Yet what finally converts the pagan in the end is not scriptural truth but witnessing the raw miracle of the saint exorcising a terrifying demoniac.[20]

Like much Christian hagiography, the *Vita Epiphanii* is structured primarily through geographic movement: in Palestine, Persia, Egypt, Cyprus, Jerusalem, Rome, and Constantinople, Epiphanius is a holy monk—and then a holy bishop—on the move. As Michel de Certeau noted, "The Life of a Saint is a composition of places.... The organization of the space through which the saint passes folds and unfolds in order to display a truth which is a place."[21] The "organized space" in

---

16. Exorcisms and healings: *Vita Epiphanii* 15, 18, 20, 23, 33, 34, 40, 43, 46, 50, 51, 74, 75, 87, 100, 126 (a posthumous healing of three blind men) (Rapp, "*Vita* of Epiphanius," 2:66, 68, 72, 76, 93, 99–100, 102, 106–7, 111–12, 113, 143, 146, 161, 178, 208).

17. Divine visions: *Vita Epiphanii* 7, 40 (Epiphanius appears in a vision to someone else), 68, 90 (Epiphanius appears in another's vision), 94 (divine audition) (Rapp, "*Vita* of Epiphanius," 2:57, 100, 135–36, 163–64, 168–69). Speaking to animals: *Vita Epiphanii* 31 (Rapp, "*Vita* of Epiphanius," 2:91); later Epiphanius kills a marauding neighborhood lion on sight: *Vita Epiphanii* 35–36 (Rapp, "*Vita* of Epiphanius," 2:94–96).

18. Wine into water: *Vita Epiphanii* 14 (Rapp, "*Vita* of Epiphanius," 2:64–65). The comparison with Christ's first "sign" in John 2 is explicit in the text; this is also Epiphanius's first miracle as a Christian monk. Miraculous rainfall: *Vita Epiphanii* 53 (Rapp, "*Vita* of Epiphanius," 116–18).

19. Silencing heretics: *Vita Epiphanii* 24 (actually a Persian *magos*), 49, 105 (Rapp, "*Vita* of Epiphanius," 2:78–79, 110, 184–85). Blinding the greedy bishop John of Jerusalem: *Vita Epiphanii* 80 (Rapp, "*Vita* of Epiphanius," 2:152–53). Epiphanius only restores sight to John's right eye.

20. *Vita Epiphanii* 38–43 (Rapp, "*Vita* of Epiphanius," 2:96–103). The Syrian philosopher Epiphanius locks himself in a monastic cell when the saint goes to heal the demoniac, providing one of the few unequivocally comic moments in the *vita*.

21. De Certeau, "A Variant," 281. See also Scott F. Johnson, "Apostolic Geography: The Origins and Continuity of a Hagiographic Habit," *DOP* 64 (2010): 5–25.

which this saint's truth take shape is, as we shall see, the space of the Roman Empire. Yet the empire as both geographic site and ideological system occupies an ambivalent place in the *vita*, articulating deep questions about the all-too-recent Christianization of the Roman Empire. I explore this imperial ambivalence before turning to an even more curious (and, I suggest, related) detail in the *vita:* the Jewish childhood of the miraculous monk-bishop.

Epiphanius's Empire

From early on in his monastic career, Saint Epiphanius seems to embody not just Christian virtues but the civilizing values of the Roman Empire. Soon after settling into a monastery in Palestine, Epiphanius flees into the wilderness to avoid the fame his miracle working has brought upon him. He is taken hostage by a tribe of Saracens, whom he proceeds to civilize over several months.[22] The barbarians learn to respect Epiphanius's Christian morality ("He kept them from all mischief," we read) but notably do not convert to Christianity.[23] Just as Rome can "Romanize" provincials or barbarians without making them into Romans,[24] so too Christianity possesses the power to Christianize those outside without actually making them into

---

22. *Vita Epiphanii* 15–16 (Rapp, "*Vita* of Epiphanius," 2:66–67): "Transformed through Epiphanius's words (coming to understanding) they said that he was a God" (οἱ δὲ διὰ τῶν λόγων Ἐπιφανίου, ἐν καταστάσει ἔλθοντες, μεταβαλλόμενοι ἔλεγον θεὸν αὐτὸν εἶναι). Since they still think Epiphanius is a god at this point, *metaballomenoi* must mean something other than "converted." The "coming to understanding (*katastasis*)" seems to indicate a kind of realization or intellectual awakening on their part (symbolized by the miraculous opening of the Saracen leader's blind eye).

23. With one exception: a single Saracen converts, takes the name "John," and becomes one of Epiphanius's lifelong companions: *Vita Epiphanii* 17 (Rapp, "*Vita* of Epiphanius," 2:67–68). John is the putative author of the first half of the *vita*.

24. On the complicated place of "barbarians" in the capital, see Alan Cameron and Jacqueline Long, *Barbarians and Politics at the Court of Arcadius* (Berkeley: University of California Press, 1993); and Susanna Elm, "What the Bishop Wore to the Synod: John Chrysostom, Origenism, and the Politics of Fashion at Constantinople," *Adamantius* 19 (2013): 156–69.

Christians. The effect is to align Rome and Christianity: they both have the ability to ameliorate the "other" without erasing that other's essential difference.

This alignment of Rome and Christianity against non-Roman, non-Christian others is made explicit in an extended portion of the *vita* set across the Roman border in Persia. Epiphanius has expelled a demon from a possessed man in the Judean desert. Angered, the demon flees to the royal house of Persia, possesses the Persian king's daughter, and taunts the Persian household that only Epiphanius can cast him out. Eventually Epiphanius is found and brought to Persia, where he casts out the demon for good.[25] He remains in the royal house for ten days, teaching the king about Christ. While we might expect the denouement of this story to be the foreign king's conversion, Epiphanius's Persian sojourn reinforces religious and political boundaries. Already the king's priests had shown their ignorance of Christ by assuming that Epiphanius was one of them, a "great magos."[26] The king himself, while susceptible to the saint's power, seems no more likely to become a Christian. At the end of the ten days of instruction, Epiphanius announces:

> I shall hasten back to my homeland,
> For I long for everything that is there.
> But you will remain seated on your throne
> not roused up against the Romans.
> For if you become hostile to the Romans
> you will become an enemy of the Crucified One (*tōi estaurōmenōi*).
> If you become an enemy of the One Crucified (*tou staurōthentos*),
> you shall be wickedly consumed by your adversaries.[27]

---

25. *Vita Epiphanii* 19–23 (Rapp, "*Vita* of Epiphanius," 2:69–77). Perhaps to avoid the problem of the demon simply hopping to another victim (in yet another empire), Epiphanius clarifies that "the wolf has fled to uninhabited places (εἰς ἀοικήτους τόπους)" (*Vita Epiphanii* 23 [Rapp, "*Vita* of Epiphanius," 2:76]).

26. *Vita Epiphanii* 24 (Rapp, "*Vita* of Epiphanius," 2:78–80).

27. *Vita Epiphanii* 28 (Rapp, "*Vita* of Epiphanius," 2:84). Most of the dialogue in this part of the *vita* is metrical, leading Rapp to propose a preexisting poetic source (which she dubs the *Dialogus metricus de rebus gestis Epiphanii*); see "*Vita* of Epiphanius," 1:75–85;

Epiphanius draws a clear dividing line between Persian pagans and Roman Christians; and Epiphanius's loyalty to the Roman Empire—he "longs" to return to his "homeland" (*patrida*)—is identical to his loyalty to Christ. By the time this *vita* was composed, the Persian and Roman empires had been engaged in long-standing diplomatic and, occasionally, military confrontation: Epiphanius's assertion of Roman separation and superiority is thus quite pointed.[28] When Epiphanius at last departs Persia (after performing one more miraculous resurrection), the Persian king proclaims: "Go in peace, Epiphanius, the glory of the Romans (*hē doxa tōn Rhōmaiōn*)! Remember us as well in Persia."[29] The united power of Rome/Christ is effective across ethnic and political boundaries, but also clearly maintains those boundaries: the Saracens learn right from wrong and the Persian king learns respect for "the Crucified One" and the Romans at once. Political and religious difference is maintained and managed.

In these early chapters, as well as in other later incidents,[30] Epiphanius's Christian sanctity seems unproblematically, even naturally, allied with the interests of the Roman Empire. This natural alignment of Rome and Christianity coheres with the historical Epiphanius's own

---

and Claudia Rapp, "Frühbyzantinische Dichtung und Hagiographie am Beispiel der Vita des Epiphanius von Zypern," *Rivista di Studi Bizantini e Neoellenici* 27 (1991): 3–31, on its liturgical resonances.

28. The *vita* highlights the real military tensions between the two empires when it recounts the failed attempts of Persian agents to find Epiphanius: the first group of Persians are caught and treated as spies, while the second group must "put on Roman disguise" (λάβετε σχῆμα τῶν Ῥωμαίων) in order to successfully penetrate to Epiphanius's monastery: *Vita Epiphanii* 19 (Rapp, "*Vita* of Epiphanius," 70).

29. *Vita Epiphanii* 29 (Rapp, "*Vita* of Epiphanius," 2:89).

30. In *Vita Epiphanii* 40 (Rapp, "*Vita* of Epiphanius," 2:99–100), Epiphanius remotely exorcises an evil spirit from Callistus, "son of Aetius, the prefect of Rome (τοῦ μεγαλοῦ ἐπάρχου τῆς Ῥωμῆς)," who then comes to dwell at Epiphanius's monastery. Soon after becoming bishop of Constantia, Epiphanius uses church funds to redeem a certain "Eugnomon, who was a Roman" (ῥωμαῖος ὤν; repeated later, Εὐγνώμονα τὸν Ῥωμαῖον), from imprisonment by the "pagan" Drakon (*Vita Epiphanii* 63 [Rapp, "*Vita* of Epiphanius," 2:130]). Both of these incidents show at the least a sympathetic relationship between the saint and Rome.

imperialized Christian culture. Several stories that place Saint Epiphanius in direct contact with the imperial family, however, render that alliance more ambiguous. Some time after becoming bishop, Epiphanius is summoned to the city of Rome to heal the sister of the emperors, Arcadius and Honorius.[31] Unlike earlier monastic saints, such as Antony, Epiphanius does not even momentarily resist answering a summons from the imperial house.[32] Epiphanius (of course) heals the princess, and "when the emperors saw what Epiphanius had done, their hearts were inclined to love him and hear him and believe everything that was said by him. They called upon Epiphanius to remain with them in Rome and be their Father."[33] When they ask him to resurrect the princess's son, who has died, Epiphanius barters one resurrection for the baptism of the royal household: "If you raise the boy," they agree, "we will believe and be baptized."[34] The boy is raised from the dead and baptized along with his uncles and mother;[35] after a week of instruction from the bishop, the young boy dies once more, but the imperial household has already become fully Christian.[36]

The similarity to the healing in the Persian royal household is telling: a saint summoned, a princess healed, a king (or two) enraptured by the miraculous saint, religious instruction. The only difference comes at the end: while the Persians remain pagan (but respectful), the Roman

---

31. Later in the *vita* it is explained that Arcadius and Honorius were sojourning in Rome to keep their sick sister (who was married to a man in Rome) company (*Vita Epiphanii* 101 [Rapp, "*Vita* of Epiphanius," 2:180]).

32. See Athanasius, *Vita Antonii* 81 (SC 400:340–44), where Constantine and his sons "wrote to him, as a father" (ἔγραφον αὐτῷ ὡς πατρὶ) (notably, Epiphanius in the *vita* acts "as a father" to the members of the imperial house; see below), and he only reluctantly replies; more sharply, in the *Apophthegmata Patrum Antony* 31 (PG 65:85), when Antony receives a letter from Constantine summoning him to Constantinople, he receives counsel that attendance upon an emperor is inconsistent with the monastic life ("If you go, you will be called 'Antony'; if you do not, 'Abba Antony'").

33. *Vita Epiphanii* 87 (Rapp, "*Vita* of Epiphanius," 2:160).

34. *Vita Epiphanii* 88 (Rapp, "*Vita* of Epiphanius," 2:161).

35. *Vita Epiphanii* 89–90 (Rapp, "*Vita* of Epiphanius," 2:162–64); only at the baptism do we learn the sister's name: Proklianē.

36. *Vita Epiphanii* 91 (Rapp, "*Vita* of Epiphanius," 2:165).

emperors become Christians. Yet we, along with the *vita*'s late fifth-century audience, might pause to wonder that the Roman imperial household, at the end of the fourth century, has not already converted to Christianity.[37] The strangely belated piety of the imperial family, in the old capital of Rome itself, disrupts the easy alignment of "Christ" and "Rome" in the saint's life.

When, some time later, Epiphanius is summoned to Constantinople by the emperor Theodosius, the values of empire and saint are once more uneasily juxtaposed. The emperor is bedridden with a foot ailment. In contrast to his reaction to the summons to Rome, just a few chapters before, here Epiphanius resists going with Theodosius's messengers. After a back-and-forth, "they barely persuaded Epiphanius to sail away with them."[38] Epiphanius, of course, heals Theodosius on sight, and the grateful emperor (like his sons earlier) implores the bishop to stay and "be my father."[39] Unlike his sons, Theodosius seems already to be baptized, and once he finds out Epiphanius has baptized his own sons, "he rejoiced greatly."[40] Arcadius and Honorius end their five-year sojourn in Rome and return to Constantinople, reunited with their imperial father and their spiritual father. Here, in one tableau, we envision the unity of Roman empire and Christian faith.

Immediately thereafter, however, a crack forms between these two institutions. By chance one Faustinianus, an enemy of Epiphanius's, one of the last recalcitrant pagans of Cyprus, is arrested on a charge of *lèse-majesté* (*loidoria basilikē*) and brought to the capital city. He refuses Epiphanius's attempts to help him and the next day is reported dead.

---

37. It doesn't simply seem to be a question of the *baptism* of the royal family (since they also claim they are willing "to believe" what Epiphanius believes), but rather their conversion to Christianity. It is possible that Theodosius's sons were not baptized until adulthood (although certainly not by Epiphanius and not under the circumstances narrated in the *vita*); it is not possible that they were not raised Christians.

38. *Vita Epiphanii* 99 (Rapp, "*Vita* of Epiphanius," 2:177).

39. *Vita Epiphanii* 100 (Rapp, "*Vita* of Epiphanius," 2:179): γίνου μοι πατήρ.

40. *Vita Epiphanii* 101 (Rapp, "*Vita* of Epiphanius," 2:180): hearing that ἐφώτισεν Ἀρκάδιον καὶ Ὀνώριον, ἐχάρη χαρὰν μεγάλην.

The *vita* is circumspect on the cause of death ("he ended his life" [*katelusen ton bion*]), but a reader would likely infer that he was executed for his crime on the emperor's order. The author's coyness on the cause of death gives us our first hint that saintly values and imperial ones may not perfectly align. Epiphanius then learns that the emperor plans to appropriate all of Faustinianus's property for the imperial fisc. Epiphanius has a better, more Christian idea: "Look, child, he said; do not be sinful (*mē hamartēsēis*). Faustinianus has a wife who worships God from the heart. Have faith in Epiphanius's words and it will be a gift to you from the Most High."[41] Theodosius obeys his spiritual "father," and when Epiphanius returns to Cyprus he baptizes Faustinianus's widow, ordains her a deaconess, and helps her distribute her late husband's property to the poor.[42] Once instructed, the emperor ceases his "sinful" behavior and toes a more Christian line.[43] But this moral gap between emperor and saint places some distance between the politics of empire and the aspirations of faith, and foreshadows a more dire conflict at the end of the *vita*.

The last chapters of the *vita* are taken up with a transformed version of the Origenist controversy.[44] In the *vita*, the cause of the conflict is the excommunication of three monks who refuse to take up their clerical obligations in Egypt.[45] The monks flee to Constantinople, where they are given shelter by the bishop, John. At the same time, John has come

---

41. *Vita Epiphanii* 103 (Rapp, "*Vita* of Epiphanius," 2:182–83).

42. *Vita Epiphanii* 104 (Rapp, "*Vita* of Epiphanius," 2:184).

43. Similarly, in the next chapter, Theodosius passes a rescript (τύπος) banning heresy in Cyprus, but only after prompting from Epiphanius: *Vita Epiphanii* 106 (Rapp, "*Vita* of Epiphanius," 2:185–86).

44. See Rapp, "*Vita* of Epiphanius," 1:174–76, 188–212, on how the hagiographer minimizes Epiphanius's role in the fall of John Chrysostom and the excesses of the Origenist controversy. Contrast the explicit anti-Origenism of a miracle story edited by Claudia Rapp, "Der heilige Epiphanius im Kampf mit dem Dämon des Origenes: Kritische Erstausgabe des Wunders BHG 6011," in *Symbolae Berolinenses für Dieter Harlfinger*, ed. Friederike Berger et al. (Amsterdam: Adolf M. Hakkert, 1993), 249–64, originating out of the later, sixth-century Origenist controversy in Palestine.

45. *Vita Epiphanii* 107–8 (Rapp, "*Vita* of Epiphanius," 2:186–88).

into conflict with the empress Eudoxia over her immoral seizure of a widow's vineyard.[46] The conniving bishop of Alexandria and the immoral empress both attempt to enlist Epiphanius in bringing down Bishop John on trumped-up charges of heresy.[47] When Epiphanius at last arrives in Constantinople—after drawing John's anger by ordaining priests in a local monastery[48]—he is summoned to meet the empress. Eudoxia explains how the two of them represent the church and empire working in concert: "Father Epiphanius, the entire Roman Empire is mine and all of the priesthood of the churches under my empire is yours."[49] She proposes that Epiphanius's authority will allow him to appoint a new bishop of Constantinople by himself, and she will send John into exile, without the need for any messy or complicated synods.

Epiphanius is unmoved by Eudoxia's proposal. He agrees that if John is indeed a heretic, he will be condemned and found unworthy of his priesthood.

> But [he warns] if this is about your pride (*peri tēs humeteras hubreōs*) that you seek to exile John from the church, your Epiphanius will not agree to this. For it is better, child, of emperors that they should be mistreated and forgive (*hubrizesthai kai sunchōrein*), since even you have an emperor in heaven against whom you customarily sin and he forgives you.[50]

---

46. *Vita Epiphanii* 109–11 (Rapp, "*Vita* of Epiphanius," 2:188–92).

47. *Vita Epiphanii* 112 (Rapp, "*Vita* of Epiphanius," 2:192–93): "When Theophilus heard that the empress wished to exile John, he fabricated to an excessive degree. Theophilus wrote made-up letters to Epiphanius against John, that John held the opinions of Origen and the empress was moved to exile him. Then Epiphanius was persuaded quickly by Theophilus, for he did not know that Theophilus was John's enemy."

48. On the historical background of Epiphanius's extracanonical ordinations, see my discussion in chapter 3.

49. *Vita Epiphanii* 114 (Rapp, "*Vita* of Epiphanius," 2:194): πᾶσα ἡ βασιλεία τῶν Ῥωμαίων ἐμή ἐστιν, καὶ πᾶσα ἡ ἱερωσύνη τῶν ἐκκλησιῶν τῶν ὑπὸ τὴν ἐμὴν βασιλείαν σή ἐστιν. There is no mention of Theodosius, who is presumably dead at this point in the narrative (although his death goes unmentioned). Arcadius, Eudoxia's husband, appears only at the end of this story as Epiphanius sets sail for his last journey to Cyprus: *Vita Epiphanii* 118 (Rapp, "*Vita* of Epiphanius," 2:199).

50. *Vita Epiphanii* 115 (Rapp, "*Vita* of Epiphanius," 2:195).

Whereas Eudoxia had suggested a kind of partnership between king and bishop—"my empire" and "your priesthood"—Epiphanius explains that both of them are loyal to a higher "emperor." Eudoxia wails and threatens Epiphanius: "If you make an impediment, Father Epiphanius, to my exiling of John, I will restore the shrines of idols and I will make the people bow down to them!"[51] Fragile indeed, it seems, is the Christian faith of the house of Theodosius—and of the entire Roman Empire, which could be made, at a word, to bow down to idols again.

To be sure, Eudoxia is not a sympathetic figure in the *vita*. But what I want to point out here is that, taken together with the previous encounters between Epiphanius and the imperial household, she highlights the always latent moral tension between Christianity and Rome. Theodosius, too, had reflexively thought to confiscate the money of a pious widow rather than place his imperial power in service of the church. Epiphanius, who civilized barbarians and warned the Persian king that Christ protects Rome, who baptized emperors and advised Theodosius the Great, ends his life in conflict with the empire. He dies on board the ship during the journey from Constantinople back to Cyprus, alienated from the imperial household that had called him "father."

Epiphanius's Jewish Past

The disrupted relationship between Christianity and empire relates to another curious detail of the *vita:* until his sixteenth year, we learn, Epiphanius was Jewish. The tradition that Epiphanius was a Jew who converted to Christianity and became a monk after a divine vision seems to originate with the *vita*.[52] (It persists in the saints' calendars of

---

51. *Vita Epiphanii* 115 (Rapp, "*Vita* of Epiphanius," 2:196).
52. It is not mentioned by the church historian Sozomen, who includes Epiphanius among his famous Palestinian bishops (*Historia ecclesiastica* 6.32.2 [GCS n.F. 4:288]), nor by Epiphanius's colleague and admirer Jerome.

several modern orthodox denominations.⁵³) The opening of the *vita* is actually somewhat coy on its subject's religio-ethnic origins: "Epiphanius," it begins, "was of the Phoenician people (*Epiphanios genos men ēn Phoinikōn*)."⁵⁴ This geographical circumlocution of "Phoenicia" for "Palestine" occurs at several points in the *vita*, but here it is used to describe Epiphanius's *genos*.⁵⁵ Soon it becomes clear that *Phoenician* is a covert way of describing Epiphanius as *Jewish*.⁵⁶ When his family falls on hard times after his father's death, Epiphanius goes to the market to sell an "unruly donkey." He meets "a certain Jewish businessman named James" who asks Epiphanius: "What religion (*poias thrēskeias*) do you follow?" When Epiphanius replies ("Jewish" [*Ioudaios*]), the businessman replies: "We are of the same *ethnos*."⁵⁷ In this brief exchange, Epiphanius's Jewish identity is now defined as both a religion (*thrēskeia*) and a nation or people (*ethnos*).

The depth of Epiphanius's Jewishness builds throughout this opening section. After his exchange with James the Jew, he meets a Christian named Cleobius, also interested in the donkey. In the midst of their discussion, the unruly donkey throws Epiphanius to the ground.

---

53. See, for instance, the summary of Epiphanius's life by the Greek Orthodox Church in America, at www.goarch.org/chapel/saints_view?contentid = 51. The *Prologue from Ochrid*, by the Serbian saint Nikolai Velimirovic (known as "the new Chrysostom"), contains summaries for each saint's day that are still used by modern Serbian Orthodox Christians; see www.serbianorthodoxchurch.net/cgi-bin/saints.cgi?view = 091571793632. The autocephalous Orthodox Church in America has its own summary of Epiphanius's life; see http://oca.org/saints/lives/2014/05/12/101356-st-epiphanius-the-bishop-of-cyprus.

54. *Vita Epiphanii* 1 (Rapp, "*Vita* of Epiphanius," 2:49). As Rapp points out in her commentary to the *vita* ("*Vita* of Epiphanius," 2:221), this opening line mimics the opening of Athanasius's *Vita Antonii* 1: Ἀντώνιος γένος μὲν ἦν Αἰγύπτιος (SC 400:130).

55. The archaic use of "Phoenicia" for "Palestine" occurs elsewhere in the text: *Vita Epiphanii* 29, 32, 40, 53, 102, 120 (Rapp, "*Vita* of Epiphanius," 2:89, 92, 100, 116, 181, 201).

56. Twice more the *vita* describes Epiphanius as being of the Phoenician *genos*: *Vita Epiphanii* 19, the demon possessing the Persian king's daughter describes him as "of the Phoenician *genos*" (τὸ γένος τῶν Φοινίκων); 40, Epiphanius appears in a vision to the prefect's son Callistus and describes himself as "the Phoenico-Palestinian" (ὁ φοινικοπαλαιστινός) (Rapp, "*Vita* of Epiphanius," 2:70, 100).

57. *Vita Epiphanii* 3 (Rapp, "*Vita* of Epiphanius," 2:51): Σύνεθνοι ὄντες.

Cleobius seizes Epiphanius's wounded thigh, makes the sign of the cross, and heals him. Cleobius then invokes "Jesus the Crucified," and curses the donkey who falls down dead. When Epiphanius asks about "Jesus the Crucified," Cleobius answers: "He is Jesus, the son of God, whom the Jews crucified." The narrator reports: "Epiphanius was afraid to tell Cleobius that he was a Jew."[58] Epiphanius's Jewishness has been constructed as a religion, an ethnicity, and now as a marker of social difference. In the next chapters, Jewishness is further constructed as a body of knowledge. Epiphanius is adopted by a learned Jew named Trypho,[59] who "instructed him diligently in all the matters of the Law and the Hebrew parts of speech with precision."[60] By the end of this section of the *vita*, Epiphanius's Jewish identity is ethnic, religious, social, and cultural.

At this precise moment when Epiphanius's Jewishness has achieved these many layers, his conversion narrative begins. Trypho has died and left all of his property to Epiphanius. While going out to inspect his property, Epiphanius sees a Christian monk giving his cloak to a beggar, and has a vision of a shining garment descending from heaven to replace it. Epiphanius is awestruck. He asks who the stranger is, and is asked his religion in return. "I am a Jew," he answers.[61] The monk is leery: "How is it that you, who are a Jew, inquire of a Christian to learn who I am? For the Jews are an abomination to the Christians, and Christians to the Jews."[62] Epiphanius's response is immediate: "What is

---

58. *Vita Epiphanii* 4 (Rapp, "*Vita* of Epiphanius," 2:52–54).

59. *Vita Epiphanii* 5 (Rapp, "*Vita* of Epiphanius," 2:54–55). Trypho's intention is to marry Epiphanius to his daughter. Both Trypho and his daughter die soon after.

60. *Vita Epiphanii* 6 (Rapp, "*Vita* of Epiphanius," 2:55): ἐπαίδευσεν αὐτὸν ἐμπόνως πάντα τὰ τοῦ νόμου καὶ τὰ στοιχεῖα τὰ ἑβραϊκὰ μετὰ ἀκριβείας.

61. *Vita Epiphanii* 7 (Rapp, "*Vita* of Epiphanius," 2:57): Ἰουδαῖος εἰμι. The simple declaration recalls the confession of martyrs (*Christianus sum*), but here signals a (pending) renunciation rather than an affirmation of religious identity.

62. *Vita Epiphanii* 7 (Rapp, "*Vita* of Epiphanius," 2:57–58). "Abomination" translates βδέλυγμα, recalling the "abomination of desolation" in Dan 9:27, 1 Macc 1:54, and Matt 24:15, passages that discuss the destruction of the Jewish Temple—a charged term to characterize the antipathy of Jews and Christians.

to prevent (*ti kōluei*) me from becoming a Christian?"[63] Epiphanius's words recall those of the Ethiopian eunuch to the apostle Philip in the Acts of the Apostles (Acts 9:36), another moment when ethnicity and religion are overwritten in the act of Christianization. Over the next few chapters Epiphanius and his dependent sister are baptized, and both embrace the monastic life.[64]

At no point in the rest of *vita*—until a strange moment at the very end—do we hear explicit mention of Epiphanius's Jewish origins. The absence of Epiphanius's Jewishness might suggest the absolute absorption of one religion into another, a tale of supersession so total that no trace of the previously textured and layered Jewish identity remains. Yet, I would argue, the *vita* is actually artfully coy on the matter. Later in the *vita*, as Epiphanius and his companion begin a journey in Egypt, they encounter an Alexandrian Jew named Aquila, "learned in the Law" (*nomodidaskalos*).[65] It is probably not a coincidence that the *vita* had applied the same epithet to Epiphanius's adoptive Jewish father, Trypho.[66] Should we not indeed be reminded of Epiphanius's rigorous education "in all matters of the Law" when he engages in a two-day "debate about the Law" (*apo tou nomou dialegesthai*) with Aquila?[67] Were it not for the opening chapters of the *vita*,

---

63. *Vita Epiphanii* 7 (Rapp, "*Vita* of Epiphanius," 2:58).

64. *Vita Epiphanii* 8–12 (Rapp, "*Vita* of Epiphanius," 2:58–62). The course of events (inheritance, inspiration, delivery of sister to a convent) roughly (and surely deliberately) parallels Athanasius, *Vita Antonii* 2–3 (SC 400:132–38).

65. *Vita Epiphanii* 47 (Rapp, "*Vita* of Epiphanius," 2:107).

66. *Vita Epiphanii* 5 (Rapp, "*Vita* of Epiphanius," 2:55).

67. *Vita Epiphanii* 47 (Rapp, "*Vita* of Epiphanius," 2:108). The two-day debate recalls Justin Martyr's *Dialogue with Trypho the Jew* (another echo of Epiphanius's own Jewish education). The name of the Jewish interlocutor here, Aquila, perhaps shows knowledge of the *Dialogue of Timothy and Aquila*. Surviving manuscripts of that *Dialogue* claim it took place in fifth-century Alexandria, during the episcopacy of Cyril (d. 444 CE). Jacqueline Z. Pastis, "Dating the *Dialogue of Timothy and Aquila*: Revisiting the Earlier Vorlage Hypothesis," *HTR* 95 (2002): 169–95, revives early twentieth-century theories that the *Dialogue* underwent at least two periods of redaction and dates originally to the third century. The name Aquila, in both the *Dialogue* and in the *Vita Epiphanii*, would likely invoke the Jewish (and, according to multiple Christian sources, anti-Christian) translator of the Greek Old Testament.

we might view this incident like any of the numerous conversion stories that populate Epiphanius's life.[68] But echoes of Epiphanius's former Judaism, conspicuous by their very faintness, linger in this passage. Likewise, later in the *vita*, another Jew named Isaac "attached himself to Epiphanius and was instructed by him and was baptized." In this case, too, there is a subtle verbal allusion to Epiphanius's Jewish education: like the young Epiphanius, this Isaac "observed the Law of Moses with precision (*meta akribeias*)."[69] Isaac is a double of Epiphanius: a convert from Judaism who becomes a monk and the bishop's lifelong companion.[70]

These hints at a seemingly forgotten Jewish life are compounded by an incident just after Epiphanius's death. After his painful confrontation with John Chrysostom in Constantinople, Epiphanius sails home. He dies aboard the boat during a storm. As his body is laid out, before the ship makes port at Cyprus, one of the curious sailors approaches the body:

> Now one of the sailors, to whom Epiphanius said while he was yet living, "Do not test, lest you be tested," moving toward Epiphanius's feet, wished to lift up Epiphanius's cloak and see if he was circumcised (*idein ei emperitomos estin*). But Epiphanius, even though he lay dead, raised up his right foot and gave it to him in the face, and cast him to the stern of the ship. For two days [the sailor] lay as if dead. On the third day, the sailors lifted him and brought him to Epiphanius. When they set him down at his feet and he touched his feet, straightaway he stood up.[71]

---

68. In addition to the conversion of Epiphanius and his sister, there is the conversion of the Saracen, subsequently named John; a philosopher also named Epiphanius; another philosopher, named Eudaimon; and (as we have seen above) the imperial siblings Arcadius, Honorius, and Proklianē (*Vita Epiphanii* 17, 38–43, 51, 83–91 [Rapp, "*Vita* of Epiphanius," 2:67, 96–103, 112–14, 155–65]). Notably, all of these conversions are effected by Epiphanius's performance of miracles or healings; only Aquila is converted through discourse with Epiphanius.

69. *Vita Epiphanii* 82 (Rapp, "*Vita* of Epiphanius," 2:155); the same phrase was used of Epiphanius's tutelage in the Law and Hebrew by Trypho (see above, n. 60).

70. Isaac is one of several doubles in the *vita*, along with the Syrian philosopher Epiphanius (see above), who becomes the abbot of Epiphanius's monastery and a demon who takes Epiphanius's shape to possess one of his fellow monks (*Vita Epiphanii* 33 [Rapp, "*Vita* of Epiphanius," 2:92–93]).

71. *Vita Epiphanii* 124 (Rapp, "*Vita* of Epiphanius," 2:206–7).

We are not told how or why this sailor thought to make this postmortem inspection and, tantalizingly, neither he nor we get to see beyond Epiphanius's high-kicking foot. Of course, we know, based on the opening chapters of the *vita*, what the sailor would have seen; so why don't we see it?

We might be reminded of the curious ending of the perhaps contemporaneous *Life of Pelagia*, in which narrative fulsomeness gives way to postmortem reticence. In this story, a wealthy prostitute and actress named Pelagia is converted by a bishop and, after her baptism, sneaks away and lives as a eunuch (named Pelagios) on the Mount of Olives near Jerusalem. When "he" dies, the clergy and monks of Jerusalem, upon finding out the true gender of their beloved local monk, try (in vain) to keep the truth from local mourners.[72] In Patricia Cox Miller's elegant reading of the *Life of Pelagia*, this "luminous detail" opens up to view the contradictions of the concept of "holy women" in late antiquity: "paradoxes whose allure is the truth of female holiness."[73] Both of these narratives try to cover up what we know is there, a truth that embodies impossibilities and contradictions. The coyness at this last moment of Epiphanius's life amplifies the teasing nature of Epiphanius's former Jewishness at multiple moments in the *vita*: it is present even when not invoked. A Jewish past only barely concealed—like Pelagia's impossible feminine sanctity—makes itself known at the end of the Christian saint's life. Epiphanius's saintly difference is at once exemplary, demonstrating the transformative power of Christian

---

72. Latin text: *Vita Pelagiae meretricis* 15 (PL 73:670); Syriac text: *Life of Pelagia* 49–50, in *Acta sanctae Pelagiae syriace*, ed. J. Gildemeister (Bonn: Adolphus Marcus, 1879), 11–12 (Syr.); 13–14 (Lat.). English translation of Syriac in Susan Ashbrook Harvey and Sebastian Brock, *Holy Women of the Syrian Orient* (Berkeley: University of California Press, 1987), 61.

73. Patricia Cox Miller, "Is There a Harlot in This Text? Hagiography and the Grotesque," in *The Cultural Turn in Late Ancient Studies: Gender, Asceticism, and Historiography*, ed. Patricia Cox Miller and Dale B. Martin (Durham, NC: Duke University Press, 2005), 87–102; the "luminous detail" (from Ezra Pound via New Historicism) of the "attempted cover-up" is at p. 91; the final quote at p. 97.

conversion, yet impossible, exposing the ineradicable trace of Jewish otherness in the heart of Christian sanctity.

Like so many subjects of hagiography, Saint Epiphanius in his Greek life creates a space to contemplate and interrogate the cultural values of its time. The *vita* seems, above all, concerned with the proper maintenance of boundaries, a clear sense of the difference between a (Roman, Christian, orthodox) self and an (pagan, foreign, Jewish) other. In the idealized world of the saint (echoing, in a way, the work of the historical Epiphanius), piety and power work in concert to maintain these boundaries. Yet the text also uses the figure of the saint to trouble this ideological totality. In a text concerned with protecting boundaries, Epiphanius transgresses them routinely: geographic boundaries (as in the case of the Persian empire), religious boundaries (from Jew to Christian), even the boundary between animal and human (when he speaks to animals ransacking his monastery's garden). Epiphanius more than crosses boundaries; as his lingering Jewish past reminds us, even at the moment of his death, he blurs them. Both Epiphanius's troublesome excess and the questionable Christianity of the imperial household disturb the boundaries of the Christian Roman Empire. The unbridled otherness of the saint and the moral failure of the imperial center together produce a textual space for the *vita*'s audience to question the unity of Christ and Rome.

SAINT EPIPHANIUS: "IN ALL THINGS CATHOLIC"

The Greek *vita* remains untranslated into English,[74] and has received little attention in modern scholarship.[75] This was not always the case:

---

74. It has been translated into French by Fr. Steven Bigham, working from the Migne text (PG 41:23–114) in consultation with Rapp's critical edition: http://srbigham.com/articles/vie-epiphane.html.

75. One exception seems to be the use of the chapters recounting Epiphanius's encounter with Hieracas (*Vita Epiphanii* 49 [Rapp, "*Vita* of Epiphanius," 109–10]). Historians of monasticism use this account as "evidence" for Hieracas's activities in the Egyptian

Greek and Latin versions of the *vita* circulated throughout the Middle Ages and, in the Middle Byzantine period, Epiphanius's Jewish origins played a key role in the iconoclast controversy.[76] Iconoclasts had collated various writings of Epiphanius to support their position, including a letter of Epiphanius to the emperor Theodosius in which the bishop claimed that "he followed the faith of the Nicene fathers from an early age, and his parents were raised in it and held the same confession."[77] In his refutation of the iconoclasts, the iconophile patriarch Nicephorus claimed the letter must be a forgery, based on Epiphanius's *vita:* "But that holy Epiphanius, as we know, was born a 'Hebrew of Hebrews' [cf. Phil 3:5]. And his parents died in that Hebrew religion; but not until he was sixteen years old was he initiated into the Christian faith and received the divine baptism."[78] For Nicephorus, and his medieval opponents, Epiphanius's *vita* held not just hagiographic but historical significance in their dogmatic controversies.

The *vita* emerged as a full-fledged historical source for the life of Epiphanius in post-Reformation church histories,[79] boosted particularly

---

desert; see James Goehring, "Hieracas of Leontopolis: The Making of a Desert Ascetic," in *Ascetics, Society, and the Desert: Studies in Early Egyptian Monasticism* (Harrisburg, PA: Trinity Press, 1999), 110–36.

76. Steven Bigham, *Epiphanius of Salamis, Doctor of Iconoclasm? Deconstruction of a Myth* (Boston: Orthodox Research Institute, 2008), surveys the debates from the Byzantine era to the present and produces a strongly iconophile interpretation of Epiphanius in the course of which he ultimately suggests that the *vita* accurately represents Epiphanius's Jewish birth (103–12).

77. It is numbered as fr. 20 of the *Epistula ad imperatorem Theodosium* by K. Holl, *Gesammelte Aufsätze zur Kirchengeschichte* (Tübingen: Mohr-Siebeck, 1928), 2:360 (the italicized words are not considered part of the "fragment" by Holl): εἰσφέρει ἑαυτὸν ἐν τῇ ἐπιστολῇ τῇ πίστει τῶν ἐν Νικαίᾳ πατέρων ἐκ νέας ἡλικίας ἠκολουθηκέναι καὶ ὡς οἱ γονεῖς αὐτοῦ ἐν ταύτῃ γεγέννηνται καὶ τὴν αὐτὴν εἶχον ὁμολογίαν.

78. Nicephorus I, *Antirrhetica adversus Eusebium et Epiphanidem* 15.61; text in *Spicilegium solesmense complectens sanctorum patrum scriptorumque ecclesiasticorum anecdota hactenus opera*, ed. Jean-Baptiste Pitra (Paris: Firmin Didot Frères, 1858), 4:340. The treatise is "against Epiphanides" because Nicephorus argues that the anti-icon materials ascribed to Epiphanius of Salamis should be ascribed to (an otherwise unknown) Epiphanides: Nicephorus, *Antirrhetica* 1.1 (Pitra, *Spicilegium*, 4:294–95).

79. William Cave's widely read and translated *Scriptorum ecclesiasticorum historia litteraria a Christo nato usque ad saeculum XIV* (London: Richard Chiswell, 1688), 184,

by the Catholic French historian François-Armand Gervaise, who defended his historical use of the *vita* in a lengthy and prickly preface.[80] By the nineteenth century, the historical "kernel" of the *vita*, divorced from its more miraculous (indeed, saintly) aspects, had secured a tenuous place in various European church histories (biblical, Jewish, and Christian).[81] Yet in the fraught religio-political climate of Victorian England, Epiphanius once more took a turn toward the hagiographic, now in a new literary style.

England throughout the nineteenth century roiled with religious struggles set on a political stage. Acts of Parliament in 1828 and 1829 granted full political rights to non-Anglican Christians (Nonconformists and Catholics), and throughout the century evangelicals, liberals, Anglo-Catholics, and Broad Churchmen tangled over the role of government in administering the "state" Church of England.[82] Jews were

---

describes the *vita* as "magnam partem fabulosa," but still reports that Epiphanius's parents were Jewish ("parentibus, ut videtur, ortus Judaeis").

80. François-Armand Gervaise, *L'histoire et la vie de St Epiphane, archevêque de Salamine & docteur de l'Eglise, où l'on voit ce qui s'est passé de plus curieux & de plus intéressant dans l'Eglise, depuis l'An 310 jusqu'en 403 avec l'Analyse des Ouvrages de ce Saint, son Apologie contre les Protestants, & des Notes Critiques & Historiques* (Paris: Jean-Baptiste Lamesle and Pierre-François Giffart, 1738), v-xvi and 3 (on Epiphanius's Jewish childhood). Gervaise is clear that he is only using the *vita* as a historical, not a hagiographical, source (for instance, he does not credit the miracles and has no difficulty declaring some details in the *vita* erroneous).

81. One example: Philip Smith, *The History of the Christian Church during the First Ten Centuries*, The Student's Ecclesiastical History (New York: Harper & Brothers, 1879), 323: Epiphanius was born "of poor Jewish parents"; and n. 1: "This tradition is found in the biography of his pupil John; it is accepted by [William] Cave [see above, n. 79], and derives some support from the knowledge of Hebrew which was possessed by Epiphanius alone of the Fathers, except Jerome."

82. Multiple government interventions into the "state" churches of Great Britain prompted vociferous debate throughout the period. John Keble's 1833 Assize Sermon, entitled "National Apostasy," was a broadside against "Erastianism" (state control of the church) following parliamentary acts dissolving multiple parishes of the Church of Ireland. John Henry Newman would later recall this sermon as the beginning of the Oxford Movement; see C. Brad Faught, *The Oxford Movement: A Thematic History of the Tractarians and Their Times* (University Park: Pennsylvania State University Press, 2003), 3–15.

also slowly achieving parity in British political life, even as images of Judaism (both ancient and modern) became powerful wedges in debates over faith among rival Christian groups.[83] Imperial expansion abroad brought home the new possibility that "other" faiths and practices might intermingle with or even compete with the Christian truth.[84] These discourses about religious difference and national identity found expression in diverse cultural forms, including a subgenre of Victorian novel set in the days of the early church.[85] These novels—written by evangelicals, Catholics, men, and women—imagined the centuries of "primitive Christianity" as a time when church and state clashed, true Christians suffered (but triumphed in their suffering), and exotic and distracting philosophies abounded (including a hauntingly not quite past-tense Judaism).

The most famous trio of these novels, published in the 1850s, makes clear their role in the ongoing religious partisanship. In 1853, Charles Kingsley, an evangelical proponent of "muscular Christianity" and an

---

83. Virginia Burrus, "Hailing Zenobia: Anti-Judaism, Trinitarianism, and John Henry Newman," *Culture and Religion* 3 (2002): 163–77, discusses the alignment of "Catholic" and "Jew" in late nineteenth-century religious politics.

84. On the entanglements of colonialism (particularly in India) and religious emancipations and new religious movements in Britain, see Gaura Viswanathan, *Outside the Fold: Conversion, Modernity, and Belief* (Princeton, NJ: Princeton University Press, 1998).

85. The fullest study of these novels is Royal W. Rhodes, *The Lion and the Cross: Early Christianity in Victorian Novels* (Columbus: The Ohio State University Press, 1995). See also Margaret M. Maison, *The Victorian Vision: Studies in the Religious Novel* (New York: Sheed & Ward, 1961), 117–18, 124–37, 144–47, 156–67, 297; Curtis Dahl, "Pater's *Marius* and Historical Novels on Early Christian Times," *Nineteenth-Century Fiction* 28 (1973): 1–24; Leon B. Litvack, "Callista, Martyrdom, and the Early Christian Novel in the Victorian Age," *Nineteenth-Century Context* 17 (1993): 159–73; and Vincent A. Lankewish, "Love among the Ruins: The Catacombs, the Closet, and the Victorian 'Early Christian' Novel," *Victorian Literature and Culture* 28 (2000): 239–73. The genre "early Christian novels" was an object of literary criticism already by the end of the nineteenth century; see Andrew Lang, "At the Sign of the Ship," *Longman's Magazine* 32.187 (May 1898): 85–88 (who seems to be the first to coin the term "early Christian novels"); and Edward Mortimer Chapman, *English Literature and Religion, 1800–1900* (London: Constable, 1910), 509–11.

ardent anti-Catholic, published the novel *Hypatia, or New Foes with an Old Face*.[86] For Kingsley, the tumultuous period of fifth-century Alexandria provides a chilling warning of the ill effects of modern Catholic appeal to the postapostolic, ascetic "Fathers": decadence, effeminacy, faithless aristocrats weakening the strength of empire by eroding the healthy bonds of marriage and family.[87] Over the next three years, two Catholic-authored novels appeared in response: *Fabiola, or The Church of the Catacombs*, by the recently restored English Catholic cardinal Nicholas Wiseman;[88] and *Callista: A Tale of the Third Century*, by former Tractarian and famous Catholic convert John Henry Newman.[89] These novels, set during the persecutions of Diocletian and Decius, more sentimental than Kingsley's epic tale, lionize ante-Nicene Christians, focusing on their heroism (and martyrdom) as they chose solitude in God against the predations of an irreligious state.[90] Among the dozens of early

---

86. Charles Kingsley, *Hypatia, or New Foes with an Old Face*, 2 vols. (London: John W. Parker and Son, 1853). See Rhodes, *Lion and the Cross*, 86–98; Maison, *Victorian Vision*, 124–37; Andrew Sanders, *The Victorian Historical Novel, 1840–1880* (New York: St. Martin's Press, 1979), 120–48.

87. Joseph Ellis Baker, *The Novel and the Oxford Movement* (1932; repr., New York: Russell & Russell, 1965), 95: "The new foes are those nineteenth-century currents that might break up the family and the rule of the people in a nation: asceticism, skepticism, aristocracy, theocracy. The old face is the Empire of the fifth century." *Hypatia* was originally serialized (in 1851–52) in *Fraser's Magazine*, and revisions before the book publication also served to highlight manliness, family, and the deleterious effects of Catholic asceticism on the nation-state; see Larry K. Uffelman, "*Hypatia:* Revisions in Context," *Nineteenth-Century Literature* 41 (1986): 87–96.

88. Nicholas Cardinal Wiseman, *Fabiola, or The Church of the Catacombs* (London: Burns & Oates, Limited, 1854). *Fabiola* was the first volume in a planned Catholic Popular Library, which printed edifying volumes for lay readers from 1854 to 1861; see Charlotte E. Crawford, "Newman's 'Callista' and the Catholic Popular Library," *Modern Language Review* 45 (1950): 219–21.

89. John Henry Newman, *Callista: A Tale of the Third Century* (London: Burns & Oates, 1856); some editions were titled *Callista: A Sketch of the Third Century*, an earlier title Newman abandoned (Rhodes, *Lion and the Cross*, 114). See Susann Dorman, "*Hypatia* and *Callista:* The Initial Skirmish between Kingsley and Newman," *Nineteenth-Century Fiction* 34 (1979): 173–93. *Callista* also appeared as a volume in the Catholic Popular Library (see above, n. 88).

90. Rhodes, *Lion and the Cross*, 82–141, considers these novels together.

Christian novels that appeared throughout the nineteenth century,[91] these three were the most prominent and most clearly demonstrated the partisan appeal of the genre: all of these competing Christian groups found authoritative historical lessons in the distant past.[92] These novels also show some of the major themes and tropes that characterized the genre: anxiety about the relation between church and state (often figured as a persecuting empire); uncertainty about the relationship of Judaism to Christianity; and debates about ritual and church hierarchy.

In addition to approaching common themes, these novels had a common interest in reimagining the uses of the past. Kingsley, Wiseman, and Newman—despite their vastly different understandings of the value of the "patristic" past—all rejected an earlier, rationalist idea of ancient history, particularly the Enlightenment narrative (and anti-Christianity) of Edward Gibbon.[93] Instead, their romanticized depictions of the early church allowed for a dramatic, even excessive portrayal of characters achieving an exemplary, yet also impossible, religious perfection. In short, these novels transformed the "historical" figures of early Christianity once more into hagiographic ones.[94]

91. There is no definitive list of early Christian novels. A good starting place (although it contains some errors) is Doris B. Kelley, "A Check List of Nineteenth-Century English Fiction about the Decline of Rome," *Bulletin of the New York Public Library* 72 (1968): 400–413, along with the bibliography of Primary Material in Rhodes, *Lion and the Cross*, 357–63.

92. The rise of historicism generally, and the allure of "antiquity" more specifically in this period (following archaeological and textual discoveries, and the popularity of Walter Scott's novels), contributed to the appeal of novels about the past; Rhodes, *Lion and the Cross*, 8–10. See also Maria Poggi Johnson, "Critical Scholarship, Christian Antiquity, and the Victorian Crisis of Faith in the Historical Novels of Edwin Abbot," *Clio* 37 (2008): 399: "The search for the historical church was almost as crucial to nineteenth-century religious sensibilities as was that for the historical Jesus, and both were entwined with the pervasive Victorian preoccupation with origins and development."

93. Sanders, *Victorian Historical Novel*, 122, on the rejection of Gibbon. See, more generally, Linda Dowling, "Roman Decadence and Victorian Historiography," *Victorian Studies* 28 (1985): 597–607.

94. Sanders, *Victorian Historical Novel*, 134: "*Fabiola* is really only hagiography re-dressed as Victorian fiction"; Rhodes, *Lion and the Cross*, 132: "Indeed, much of *Callista* much be seen as part of the hagiographical tradition." Rhodes, *Lion and the Cross*, 91, also

Epiphanius rarely appeared in these semihagiographical early Christian novels.[95] One late Victorian author, however, crafted his own version of the saintly life of Epiphanius, invoking—like both his ancient predecessor and his Victorian contemporaries—the excessive figure of the saint to confront and interrogate issues of empire, religion, and difference. Thomas Wimberley Mossman, an Anglo-Catholic clergyman with a penchant for "primitive" church history,[96] wrote a slim novel in 1874 entitled *Epiphanius: The History of His Childhood and Youth Told by Himself; A Tale of the Early Church*.[97] Mossman (1826–85) was an Oxford-educated Anglican clergyman who embraced increasingly Catholic ritualism during his career. An author of several works of early church history, Mossman ended his life being baptized into the Roman Catholic Church and may even have received covert ordination into a "unionist" Catholic priesthood earlier.[98]

Although Mossman protests in his introduction that "with two or three exceptions, nothing has been taken from the Greek Life of Saint Epiphanius in Metaphrastes but a bare outline of names and alleged

---

points out that Kingsley attacked the Catholic cult of saints in *Hypatia*; even still, I would argue, his portrayal of certain heroic characters (not only Raphael the Jewish convert to Christianity, but the Gothic prince Wulf) is hagiographic in the sense I discuss at the beginning of this paper: putatively exemplary figures who exceed the readers' normative bounds of personhood.

95. Most novels are set either during periods of persecution or, if later, in ancient Britain or Gothic Europe. Epiphanius does appear in the later novel by Frederic William Farrar, *Gathering Clouds: A Tale of the Days of St. Chrysostom* (London: Longman, Green, 1895), 376–85, in a distinctly unsympathetic role ("To Epiphanius the sole norm of orthodoxy was agreement with himself" [379]); on this novel by an evangelical author, see Rhodes, *Lion and the Cross*, 275–82.

96. The year before he published his novel on Epiphanius, Mossman published a church history: *A History of the Catholic Church of Jesus Christ: From the Death of Saint John to the Middle of the Second Century, Including an Account of the Original Organisation of the Christian Ministry and the Growth of the Episcopacy* (London: Longman, Green, 1873).

97. The frontispiece also contains the sparer title *Saint Epiphanius* (London: J. T. Hayes, 1874). I first learned of Mossman's novella from Rapp, "*Vita* of Epiphanius," 1:2.

98. Biographical details were collated from several obituaries by Thompson Cooper, "Mossman, Thomas Wimberley," in *Dictionary of National Biography*, vol. 39, *Morehead—Myles*, ed. Sidney Lee (London: Smith, Elder, 1894), 185–86.

facts,"[99] he in fact follows the first section of the ancient *vita* fairly closely. We meet Epiphanius as a young Jewish boy in Palestine whose family is left bereft after the death of his father. He attempts to sell an unruly donkey, and encounters a Jew and a Christian. After being adopted and educated by a wealthy Jew named Tryphon, and surviving to inherit his estate, Epiphanius is converted to Christianity and monasticism after witnessing a monk's act of kindness. He lives for a time in the Judean desert as a monk, reading and translating Scriptures, and travels to Egypt.[100] Here the Victorian life deviates from the Greek *vita*, as Mossman inserts his version of a famous incident from the *Panarion:* Epiphanius's encounter with a seductive sect of female gnostics.[101] (More on this scene below.)

---

99. Mossman, *Epiphanius*, v-vi. Luigi Lippomano (Aloys Lipomanus) produced the first Latin translation of the Greek *vita* in his *Vitae sanctorum priscorum patrum* (1558), which was then edited and reprinted by Laurentius Surius in his compendious *De probatis sanctorum* (1579). Surius misidentified the *Vita Epiphanii* as the work of Simeon Metaphrastes. When Denis Pétau (in 1622) published his bilingual edition of the *vita*, he included Surius's mistaken ascription. Migne's reprint of Pétau's Greek and Latin in the Patrologia Graeca (1863) finally removed the Metaphrast's name, and Dindorf's edition (based on Pétau's, in 1854) simply identifies the text as the ΒΙΟΣ ΕΠΙΦΑΝΙΟΥ. It seems likely Mossman was working from the Latin text (e.g., he refers to the baptismal sponsor of Epiphanius's sister as "Veronica" [Mossman, *Epiphanius*, 76], whereas in the Greek *vita* she is called "Bernikē" [Rapp, "*Vita* of Epiphanius," 2:62]), possibly in Pétau's edition.

100. In addition to the broad outlines of the story, Mossman retains many specific details from the *vita:* the conversation with Cleobius the Christian is nearly verbatim; Lucian the monk protests he cannot baptize Epiphanius without the local bishop; Epiphanius loses his sandals as he goes to be baptized, and walks barefoot for the rest of his life; after divesting himself of all of his property, Epiphanius keeps a small sum for the purchase of books (calligraphy equipment in the *vita*); Epiphanius's monastery is called "Spanhydrion"; Epiphanius encounters Saracens, and one of them becomes his companion, John (Mossman, *Epiphanius*, 37; 78–79; 81; 97; 123; 126–33).

101. Mossman may actually be taking inspiration from a line in the *vita* (which also seems to be acknowledging this famous scene): on his deathbed on the boat back to Cyprus, Epiphanius recalls: "Such evil happened to me in Phoenicia from the unruly Simonians, such [evil] in Egypt from the impure Gnostics, and such [evil] in Cyprus from the lawless Valentinians and other heresies" (*Vita Epiphanii* 120 [Rapp, "*Vita* of Epiphanius," 2:201]).

While generally faithful to the Greek *vita,* Mossman has made several modifications that signal his particular late Victorian, Anglo-Catholic sensibilities. For instance, it is no longer Epiphanius who convinces animals not to despoil a monastic garden but a simple, illiterate monk named Laetus.[102] The ascription of this saintly moment to Laetus allows Epiphanius—the first-person narrator of the novel—to strike a moderately skeptical pose toward miracles characteristic of Anglo-Catholics of Mossman's generation.[103] Mossman has also inserted several lengthy depictions of religious ritual; Epiphanius's father's funeral, his own baptism (in what is actually the longest scene in the novel), and his ordination are all depicted in loving detail that reflects Mossman's late Anglo-Catholic ritualism.[104] Finally, characters who appear briefly in the Greek *vita* receive names and fuller roles: Epiphanius's sister Callitrope and Tryphon's daughter (and Epiphanius's betrothed) Salome. More interesting, perhaps, than the modifications Mossman has made to the life are those elements he has retained and even enhanced: specifically, the ambivalent role of the Roman Empire and the equally ambivalent significance of Epiphanius's Jewish origins.[105]

---

102. Mossman, *Epiphanius,* 120–23.

103. A longer excursus on miracles appears in Mossman, *Epiphanius,* 34–36. On Mossman's typical skepticism, see Rhodes, *Lion and the Cross,* 189–90. Rhodes doesn't note that the incident, ascribed to Epiphanius, appears in the Greek *vita,* and suggests (also possibly correctly) that the scene was influenced by a popular biography on Saint Francis of Assisi that had been published in 1868: Mrs. [Margaret] Oliphant, *Saint Francis,* The Sunday Library for Household Reading (London: Macmillan, 1868).

104. Father's funeral: Mossman, *Epiphanius,* 10–20; Epiphanius's baptism: Mossman, *Epiphanius,* 81–95; Epiphanius's ordination: Mossman, *Epiphanius,* 136–39. Rhodes, *Lion and the Cross,* 179, describes Mossman as a "prominent leader of the extreme Ritualist party." On the Ritualist strain of late Anglo-Catholicism, see J.E.B. Munson, "The Oxford Movement by the End of the Nineteenth Century: The Anglo-Catholic Clergy," *CH* 44 (1975): 382–95; Nigel Yates, *Anglican Ritualism in Victorian Britain, 1830–1910* (Oxford: Oxford University Press, 1999); Faught, *Oxford Movement,* 44–45 and 123–24.

105. As I noted above, Judaism and empire played a significant role in many early Christian novels of the Victorian era: it is even possible that the complexity of these tropes in the existing Greek *vita* inspired Mossman to produce his own version of the life of Saint Epiphanius.

Epiphanius's Empire

Catholic and Anglo-Catholic authors of early Christian novels rarely set their tales in the post-Constantinian period, preferring like Wiseman and Newman the more inspiring stories of ante-Nicene martyrs.[106] That Mossman has chosen to set his story squarely in the period of Constantine suggests a more tolerant, if still ambivalent, attitude toward the union of church and state.[107] Yet when Mossman does evoke the empire, he almost always pairs mentions of Christian and pagan emperors as a way of distancing the power of empire from the faith of the church. Early in the novel, before his conversion, Epiphanius climbs up a hill near his village from which he can see Mount Zion.[108] The marble of the city walls and buildings, "ablaze with crimson and gold" in the sunset, entrances young Epiphanius. Yet imperial shadows loom over his "vision of wondrous beauty ... my first sight of Zion." Of the "pure white marble" he can see from his perch, he notes, "as I learned in after years, the Emperor Adrian had rebuilt its temple and palaces" and then observes soon after: "I have lived for months in the Holy City after the British Helena adorned it with goodly stones and gifts, and built a glorious Church on every spot which had been consecrated by the presence of our Saviour Christ."[109] Epiphanius speaks positively of both the intervention of Constantine's mother to beautify the holy city and the

---

106. On martyrdom, see Rhodes, *Lion and the Cross*, 107–14; Litvack, "Callista."

107. Rhodes, *Lion and the Cross*, 183, notes Mossman's unusual chronological choice but then suggests the author maintains a "silence about empire" in the novel. As will be clear, I disagree with Rhodes's analysis here.

108. Mossman seems unconcerned with geographic realism: from a hill he could climb as "a little child," Epiphanius can see Jerusalem, "five or six leagues away" (i.e., roughly twenty miles) (Mossman, *Epiphanius*, 4–5); later in the novel, Epiphanius and his fellow monks sell their woven mats "at a large city about a hundred miles to the north-east of our oasis" (111), which he guesses is Palmyra. The distance from Judea to Palmyra is closer to 250 miles, a journey by foot that would take roughly eighteen days each way according to the Stanford Geospatial Network Model of the Roman World (http://orbis.stanford.edu).

109. Mossman, *Epiphanius*, 5. Victorian novelists often emphasized, wherever possible, ancient connections between Britain and the "primitive church"; see Rhodes, *Lion and the Cross*, 263–72.

"pure" "white" remnants of Hadrian's pagan temples.[110] What might have been approving or disapproving comments on the material imposition of empire onto sacred space recedes into the pleasant, but decidedly non-Christian, aesthetic appreciation of "Roman ruins."[111]

I have mentioned already Mossman's skepticism toward miracles throughout the novel. One exception concerns the very miracle that joined together the church and empire. Epiphanius wonders: "Can I doubt that a luminous Cross appeared in mid-heaven to the Emperor Constantine, and that he saw the words written over it in letters of fire, 'By this thou shalt conquer?'" Yet once more he pairs the good Christian emperor with a negative, pagan counterpart:

> And when I think of all the wonderful things which happened when Julian the Apostate endeavoured to rebuild the Temple in Jerusalem, to falsify, if he could, the prophecy of Christ...; when I remember that I was myself at Bethlehem at the time, on a visit to the Shrine of the Nativity, and that I saw the strange lights and appearances in the sky which hung over Jerusalem for many days, how can I doubt that the Hand of the Lord stretched out to do His marvelous works in the sight of all men now, just as much as it was before the eyes of our fathers of old?[112]

Epiphanius recalls much more fulsomely the miracles surrounding Julian, the last pagan emperor; indeed, these are miracles he has himself witnessed! The effect is, once more, to minimize the interpenetration of church and empire: pagan and Christian emperor alike provide occasions for a divine intervention that is more important than either of them.

---

110. Mossman, *Epiphanius*, 16–17, also compares Helena's Christian construction (the dome of the Church of the Holy Sepulcher) with a pagan imperial building ("the great amphitheater of Titus, which I saw in long after years in Rome"). Both buildings are inferior to the wondrous natural cathedral (a hidden cavern) in which Epiphanius's father's funeral is held.

111. On the role of reimagined Roman architecture at the start of the nineteenth-century Gothic revivalism, see Frank Salmon, *Building on Ruins: The Rediscovery of Rome and English Architecture*, Reinterpreting Classicism (Aldershot, UK: Ashgate, 2000).

112. Mossman, *Epiphanius*, 35–36.

At yet another point, Epiphanius recalls as a child seeing old, wounded men begging in his neighborhood; in later life, he realizes that these must have been "Christian Confessors," survivors of the last persecution, "when the tyrants were literally wearied with the numbers of God's servants whom they had put to death." Juxtaposed immediately with this imagery of faithful martyrdom, a favorite of Catholic and Anglo-Catholic authors, comes a moment of religious, imperial triumph:

> How little could I have thought then what my own very eyes would one day behold—the mighty Emperor of the world, the successor of Diocletian, the dread lord of a hundred legions, the glorious Constantine, treating those servants and confessors of the Lord Jesus with honour and respect greater than he paid to the highest nobles and princes of the Empire.[113]

Again, it is possible to read Epiphanius's exultation as a celebration of the Christianization of the Roman Empire. Yet when Epiphanius describes Constantine here as both "the successor of Diocletian" and the "mighty emperor" paying homage to living saints, should the reader feel the contrast between good emperor and bad, or rather sense the thin line that separates beneficent imperial power from harmful imperial power? Do these juxtapositions of Christian and pagan emperors, of patrons and persecutors, convey the triumph of an imperial Christianity, or its inherent weakness?

Two other points in the novel invoke and problematize the triumphant unity of empire and faith. As he begins to narrate his baptism, Epiphanius explains why he is going to give so much detail: "because we were baptized soon after Constantine had given peace to the Church."[114] The implication is that a memorial of Constantinian baptism would be particularly valuable, even especially authentic, to later readers.[115] Yet Epiphanius continues immediately:

---

113. Mossman, *Epiphanius*, 30–31.
114. Mossman, *Epiphanius*, 80–81.
115. Epiphanius is supposedly narrating his life in the year 400, at ninety years of age; Mossman, *Epiphanius*, 1.

And *as yet* no change had been made in the various rites and ceremonies, and prayers and addresses, which had been used in the martyr church, and which were at least as old as the immediate successors of those who had gone in and out with the Lord Jesus during the whole course of His earthly ministry.[116]

The mention of Constantine, it seems, is as much a negative as a positive milestone: he "gave peace" to the church, but also marks a moment when the original, apostolic (indeed, dominical!) rituals began to undergo changes. Similarly, when Epiphanius as a monk sets out on a Holy Land pilgrimage, he notes with appreciation: "Now that the persecutions of the heathen were at an end, pilgrims were beginning to flock from every quarter of the globe."[117] Epiphanius then lists all the places from which these pilgrims were "flocking," concluding: "From all these places and a thousand more, where Roman edicts had never run, and Roman soldiers had never fought or bled or conquered, the converts of Christianity Missionary Priests were beginning to throng to Bethlehem and Nazareth and Calvary."[118] By describing distinct "Christian missionary" activity as more widespread and effective than the political power of Rome, Mossman once more prises apart the church and empire.[119]

In all of these examples, Mossman does not place the church and empire in opposition, as do many other Catholic and Anglo-Catholic early church novelists. At the same time, he does not find any comfort in entangling the two institutional forces: the church remains distinct from, and superior to, the workings of the empire even as it benefits from occasional imperial benevolence. An optimistic yet cautious take on church-state relations in the late Victorian era, to be sure.[120] The

---

116. Mossman, *Epiphanius*, 81 (emphasis added).

117. Mossman, *Epiphanius*, 98–99.

118. Mossman, *Epiphanius*, 99.

119. Anglo-Catholics, in the latter half of the nineteenth century, placed special emphasis on the social and missionary work of the clergy apart from the welfare work of the state, at home and in the colonies; Faught, *Oxford Movement*, 124–50.

120. The parliamentary disestablishment of the Church of Ireland in 1869 increased support among Anglo-Catholics for similar disestablishment of the Church of England, especially after the anti-Ritualist legislation of 1874; Yates, *Anglican Ritualism*, 203–5.

final chapter of the novel, however, changes this relationship dramatically. In this chapter, Epiphanius embarks on a trip to Egypt and along the way stops at what he thinks is a religious establishment.[121] Despite his suspicions about Barbelio, the Christian virgin who receives him,[122] Epiphanius accepts her hospitality. He soon finds himself alone in a room filled with gnostic texts, drugged by Barbelio's wine, and—for the first time in the novel—tempted to break his monastic vows.[123] He recovers his wits and passes the night reading through the "gospels of Gehenna" on the shelves of his room, until his anger "was at a white heat."[124] Storming out and finding a church, Epiphanius consults with the "Bishop and Clergy" about his "never-to-be-forgotten night." He then reports:

> Constantine wielded at that time the scepter of the Roman Empire, and he had given large powers of jurisdiction to the Catholic Church. After listening to my story, the Bishop said he would confer with the civil magistrates about the matter, and decide about what ought to be done. This the Bishop did; and the result was, that this nest of heresy and pollution was utterly broken up, and its inmates, to the number of between sixty and seventy persons, expelled with ignominy from Bubastus.[125]

In this final scene of the novel, empire and church work hand in hand: the emperor "gives" jurisdiction to the church, which in turn "confers with the civil magistrates" to devise a punishment. (It is—perhaps deliberately—unclear who actually executes the expulsion of heretics from the city.[126]) There is no hesitation on the part of Epiphanius—or Mossman—to endorse this imperial intervention in church matters.

---

121. This scene is loosely based on *Panarion* 26.17.4–8 (GCS n.F. 10.1:297–98).

122. Mossman, *Epiphanius*, 153: "Everything seems so extraordinary, so very different from anything I had ever seen, or heard, or read of the ways of Christians. Still there was nothing wrong upon the surface of things. Men say that I am of an unsuspicious nature."

123. Mossman, *Epiphanius*, 160.

124. Mossman, *Epiphanius*, 166.

125. Mossman, *Epiphanius*, 167–68.

126. The original source text in the *Panarion* is equally vague; see my discussion in chapter 3.

Given Mossman's cautiousness about church-state relations in the rest of the novel, this ending is striking. A faith perfect in its purity and persuasiveness is suddenly insufficient, requiring the iron hand of the state to guard the borders of true Catholic Christianity. There had been few mentions of deviant heresy in the novel, and the hand of empire hovered lightly over a unified and empowered Catholic faith. At this end of the novel, a previously unknown fear of the other rears its head, and Mossman must allow for a full and clear convergence of imperial power and Catholic orthodoxy.

Epiphanius's Jewish Past

Two boundaries that preoccupied the Victorian early church novelists—between church and state and between Judaism and Christianity—play an integral, and related, role in Mossman's tale of Epiphanius. Throughout the novel, Mossman emphasizes the natural continuity between Judaism and Christianity, a continuity embodied not only in Epiphanius's conversion from Jew to Christian in the first half of the novel,[127] but in the way Jewishness remains deeply embedded in Mossman's ideal Catholic orthodoxy.

At the outset, Mossman minimizes, even de-Judaizes, Epiphanius's Jewish identity. "I should mention," Epiphanius writes, after his father has died, "that neither my father nor my mother belonged by descent to the race of Israel. They were sprung from those ancient inhabitants of the land of Canaan, most of whom were destroyed by Joshua."[128] Perhaps inspired by the ethnic circumlocution used by the author of the Greek *vita* (*genos men ēn Phoinikōn*), Mossman dislodges Epiphanius's "race" from his Jewish religion.[129] Although his "forefathers had given up

---

127. Conversion was a key element of Victorian early Christian novels, which often reflected anxieties of Victorian religious pluralism; Dahl, "Pater's *Marius*."
128. Mossman, *Epiphanius*, 9.
129. Similarly in the opening, Epiphanius situates his "little village of Palestine" in "what had been in the olden time the land of the Philistines" (Mossman, *Epiphanius*, 1).

their idols, and become worshippers of Jehovah many ages back," Epiphanius is, by race, a gentile.[130] His family's "pre-Jewish," Canaanite identity persists, as he discovers at his father's funeral: his "distant kinsmen and kinswomen" arrive speaking "in the ancient dialect of our tribe, which was spoken two thousand years ago, before the Children of Israel came out of Egypt";[131] similarly, their ancestral burial place dates back "before the Twelve Tribes of Israel under Joshua invaded the land."[132] We might relate Mossman's disentanglement of "religion" and "race" to his late nineteenth-century context, a time during which national and racial identities were seen as coterminous, and the rise of Jews and former Jews in British political life brought religious, racial, and national categories into question.[133] Epiphanius's not-*really*-Jewish identity, on this reading, has been rendered more palatable for an English audience.

It is curious, then, that Mossman augments Epiphanius's Jewish identity as the novel progresses. As in the Greek *vita,* Mossman's Epiphanius encounters three men who query his religion. Jacob, the Jewish dealer interested in buying Epiphanius's unruly ass, asks, "Of what religion art thou, my son?" to which Epiphanius replies, "I am a Jew."[134] When he encounters Cleobius, the Christian who curses the ass to die, Epiphanius is (as in the *vita*) coy about his identity: "I did not like to tell

---

130. Mossman, *Epiphanius,* 10. He continues directly: "And except for the strictness with which all true Jews preserve their genealogies, we should have been considered by them, as well as by ourselves, to be descendants of Abraham according to the flesh."

131. Mossman, *Epiphanius,* 11.

132. Mossman, *Epiphanius,* 18; see also p. 40, where Epiphanius rhapsodizes about "our little vineyard [which] had belonged to our ancestors for untold generations ... it had been theirs before the Israelites came out of Egypt." Linguistic heritage and rootedness in the land played profound roles in the articulation of national racial identity in the nineteenth century; see Peter Mandler, *The English National Character: The History of an Idea from Edmund Burke To Tony Blair* (New Haven, CT: Yale University Press, 2006), 72–86.

133. Michael Ragussis, *Figures of Conversion: "The Jewish Question" and English National Identity* (Durham, NC: Duke University Press, 1995), 130–73.

134. Mossman, *Epiphanius,* 25.

him outright that I was a Jew."[135] In both cases the phrase "I am a Jew" seems to speak solely to religion, preserving Epiphanius's racial gentileness.[136] Yet when Epiphanius encounters Lucian the monk, who asks him, "Who and what art thou, my son?" Epiphanius responds, "I am a Jew, both as to race and religion."[137] We know, of course, this is not the case. Later in the novel, Epiphanius also refers to his Israelite "forefathers" who "conquered" and displaced the Canaanites.[138] How do we explain this sudden racialization of Epiphanius's Jewishness?

Throughout Mossman's novel, Epiphanius attests to the deep affinity and continuity between the Jewish past and the Catholic present. The authentic core of Judaism is absorbed into Christianity, and the intensification of Epiphanius's Jewishness embodies this process of religious absorption. Early on, Mossman depicts the natural compatibility of Judaism and Christianity: "When I was a boy," Epiphanius recalls, "I remember that the Jews and Christians in our part of the country lived together in a very friendly and neighbourly way. I never heard of such a thing as a Jew refusing to do a good turn to a Christian, or a Christian to a Jew."[139] Jews and Christians even chant their Psalms to the same melodies.[140] The novel quickly moves from mere compatibility to deep continuity.

Epiphanius's adoptive father, Tryphon, is unquestionably a Jew, a descendant of Aaron and a Scribe. Yet his Jewishness is of a notably Catholic sort:

> Tryphon belonged to what may be called the elder school of Hebrew expositors of the Sacred Scriptures: that school which, now that I am writ-

---

135. Mossman, *Epiphanius*, 37.
136. Similarly, Mossman, *Epiphanius*, 55: "No one of the race of Israel might, at this time, enter *their own* holy city on pain of death" (emphasis added).
137. Mossman, *Epiphanius*, 76; see also p. 46: "Ever since I could remember, I had an intense longing to learn all I could about the language, and history, and religion, and traditions of *our forefathers*" (emphasis added).
138. Mossman, *Epiphanius*, 108.
139. Mossman, *Epiphanius*, 28.
140. Mossman, *Epiphanius*, 15, 82, 103.

ing in extreme old age, is almost, if not entirely extinct among the Jews themselves, but whose traditionary expositions of the Messianic prophecies have become the priceless heritage of the Catholic Church.[141]

If Tryphon represents the Jewish "preparation for the gospel," his daughter Salome (Epiphanius's betrothed) embodies utterly the transfiguration of Jew into Christian. Blonde and blue-eyed, "of that rare type among the daughters of Abraham, with which one stream of tradition in the Catholic Church loves to represent the Virgin Mother of God as endowed,"[142] Salome sees quite clearly the truth of Christ in the Old Testament, which she then attempts to impart to her father and to Epiphanius.[143] When Salome grows weak and approaches death, she even intuits the sign of the cross from her reading of the prophets, and begs Epiphanius to bless her with this sign. She then weeps so profusely in her realization of Christian truth that (Epiphanius reports) she "was indeed baptized with the baptism of her own tears, and was sealed for everlasting salvation with the life-giving sign of the Cross."[144] The naturalness with which Salome moves from an authentic, messianic Judaism to the truth of the "Catholic" faith presages Epiphanius's own conversion in the next chapter.

When Epiphanius does convert, he finds he is already prepared, both intellectually and emotionally: "We had nothing to unlearn; we had no prejudices to renounce; we were waiting for this teaching of the Cross, and drank it in, as the parched land drinks in the rain and the dew from

---

141. Mossman, *Epiphanius*, 43. Epiphanius learned these "Messianic traditions" from Tryphon and "these traditions I have embodied in various parts of those works which I have endeavoured to write for the honour and glory of God" (44).

142. Mossman, *Epiphanius*, 50. Salome also recalls the biblical figures of Miriam, Jephthah's daughter, and "above all" Judith (54–55).

143. Mossman, *Epiphanius*, 59–62: Salome has a discussion with her father in which she proposes that "Jesus of Nazareth, Whom the Christians worship, is after all our own Messiah" (59), replicating in miniature Justin Martyr's more famous dialogue with Trypho(n).

144. Mossman, *Epiphanius*, 68. Salome's protracted deathbed scene plays on familiar tropes of martyrdom and death in other early church novels; Litvack, "Callista."

heaven."[145] His Jewish past informs and enriches his pursuit of a Catholic, monastic life. As he and his monastic mentor Hilarion tour the Holy Land, he can see "with his spirit's eyes" the rich biblical history—Jewish and Christian—flowing around him.[146] He studies the Scriptures, and exclaims: "As I read the Hebrew, I could not help feeling how tame in comparison was the Septuagint Version, or indeed any other translation I had ever seen."[147] Epiphanius even translates portions of Exodus for his (Christian) reader, including a brief disquisition on the "reflexive verb *mithlakkachath*."[148] Epiphanius's knowledge and love of Hebrew is quite explicitly a remainder of his Jewish education under Tryphon,[149] yet at the same time grounds Epiphanius in an unchanging Christian tradition. Epiphanius's knowledge of Hebrew allows him to discount a rationalizing interpretation of the ravens feeding Elijah (1 Kings 17), and he remarks: "In all these things I prefer to follow the tradition of the Catholic Church," a tradition deeply embedded in—if not coterminous with—his pious Jewish education.[150] Not only is Epiphanius after his conversion "in all things Catholic," but he always has been: from his Jewish childhood through his ordination to the priesthood, Epiphanius has embodied an eternal truth that has existed unchanging from the first moments of sacred history. This eternal and unchanging truth naturally absorbs and perpetuates its pristine Jewish past. The incorpora-

---

145. Mossman, *Epiphanius*, 80.
146. Mossman, *Epiphanius*, 101–6.
147. Mossman, *Epiphanius*, 113.
148. Mossman, *Epiphanius*, 114.
149. Mossman, *Epiphanius*, 45–48, 65. Salome, Tryphon's daughter, has learned even more of the Hebrew language and biblical texts (64–65).
150. Mossman, *Epiphanius*, 124–25: "Some learned men, among them Hieronymus of Dalmatia, whom I once met with at Bethlehem, are of opinion that when it is said in the Book of Kings, the ravens, by the command of God, brought unto Elijah bread and flesh in the morning, and bread and flesh in the evening, the word ravens out to be translated Arabians. I do not think so myself, although it is quite true that the Hebrew word *Oreb*, may mean Arab, or a raven." The minimization of the historical Epiphanius's friendship with Jerome is notable here, perhaps reflective of the more sublimated distance between the saintly Epiphanius and the historical Epiphanius (with whom Jerome was so close).

tion of a true, ancient, and pristine Judaism into the eternal truth of Catholic Christianity explains the fulsome—even growing—Jewishness of Mossman's saintly hero.

This deep continuity between Judaism and Christianity also, I suggest, illuminates the strange role of empire in the novel: evanescently, even benignly, present, until the sudden threat of heresy brings it into sharp focus and total alignment with the church. Mossman's novel imagines a world in which religious truth is clear and eternal, stretching from the origins of God's contact with humanity into his own Victorian present. There is no true religious difference, since the truth of the Jewish other is the truth of the Catholic self. Epiphanius—the ex-Jew whose essential Jewishness feeds directly into his Catholic sainthood—embodies this eternal truth. In a world in which primitive otherness flows naturally into eternal truth, imperial intervention is unnecessary. In Mossman's own day, however, religious truth was not clear and eternal but fragmentary and contested. Jews and ex-Jews did not so much illuminate the truth of God's eternal message, but rather confused it. Benjamin Disraeli, the most famous ex-Jew of Mossman's day, represents this confusion in multiple contexts: religion, letters, and politics.[151] So at the end of the story Epiphanius's saintly certainty begins to slip—under the influence of a "demonic wine" (*oinos daimonōn*)[152]—at which point the Roman Empire steps in to steady the momentarily teetering edifice of Christian truth. The threat of religious difference, so easily contained before, irrupts in the final chapter of Mossman's novel, requiring the iron hand of empire to secure the hoped-for, but ultimately impossible, absorption and expulsion of religious difference.

151. Richard Dellamora, "Benjamin Disraeli, Judaism, and the Legacy of William Beckford," in *Mapping Male Sexuality: Nineteenth-Century England*, ed. Jay Losey and William Dean Brewer (Cranbury, NJ: Associated University Presses, 2000), 145–77; and Dellamora, *Friendship's Bonds: Democracy and the Novel in Victorian England* (Philadelphia: University of Philadelphia Press, 2004), 47–69; Ragussis, *Figures of Conversion*, 174–233.

152. Mossman, *Epiphanius*, 160.

EPIPHANIUS, THE SAINT AND THE MAN

To quote Meltzer and Elsner once more, the saint's world "is a world of transgressions." Hagiography presents us with a familiar world rendered slightly askew, bounded by familiar borders, which the saint routinely, even profligately, transgresses. The worlds evoked in our two lives of Epiphanius bear remarkable similarities, despite their chronological and geographic distance. Indeed, it is because of these thematic similarities that I have brought together these two lives. Both texts, on the surface, depict a familiar world in which imperial power and religious faith have been brought into a precarious balance, a world in which religious difference, symbolized by the saint's Jewish past, has been overcome and absorbed into a triumphant, imperial Christian present. Yet both of these saintly representations also hint at their own impossibilities. The ancient saint's Christian Roman Empire is ultimately unable to match the excessive piety of the saint who—after all—has not totally overcome his own Jewish difference. The Victorian saint's ability to transform religious difference into Catholic truth also fails in the face of devious otherness, requiring the intervention of a previously unnecessary imperial hand. In both contexts, the life of a saint opens up a space to confront acute anxieties over religion and difference in the context of empire. The Byzantine life of the saint prompts its audience to ask, if only the supernatural power and authority of the saint can control and manage difference, can the imperial authorities entrusted with religious border control possibly succeed? The Victorian life of the saint poses a similar question from a different angle: if even the saintly embodiment of eternal truth cannot fend off otherness without the secular arm of the law, will Catholic Christianity ever be free of the interventions of the state? Impossible hopes for difference contained or expelled, with or without the power of empire, oscillate uneasily in the life of a saint.

I want to conclude this comparison of two hagiographic moments with a question: how did Epiphanius become, in these two distant moments, the patron saint of the anxieties of religious difference in the space of empire? Here, I suggest, the historical Epiphanius lurks behind his hagiographic doppelgänger. As we have seen throughout this chapter, the saintly Epiphanius, in the fifth century and the nineteenth, cuts a holy figure rather different from the historical Epiphanius. The fifth-century saint is a demon-expelling wonder-worker; the nineteenth-century saint is a softhearted, intellectual renunciant. Yet behind these saintly lives hides a more familiar Epiphanius: the author of an encyclopedia of heresies who spent his final decades facing off against "heretical" bishops across the eastern Mediterranean. We have already seen that Mossman draws on Epiphanius's *Panarion* for his final chapter. The Greek *vita* likewise makes a cursory reference to the *Panarion* in Epiphanius's deathbed speech.[153] Both hagiographers suppress the heresiological Epiphanius, all the while making clear that they—and we—know he is there.

In both of these hagiographical transfigurations of Epiphanius, we can sense a nascent discomfort with the cultural formations promulgated by the bishop himself, grounded so deeply in imperial forms of power and control over modes of otherness and difference. What had been seemingly persuasive during Epiphanius's lifetime began, in the centuries after his death and well into the modern period, to seem less compelling. While his celebrity endured (at least into the twentieth century), his cultural ideas did not. Yet even so, the historical master of "otherness" lies like a dark shadow behind the embodied, queered Christian "other" of these lives of Saint Epiphanius.

---

153. *Vita Epiphanii* 120 (Rapp, "*Vita* of Epiphanius," 2:202): "Turn away from every heresy as from beasts plump with fatal poison (θηρία μεστὰ ἰοῦ θανατικοῦ): concerning these also I have handed over to you in writing the books called *Panarion*." Certainly Mossman was also more than just passingly familiar with Epiphanius's heresiology, as he cites him more than a dozen times as a source in his history of ante-Nicene Christianity, written just before *Epiphanius* the novel; Mossman, *History of the Catholic Church*. In an appendix on the Arian controversy, Mossman even includes himself among the "careful" readers of Epiphanius (483 n. 1).

Conclusion

The two saint's lives under examination in chapter 6 reveal a nascent discomfort with the historical Epiphanius as we have encountered him in the previous chapters: the shadow of Epiphanius the activist bishop and indefatigable heresiologist lingers uneasily behind the haloed image of Epiphanius the saint. This discomfort has only become amplified in the modern historiographic field of late antiquity, a field that has reified and canonized a certain set of persons, themes, and desires—all of which demand the exclusion or, at least, the marginalization of Epiphanius. I have alluded in several chapters to the low opinion of Epiphanius held in most modern scholarship and, indeed, it has become something of a commonplace in rare studies of Epiphanius to quote these poor reviews like something of a prophylactic mantra.[1] Many of the criticisms of Epiphanius seem to pertain to his personality: he is, as one scholar said to me, "horrible," an intolerant and mean-spirited

---

1. See Young Richard Kim, *Saint Epiphanius of Cyprus, Ancoratus*, FC 128 (Washington, DC: Catholic University of America Press, 2013), 10–11, 14–15; *The Panarion of Epiphanius of Salamis*, vol. 1, *Book I (Sects 1–46)*, ed. Frank Williams, NHMS 63 (Leiden: Brill, 2009), xxxi-xxxii; Jon Dechow, *Dogma and Mysticism in Early Christianity: Epiphanius of Cyprus and the Legacy of Origen*, PMS 13 (Macon, GA: Mercer University Press, 1988), 26–27; Andrew S. Jacobs, "Epiphanius of Salamis and the Antiquarian's Bible," *JECS* 21 (2013): 440–41; and my comments in the introduction.

bully. Yet it is hard to say that Epiphanius's personality, such as we have access to it, is substantially more intolerant or unpleasant than those of many of his contemporaries. No doubt this disgust with Epiphanius's personality relates to his best-known work: a vituperative catalogue of heresies that reduces fellow Christians to poisonous insects to be crushed underfoot. If we view Epiphanius solely through the lens of the *Panarion*, he comes off as a perhaps uniquely disagreeable character. And it may be that, in fact, he was personally unpleasant, although we can infer moments of intimacy and camaraderie from writings that mention Epiphanius. Unlike his hagiographers, I have no desire to rescue the person of Epiphanius from his unfortunate reputation.[2]

Routine critiques and dismissals of Epiphanius, however, boil down to his incompatibility with our present notion of "late antiquity." Where Epiphanius strikes us as narrow, intransigent, and antiphilosophical, the cultural construction of late antiquity as it has taken root since the 1970s emphasizes expansion, openness, and intellectual flowering.[3] If our view of late antiquity is correct, Epiphanius must be an outlier. Our distaste for him is therefore historically as well as ethically justified. Here my aim is to push back against this trend in scholarship. We may indeed find Epiphanius objectionable on all sorts of grounds, but we should not, I argue, dismiss him outright from our construction of late antiquity. Young Richard Kim has gone so far as to assert that "Epiphanius of

---

2. Gabriella Aragione, "Una 'storia' universale dell'eresia: Il *Panarion* di Epifanio," in *Epifanio di Salamina: Panarion, Libro primo*, ed. Giovanni Pini, Letteratura Cristiana Antica, nuova serie 21 (Brescia: Morcelliana, 2010), 5, asserts that "la ricerca scientifica più recente cerca, tuttavia, di recuperare l'importanza storica del vescovo di Costanza." Such "recuperation," I think, is less evident in Anglophone scholarship.

3. A typical recent statement: "Late Antiquity witnessed the growth and development of major religious movements while at the same time witnessing the transformation of ancient religious traditions under the influence of a plethora of multi-cultural social and political changes" (Richard Valantasis, introduction to *Religions of Late Antiquity in Practice*, ed. Richard Valantasis, Princeton Readings in Religions [Princeton, NJ: Princeton University Press, 2000], 5).

Cyprus was late antiquity."[4] My argument throughout this volume has been that we need to integrate Epiphanius into our historical vision of the late fourth century, to take him as seriously as his contemporaries did. In this concluding chapter, I assess the modern assumptions and contexts for the Anglo-American understanding of "late antiquity," and the ways in which Epiphanius seems not to fit. I then ask how late antiquity, at least in its fourth-century incarnation, would look differently with Epiphanius at its center (or at least drawn in from the margins).

LATE ANTIQUITY IN THE MODERN ERA

Several historiographic essays in the past decades have considered how we arrived at our present, generally Anglo-American disciplinary field of late antiquity or late ancient studies.[5] Since Peter Brown's landmark publications of the 1970s and 1980s,[6] which indubitably established late antiquity in our canonical list of historical periods to be studied,[7]

---

4. Young Richard Kim, *Epiphanius of Cyprus: Imagining an Orthodox World* (Ann Arbor: University of Michigan Press, 2015), 1.

5. Among those I have consulted closely in this chapter are Clifford Ando, "Decline, Fall, and Transformation," *JLA* 1 (2008): 31–60; Andrea Giardina, "Esplosione di tardoantica," *Studi Storici* 40 (1999): 157–80; and the several essays in *Symbolae Osloenses* 72 (1997): 5–85, on "The World of Late Antiquity Revisited." I refer, throughout this conclusion, to the "Anglo-American" field of late antiquity, since English-language scholarship has predominated in the institutional inscription of this period. That is not to say that Continental thought has not been deeply influential in the field since its inception; see Mark Vessey, "The Demise of the Christian Writer and the Remaking of 'Late Antiquity': From H.-I. Marrou's Saint Augustine (1938) to Peter Brown's Holy Man (1983)," *JECS* 6 (1998): 377–411.

6. Particularly the popular book *The World of Late Antiquity, AD 150–750* (London: Thames & Hudson, 1971) and his essay collections *Religion and Society in the Age of Augustine* (London: Faber & Faber, 1972); *The Making of Late Antiquity* (Cambridge: Harvard University Press, 1978); and *Society and the Holy in Late Antiquity* (Berkeley: University of California Press, 1982).

7. In the past thirty years "late antiquity" has gained not only popular momentum (note the inclusion of "Late Antiquity" as one of the "Periods of the History of Europe" on Wikipedia [http://en.wikipedia.org/wiki/Late_Antiquity]) but institutional presence: a regular North American conference (Shifting Frontiers in Late Antiquity, which first met at the University of Kansas in 1995 and has met every other year since);

one of the defining features of this field has been its attention to culture. Culture stands at the productive center of the modern historiographic creation of "late antiquity" in two, related senses. First, the integration of sociocultural methods and theories into the study of the late ancient Mediterranean and Near East shifted scholarship away from the predominating attention to more "social scientific" areas of study in the 1950s and 1960s.[8] Studies of the military, politics, and economy have certainly not disappeared from the examination of the late Roman Empire,[9] but they have arguably taken a backseat to studies of religion, philosophy, and literature in the Anglo-American context.[10] Culture has become the primary focus of study for scholars of late antiquity.

The second sense in which culture has shaped the field of late antiquity is in how we assign and do not assign value to cultural production. What had once been demeaned as a period of "decadence" and artistic decline—"The poetical fame of Ausonius condemns the taste of his age," Gibbon famously quipped as an aside in a footnote[11]—has been

---

a peer-reviewed journal (*Journal of Late Antiquity*, which began appearing in 2008); as well as series (Oxford Studies in Late Antiquity), graduate programs (University of Illinois at Urbana-Champaign), and innumerable books, journals, and conference talks.

8. See Dale B. Martin, introduction to *The Cultural Turn in Late Ancient Studies: Gender, Asceticism, and Historiography*, ed. Dale B. Martin and Patricia Cox Miller (Durham, NC: Duke University Press, 2005), 1–21; and Peter Brown, "The Rise and Function of the Holy Man, 1971–1997," *JECS* 6 (1998): 353–76.

9. The two volumes on late antiquity added to the updated *Cambridge Ancient History* reference series certainly give more than equal time to traditional categories such as "Government and Institutions," "Economy and Society," and "Foreign Relations" before turning to "Religion" and "Art and Culture" (or, in volume 14, "Religion and Culture"). See the review essay of Garth Fowden, "Elefantiasi del tardoantico?," *Journal of Roman Archaeology* 15 (2002): 681–86, the title of which alludes to Giardina, "Esplosione," 168, who refers (without the question mark) to "L'elefantiasi del tardoantico."

10. Bryan Ward-Perkins, *The Fall of Rome and the End of Civilization* (Oxford: Oxford University Press, 2005), 178–80.

11. Edward Gibbon, *The History of the Decline and Fall of the Roman Empire* (London: W. Strahan, 1783), 5:3–4 n. 1: "Valentinian was less attentive to the religion of his son; since he entrusted the education of Gratian to Ausonius, a professed pagan (Mem. de l'Academie des Inscriptions, tom. xv. p. 125–138). The poetical fame of Ausonius condemns the taste of his age." Peter Brown early on held up Gibbon as a foil in the

redeemed under a new name. Alois Riegl, at the turn to the twentieth century, denominated the period of "late antiquity" (*spätere Antike*) precisely in order to recuperate previously unappreciated formal aspects of late Roman art.[12] Attention to the cultural production of late antiquity (art, religion, literature, and so forth) has consistently sought to evaluate these products on their own terms, rather than inscribing their inferiority to "classical" models.[13] Taking a page from the new anthropology initiated in the 1960s by Mary Douglas and Clifford Geertz,[14] scholars of late antiquity study its cultures in a spirit of positive discovery rather than negative contrast.[15]

Two additional facets of the study of late antiquity follow from this cultural turn: its reflexivity and its focus on religion. From its very

---

cultural revaluation of this period; see Brown, "Gibbon's Views on Culture and Society in the Fifth and Sixth Centuries" and "In Gibbon's Shade," two essays from the 1970s reprinted in *Society and the Holy in Late Antiquity* (Berkeley: University of California Press, 1982), 22–62.

12. Giardina, "Esplosione," 158–59, citing Alois Riegl, *Spätrömische Kunst-Industrie nach den Funden in Österreich-Ungarn* (Vienna: Österreichische archäologische Institut, 1901), 2, who refers for the first time to "den Werken der spätesten Antike" and subsequently to "spätantike Kunstwollen" (38, 41, 190), a double neologism that seems to indicate something both more and less than "late ancient Zeitgeist"; see the helpful overview of Otto Pächt, "Art Historians and Art Critics, vi: Alois Riegl," in *Historiography: Critical Concepts in Historical Studies*, vol. 3, *Ideas*, ed. Robert Burns (London: Routledge, 2006), 268–81.

13. Tim Whitmarsh has recently attempted a similar aesthetic appreciation and recuperation of late ancient Greek literature under the rubric "postclassicism": *Beyond the Second Sophistic: Adventures in Greek Postclassicisim* (Berkeley: University of California Press, 2013), esp. his introduction (1–7).

14. On Geertz's influence on the study of early Christianity, see Elizabeth A. Clark, *History, Theory, Text: Historians and the Linguistic Turn* (Cambridge, MA: Harvard University Press, 2004), 145–55. Geertz begins appearing in Peter Brown's footnotes in the 1970s; see "The View from the Precipice," in *Society and the Holy*, 204 n. 20 (this essay appeared earlier in the *New York Review of Books* 21.15 [October 3, 1974], but without footnotes and thus without explicit reference to Geertz); Brown, "Holy Man, 1971–1997," 360, credits his reading of (and conversations with) Mary Douglas for a dawning awareness that "cultural and religious judgments as to ... relative worth were deemed irrelevant."

15. Peter Brown, "The World of Late Antiquity Revisited," *Symbolae Osloenses* 72 (1997): 10, speaks of his desire to view the late Roman Empire "in a different, less sinister light."

origins, the cultural (and cultured) study of late antiquity connected profoundly to anxieties about the values of the modern era. Alois Riegl explicitly linked his recuperation of "late ancient" art genealogically and conceptually to a positive appreciation of "modern" artists who drew on non-Western artistic forms. Since the 1960s, late antiquity has served implicitly and, at times, explicitly as a historical mirror in which to gaze upon our own particular preoccupations with empire, colonialism, multiculturalism, and social politics.[16] A period once characterized by the decline of "traditional" society, by the destructive triumph of "outsiders" (barbarians and Christians), was now reimagined as a period of positive "transformation." So too a postcolonial modernity might learn to view the fall of European empires not as the twilight of civilization, heralded by the destructive triumph of non-Western culture and the decline of traditional religion, but as the beginning of a new, transformative age.[17]

As the culture of late antiquity was refashioned in modern eyes, it was religion that took center stage in this new field of study.[18] If

---

16. Giardina, "Esplosione," 162: "L'esaltazione della modernità tardoantica potrebbe essere definita come un neoclassicismo intriso di cristianesimo e di pluralismo etnico"; Ward-Perkins, *Fall of Rome*, 176: "The vision of Late Antiquity as full of positive cultural achievements also has obvious roots in modern attitudes to the world."

17. Giardina, "Esplosione," 158–63; Brown, "Holy Man, 1971–1997," 355–58; Brown, "World of Late Antiquity," 7–9; G.W. Bowersock, "The World of Late Antiquity Revisited," *Symbolae Osloenses* 72 (1997): 32: "There was something about the late sixties that impelled younger ancient and medieval historians of the time to look to more exotic cultures"; Peter Brown, "Reply to the Comments," *Symbolae Osloenses* 72 (1997): 79–80; Ward-Perkins, *Fall of Rome*, 178.

18. Hervé Inglebert, "Introduction: Late Antique Conceptions of Late Antiquity," in *The Oxford Handbook of Late Antiquity*, ed. Scott Fitzgerald Johnson (Oxford: Oxford University Press, 2012), 16: "In the late antique world, religious values became the central values, even the supreme values, for conceiving of the world and for justifying discourse and action"; and Ando, "Fall and Transformation," 49: "Much of what is 'new' in Late Antiquity falls within the domain of religion." On the degree to which this religiosity is Christian, see Alan Cameron, *The Last Pagans of Rome* (Oxford: Oxford University Press, 2011); and the review by Peter Brown, "Paganism: What We Owe the Christians," *New York Review of Books* 58.6 (April 2011): 68–73.

Gibbon had shown his Enlightenment colors in his cultured rejection of nascent Christianity, a new generation of scholars of late antiquity could find in the rise of Christianity not a grim, repressive, and irrational superstition but a productive and creative cultural movement that could become exemplary for a particularly modern liberal society. To take one prominent example of this historiographic alchemy we can consider the study of late ancient monasticism. What had been for Gibbon the clearest symptom of the creeping rot of superstitious Christianity, populated by "unhappy exiles from social life ... impelled by the dark and implacable genius of superstition,"[19] has become a series of complex and even admirable "technologies of the self,"[20] in which new possibilities of personhood—and even personal liberation—might be explored.[21]

Of course, I am not suggesting that all studies of late antiquity are unremittingly positive.[22] Nonetheless the remarkable scholarly transformation of the late Roman Empire into late antiquity has fundamentally altered our approach to this period. Like post-Geertzian anthropologists, we are open to taking late antique culture "on its own terms," as possessing an inherent logic and sensibility that it is our job to understand. By making late antiquity culturally sensible, we also render it potentially compatible with our own cultural ideals. We are open to seeing ourselves reflected embryonically in the past laid out before us, and the

---

19. Edward Gibbon, *The History of the Decline and Fall of the Roman Empire* (London: W. Strahan, 1783), 6:247.

20. The influence of French philosophy, particularly Michel Foucault, on the study of asceticism has been traced by Averil Cameron, "Redrawing the Map: Early Christian Territory after Foucault," *JRS* 76 (1986): 266–71; see also Elizabeth A. Clark, "Foucault, the Fathers, and Sex," *JAAR* 56 (1988): 619–41.

21. The bibliography of late ancient asceticism is vast, beginning with Brown's own *The Body and Society: Men, Women, and Sexual Renunciation in Early Christianity* (1988; repr., New York: Columbia University Press, 2008).

22. Already in *World of Late Antiquity*, Brown noted: "The Christian congregations of the 380s wanted a 'Christian' empire, purged of the heavy legacy of the gods, and ruled by an emperor who shared their prejudices against Jews, heretics, and pagans" (104).

canon of "late ancient authors" upon whom we tend to labor possesses a glint of cultural possibility. Augustine has long been a kind of late ancient mascot, the troubled but brilliant spokesman of a troubled but brilliant age.[23] Other canonical figures of late antiquity, and of late antique Christianity in particular, have value in their illumination of aspects of late ancient culture; as new figures enter into the historiographic world of late antiquity their cultural potential likewise secures their place.

To take one recent example, the Egyptian monastic leader Shenoute (whom I discuss briefly in chapter 5) has relatively recently entered into late ancient scholarship. Although he was a notoriously violent and difficult character, scholars nonetheless find in him and his writings new ways of understanding bodily discipline, moral authority, and social institutions, such as the family, poverty, and health care.[24] It is fair to say that the scholars doing such innovative work on Shenoute do not particularly like him or identify with him as a personal role model. Rather, despite any personal feelings toward an often disturbing person, scholars of late antiquity can find in him some kind of cultural value that resonates with our own modern and postmodern concerns about personhood, gender, self-fashioning, communal care, and social justice. It is a question, I suggest, of historiographic orientation, beginning either implicitly or explicitly with particular contemporary concerns that find illuminating resonance in the fertile grounds of late antiquity.[25]

---

23. Vessey, "Demise of the Christian Writer."

24. Rebecca Krawiec, *Shenoute and the Women of the White Monastery* (New York: Oxford University Press, 2002); Andrew Crislip, *From the Monastery to the Hospital: Christian Monasticism and the Transformation of Health Care in Late Antiquity* (Ann Arbor: University of Michigan Press, 2005); Caroline T. Schroeder, *Monastic Bodies: Discipline and Salvation in Shenoute of Atripe,* Divinations (Philadelphia: University of Pennsylvania Press, 2007); Ariel Lopez, *Shenoute of Atripe and the Uses of Poverty: Rural Patronage, Religious Conflict, and Monasticism in Late Antique Egypt,* TCH 50 (Berkeley: University of California Press, 2013); Bentley Layton, *The Canons of Our Fathers: Monastic Rules of Shenoute,* OECS (Oxford: Oxford University Press, 2014).

25. See Claudia Rapp, "Church and State, Religion and Power in Late Antique and Byzantine Scholarship of the Last Five Decades," in *The Church and Its Past,* ed. Peter D. Clarke and Charlotte Methuen, Studies in Church History 49 (Woodbridge, UK: Boydell, 2013), 447–67.

EPIPHANIUS AND LATE ANTIQUITY

Epiphanius has not benefited from this historiographic reorientation that we call "late antiquity." It is difficult to ascribe his marginalization solely to his difficult or unpleasant personality. My suggestion is that something more fundamental about Epiphanius's distinctive (but, we must recall, incredibly influential) worldview in the late fourth century raises issues about this period that we do not find congenial to our own cultural concerns. Epiphanius, I posit, is the impresario of an imperial culture that fixes otherness and difference at the uncomfortable center of Christian identity. His approach to self, other, community, society, and power moves us away from many of the values scholars have found so readily at work in the cultures of late antiquity into an uneasy realm of irresoluble otherness.

Let me begin by recapping briefly my insights about Epiphanius from the previous chapters. In chapter 1, I asked us to reimagine the social function of episcopal authority in the late fourth century not as an increasingly "talent-based" sign of cultural value,[26] but rather as a free-floating signifier of importance more akin to modern notions of celebrity. In chapter 2, we saw Epiphanius scripting the processes of religious status change (conversion) not as the interior process of a soul or a subjectivity,[27] but as the public management of identity and difference. In chapter 3 I traced Epiphanius's modes of discipline not as sites of increasingly complex "technologies of the self" (or of the community),[28] but rather as occasions for improvisational displays that naturalize forms of

---

26. See, among recent studies, Allen E. Jones, *Social Mobility in Late Antique Gaul: Strategies and Opportunities for the Non-Elite* (Cambridge: Cambridge University Press, 2009), building on the earlier work of M. Keith Hopkins, "Social Mobility in the Later Roman Empire: The Case of Ausonius," *CQ* n.s. 11 (1961): 239–49.

27. See, most recently, the perceptive account of Jason BeDuhn, *Augustine's Manichaean Dilemma*, vol. 1, *Conversion and Apostasy, 373–388 C.E.*, Divinations (Philadelphia: University of Pennsylvania Press, 2010).

28. See Schroder, *Monastic Bodies;* Catherine M. Chin, "Cassian, Cognition, and the Common Life," in *Ascetic Culture: Essays in Honor of Philip Rousseau*, ed. Blake Leyerle and Robin Darling Young (South Bend, IN: University of Notre Dame Press, 2013), 147–66.

power and control over others. In chapter 4, we saw how Scriptures for Epiphanius are not intellectualized through philosophical and christological discourses,[29] but become a site for alternative forms of bewildering intellectual production through antiquarianism. Epiphanius, as we saw in chapter 5, articulates a theology of salvation not through complicated metaphysical discourse,[30] but as a fundamentally moral program in which the self is not only reflected in the divine but enacted through the unstable multiplicity and unity of Christian community.

In sum, Epiphanius represents to us a late ancient Christian culture of display and performance centered on difference: different modes of status and power, different forms of knowledge, different types of Christians multiplying almost without end across a backdrop of anxiously incomplete orthodoxy. Difference, for Epiphanius, is not a problem in but rather a feature of his late ancient culture, a culture that differentiates but never excludes, that identifies the "other"—indeed, myriad others—and incorporates them into the fabric of an imperial Christian world. Here, I think, we begin to approach our discomfort with Epiphanius. To be sure, many Christians were concerned with the problem of otherness, difference, and identity.[31] Yet it remains, for them, precisely that: a *problem,* a disruption in the construction of Christian culture to be addressed and (ideally, if never actually) resolved. For Epiphanius, otherness is to be collected, catalogued, memorialized, even publicly condemned, but it will never—can never—be eradicated.[32]

29. See, among recent studies, Blossom Stefaniw, *Mind, Text, and Commentary: Noetic Exegesis in Origen of Alexandria, Didymus the Blind, and Evagrius Ponticus,* Early Christianity in the Context of Antiquity 6 (Frankfurt am Main: Peter Lang, 2010); Matthew R. Crawford, *Cyril of Alexandria's Trinitarian Theology of Scripture,* OECS (Oxford: Oxford University Press, 2014).

30. See, among recent studies, Christopher A. Beeley, *The Unity of Christ: Continuity and Conflict in Patristic Tradition* (New Haven, CT: Yale University Press, 2012).

31. Indeed, arguably such concern for "the other" characterizes Christianity at its origins: see Judith Lieu, *Christian Identity in the Jewish and Graeco-Roman World* (Oxford: Oxford University Press, 2004); and E.P. Sanders et al., eds., *Jewish and Christian Self-Definition,* 3 vols. (Philadelphia: Fortress Press, 1980–81).

32. Averil Cameron, "The Cost of Orthodoxy," *Church History and Religious Culture* 93 (2013): 339–61, traces some societal effects of a heresiological culture.

Epiphanius provides a vision of Christian culture centered on the productive persistence of otherness, one that could resurrect a third-century theologian and enact from his literary remains a veritable holy war. Perhaps scholarly distaste for Epiphanius's anti-Origenism stems not solely from its seeming anti-intellectualism, but from its sheer inexhaustibility: if Epiphanius had not died on that boat home from Constantinople, where would his invective have landed next? Origenism, at the end of Epiphanius's life, came to embody that otherness permanently fixed at the wobbly center of imperial Christian culture; it required constant management, negotiation, intervention, and disruption. In many ways, Epiphanius's Christianity hews rather closely to the political style of the Roman Empire itself, which managed but never eradicated the difference of its endless parade of "others."[33] Perhaps, for this reason, Epiphanius's contemporaries found him such a compelling and authoritative Christian leader.

Perhaps, for similar reasons, we as scholars of late antiquity have found Epiphanius less compelling. Epiphanius's attention to the other is *excessive*. There is seemingly nothing else *to* him but a frothing desire to find, even invent, others for his unceasing delectation and invective. I am struck by how often very smart colleagues, when they find out I am working on Epiphanius, accuse him of *lying*, of fabricating details large and small in the service of heresiology. I can't imagine many historical characters from late antiquity whom we study who might not be accused of dishonesty (even the venerable church father Augustine, who wrote not one but *two* treatises "against lying"), and obviously Epiphanius is no different.[34] Yet we come back again and again to Epiphanius's *lying* because it signals the

---

33. See my discussion in *Christ Circumcised: A Study in Early Christian History and Difference*, Divinations (Philadelphia: University of California Press, 2012), 6–10 and 15–19.

34. In his propensity for invention Epiphanius is also, of course, following in the tradition of most classical historians and ethnographers; see Hervé Inglebert, *Interpretatio Christiana: Les mutations des savoirs (cosmographie, géographie, ethnographie, histoire) dans l'Antiquité chrétienne, 30–630 après J.-C.*, Collection des Études Augustiniennes, Série Antiquité 166 (Paris: Institut d'Études Augustiniennes, 2001).

depths of his obsessive desire to castigate an(y) other. The uncomfortable difference already permeating his world is not enough for Epiphanius's voracious heresiographic appetite: he must *invent* others to populate his Christian cultural history and landscape.

Yet this ability to conjure and master others, this performance of difference, satisfied an imperial desire in Epiphanius's fourth-century context. Epiphanius is the heresy-hunter who does not care to imagine a Christian world without heresy; he is the biblical interpreter whose Bible spills over not with philosophical insight, but with undigested bits of Greco-Roman flotsam and jetsam; he is the bishop who exercises improvisational authority, who enforces orthodoxy but skips (or at least does not sign off on) the major ecumenical council of his day. How does our image of late antiquity shift if we place such a figure at its center? What would a late antiquity in Epiphanius's image look like, and why have we shied away from it for these past decades?

A late antiquity invested in the promotion and stigmatization of difference does not cohere with the blossoming period of liberalism, diversity, and expansiveness that has beckoned (in various shades) since the 1970s. In a frank retrospective of the writing of *The World of Late Antiquity* on the occasion of its twenty-fifth anniversary, Peter Brown recalled the heady optimism that granted him

> the hubris of narrating the entire history of the religious and cultural revolution associated with the end of the ancient world without invoking an intervening catastrophe and without pausing, for a moment, to pay lip service to the widespread notion of decay. I proposed a social and cultural history that could be narrated, from end to end, almost in terms of ever-widening ripples of change, as different strata of the Roman world, and eventually, indeed, much of its non-Roman periphery, came to participate in a core of central concerns. "New" men ... brought with them to the centers of power new ideas, new, distinctly "non-classical" religious options and, with these, a heightened need to find, within the continuing classical tradition itself, the basis for a new equilibrium between the old and the new. Put bluntly: from the point of view of religious and cultural creativity,

"the shaking of an *ancien regime*" could do nothing but good to a traditional society (Brown 1971b, 37).[35]

In contrast with this hopeful vision, Epiphanius's Christian culture was not characterized by "ever-widening ripples of change"; difference and novelty, for Epiphanius, did not drift in from the periphery to reform culture but were invented and deployed—often maliciously—from the center. In Epiphanius we catch a glimpse of a Christian imperial culture that did not embody transformation and a "new equilibrium," but precisely the "traditional society" whose end Brown found so exhilarating.[36] Epiphanius *was* the bishop of the *ancien régime*.

Averil Cameron has recently and sensitively written about the historiographic marginalization of Byzantine studies in the Anglo-American academy. "Part of the reason for Byzantium's absence from the wider historical discourse," she explains, "is that it has been relegated to the sphere of negativity."[37] "Negativity" both in the sense that historians associate the "Byzantine" with derogatory traits such as "autocracy, bureaucracy, deviousness, and stultifying lack of originality" and in the sense that it becomes a negative foil against which to measure modernity's own positive achievements.[38] "The field of Byzantine studies," Cameron concludes, "must be rescued from its continuing association with the competing clams of negativity and exoticism."[39]

35. Brown, "World of Late Antiquity Revisited," 15. Brown cites from the original 1971 British edition of *World of Late Antiquity*; in the US edition, the quotation at the end falls on p. 33 and reads: "In the later empire, indeed, one feels a sudden release of talent and creativity such as often follows the shaking of an *ancien régime*." See also Philip Rousseau, "Can 'Late Antiquity' Be Saved?," *Marginalia Review of Books*, http://marginalia.lareviewofbooks.org/can-late-antiquity-be-saved-by-philip-rousseau/.

36. See also Ando, "Fall and Transformation," 35: "In the middle of the twentieth century ... traditional, classicizing analysis gave way to new readings, which found distinct vibrancy, creativity, and flexibility in the late classical elements of late antique culture."

37. Averil Cameron, *Byzantine Matters* (Princeton, NJ: Princeton University Press, 2014), 10.

38. Cameron, *Byzantine Matters*, 10–13.

39. Cameron, *Byzantine Matters*, 115.

Indeed, we might see the rise of a negative Byzantium as the counterpart of the rise of a positive "late antiquity," its marginalized shadow.⁴⁰ The "Byzantine" becomes the historiographic container for the antiquity that we do not want to see, that we cannot take on its own terms, that does not reflect meaningfully back at us.⁴¹ Epiphanius (in historiographic terms) may seem to us more Byzantine than late antique.⁴² Lacking cultural value, he becomes a negative space in the bright firmament of late antiquity: an ethical dark spot and a historiographic absence.

Restored to the center of that late ancient cultural sphere, Epiphanius's negativity (in these two, Byzantine senses) must alter our perception of this historical period. Indeed, perhaps Epiphanius the late antique man forces us to question our own motives and desires in identifying, promoting, and studying any historical period. In her study of history and theory, Elizabeth Clark argued for a clear acknowledgment of the relationship between historians and their pasts:

> I claim that such histories should acknowledge that, as intellectual constructions, they differ from "the past," vanished and now available only through "traces," and that no historical construction is "politically innocent" but is driven by the problems and questions set by the historian in the present.⁴³

Clark's insistence on the ethical stakes in history writing draws on a long historiographic tradition, dating back even to the "father" of modern, positivist history, Leopold van Ranke.⁴⁴ What, we might ask, are

---

40. Cameron, *Byzantine Matters*, 113–15.

41. Cameron, *Byzantine Matters*, 27: "Byzantium has suffered from what an Italian historian writing in 1999 ... called the 'explosion' of late antiquity as a historical period" (citing Giardina, "Esplosione").

42. Averil Cameron, "How to Read Heresiology," in Martin and Miller, *Cultural Turn*, 193–212, traces Epiphanius's influence on later Byzantine writing against heresy.

43. Clark, *History, Theory, Text*, 7.

44. On von Ranke, see Clark, *History, Theory, Text*, 9–13; Clark is most interested in the American appropriation of von Ranke's famous quest for the past "wie es eigentlich gewesen" into an "objective" historical science (see pp. 13–17), which (she acknowledges) stripped von Ranke's Positivism of its moral fervor. On Ranke's own ethical

we looking for in the late antique past? What questions about ourselves are we seeking to answer there? Since the 1970s, we have been willing to see in this period growing possibility: not only for the "new men" Brown considered at the time, but for other figures in the margins.[45] *Difference*, in late antiquity, becomes a positive cultural force, reflecting our own ideals about a liberal, multicultural society.

Epiphanius's late antiquity complicates our ideas about difference in society: in this late antiquity, a bishop achieves prominence by twisting the possibilities of difference into an opportunity for the performative exercise of power and control. To take Epiphanius seriously as a representative figure of late antiquity, a late antiquity in which (so often) we find shadows of our own cultural concerns, leads us to ask, to what extent does our own multicultural society make similarly twisted uses of "difference" in the public sphere? By marginalizing certain uncomfortable figures from our canonical field of late antiquity, what "problems and questions" of our own might we be refusing to bring to the forefront? It may be that, at the end of the day, remembering Epiphanius will allow us not only to bring historiographic nuance to the field of late antiquity, but ethical nuance to our own considerations of the past, and the present.

---

hopes, see the extensive introduction to and collection of von Ranke's writings in Leopold von Ranke, *The Theory and Practice of History*, ed. Georg G. Iggers, 2nd ed. (London: Routledge, 2011).

45. Attention to women's history stands as a prime example. Brown himself has most recently moved on to the poor: *Through the Eye of the Needle: Wealth, the Fall of Rome, and the Making of Christianity in the West, 350–550 AD* (Princeton, NJ: Princeton University Press, 2012) and *The Ransom of the Soul: Afterlife and Wealth in Early Western Christianity* (Cambridge: Cambridge University Press, 2015).

BIBLIOGRAPHY

For full titles of book series, journals, and critical editions abbreviated below, see the list of abbreviations.

PRIMARY SOURCES

English translations given when consulted; otherwise, all translations from Greek and Latin are my own.

Apophthegmata Patrum. Alphabetical collection in PG 65:72–440. Anonymous collection in *The Anonymous Sayings of the Desert Fathers: A Select Edition and Complete English Translation,* edited and translated by John Wortley. Cambridge: Cambridge University Press, 2014. Systematic collection in *Les apophtegmes des pères: Collection systématique,* edited by Jean-Claude Guy. SC 387, 474. Paris: Éditions du Cerf, 1993–2013.

Athanasius. *Epistula* 64. PG 26:1261–62.

———. *Epistulae ad Serapionem.* Text in *Athanasius Werke,* vol. 1.1, *Die dogmatischen Schriften,* pt. 4, *Epistulae I-IV ad Serapionem,* edited by Kyriakos Savvidis. Berlin: De Gruyter, 2010.

———. *Vita Antonii.* Text in *Vie d'Antoine,* edited by G. J. M. Bartelink. SC 400. Paris: Cerf, 2004.

Augustine. *Contra Iulianum opus imperfectum.* PL 45:1049–1608.

———. *De haeresibus.* PL 42:21–50.

———. *Epistulae.* Text in *Sancti Aureli Augustini Hipponiensis episcopi epistulae.* CSEL 34.1–2, 44, 47–58, edited by A. Goldbacher. Vienna: Tempsky, 1895–1923.

———. *Sermones.* PL 38–39.

Basil of Caesarea. *Epistulae.* PG 32:219–1112.

Canons of Ephesus (431). Text in Karl Joseph von Hefele, *Histoire des conciles,* vol. 2, pt. 1:332–40. Paris: Letouzey et Ané, 1908.

Canons of Nicaea (325). Text in Karl Joseph von Hefele, *Histoire des conciles,* vol. 1, pt. 1:528–620. Paris: Letouzey et Ané, 1907.

Chronicon Paschale. PG 92:70–1028.

Collectio Avellana. Text in *Epistulae imperatorum pontificum aliorum avellana quae dicitur collectio,* edited by Otto Günther. CSEL 35. Vienna: F. Tempsky, 1898.

Epiphanius. *Ancoratus.* Text in *Epiphanius I: Ancoratus und Panarion haer. 1–33,* edited by Karl Holl, Marc Bergermann, and Christian-Friedrich Collatz, 1–149. GCS n.F. 10.1. Berlin: De Gruyter, 2013. English translation in *Saint Epiphanius of Cyprus: Ancoratus,* translated by Young Richard Kim. FC 128. Washington, DC: Catholic University of America Press, 2014.

———. Collected works in Dionsyius Petavius [Denis Pétau], *Sancti Patris Nostri Epiphanii Constantiae sive Salaminis in Cypro, episcopi, opera omnia.* 2 vols. Paris: Sumptibus Michaelis Sonnii, Claudii Morelli, et Sebastiani Cramoisy, 1622.

———. *De XII gemmis.* Old Georgian and Coptic text and English translation in *Epiphanius "De Gemmis": The Old Georgian Version and the Fragments of the Armenian Version,* edited by Robert P. Blake and Henri de Vis. Studies and Documents. London: Christophers, 1934. Armenian text and German translation in *Epiphanius von Salamis, Über die zwölf Steine im hohpriesterlichen Brustschild (De duodecim gemmis rationalis),* edited by Felix Albrecht and Arthur Manukyan. Gorgias Eastern Christian Studies 37. Piscataway, NJ: Gorgias Press, 2014.

———. *De fide.* Text in *Epiphanius III: Panarion haer. 65–80; De fide,* edited by Karl Holl and Jürgen Dummer, 496–526. GCS 37. Berlin: Akademie Verlag, 1985. English translation in *The Panarion of Epiphanius of Salamis,* vol. 2, *Books II and III, De fide,* translated by Frank Williams, 655–82. 2nd rev. ed. NHMS 79. Leiden: Brill, 2013.

———. *De mensuris et ponderibus.* Syriac text and English translation in *Epiphanius' Treatise on Weights and Measures: The Syriac Version,* edited by James Elmer Dean. Studies in Ancient Oriental Civilizations 11. Chicago: University of Chicago, 1935. Greek text in Elias Moutsoulas, "Τὸ Περὶ μέτρων καὶ σταθμῶν ἔργων Ἐπιφανίου τοῦ Σαλαμῖνος." Θεολογία 44 (1973): 157–98. Georgian text in *Les versions géorgiennes d'Épiphane de Chypre, Traité des poids et de mésures,* edited by Michel van Esbroeck. CSCO 460–61. Leuven: Peeters, 1984. Armenian text in *The Armenian Texts of Epiphanius of Salamis "De mensuris et ponderibus,"* edited by Michael Stone and Roberta Ervine. CSCO 583. Leuven: Peeters, 2000.

———. *Epistula ad Ioannem.* Latin text in Jerome, *Epistulae.* CSEL 54:395–412.

———. *Panarion.* Text in *Epiphanius I: Ancoratus und Panarion haer. 1–33,* edited by Karl Holl, Marc Bergermann, and Christian-Friedrich Collatz, 150–464. GCS n.F. 10.1. Berlin: De Gruyter, 2013; *Epiphanius II: Panarion haer. 34–64,* edited by Karl Holl and Jürgen Dummer. GCS 31. Berlin: Akademie Verlag, 1980; *Epiphanius III: Panarion haer. 65–80; De fide,* edited by Karl Holl and Jürgen Dummer, 1–496. GCS 37. Berlin: Akademie Verlag, 1985. English translation in *The Panarion of Epiphanius of Salamis,* translated by Frank Williams. 2nd rev. ed. 2 vols. NHMS 63 and 79. Leiden: Brill, 2009–13.

Eusebius. *Historia ecclesiastica.* Text in *Eusebius Werke II: Die Kirchengeschichte,* edited by Eduard Schwartz. GCS 9. Leipzig: J.C. Hinrichs, 1903–8.

———. *Onomastikon.* Text in *Eusebius Werke III.1: Das Onomastikon,* edited by Erich Klostermann. GCS 11.1. Leipzig: J.C. Hinrichs, 1904.

Florilegium Edessenum Anonymum. Text in Ignaz Rucker, *Florilegium Edessenum Anonymum (Syriace ante 562),* Sitzungberichte der Bayerischen Akademie der Wissenschaften, Phil.-Hist. Abteilung 5. Munich: Verlag der Bayerischen Akademie der Wissenschaften, 1933.

Irenaeus. *Adversus haereses.* Text in *Contre les heresies,* edited by P. Doutreleau et al. SC 263–64, 293–94, 210–11, 34, 100, 152–53. Paris: Éditions du Cerf, 1952–69.

Itinerarium Antonini Placentini. Text in *Itineraria et alia geographica,* edited by P. Geyer and O. Cuntz, 1–26. CCL 175. Turnhout: Brepols, 1965.

Jerome. *Adversus Iovinianum.* PL 23:205–338.

———. *Apologia contra Rufinum.* Text in *Apologie contre Rufin,* edited by Pierre Lardet. SC 303. Paris: Éditions du Cerf, 1983.

———. *Commentarius in Ezechielem.* PL 25:15–490.

———. *Commentarius in Isaiam.* PL 24:17–678.

———. *Contra Ioannem Hierosolymitanum.* PL 23:351–96.

———. *De viris inlustribus.* Text in *Hieronymus: Liber de viris inlustribus; Gennadius: Liber de viris inlustribus,* edited by E.C. Richardson. Texte und Untersuchungen zur Geschichte der altchristlichen Literatur 14.1a. Leipzig: J.C. Hinrichs, 1896.

———. *Epistulae*. Text in *Sancti Hieronymi Eusebii epistulae*, edited by I. Hilberg and M. Kamptner. CSEL 54–56. Vienna: Österreichischen Akademie der Wissenschaften, 1996.

———. *Vita Hilarionis*. PL 23:29–54.

Justin Martyr. *Apologia*. Text in *Iustini Martyris Apologiae pro Christianis*, edited by Miroslav Marcovich. Patristische Texte und Studien 38. Berlin: De Gruyter, 1994.

Nicephorus I. *Antirrhetica adversus Eusebium et Epiphanidem*. Text in *Spicilegium solesmense complectens sanctorum patrum scriptorumque ecclesiasticorum anecdota hactenus opera*, edited by Jean-Baptiste Pitra, 4:292–380. Paris: Firmin Didot Frères, 1858.

Palladius. *Dialogus de vita sanctis Ioannis Chrysostomi*. Text in *Dialogue sur la vie de Jean Chrysostome*, edited by Anne-Marie Malingrey and Philippe Leclercq. SC 341–42. Paris: Éditions du Cerf, 1988.

———. *Historia Lausiaca*. Text and translation in *The Lausiac History of Palladius*, edited by Dom Cuthbert Butler. 2 vols. Texts and Studies 6. Cambridge: Cambridge University Press, 1898.

Philostratus. *Vitae sophistarum*. Text in *Philostratus: Lives of the Sophists; Eunapius: Lives of the Philosophers and Sophists*, translated by William C. Wright, 2–315. Loeb Classical Library 134. Cambridge, MA: Harvard University Press, 1922.

Photius. *Bibliotheca*. Text in *Photius, Bibliothèque*, edited by René Henry. Collection Byzantine. Paris: Éditions 'Les Belles Lettres,' 1960.

Rufinus of Aquileia. *De adulteratione librorum Origenis*. Text in *Pamphile et Eusèbe de Césarée, Apologie pour Origène suivi de Rufin d'Aquilée; Sur la falsification des livres d'Origène*, edited by René Amacker and Éric Junod. SC 464–65. Paris: Éditions du Cerf, 2002.

———. *Historia ecclesiastica*. PL 21:461–540.

Severus of Antioch. *Contra impium Grammaticum*. Text in *Seueri Antiocheni liber contra impium Gramamaticum*, edited by Joseph Lebon. CSCO 101–2. Leuven: CSCO, 1938–52.

Shenoute of Atripe. *I Am Amazed* (= *Contra Origenistas*). Text and German translation in *Schenute von Atripe: Contra Origenistas*, edited by Hans-Joachim Criste. Studien und Texte zu Antike und Christentum 60. Tübingen: Mohr-Siebeck, 2011. Text and Italian translation in *Shenute, Contra Origenistas, testo con introduzione e traduzione*, edited by Tito Orlandi. Rome: C.I.M., 1985. English translation in (1) Michael Foat, "I Myself Have Seen: The Representation of Humanity in the Writings of Apa Shenoute of Atripe."

PhD diss., Brown University, 1996; (2) *Selected Discourses of Shenoute the Great: Community, Theology, and Social Conflict in Late Antique Egypt*, edited and translated by Andrew Crislip and David Brakke, 54–82. Cambridge: Cambridge University Press, 2015.

Socrates. *Historia ecclesiastica*. Text in *Socrates, Kirchengeschichte*, edited by G.C. Hansen. GCS n.F. 1. Berlin: Akademie Verlag, 1995.

Sozomen, *Historia ecclesiastica*. Text in *Sozomenus, Kirchengeschichte*, edited by G.C. Hansen. GCS n.F. 4. Berlin: Akademie Verlag, 1995.

Theodoret of Cyrus. *Historia ecclesiastica*. Text in *Theodoret, Kirchengeschicte*, edited by Léon Parmentier. GCS 19. Leipzig: J.C. Hinrichs, 1911.

Theophilus of Alexandria. *Epistula ad Epiphanium*. Latin text in Jerome, *Epistulae*. CSEL 55:143–45.

———. *Epistulae festales*. Latin text in Jerome, *Epistulae*. CSEL 55:159–81, 185–211, 213–32.

———. *Epistula synodica*. Latin text in Jerome, *Epistulae*. CSEL 55:147–55.

Vita Epiphanii. Text in Claudia Rapp, "The *Vita* of Epiphanius of Salamis: An Historical and Literary Study." 2 vols. D.Phil. thesis, Oxford University, 1991.

Vita Olympiadis. Text in Hippolyte Delehaye, "Vita Sanctae Olympiadis et narratio Sergiae." *Analecta Bollandiana* 15 (1896): 400–423.

Vita Pelagiae meretricis. Latin text in PL 73:663–71. Syriac text in *Acta Sanctae Pelagiae syriace*, edited by J. Gildemeister. Bonn: Adolphus Marcus, 1879. English translation in Susan Ashbrook Harvey and Sebastian Brock, *Holy Women of the Syrian Orient*, 41–62. Berkeley: University of California Press, 1987.

SECONDARY SOURCES

Abt, Jeffrey. "The Origins of the Public Museum." In *A Companion to Museum Studies*, edited by Sharon MacDonald, 115–34. Companions to Cultural Studies 12. Malden, MA: Wiley-Blackwell, 2006.

Adler, William. "*Ad Verbum* or *Ad Sensum:* The Christianization of a Latin Translation Formula in the Fourth Century." In *Pursuing the Text: Studies in Honor of Ben Zion Wacholder on the Occasion of His Seventieth Birthday*, edited by John C. Reeves and John Kampen, 321–48. Sheffield: Sheffield Academic Press, 1994.

———. "The Origins of the Proto-Heresies: Fragments from a Chronicle in the First Book of Epiphanius' *Panarion*." *JTS* n.s. 41 (1990): 472–501.

Albl, Martin C. *"And Scripture Cannot Be Broken": The Form and Function of the Early Christian Testimonia Collections.* Supplements to *Novum Testamentum* 96. Leiden: Brill, 1999.

Alexander, Jeffrey. "The Celebrity-Icon." *Cultural Sociology* 4 (2010): 323–36.

Alperson, Philip. "On Musical Improvisation." *Journal of Aesthetics and Art Criticism* 42 (1984): 17–29.

Altaner, Berthold. "Augustinus und Epiphanius von Salamis: Eine quellenkritische Studie." In *Mélanges Joseph de Ghellinck*, 265–75. Gembloux: J. Duculot, 1951.

Amory, Patrick. *People and Identity in Ostrogothic Italy, 489–554.* Cambridge: Cambridge University Press, 1997.

Ando, Clifford. "Decline, Fall, and Transformation." *JLA* 1 (2008): 31–60.

Anzaldúa, Gloria. *Borderlands/La Frontera.* Ann Arbor: University of Michigan Press, 1987.

Aragione, Gabriella. "Una 'storia' universale dell'eresia: Il *Panarion* di Epifanio." In *Epifanio di Salamina: Panarion, Libro primo*, edited by Giovanni Pini, 6–19. Letteratura Cristiana Antica, nuova serie 21. Brescia: Morcelliana, 2010.

Asad, Talal. *Genealogies of Religion: Discipline and Reasons of Power in Christianity and Islam.* Baltimore: Johns Hopkins University Press, 1993.

Ayres, Lewis. *Nicaea and Its Legacy: An Approach to Fourth-Century Trinitarian Theology.* Oxford: Oxford University Press, 2004.

Baker, Joseph Ellis. *The Novel and the Oxford Movement.* 1932. Reprint, New York: Russell & Russell, 1965.

Banev, Krastu. *Theophilus of Alexandria and the First Origenist Controversy: Rhetoric and Power.* OECS. Oxford: Oxford University Press, 2015.

Barbas, Samantha. *Movie Crazy: Fans, Stars, and the Cult of Celebrity.* New York: Palgrave, 2001.

Bartelink, G. J. M. *Hieronymus: Liber de optimo genere interpretandi (Epistula 57); Ein Kommentar.* Mnemosyne Supplement 61. Leiden: Brill, 1980.

Bassi, Dominicus. *Catalogus codicum graecorum Bibliothecae Ambrosianae.* Vol. 2. Milan: Impensis u. Hoepli, 1906.

Bauckham, Richard. "The Parable of the Royal Wedding Feast (Matthew 22:1–14) and the Parable of the Lame Man and the Blind Man (*Apocryphon of Ezekiel*)." *JBL* 115 (1996): 471–88.

BeDuhn, Jason. *Augustine's Manichaean Dilemma.* Vol. 1, *Conversion and Apostasy, 373–388 C.E.* Divinations. Philadelphia: University of Pennsylvania Press, 2010.

Beeley, Christopher A. *The Unity of Christ: Continuity and Conflict in Patristic Tradition.* New Haven, CT: Yale University Press, 2012.

Bennett, Tony. *The Birth of the Museum: History, Theory, Politics.* London: Routledge, 1995.

Berzon, Todd S. *Classifying Christians: Ethnography, Heresiology, and the Limits of Knowledge in Late Antiquity.* Oakland: University of California Press, 2016.

Bigham, Steven. *Epiphanius of Salamis, Doctor of Iconoclasm? Deconstruction of a Myth.* Patristic Theological Library. Rollinsford, NH: Orthodox Research Institute, 2008.

Blair-Dixon, Kate. "Memory and Authority in Sixth-Century Rome: The *Liber Pontificalis* and the *Collectio Avellana.*" In *Religion, Dynasty, and Patronage in Early Christian Rome, 300–900,* edited by Kate Cooper and Julia Hillner, 59–76. Cambridge: Cambridge University Press, 2007.

Bloomer, W. Martin. "Schooling in Persona: Imagination and Subordination in Roman Education." *CA* 16 (1997): 57–78.

Boorstin, Daniel. "From Hero to Celebrity: The Human Pseudo-event." In *The Image: A Guide to Pseudo-Events in America,* 45–76. 1961. Reprint, New York: Vintage Books, 2012.

Bowersock, G. W., Peter Brown, and Oleg Grabar, eds. *Late Antiquity: A Guide to the Postclassical World.* Cambridge, MA: Belknap Press of Harvard University Press, 1999.

Boyarin, Daniel. *Border Lines: The Partition of Judaeo-Christianity.* Divinations. Philadelphia: University of Pennsylvania Press, 2004.

Brakke, David. "Athanasius' *Epistula ad Epiphanium* and Liturgical Reform in Alexandria." *SP* 36 (2001): 482–88.

———. *Demons and the Making of the Monk: Spiritual Combat in Early Christianity.* Cambridge, MA: Harvard University Press, 2006.

———. "The Egyptian Afterlife of Origenism: Conflicts over Embodiment in Coptic Sermons." *Orientalia Christiana Periodica* 66 (2000): 277–93.

———. *The Gnostics: Myth, Ritual, and Diversity in Early Christianity.* Cambridge, MA: Harvard University Press, 2010.

Braudy, Leo. *The Frenzy of Renown: Fame and Its History.* Oxford: Oxford University Press, 1986.

Brock, Sebastian. "Two Syriac Translations of the Life of Epiphanios." In *Mosaic: Festschrift for A. H. S. Megaw,* edited by Judith Herrin, Margaret Mullett, and Catherine Otten-Froux, 19–25. British School at Athens Studies 8. London: British School at Athens, 2001.

Broek, Roelof van den. "Archontics." In *Dictionary of Gnosis and Western Esotericism,* edited by W. J. Hanegraaff, 89–91. Leiden: Brill, 2006.

Brown, Peter. *Augustine of Hippo: A Biography*. 2nd ed. Berkeley: University of California Press, 2000.

———. *The Body and Society: Men, Women, and Sexual Renunciation in Early Christianity*. Lectures on the History of Religions, n.s. 13. New York: Columbia University Press, 1988.

———. "Conversion and Christianization in Late Antiquity: The Case of Augustine." In *The Past before Us: The Challenge of Historiographies of Late Antiquity*, edited by Carole Straw and Richard Lim, 103–17. Turnhout: Brepols, 2004.

———. *The Making of Late Antiquity*. Cambridge, MA: Harvard University Press, 1978.

———. "Paganism: What We Owe to the Christians." *New York Review of Books* 58.6 (April 2011): 68–73.

———. *Power and Persuasion in Late Antiquity: Toward a Christian Empire*. Curti Lectures. Madison: University of Wisconsin Press, 1992.

———. *The Ransom of the Soul: Afterlife and Wealth in Early Western Christianity*. Cambridge, MA: Harvard University Press, 2015.

———. *Religion and Society in the Age of Augustine*. London: Faber & Faber, 1972.

———. "The Rise and Function of the Holy Man in Late Antiquity." *JRS* 61 (1971): 80–101.

———. "The Rise and Function of the Holy Man in Late Antiquity, 1971–1997." *JECS* 6 (1998): 353–76.

———. *Society and the Holy in Late Antiquity*. Berkeley: University of California Press, 1982.

———. *Through the Eye of the Needle: Wealth, the Fall of Rome, and the Making of Christianity in the West, 350–550 AD*. Princeton, NJ: Princeton University Press, 2012.

———. *The World of Late Antiquity, AD 150–750*. London: Thames & Hudson, 1971.

Brown, Peter, et al. "The World of Late Antiquity Revisited." *Symbolae Osloenses* 72 (1997): 5–90.

Burrus, Virginia. *"Begotten Not Made": Conceiving Manhood in Late Antiquity*. Figurae. Stanford, CA: Stanford University Press, 2000.

———. "Hailing Zenobia: Anti-Judaism, Trinitarianism, and John Henry Newman." *Culture and Religion* 3 (2002): 163–77.

———. "A Saint of One's Own: Emmanuel Levinas, Eliezer ben Hyrcanus, and Eulalia of Mérida." *L'Esprit Créateur* 50 (2010): 6–20.

———. *The Sex Lives of Saints*. Divinations. Philadelphia: University of Pennsylvania Press, 2004.

Burton-Christie, Douglas. *The Word in the Desert: Scripture and the Quest for Holiness in Early Christian Monasticism.* Oxford: Oxford University Press, 1993.

Cain, Andrew. *Jerome's Epitaph on Paula: A Commentary on the "Epitaphium Sanctae Paulae" with an Introduction, Text, and Translation.* OECT. Oxford: Oxford University Press, 2013.

———. *Letters of Jerome: Asceticism, Biblical Exegesis, and the Construction of Christian Authority in Late Antiquity.* OECS. Oxford: Oxford University Press, 2009.

Cameron, Alan. *The Last Pagans of Rome.* Oxford: Oxford University Press, 2011.

Cameron, Alan, and Jacqueline Long. *Barbarians and Politics at the Court of Arcadius.* Berkeley: University of California Press, 1993.

Cameron, Averil. "Ascetic Closure and the End of Antiquity." In *Asceticism,* edited by Vincent Wimbush and Richard Valantasis, 147–61. New York: Oxford University Press, 2002.

———. *Byzantine Matters.* Princeton, NJ: Princeton University Press, 2014.

———. "Christian Conversion in Late Antiquity: Some Issues." in *Conversion in Late Antiquity: Christianity, Islam, and Beyond,* edited by Arietta Papaconstantinou, Neil McLynn, and Daniel Schwartz, 3–21. Burlington, VT: Ashgate, 2015.

———. *Christianity and the Rhetoric of Empire: The Development of Christian Discourse.* Sather Classical Lectures 55. Berkeley: University of California Press, 1994.

———. "The Cost of Orthodoxy." *Church History and Religious Culture* 93 (2013): 339–61.

———. *Dialoguing in Late Antiquity.* Hellenic Studies Series 65. Washington, DC: Center for Hellenic Studies, 2014.

———. "How to Read Heresiology." In *The Cultural Turn in Late Ancient Studies,* edited by Dale B. Martin and Patricia Cox Miller, 193–212. Durham, NC: Duke University Press, 2005.

———. "Redrawing the Map: Early Christian Territory after Foucault." *JRS* 76 (1986): 266–71.

Caner, Daniel. *Wandering, Begging Monks: Spiritual Authority and the Promotion of Monasticism in Late Antiquity.* TCH 33. Berkeley: University of California Press, 2002.

Carter, Curtis L. "Improvisation in Dance." *Journal of Aesthetics and Art Criticism* 58 (2000): 181–90.

Cave, William. *Scriptorum ecclesiasticorum historia litteraria a Christo nato usque ad saeculum XIV.* London: Richard Chiswell, 1688.

Certeau, Michel de. "A Variant: Hagio-Graphical Edification." In *The Writing of History*, translated by Tom Conley, 269–83. New York: Columbia University Press, 1988.

Chadwick, Henry. *The Early Church*. London: Penguin Books, 1967.

Chapman, Edward Mortimer. *English Literature and Religion, 1800–1900*. London: Constable, 1910.

Cherry, David. *Frontier and Society in Roman North Africa*. Oxford: Oxford University Press, 2002.

Chew, Kathryn. "Virgins and Eunuchs: Pulcheria, Politics, and the Death of Emperor Theodosius II." *Historia* 55 (2006): 207–27.

Chidester, David. *Savage Systems: Colonialism and Comparative Religion in Southern Africa*. Charlottesville: University of Virginia Press, 1996.

Chin, Catherine M. "Cassian, Cognition, and the Common Life." In *Ascetic Culture: Essays in Honor of Philip Rousseau*, edited by Blake Leyerle and Robin Darling Young, 147–66. South Bend, IN: University of Notre Dame Press, 2013.

———. *Grammar and Christianity in the Late Roman World*. Divinations. Philadelphia: University of Pennsylvania Press, 2008.

———. "Rufinus of Aquileia and Alexandrian Afterlives: Translation as Origenism." *JECS* 18 (2010): 617–47.

———. "Short Words on Earth: Theological Geography in Rufinus's *Commentary on the Apostles' Creed*." *JECS* 21 (2013): 391–412.

Clark, Elizabeth A. "Elite Networks and Heresy Accusations: Toward a Social Description of the Origenist Controversy." *Semeia* 56 (1991): 79–117.

———. "Foucault, the Fathers, and Sex." *JAAR* 56 (1988): 619–41.

———. *History, Theory, Text: Historians and the Linguistic Turn*. Cambridge, MA: Harvard University Press, 2004.

———. "Introduction to the *Life of Olympias* and Sergia's *Narration Concerning St. Olympias*." In *Jerome, Chrysostom, and Friends: Essays and Translations*, 107–26. Studies in Women and Religion 1. New York: Edwin Mellen Press, 1979.

———. *The Origenist Controversy: The Cultural Construction of an Early Christian Debate*. Princeton, NJ: Princeton University Press, 1992.

———. *Reading Renunciation: Asceticism and Scripture in Early Christianity*. Princeton, NJ: Princeton University Press, 1999.

———. "Sex, Shame, and Rhetoric: En-Gendering Early Christian Ethics." *JAAR* 59 (1991): 221–45.

Conybeare, Fred. *The Dialogues of Athanasius and Zacchaeus and of Timothy and Aquila*. Anecdota Oxoniensia. Oxford: Clarendon Press, 1898.

Cook, Zeba. *Reconceptualising Conversion: Patronage, Loyalty, and Conversion in the Religions of the Ancient Mediterranean.* Beihefte zur Zeitschrift für die neutestamentlische Wissenschaft und die Kunde der älteren Kirche 130. Berlin: De Gruyter, 2004.

Cooper, Kate. "Poverty, Obligation, and Inheritance: Roman Heiresses and the Varieties of Senatorial Christianity in Fifth-Century Rome." In *Religion, Dynasty, and Patronage in Early Christian Rome, 300–900,* edited by Kate Cooper and Julia Hillner, 165–89. Cambridge: Cambridge University Press, 2007.

Cooper, Thompson. "Mossman, Thomas Wimberley." In *Dictionary of National Biography,* vol. 39, *Morehead—Myles,* edited by Sidney Lee, 185–86. London: Smith, Elder, 1894.

Cowen, Tyler. *What Price Fame?* Cambridge, MA: Harvard University Press, 2000.

Crawford, Charlotte E. "Newman's 'Callista' and the Catholic Popular Library." *Modern Language Review* 45 (1950): 219–21.

Crawford, Matthew R. *Cyril of Alexandria's Trinitarian Theology of Scripture.* OECS. Oxford: Oxford University Press, 2014.

Crislip, Andrew. *From the Monastery to the Hospital: Christian Monasticism and the Transformation of Health Care in Late Antiquity.* Ann Arbor: University of Michigan Press, 2005.

Crouzel, Henri. "Encore sur divorce et remariage selon Épiphane." *VC* 38 (1984): 271–80.

Dahl, Curtis. "Pater's *Marius* and Historical Novels on Early Christian Times." *Nineteenth-Century Fiction* 28 (1973): 1–24.

Davidson, Ivor. "Staging the Church? Theology as Theater." *JECS* 8 (2000): 413–51.

Davis, Stephen J. *Coptic Christology in Practice: Incarnation and Divine Participation in Late Antique and Medieval Egypt.* OECS. Oxford: Oxford University Press, 2008.

Dawson, Lorne L. "Who Joins New Religious Movements and Why: Twenty Years of Research and What Have We Learned?" In *Cults and New Religious Movements: A Reader,* edited by Lorne L. Dawson, 116–30. Oxford: Blackwell, 2003. Originally published in *Studies in Religion/Sciences Religieuses* 25 (1996): 141–61.

Dechow, Jon. *Dogma and Mysticism in Early Christianity: Epiphanius of Cyprus and the Legacy of Origen.* PMS 13. Macon, GA: Mercer University Press, 1988.

———. "From Methodius to Epiphanius in Anti-Origenist Polemic." *Adamantius* 19 (2013): 10–29.

Dekkers, E. "Les traductions grecques des écrits patristiques latins." *Sacris Erudiri* 5 (1953): 193–233.
Del Bello, Davide. *Forgotten Paths: Etymology and the Allegorical Mindset.* Washington, DC: Catholic University of America Press, 2007.
DelCogliano, Mark. "Basil of Caesarea on Proverbs 8:22 and the Sources of Pro-Nicene Theology." *JTS* n.s. 59 (2008): 183–90.
———. "Situating Sarapion's Sorrow: The Anthropomorphite Controversy as the Historical and Theological Context of Cassian's Tenth Conference on Pure Prayer." *Cistercian Studies Quarterly* 38.4 (2003): 377–421.
Dellamora, Richard. "Benjamin Disraeli, Judaism, and the Legacy of William Beckford." In *Mapping Male Sexuality: Nineteenth-Century England,* edited by Jay Losey and William Dean Brewer. Cranbury, NJ: Associated University Presses, 2000, 145–77.
———. *Friendship's Bonds: Democracy and the Novel in Victorian England.* Philadelphia: University of Pennsylvania Press, 2004.
Denzey, Nicola. "'Enslavement to Fate,' 'Cosmic Pessimism,' and Other Explorations of the Late Roman Psyche: A Brief History of a Historiographical Trend." *Studies in Religion/Sciences Religieuses* 33 (2004): 277–99.
Derby, Josiah. "Rashi's Conjectures." *Jewish Bible Quarterly* 32 (2004): 125–29.
Doerfler, Maria. "'Hair!' Remnants of Ascetic Exegesis in Augustine of Hippo's *De Opere Monachorum.*" *JECS* 22 (2014): 79–111.
Dorman, Susann. "*Hypatia* and *Callista:* The Initial Skirmish between Kingsley and Newman." *Nineteenth-Century Fiction* 34 (1979): 173–93.
Dowling, Linda. "Roman Decadence and Victorian Historiography." *Victorian Studies* 28 (1985): 597–607.
Dugan, John. *Making a New Man: Ciceronian Self-Fashioning in the Rhetorical Works.* Oxford: Oxford University Press, 2005.
Dummer, Jürgen. "Ein naturwissenschaftliches Handbuch als Quelle für Epiphanius von Constantia." *Klio* 55 (1973): 289–99. Reprinted in Dummer, *Philologia sacra et profana: Ausgewählte Beiträge zur Antike und zu ihrer Wirkungsgeschichte,* edited by Meinolf Vielberg, 82-95. Altertumswissenschaft Kolloquium 16. Stuttgart: Franz Steiner Verlag, 2006.
———. "Die Sprachskenntnisse des Epiphanius." In *Die Araber in der alten Welt,* edited by F. Altheim and R. Stiehl, 392–435. Berlin: De Gruyter, 1968. Reprinted in Dummer, *Philologia sacra et profana: Ausgewählte Beiträge zur Antike und zu ihrer Wirkungsgeschichte,* edited by Meinolf Vielberg, 29–73. Altertumswissenschaft Kolloquium 16. Stuttgart: Franz Steiner Verlag, 2006.

Dyer, Richard. *Stars*. London: British Film Institute, 1979.
Ebbeler, Jennifer. *Disciplining Christians: Correction and Community in Augustine's Letters*. OSLA. Oxford: Oxford University Press, 2012.
Ehrman, Bart D. *Forgery and Counterforgery: The Use of Literary Deceit in Early Christian Polemics*. Oxford: Oxford University Press, 2013.
Elliott, Mark. *The Song of Songs and Christology in the Early Church, 381–451*. Studies and Texts in Antiquity and Christianity 7. Tübingen: Mohr-Siebeck, 2000.
Elm, Susanna. "Introduction." *JECS* 6 (1998): 343–51.
———. "What the Bishop Wore to the Synod: John Chrysostom, Origenism, and the Politics of Fashion at Constantinople." *Adamantius* 19 (2013): 156–69.
Emmel, Stephen. *Shenoute's Literary Corpus*. 2 vols. CSCO Subsidia 111–12. Leuven: Peeters, 2004.
Englezakis, Benedict. "Epiphanius of Salamis, the Father of Cypriot Autocephaly." In *Studies on the History of the Church of Cyprus, 4th-20th Centuries*, translated by Normal Russell, 29–40. Aldershot, UK: Ashgate, 1995.
Erskine, Andrew. "Culture and Power in Ptolematic Egypt: The Museum and Library of Alexandria." *Greece & Rome* 62 (1995): 38–48.
Farrar, Frederic William. *Gathering Clouds: A Tale of the Days of St. Chrysostom*. London: Longman, Green, 1895.
Fatti, Federico. "*Pontifex tantus:* Giovanni, Epifanio e le origini della prima contrversia origenista." *Adamantius* 19 (2013): 30–49.
Faught, C. Brad. *The Oxford Movement: A Thematic History of the Tractarians and Their Times*. University Park: Pennsylvania State University Press, 2003.
Ferguson, Everett. "Community and Worship." In *The Routledge Companion to Early Christian Thought*, edited by D. Jeffrey Bingham, 313–30. London: Routledge, 2010.
Ferguson, Everett, et al., eds. *Encyclopedia of Early Christianity*. London: Taylor & Francis, 1998.
Flemming, Rebecca. "Empires of Knowledge: Medicine and Health in the Hellenistic World." In *A Companion to the Hellenistic World*, edited by Andrew Erskine, 449–63. Malden, MA: Blackwell, 2003.
Flower, Richard. "Genealogies of Unbelief: Epiphanius of Salamis and Heresiological Authority." In *Unclassical Traditions*, vol. 2, *Perspectives from the East and West in Late Antiquity*, edited by Christopher Kelly, Richard Flower, and Michael Stuart Williams, 70–87. Cambridge: Cambridge University Press, 2011.

Foucault, Michel. "What Is an Author?" In *Textual Strategies: Perspectives in Post-Structuralist Criticism*, edited by Josué V. Harari, 41–60. Ithaca, NY: Cornell University Press, 1979.

Fowden, Garth. "Elefantiasi del tardoantico?" *Journal of Roman Archaeology* 15 (2002): 681–86.

Fraenkel, Pierre. "Histoire sainte et hérésie chez Saint Épiphane de Salamine d'après le tome I du *Panarion*." *Revue de Théologie et de Philosophie* 12 (1962): 175–91.

Fredriksen, Paula. "Mandatory Retirement: Ideas in the Study of Christian Origins Whose Time to Go Has Come." *Studies in Religion/Sciences Religieuses* 35 (2006): 231–46.

———. "Paul and Augustine: Conversion Narratives, Orthodox Traditions, and the Retrospective Self." *JTS* n.s. 37 (1986): 3–34.

Freeman, Charles. *A New History of Early Christianity*. New Haven, CT: Yale University Press, 2009.

French, Todd Edison. "Just *Deserts*: Losing Origen and Gaining Retributive Judgment in the Hagiographical Literature of the Early Byzantine World." PhD diss., Columbia University, 2013.

Gallagher, Eugene V. "Conversion and Community in Late Antiquity." *JR* 73 (1993): 1–15.

Galvão-Sobrinho, Carlos R. *Doctrine and Power: Theological Controversy and Christian Leadership in the Later Roman Empire*. TCH 51. Berkeley: University of California Press, 2013.

Gannon, Shane. "Conversion as a Thematic Site: Academic Representations of Ambedkar's Buddhist Turn." *Method and Theory in the Study of Religion* 23 (2011): 1–28.

Garland, Robert. "Celebrity Ancient and Modern." *Society* 47 (2010): 484–88.

———. "Celebrity in the Ancient World." *History Today* 55.3 (March 2005): 24–30.

———. *Celebrity in Antiquity: From Media Tarts to Tabloid Queens*. Classical Interfaces. London: Duckworth, 2006.

Gervaise, François-Armand. *L'histoire et la vie de St Epiphane, archevêque de Salamine & docteur de l'Eglise, où l'on voit ce qui s'est passé de plus curieux & de plus intéressant dans l'Eglise, depuis l'An 310 jusqu'en 403 avec l'Analyse des Ouvrages de ce Saint, son Apologie contre les Protestans, & des Notes Critiques & Historiques*. Paris: Jean-Baptiste Lamesle and Pierre-François Giffart, 1738.

Giacchi, G., et al. "The Wood of 'C' and 'F' Roman Ships Found in the Ancient Harbour of Pisa (Tuscany, Italy): The Utilisation of Different Timbers and the Probable Geographical Area Which Supplied Them." *Journal of Cultural Heritage* 4 (2003): 269–83.

Giardina, Andrea. "Esplosione di tardoantica." *Studi Storici* 40 (1999): 157–80.

Gibbon, Edward. *The History of the Decline and Fall of the Roman Empire*. 6 vols. London: W. Strahan, 1776–89.

Gleede, Benjamin. *The Development of the Term ἐνυπόστατος from Origen to John of Damascus*. Supplements to *Vigiliae Christianae* 113. Leiden: Brill, 2012.

Goehring, James. "Hieracas of Leontopolis: The Making of a Desert Ascetic." In *Ascetics, Society, and the Desert: Studies in Early Egyptian Monasticism*, 110–36. Harrisburg, PA: Trinity Press, 1999.

Goranson, Stephen. "The Joseph of Tiberias Episode in Epiphanius: Studies in Jewish and Christian Relations." PhD diss., Duke University, 1990.

———. "Joseph of Tiberias Revisited: Orthodoxies and Heresies in Fourth-Century Galilee." In *Galilee through the Centuries: A Confluence of Cultures*, edited by Eric M. Meyers, 335–43. Duke Judaic Studies 1. Winona Lake, IN: Eisenbrauns, 1999.

Gould, Carol S., and Kenneth Keaton. "The Essential Role of Improvisation in Musical Performance." *Journal of Aesthetics and Art Criticism* 58 (2000): 143–48.

Gould, Graham. *The Desert Fathers on Monastic Community*. OECS. Oxford: Oxford University Press, 1993.

Grafton, Anthony, and Megan H. Williams. *Christianity and the Transformation of the Book: Origen, Eusebius, and the Library of Caesarea*. Cambridge, MA: Harvard University Press, 2006.

Greenblatt, Stephen. "The Improvisation of Power." In *Renaissance Self-Fashioning: From More to Shakespeare*, 222–54. Chicago: University of Chicago Press, 1980.

Grillmeier, Aloys. *Christ in the Christian Tradition*. Translated by O.C. Dean. Vol. 2, pt. 4. Louisville, KY: Westminster/John Knox Press, 1996.

Groh, Dennis, and Robert Gregg. *Early Arianism: A View to Salvation*. Philadelphia: Fortress Press, 1981.

Gunderson, Erik, ed. *Cambridge Companion to Ancient Rhetoric*. Cambridge: Cambridge University Press, 2009.

———. *Declamation, Paternity, and Roman Identity: Authority and the Rhetorical Self*. Cambridge: Cambridge University Press, 2003.

———. *Nox philologiae: Aulus Gellius and the Fantasy of the Roman Library*. Wisconsin Studies in Classics. Madison: University of Wisconsin Press, 2009.

Habinek, Thomas. *The Politics of Latin Literature: Writing, Identity, and Empire in Ancient Rome*. Princeton, NJ: Princeton University Press, 2001.

———. "Seneca's Renown: *Gloria, Claritudo*, and the Replication of the Roman Elite." *CA* 19 (2000): 264–303.

Hadot, Pierre. *Philosophy as a Way of Life: Spiritual Exercises from Socrates to Foucault*. Translated by Arnold Davidson. Oxford: Blackwell, 1995.

Hall, J. B. "Review of *The Jeweled Style: Poetry and Poetics in Late Antiquity*." *Classical Review* n.s. 41 (1991): 359–61.

Hanson, F. Allan. *The Trouble with Culture: How Computers Are Calming the Culture Wars*. Albany: SUNY Press, 2007.

Hanson, R. P. C. *The Search for the Christian Doctrine of God: The Arian Controversy, 318–381*. Edinburgh: T. & T. Clark, 1998.

Harmless, William. *Augustine and the Catechumenate*. Collegeville, MN: Liturgical Press, 1995.

Harvey, Graham. *The True Israel: Uses of the Names Jew, Hebrew, and Israel in Ancient Jewish and Early Christian Literature*. Leiden: Brill, 1996.

Harvey, Susan Ashbrook, and David G. Hunter, eds. *The Oxford Handbook of Early Christian Studies*. Oxford: Oxford University Press, 2008.

Hengstenberg, W. "Review of *Epiphanius's 'De Gemmis': The Old Georgian Version and the Fragments of the Armenian Versian*, ed. Robert P. Blake and Henri de Vis." *BZ* 37.2 (1937): 400–440.

Holcomb, Chris. "'The Crown of All Our Study': Improvisation in Quintilian's *Institutio Oratoria*." *Rhetoric Society Quarterly* 31.3 (2001): 53–72.

Holl, Karl. "Ein Bruchstück aus einem bisher unbekannten Brief des Epiphanius." In *Festgabe für Adolf Jülicher zum 70. Geburtstag*, edited by R. Bultmann and H. Soden, 159–89. Tübingen: J. C. B. Mohr, 1927.

———. *Gesammelte Aufsätze zur Kirchengeschichte*. Tübingen: Mohr-Siebeck, 1928.

———. *Die handschriftliche Überlieferung des Epiphanius (Ancoratus und Panarion)*. Texte und Untersuchungen zur Geschichte der altchristlichen Literatur 36. Leipzig: J. C. Hinrichs, 1910.

Hopkins, M. Keith. "Social Mobility in the Later Roman Empire: The Case of Ausonius." *CQ* n.s. 11 (1961): 239–49.

Huebner, Sabine. "Currencies of Power: The Venality of Offices in the Later Roman Empire." In *The Power of Religion in Late Antiquity*, edited by Andrew Cain and Noel Lenski, 167–79. Burlington, VT: Ashgate, 2009.

Huffman, Joseph P. "The Donation of Zeno: St. Barnabas and the Origins of the Cypriot Archbishops' Regalia Privileges." *JEH* 66 (2015): 235–60.

Inglebert, Hervé. *Interpretatio Christiana: Les mutations des savoirs (cosmographie, géographie, ethnographie, histoire) dans l'Antiquité chrétienne, 30–630 après J.-C.* Collection des Études Augustiniennes, Série Antiquité 166. Paris: Institut d'Études Augustiniennes, 2001.

———. "Introduction: Late Antique Conceptions of Late Antiquity." In *The Oxford Handbook of Late Antiquity*, edited by Scott Fitzgerald Johnson, 3–28. Oxford: Oxford University Press, 2012.

Inglis, Fred. *A Short History of Celebrity*. Princeton, NJ: Princeton University Press, 2010.

Jacobs, Andrew S. *Christ Circumcised: A Study in Early Christian History and Difference*. Divinations. Philadelphia: University of Pennsylvania Press, 2013.

———. "Epiphanius of Salamis and the Antiquarian's Bible." *JECS* 21 (2013): 437–64.

———. "The Lion and the Lamb: Reconsidering 'Jewish-Christian Relations' in Antiquity." In *The Ways That Never Parted: Jews and Christians in Antiquity and the Middle Ages,* edited by Adam H. Becker and Annette Yoshiko Reed, 95–118. Texts and Studies in Ancient Judaism 95. Tübingen: Mohr-Siebeck, 2003.

———. *Remains of the Jews: The Holy Land and Christian Empire in Late Antiquity*. Divinations. Stanford, CA: Stanford University Press, 2004.

———. "'What Has Rome to Do with Bethlehem?' Cultural Capital(s) and Religious Imperialism in Late Ancient Christianity." *Classical Receptions Journal* 2 (2011): 29–45.

James, William. *The Varieties of Religious Experience*. New York: Longman & Green, 1902.

Jaeger, Werner. *Early Christianity and Greek Paideia*. Cambridge, MA: Belknap Press of Harvard University Press, 1961.

Jellicoe, Sidney. *The Septuagint and Modern Study*. Oxford: Clarendon Press, 1968.

Jensen, Robin. *Understanding Early Christian Art*. London: Routledge, 2000.

Johnson, Maria Poggi. "Critical Scholarship, Christian Antiquity, and the Victorian Crisis of Faith in the Historical Novels of Edwin Abbot." *Clio* 37 (2008): 395–412.

Johnson, Scott F. "Apostolic Geography: The Origins and Continuity of a Hagiographic Habit." *DOP* 64 (2010): 5–25.

Jones, Allen E. *Social Mobility in Late Antique Gaul: Strategies and Opportunities for the Non-Elite*. Cambridge: Cambridge University Press, 2009.

Kaldellis, Anthony. *Hellenism in Byzantium: The Transformations of Greek Identity and the Reception of the Classical Tradition*. Greek Culture in the Roman World. Cambridge: Cambridge University Press, 2007.

Kaster, Robert. "Controlling Reason: Declamation in Rhetorical Education at Rome." In *Education in Greek and Roman Antiquity*, edited by Yun Lee Too, 317–37. Leiden: Brill, 2001.

Kelley, Doris B. "A Check List of Nineteenth-Century English Fiction about the Decline of Rome." *Bulletin of the New York Public Library* 72 (1968): 400–413.

Kelly, J. N. D. *Jerome: His Life, Writings, Controversies*. London: Duckworth, 1975.

Kim, Young Richard. *Epiphanius of Cyprus: Imagining an Orthodox World*. Ann Arbor: University of Michigan Press, 2015.

———. "Epiphanius of Cyprus and the Geography of Heresy." In *Violence in Late Antiquity: Perceptions and Practices*, edited by Harold Drake, 235–51. Burlington, VT: Ashgate, 2006.

———. "Epiphanius of Cyprus vs. John of Jerusalem: Improper Ordination and the Escalation of the Origenist Controversy." In *Episcopal Elections in Late Antiquity*, edited by Johan Leemans, Peter van Nuffelen, Shawn W. J. Keough, and Carla Nicolaye, 411–22. Arbeiten zur Kirchengeschichte 119. Berlin: De Gruyter, 2011.

———. "The Imagined Worlds of Epiphanius of Cyprus." PhD diss., University of Michigan, 2006.

———. "Jerome and Paulinian, Brothers." *VC* 67 (2013): 517–30.

———. "The Pastoral Care of Epiphanius of Salamis." *SP* 67 (2013): 247–56.

———. "Reading the *Panarion* as Collective Biography: The Heresiarch as Unholy Man." *VC* 64 (2010): 382–413.

———. *Saint Epiphanius of Cyprus: Ancoratus*. FC 128. Washington, DC: Catholic University of America Press, 2014.

———. "The Transformation of Heresiology in the *Panarion* of Epiphanius of Cyprus." In *Shifting Genres in Late Antiquity*, edited by Hugh Elton and Geoffrey Greatrex, 53–65. Burlington, VT: Ashgate, 2015.

King, Karen. *What Is Gnosticism?* Cambridge, MA: Belknap Press of Harvard University Press, 2003.

Kingsley, Charles. *Hypatia, or New Foes with an Old Face*. 2 vols. London: John W. Parker and Son, 1853.

Kitzinger, Ernest. *Byzantine Art in the Making: Main Lines of Stylistic Development in Mediterranean Art, 3rd–7th Century*. Cambridge, MA: Harvard University Press, 1977.

———. "Byzantine Art in the Period between Justinian and Iconoclasm." In *Berichte zum XI. internationalen Byzantinisten-Kongress, München 1958*, 4.1:1–50. Munich: C. H. Beck, 1958.

———. "The Cult of Images in the Age before Iconoclasm." *DOP* 8 (1954): 83–150.

Kolb, Frank. *Diokletian und die erste Tetrarchie: Improvisation oder Experiment in die Organisation monarchischer Herrschaft?* Berlin: De Gruyter, 1987.

Kollman, Bernd. *Joseph Barnabas: His Life and Legacy*. Collegeville, MN: Liturgical Press, 2004.

König, Alice. "Knowledge and Power in Frontinus' *On Aqueducts*." In *Ordering Knowledge in the Roman Empire*, edited by Jason König and Tim Whitmarsh, 177–205. Cambridge: Cambridge University Press, 2007.

König, Jason, and Tim Whitmarsh. "Introduction: Ordering Knowledge," in *Ordering Knowledge in the Roman Empire*, edited by Jason König and Tim Whitmarsh, 3-40. Cambridge: Cambridge University Press, 2007.

Korenjak, Martin. *Publikum und Redner: Ihre Interaktion in der sophistischen Rhetorik der Kaiserzeit*. Zetemata 104. Munich: C. H. Beck, 2000.

Kösters, Oliver. *Die Trinitätslehre des Epiphanius von Salamis: Ein Kommentar zum "Ancoratus."* Forschungen zur Kirchen- und Dogmengeschichte 86. Göttingen: Vandenhoek & Ruprecht, 2003.

Kraft, Robert. *Exploring the Scripturesque: Jewish Texts and Their Christian Contexts*. Supplements to the *Journal for the Study of Judaism* 137. Leiden: Brill, 2009.

Krawiec, Rebecca. *Shenoute and the Women of the White Monastery*. New York: Oxford University Press, 2002.

Kuefler, Mathew. *The Manly Eunuch: Masculinity, Gender Ambiguity, and Christian Ideology in Late Antiquity*. Chicago Series on Sexuality, History, and Society. Chicago: University of Chicago Press, 2001.

Kurzman, Charles, et al. "Celebrity Status." *Sociological Theory* 25 (2007): 346–67.

Labendz, Jenny R. "Aquila's Bible Translation in Late Antiquity: Jewish and Christian Perspectives." *HTR* 102 (2009): 353–88.

Lang, Andrew. "At the Sign of the Ship." *Longman's Magazine* 32.187 (May 1898): 85–88.

Lankewish, Vincent A. "Love among the Ruins: The Catacombs, the Closet, and the Victorian 'Early Christian' Novel." *Victorian Literature and Culture* 28 (2000): 239–73.

Lardet, Pierre. *L'apologie de Jérôme contre Rufin: Un commentaire*. Supplements to *Vigiliae Christianae* 15. Leiden: Brill, 1993.

Lawler, Peter A. "Celebrity Studies Today." *Society* 57 (2010): 419–23.

Layton, Bentley. *The Canons of Our Fathers: Monastic Rules of Shenoute*. OECS. Oxford: Oxford University Press, 2014.

Leach, Eleanor W. "The Politics of Self-Presentation: Pliny's 'Letters' and Roman Portrait Sculpture." *CA* 9 (1990): 14–39.

Lebon, Joseph. "Sur quelques fragments de lettres attribués à S. Épiphane de Salamine." In *Miscellanea Giovanni Mercati*, vol. 1, *Bibbia—Letteratura cristiana antica*, 145–74. Studi e Testi 121. Vatican City: Biblioteca Apostolica Vaticana, 1946.

Leyerle, Blake. *Theatrical Shows and Ascetic Lives: John Chrysostom's Attack on Spiritual Marriage*. Berkeley: University of California Press, 2001.

Lieu, Judith. *Christian Identity in the Jewish and Graeco-Roman World*. Oxford: Oxford University Press, 2004.

———. "'Impregnable Ramparts and Walls of Iron': Boundary and Identity in 'Judaism' and 'Christianity.'" *New Testament Studies* 48 (2002): 297–313.

Litvack, Leon B. "Callista, Martyrdom, and the Early Christian Novel in the Victorian Age." *Nineteenth-Century Context* 17 (1993): 159–73.

Lofton, Kathryn. "Religion and the American Celebrity." *Social Compass* 58 (2011): 346–52.

Lopez, Ariel. *Shenoute of Atripe and the Uses of Poverty: Rural Patronage, Religious Conflict, and Monasticism in Late Antique Egypt*. TCH 50. Berkeley: University of California Press, 2013.

Lössl, Josef. "'Apocalypse? No.'—The Power of Millennialism and Its Transformation in Late Antique Christianity." In *The Power of Religion in Late Antiquity*, edited by Andrew Cain and Noel Lenski, 31–44. Burlington, VT: Ashgate, 2009.

Lucchesi, Enzo. "Un corpus épiphanien en copte." *Analecta Bollandiana* 99 (1981): 95–99.

Lyman, J. Rebecca. "Ascetics and Bishops: Epiphanius on Orthodoxy." In *Orthodoxie, Christianisme, Histoire/Orthodoxy, Christianity, and History*, edited by Susanna Elm, Éric Rebillard, and Antonella Romano, 149–61. Collections de l'École Française de Rome 270. Paris: de Boccard, 2000.

———. "The Making of a Heretic: The Life of Origen in Epiphanius *Panarion* 64." *SP* 31 (1997): 445–51.

———. "Origen as Ascetic Theologian: Orthodoxy and Authority in the Fourth-Century Church." In *Origeniana Septima*, edited by Wolfgang Bienert and Uwe Kühneweg, 187–94. Leuven: Peeters, 1999.

Lynch, Joseph. *Early Christianity: A Brief History*. New York: Oxford University Press, 2010.

Maas, Michael. *John Lydus and the Roman Past: Antiquarianism and Politics in the Age of Justinian*. London: Routledge, 1992.

Maas, P. "Die ikonoklastische Episode in dem Brief des Epiphanios an Johannes." *BZ* 30 (1929–30): 279–86.
Maguire, Henry. *The Icons of Their Bodies: Saints and Their Images in Byzantium*. Princeton, NJ: Princeton University Press, 1981.
Maison, Margaret M. *The Victorian Vision: Studies in the Religious Novel*. New York: Sheed & Ward, 1961.
Mandler, Peter. *The English National Character: The History of an Idea from Edmund Burke to Tony Blair*. New Haven, CT: Yale University Press, 2006.
Manor, Timothy Scott. "Epiphanius' Account of the *Alogi:* Historical Fact or Heretical Fiction?" *SP* 52 (2012): 161–70.
———. "Epiphanius' *Alogi* and the Question of Early Ecclesiastical Opposition to the Johannine Corpus." PhD diss., University of Edinburgh, 2012.
Marrou, H.-I. *A History of Education in Antiquity*. Translated by G. Lamb. Madison: University of Wisconsin Press, 1956.
Marshall, P. David. *Celebrity and Power: Fame in Contemporary Culture*. Minneapolis: University of Minnesota Press, 1997.
———, ed. *The Celebrity Culture Reader*. London: Routledge, 2006.
Martens, Peter. *Origen and Scripture: The Contours of the Exegetical Life*. OECS. Oxford: Oxford University Press, 2012.
Martin, Dale B. *The Corinthian Body*. New Haven, CT: Yale University Press, 1995.
———. Introduction to *The Cultural Turn in Late Ancient Studies*, edited by Dale B. Martin and Patricia Cox Miller, 1–21. Durham, NC: Duke University Press, 2005.
Maslakov, G. "The Roman Antiquarian Tradition in Late Antiquity." In *History and Historians in Late Antiquity*, edited by Brian Croke and Alanna M. Emmett, 100–106. Sydney: Pergamon Press, 1983.
McClure, Judith. "Handbooks against Heresy in the West from the Late Fourth to the Late Sixth Centuries." *JTS* n.s. 30 (1979): 186–79.
McKeown, J. C. *A Cabinet of Roman Curiosities: Strange Tales and Surprising Facts from the World's Greatest Empire*. New York: Oxford University Press, 2010.
Meier, Christel. *Gemma spiritalis: Methode und Gebrauch der Edelsteinallegorese vom frühen Christentum bis ins 18. Jahrhundert*. Vol. 1. Münstersche Mittelalter-Schriften 34.1. Munich: Fink, 1977.
Meltzer, Françoise, and Jaś Elsner, eds. *Saints: Faith without Borders*. Chicago: University of Chicago Press, 2011.
Miller, Patricia Cox. "1997 NAPS Presidential Address; 'Differential Networks': Relics and Other Fragments of Late Antiquity." *JECS* 6 (1998): 113–38.

———. *The Corporeal Imagination: Signifying the Holy in Late Ancient Christianity.* Divinations. Philadelphia: University of Pennsylvania Press, 2009.

———. "Is There a Harlot in This Text? Hagiography and the Grotesque." In *The Cultural Turn in Late Ancient Studies,* edited by Dale B. Martin and Patricia Cox Miller, 87–102. Durham, NC: Duke University Press, 2005.

Miller, Peter N. *Momigliano and Antiquarianism: Foundations of the Modern Cultural Sciences.* Toronto: University of Toronto Press, 2007.

Mills, Kenneth, and Anthony Grafton. *Conversion in Late Antiquity and the Early Middle Ages: Seeing and Believing.* Rochester, NY: University of Rochester Press, 2003.

———. *Conversion: Old Worlds and New.* Rochester, NY: University of Rochester Press, 2003.

Milner, Murray, Jr. "Is Celebrity a New Kind of Status System?" *Society* 57 (2010): 379–87.

Momigliano, Arnaldo. "Ancient History and the Antiquarian." *Journal of the Warburg and Courtauld Institutes* 13 (1950): 285–315.

———. "The Rise of Antiquarian Research." In *The Classical Foundations of Modern Historiography,* 54–79. Sather Lectures 54. Berkeley: University of California Press, 1990.

Moorhead, John. "*Papa* as 'Bishop of Rome.'" *JEH* 36 (1985): 337–50.

Mossman, Thomas Wimberley. *Epiphanius: The History of His Childhood and Youth Told by Himself: A Tale of the Early Church.* London: J. T. Hayes, 1874.

———. *A History of the Catholic Church of Jesus Christ: From the Death of Saint John to the Middle of the Second Century, Including an Account of the Original Organisation of the Christian Ministry and the Growth of the Episcopacy.* London: Longman, Green, 1873.

Moutsoulas, Elias. "Der Begriff 'Häresie' bei Epiphanius von Salamis." *SP* 7 (1966): 362–71.

Muehlberger, Ellen. "The Legend of Arius' Death: Imagination, Space, and Filth in Late Ancient Historiography." *Past & Present* 227 (2015): 3–29.

———. "On Authors, Fathers, and Holy Men." *Marginalia Review of Books.* http://marginalia.lareviewofbooks.org/on-authors-fathers-and-holy-men-by-ellen-muehlberger/.

Mueller, James. *The Five Fragments of the Apocryphon of Ezekiel: A Critical Study.* Journal for the Study of the Pseudepigrapha 5. Sheffield: Journal for the Study of the Old Testament Press, 1994.

Muldoon, James. *Varieties of Religious Conversion in the Middle Ages.* Gainesville: University of Florida Press, 1997.

Munson, J.E.B. "The Oxford Movement by the End of the Nineteenth Century: The Anglo-Catholic Clergy." *CH* 44 (1975): 382–95.

Murphy, Trevor. *Pliny the Elder's "Natural History": The Empire in the Encyclopedia.* Oxford: Oxford University Press, 2004.

Nasrallah, Laura. "The Rhetoric of Conversion and the Construction of Experience: The Case of Justin Martyr." *SP* 40 (2006): 467–74.

Nautin, Pierre. "Divorce et remariage chez Saint Épiphane." *VC* 37 (1983): 157–73.

———. "Épiphane (Saint), de Salamine." *Dictionnaire d'histoire et de géographie ecclésiastiques* 15 (1963): 617–31.

Nettl, Bruno. "Thoughts in Improvisation: A Comparative Approach." *Musical Quarterly* 60 (1974): 1–19.

Newman, John Henry. *Callista: A Tale of the Third Century.* London: Burns & Oates, 1856.

Nock, A.D. *Conversion: The Old and the New in Religion from Alexander the Great to Augustine of Hippo.* Oxford: Oxford University Press, 1933.

Noreña, Carlos F. "The Communication of the Emperor's Virtues." *JRS* 91 (2001): 146–68.

Norton, Glyn P. "Improvisation and Inspiration in Quintilian: The Extemporalizing of Technique in the *Institutio Oratoria*." In *Inspiration and Technique: Ancient to Modern Views on Beauty and Art*, edited by John Roe and Michele Stanco, 83–104. Bern: Peter Lang, 2007.

Norton, Peter. *Episcopal Elections, 250–600: Hierarchy and Popular Will in Late Antiquity.* OCM. Oxford: Oxford University Press, 2007.

O'Keefe, John, and R.R. Reno. *Sanctified Vision: An Introduction to Early Christian Interpretations of the Bible.* Baltimore: Johns Hopkins University Press, 2005.

Oliphant, Mrs. [Margaret]. *Saint Francis.* The Sunday Library for Household Reading. London: Macmillan, 1868.

Pächt, Otto. "Art Historians and Art Critics, vi: Alois Riegl." In *Historiography: Critical Concepts in Historical Studies*, vol. 3, *Ideas*, edited by Robert Burns, 268–81. London: Routledge, 2006.

Papaconstantinou, Arietta. Introduction to *Conversion in Late Antiquity: Christianity, Islam, and Beyond*, edited by Arietta Papaconstantinou, with Neil McLynn and Daniel Schwartz, xv–xxxvii. Burlington, VT: Ashgate, 2015.

Parvis, Sara. "'Τὰ τίνων ἄρα ῥήματα θεολογεῖ?' The Exegetical Relationship between Athanasius' *Orationes Contra Arianos I-III* and Marcellus of Ancyra's *Contra Asterium*." In *The Reception and Interpretation of the Bible in Late Antiquity*, edited by Lorenzo DiTommaso and Lucian Turcescu, 337–67. Bible in Ancient Christianity 6. Leiden: Brill, 2008.

Pastis, Jacqueline Z. "Dating the *Dialogue of Timothy and Aquila:* Revisiting the Earlier Vorlage Hypothesis." *HTR* 95 (2002): 169–95.

Patlagean, Evelyne. "Ancienne hagiographie byzantine et histoire sociale." *Annales ESC* 23 (1968): 106–26.

Patterson, Paul A. *Visions of Christ: The Anthropomorphite Controversy of 399 C.E.* Studien und Texte zu Antike und Christentum 68. Tübingen: Mohr-Siebeck, 2012.

Peraki-Kyriakido, Helen. "Aspects of Ancient Etymologizing." *CQ* n.s. 52 (2002): 478–93.

Petrey, Taylor G. *Resurrecting Parts: Early Christians on Desire, Reproduction, and Sexual Difference.* Routledge Studies in the Early Christian World. London: Routledge, 2016.

Piotrowska, Anna G. "Expressing the Inexpressible: The Issue of Improvisation and the European Fascination with Gypsy Music in the 19th Century." *International Review of Aesthetics and Sociology of Music* 43 (2012): 325–41.

Pourkier, Aline. *L'hérésiologie chez Épiphane de Salamine.* Christianisme Antique 4. Paris: Beauchesne, 1992.

Pummer, Reinhard. *Early Christian Authors on Samaritans and Samaritanism: Texts, Translations, and Commentary.* Texts and Studies in Ancient Judaism 92. Tübingen: Mohr-Siebeck, 2002.

Quasten, Johannes. *Patrology.* 4 vols. Utrecht: Spectrum, 1966.

Ragussis, Michael. *Figures of Conversion: "The Jewish Question" and English National Identity.* Durham, NC: Duke University Press, 1995.

Rajak, Tessa. *Translation and Survival: The Greek Bible and the Ancient Jewish Diaspora.* Oxford: Oxford University Press, 2009.

Ranke, Leopold von. *The Theory and Practice of History.* Edited by Georg G. Iggers. 2nd ed. London: Routledge, 2011.

Rapp, Claudia. "Church and State, Religion and Power in Late Antique and Byzantine Scholarship of the Last Five Decades." In *The Church on Its Past*, edited by Peter D. Clarke and Charlotte Methuen, 447–67. Studies in Church History 49. Woodbridge, UK: Boydell, 2013.

———. "Epiphanius of Salamis: The Church Father as Saint." In *"The Sweet Land of Cyprus": Papers Given at the Twenty-First Jubilee Spring Symposium of Byzantine Studies,* edited by A. A. M. Bryer and G. S. Georghallides, 169–87. Nicosia: Cyprus Research Center, 1993.

———. "Frühbyzantinische Dichtung und Hagiographie am Beispiel der Vita des Epiphanius von Zypern." *Rivista di Studi Bizantini e Neoellenici* 27 (1991): 3–31.

———. "Hagiography and Monastic Literature between Greek East and Latin West in Late Antiquity." In *Cristianità d'occidente e cristianità d'oriente (secoli vi-xi)*, 1221–80. Settimane di Studio della Fondazione Centro Italiano di Studi sull'Alto Medioevo 51. Spoleto: Presso La Sede della Fondazione, 2004.

———. "Der heilige Epiphanius im Kampf mit dem Dämon des Origenes: Kritische Erstausgabe des Wunders BGH 601i." In *Symbolae Berolinenses: Für Dieter Harlfinger*, edited by Friederike Berger et al., 249–69. Amsterdam: Adolf M. Hakkert, 1993.

———. "Hellenic Identity, *Romanitas*, and Christianity in Byzantium." In *Hellenisms: Culture, Identity, and Ethnicity from Antiquity To Modernity*, edited by Katerina Zacharia, 127–48. Aldershot, UK: Ashgate, 2008.

———. *Holy Bishops in Late Antiquity: The Nature of Christian Leadership in an Age of Transition*. TCH 37. Berkeley: University of California Press, 2005.

Rebillard, Éric. "A New Style of Argument in Christian Polemic: Augustine and the Use of Patristic Citations." *JECS* 8 (2000): 559–78.

Rhodes, Royal W. *The Lion and the Cross: Early Christianity in Victorian Novels*. Columbus: The Ohio State University Press, 1995.

Riegl, Alois. *Spätrömische Kunst-Industrie nach den Funden in Österreich-Ungarn*. Vienna: Österreichische archäologische Institut, 1901.

Riggi, Calogero. "La catéchèse adaptée aux temps chez Epiphane." *SP* 17.1 (1982): 160–68.

———. "La figura di Epifanio nel IV secolo." *SP* 8.2 (1966): 86–107.

———. "Nouvelle lecture du *Panarion* LIX, 4 (Épiphane et le divorce)." *SP* 12.1 (1975): 129–34.

Roberts, Michael. *The Jeweled Style: Poetry and Poetics in Late Antiquity*. Ithaca, NY: Cornell University Press, 1989.

Rojek, Chris. *Celebrity*. London: Reaktion, 2001.

Rousseau, Philip. "Can 'Late Antiquity' Be Saved?" *Marginalia Review of Books*. http://marginalia.lareviewofbooks.org/can-late-antiquity-be-saved-by-philip-rousseau/.

Rubenson, Samuel. *The Letters of St. Antony: Monasticism and the Making of a Saint*. Studies in Antiquity and Christianity. Minneapolis: Fortress Press, 1995.

Rubin, Nissan. "*Brit Milah*: A Study of Change in Custom." In *The Covenant of Circumcision: New Perspectives on an Ancient Jewish Rite*, edited by Elizabeth Wyner Mark, 89–97. Hanover, NH: Brandeis University Press, 2003.

Russell, Fredrick H. "Persuading the Donatists: Augustine's Coercion by Words." In *The Limits of Late Ancient Christianity: Essays on Late Antique Thought and Culture in Honor of R. A. Markus,* edited by William Klingshirn and Mark Vessey, 115–30. Ann Arbor: University of Michigan Press, 1999.

Russell, Norman. *Theophilus of Alexandria.* The Early Church Fathers. London: Routledge, 2007.

Salmon, Frank. *Building on Ruins: The Rediscovery of Rome and English Architecture.* Reinterpreting Classicism. Aldershot, UK: Ashgate, 2000.

Salzman, Michele Renée. *The Letters of Symmachus.* Society of Biblical Literature Writings from the Greco-Roman World 30. Leiden: Brill, 2012.

Sanders, Andrew. *The Victorian Historical Novel, 1840–1880.* New York: St. Martin's Press, 1979.

Sanders, E. P. et al., eds. *Jewish and Christian Self-Definition.* 3 vols. Philadelphia: Fortress Press, 1980–81.

Sawyer, R. Keith. "Improvisation and the Creative Process: Dewey, Collingwood, and the Aesthetics of Spontaneity." *Journal of Aesthetics and Art Criticism* 58 (2000): 149–61.

Schmitz, Thomas. *Bildung und Macht: Zur sozialen und politischen Funktion der zweiten Sophistik in der griechischen Welt der Kaiserzeit.* Zetemata 97. Munich: C. H. Beck, 1997.

Scholten, Clemens. "Die Funktion der Häresienabwehr in der Alten Kirche." *VC* 66 (2012): 229–68.

Schor, Adam M. *Theodoret's People: Social Networks and Religious Conflict in Late Roman Syria.* TCH 48. Berkeley: University of California Press, 2011.

Schott, Jeremy. "Heresiology as Universal History in Epiphanius' *Panarion.*" *ZAC* 10 (2006): 546–63.

Schroeder, Caroline T. *Monastic Bodies: Discipline and Salvation in Shenoute of Atripe.* Divinations. Philadelphia: University of Pennsylvania Press, 2007.

Scott, Alan. "The Date of the *Physiologus.*" *VC* 52 (1998): 430–41.

———. "Origen's Use of Xenocrates of Ephesus." *VC* 45 (1991): 278–85.

Seidman, Naomi. *Faithful Renderings: Jewish-Christian Difference and the Politics of Translation.* Chicago: University of Chicago Press, 2006.

Sessa, Kristina. *The Formation of Papal Authority in Late Antique Italy: Roman Bishops and the Domestic Sphere.* Cambridge: Cambridge University Press, 2011.

Shaw, Brent. *Sacred Violence: African Christians and Sectarian Hatred in the Age of Augustine.* Cambridge: Cambridge University Press, 2011.

Shaw, Teresa M. "*Askēsis* and the Appearance of Holiness." *JECS* 6 (1998): 485–500.

Shepardson, Christine. *Controlling Contested Places: Late Antique Antioch and the Spatial Politics of Religious Controversy.* Berkeley: University of California Press, 2014.

Shoulson, Jeffrey S. *Fictions of Conversion: Jews, Christians, and Cultures of Change in Early Modern England.* Philadephia: University of Pennsylvania Press, 2013.

Simelidis, Christos. "Epiphanius." In *Encyclopedia of Ancient History,* edited by Roger Bagnall et al., 2463–64. London: Wiley/Blackwell, 2013.

Smith, Geoffrey S. *Guilt by Association: Heresy Catalogues in Early Christianity.* Oxford: Oxford University Press, 2014.

Smith, Philip. *The History of the Christian Church during the First Ten Centuries.* The Student's Ecclesiastical History. New York: Harper & Brothers, 1879.

Solovieva, Olga. "Epiphanius of Salamis between Church and State: New Perspectives on the Iconoclastic Fragments." *ZAC* 16 (2012): 344–67.

———. "Epiphanius of Salamis and His Invention of Iconoclasm in the Fourth Century A.D." *Fides et Historia* 42 (2010): 21–46.

Spoerl, Kelley McCarthy. "Athanasius and the Anti-Marcellian Controversy." *ZAC* 10 (2006): 34–55.

Stark, Rodney, and John Lofland. "Becoming a World-Saver: A Theory of Conversion to a Deviant Perspective." *American Sociological Review* 30 (1965): 863–74.

Stefaniw, Blossom. *Mind, Text, and Commentary: Noetic Exegesis in Origen of Alexandria, Didymus the Blind, and Evagrius Ponticus.* Early Christianity in the Context of Antiquity 6. Frankfurt am Main: Peter Lang, 2010.

Stendahl, Krister. "Paul and the Introspective Conscience of the West." *HTR* 56 (1963): 199–215.

Stenhouse, William. "Antiquarianism." In *The Classical Tradition,* edited by Anthony Grafton, Glenn W. Most, and Salvattore Settis, 51–53. Cambridge, MA: Belknap Press of Harvard University Press, 2010.

Sterk, Andrea. *Renouncing the World Yet Leading the Church: The Monk-Bishop in Late Antiquity.* Cambridge, MA: Harvard University Press, 2004.

Stewart, Columba. *Cassian the Monk.* Oxford: Oxford University Press, 2002.

Stewart-Sykes, Alistair. *From Prophecy to Preaching: A Search for the Origins of the Christian Homily.* Leiden: Brill, 1995.

Swann, Marjorie. *Curiosities and Texts: The Culture of Collecting in Early Modern England.* Material Texts. Philadelphia: University of Pennsylvania Press, 2001.

Swete, Henry. *An Introduction to the Old Testament in Greek.* Cambridge: Cambridge University Press, 1900.

Thomasson, Einar. *The Spiritual Seed: The Church of the "Valentinians."* NHMS 60. Leiden: Brill, 2006.

Thümmel, Hans Georg. "Die bilderfeindlichen Schriften des Epiphanius von Salamis." *Byzantinoslavica* 47 (1986): 169–88.

Tillyard, Stella. "Celebrity in 18th-Century London." *History Today* 55.6 (2005): 20–27.

Turner, Graeme. *Understanding Celebrity.* London: Sage, 2004.

Uffelman, Larry K. "*Hypatia:* Revisions in Context." *Nineteenth-Century Literature* 41 (1986): 87–96.

Urbainczyk, Theresa. "Observations on the Differences between the Church Histories of Socrates and Sozomen." *Historia* 46 (1997): 355–73.

Valantasis, Richard. Introduction to *Religions of Late Antiquity in Practice,* edited by Richard Valantasis, 3–16. Princeton Readings in Religions. Princeton, NJ: Princeton University Press, 2000.

Vance, Norman. "Anxieties of Empire and the Moral Tradition: Rome and Britain." *International Journal of the Classical Tradition* 18 (2011): 264–61.

Verheyden, Joseph. "Epiphanius of Salamis on Beasts and Heretics: Some Introductory Comments." In *Heretics and Heresies in the Ancient Church and Eastern Christianity: Studies in Honor of Adelbert Davids,* edited by Joseph Verheyden and Herman Teule, 143–73. Eastern Christian Studies 10. Leuven: Peeters, 2011.

Vessey, Mark. "Conference and Confession: Literary Pragmatics in Augustine's '*Apologia contra Hieronymum.*'" *JECS* 1 (1993): 175–213.

———. "The Demise of the Christian Writer and the Remaking of 'Late Antiquity': From H.-I. Marrou's Saint Augustine (1938) to Peter Brown's Holy Man (1983)." *JECS* 6 (1998): 377–411.

———. "The Forging of Orthodoxy in Latin Christian Literature: A Case Study." *JECS* 4 (1996): 495–513.

Viswanathan, Gauri. *Outside the Fold: Conversion, Modernity, and Belief.* Princeton, NJ: Princeton University Press, 1998.

Von Staden, Heinrich. "Galen and the 'Second Sophistic.'" In "Aristotle and After," ed. Richard Sorabji, special issue, *Bulletin of the Institute of Classical Studies* 41 (1997): 33–54.

Ward-Perkins, Bryan. *The Fall of Rome and the End of Civilization.* Oxford: Oxford University Press, 2005.

Washburn, Daniel. "Tormenting the Tormentors: A Reinterpretation of Eusebius of Vercelli's Letter from Scythopolis." *CH* 78 (2009): 731–55.

Watts, Edward. *City and School in Late Antique Athens and Alexandria.* TCH 41. Berkeley: University of California Press, 2006.
Webb, Ruth. *Demons and Dancers: Performance in Late Antiquity.* Cambridge, MA: Harvard University Press, 2008.
Weischer, Bernd. "Die urpsrüngliche nikänische Form des ersten Glaubenssymbols im Ankyrōtos des Epiphanios von Salamis: Ein Beitrag um die Enstehung des konstantinopolitanischen Glaubenssymbols im Lichte neuester äthiopistischer Forschungen." *Theologie und Philosophie* 53.3 (1978): 407–14.
Whitmarsh, Tim. *Beyond the Second Sophistic: Adventures in Greek Postclassicism.* Berkeley: University of California Press, 2013.
———. *The Second Sophistic.* Cambridge: Cambridge University Press, 2005.
Whittaker, C. R. "Frontiers." In *The Cambridge Ancient History,* vol. 11, *The High Empire, A.D. 70–192,* edited by Alan Bowman, Peter Garnsey, and Dominic Rathbone, 293–319. Cambridge: Cambridge University Press, 2000.
Williams, Frank. *The "Panarion" of Epiphanius of Salamis.* 2nd rev. ed. 2 vols. NHMS 63 and 79. Leiden: Brill, 2009–13.
Williams, Megan Hale. *The Monk and the Book: Jerome and the Making of Christian Scholarship.* Chicago: University of Chicago Press, 2008.
Williams, Michael. *Rethinking "Gnosticism": An Argument for Dismantling a Dubious Category.* Princeton, NJ: Princeton University Press, 1996.
Williams, Rowan. *Arius: Heresy and Tradition.* London: SCM Press, 2001.
Wiseman, Nicholas Cardinal. *Fabiola, or The Church of the Catacombs.* London: Burns & Oates, 1854.
Woolf, Greg. *Rome: An Empire's Story.* Cambridge: Cambridge University Press, 2012.
Wyschogrod, Edith. *Saints and Postmodernism: Revisioning Moral Philosophy.* Chicago: University of Chicago Press, 1990.
Yates, Nigel. *Anglican Ritualism in Victorian Britain, 1830–1910.* Oxford: Oxford University Press, 1999.
Young, Frances M. *Biblical Exegesis and the Formation of Christian Culture.* Cambridge: Cambridge University Press, 1997.
———. "Did Epiphanius Know What He Meant by Heresy?" *SP* 17 (1982): 199–205.

INDEX

Aaron (brother of Moses), breastplate of, 163, 173. See also *On Twelve Gems* (Epiphanius of Cyprus)
abstinence: Epiphanius on, 115n61; sexual, 109; from wine drinking, 110
Acacius (cleric): identity of, 44n47; request for *Ancoratus*, 20, 43
Acta Archelai, 83n65
Acts of Thecla, Epiphanius's use of, 146
Adam (patriarch): burial site of, 144; creation of, 135, 212; descendants of, 135; salvation of, 143–44
Adamites (ascetics), 109n46
Aerius, followers of, 129n125
Aetius (Anomoioan heretic), 78n49
Aetius (bishop of Lydda), 78, 79
Albrecht, Felix, 24, 25
Alexander (bishop of Constantinople), 87; expulsion of Arius, 86
allegorism, etymological, 161n118
Alogi, in *Panarion*, 152–53
Ambrose (bishop of Milan), 3; Origen and, 84–85; performative leadership of, 106n31
amethyst, magical properties of, 163
Ammonius (Tall Brother), 51
Amory, Patrick, 24n73

Anakephalaioses (summaries), of *Panarion*, 25, 198n84
Anatolius (amanuensis), 130n127; inscriptions by, 18–19
Ancoratus (Epiphanius of Cyprus): antiquarianism in, 141–43, 175; Bible in, 140–43, 175; body in, 214; composition of, 10, 44–45, 182n19; Coptic translation of, 19; curse of Canaan in, 151; date of, 18, 133n4, 182n19; differentiation in, 191n57; editions of, 19; end of, 43n46; Epiphanius's theology in, 181, 183–86; Genesis 1:26 in, 194; geography in, 135; God's benevolence in, 141; heresies in, 44, 135; Holy Spirit in, 203; the *homoousion* in, 189; humanity of Christ in, 185n36; image of God in, 193n69; incarnation in, 185n35, 192, 203; influence on Egyptian monasticism, 215n150; literalism of, 134; Maguseans in, 177n2; manuscript tradition of, 19; moral unity in, 182, 196; Nicene Creed in, 204; on Origen, 133, 188n46; origins of, 133n4; *ousia* and *hypostasis* in, 189;

Ancoratus (continued)
    paradise in, 133; Pneumatomachoi
        in, 182n20, 192n61; post-Septuagintal
        translators in, 149n74; prebaptismal
        teaching in, 220n172; proems to,
        183–84; proof-texts of, 140–41;
        Proverbs 8:22 in, 147n71, 192;
        readership of, 11; requests for, 43,
        183, 184; resurrection in, 184, 185n35;
        Roman emperors in, 135; Sahidic
        translation of, 215n150; salvation in,
        184; ship metaphor of, 111n50; on
        theological errors, 19, 20; title
        metaphor of, 18–19; Trinity in, 188,
        190–95, 199; unity in, 191n57
Ando, Clifford, 275n36
Anglo-Catholicism: missionary work
    in, 252n119; Mossman's, 246, 248;
    ritualist strain of, 248n104
Anomoians (anti-Nicene Christians):
    Epiphanius's refutation of, 148–49,
    201–2; Trinitarian heresy of, 201–2
anthropology: Epiphanius and, 28,
    190–91, 206; in late ancient
    historiography, 267, 269; post-
    Geertzian, 269
Antioch, episcopal controversies in, 11,
    34, 41n35, 42n40, 46n53, 119–24, 126,
    177n2, 178
antiquarianism, 28, 135–39; classical/
    Christian elements in, 173;
    digressions in, 175; in early reading
    of Bible, 138, 139, 154, 175; European,
    136n17; Hellenistic, 136; intellectual
    production through, 272; learned
    display in, 174; logic in, 138n24,
    150n81; Origen's, 145, 174;
    reassembling in, 139; in service of
    empire, 138; unexpected
    associations of, 175; visible
    assemblage of, 174
antiquarianism, Epiphanius's, 28,
    139n33, 141–54, 274; in *Ancoratus*,
    141–43, 175; biblical canon and,
    167n148; collation in, 142–43;
    digressions in, 141; ethnography in,
    153; intellectual production
    through, 272; in *Panarion*, 144–49,
    175; spiritual truth in, 150–51;
    totalizing knowledge in, 153; in *On
    Twelve Gems*, 154, 162
antiquarianism, Roman, 136–38; biblical
    interpretation and, 174; political
    aspect of, 138
antiquarian writing: aesthetics of,
    135–39; fragmentary nature of, 162;
    resistance to hierarchalization, 153;
    Roman, 136–38; specious etymology
    in, 160
Antony, Saint, 206n111, 230; life of, 225
apocrypha, Epiphanius's use of, 146–47
Apocryphon of Ezekiel, Epiphanius's use
    of, 146, 209. *See also* blind and lame
    thieves, parable of
Apollinarians, 43n46; Christologies of,
    109n39, 177n4; controversy with
    Epiphanius, 120, 123; in *Panarion*,
    186
Apollinarius of Laodicea:
    condemnation at Council of
    Constantinople, 123n98; on
    incarnation, 216n152; ordination of
    Vitalius, 119–20, 124n103; on virgin
    birth, 15n40
Apopthegmata Patrum, 230n32; ascetic
    authority in, 61; cultural concerns
    of, 46; Epiphanius in, 48n57, 54,
    56–57, 61; humility in, 57n89
apostolic succession, authority of, 116
Aquila (Bible translator), 65–66, 149,
    157, 173; biographical material on,
    65n2; double conversion of, 66;
    linguistic errors of, 148–49; in
    rabbinic literature, 66n4
Aragione, Gabriella, 264n2
Arcadius, Emperor: in *Vita Epiphanii*,
    230, 231, 233n49
architecture, Gothic revival, 250n111
Archontics (ascetics), 109n46;
    ignorance of Hebrew, 147–48

Arianism: Epiphanius's description of, 122n94; interpretation of Proverbs 8:22, 148; Melitius and, 114n59; Trinitarianism in, 190
Aristotle, speculative tradition of, 206
Arius: Alexandrian crisis over, 129n126; birth of, 87n84; comparison with Judas, 86n80; death of, 86n76, 87; Epiphanius's biography of, 85–87; external forces affecting, 86; imperial power and, 85–86; as inverse Constantine, 86; and Melitians, 200n92; misreading of Scripture, 86; Satanic inspiration of, 86–87; Trinitarian heresy of, 200–201
art, late Roman, 267
Asad, Talal, 130n128
asceticism, late ancient: bibliography of, 269n21; episcopacy and, 59, 60–61, 108n35; flexible, 115–19; heretical, 109–11; inflexibility of, 110, 115; Jerome on, 113; modern historiography on, 269n20; Palestinian, 59–60; *Panarion* on, 109; "showy," 109n46
ascetics, female: as "shaming" devices, 59n94
Asia Minor, theological controversies in, 19
askesis, Epiphanius's celebrity and, 46, 47, 56–62
Atarbius (anti-Origenist), 178n8
Athanasius (bishop of Alexandria), 3, 176; in Antiochene controversy, 120n82; in *Apopthegmata Patrum*, 48n57; on baptism, 185; correspondence with Epiphanius, 14n36, 15; correspondence with Serapion 183n25, 185; Epiphanius and, 10; on Holy Spirit, 185; and Marcella, 58n90; Paulinus and, 120; soteriology of, 185n34; Syedrans' reading of, 183; theology of, 179. Works: *Epistula ad Epiphanium*, 41; *Epistula 64*, 23n71; *Tomus ad Antiochenos*, 120n86; *Vita Antonii*, 235n54
Audians: on body of God, 194n74; use of *Didascalia apostolorum*, 117n70
Audius (ascetic), 114
Augustine of Hippo: conscription into priesthood, 76n38; on Epiphanius's expertise, 52, 53n72; on forcible ordination, 76n38; interior introspection of, 70, 94; literary ambitions of, 26n82; on lying, 273; modern studies of, 6; on Paul's transformation, 94; social management by, 71n20; as spokesman for late antiquity, 270. Works: *City of God*, 198; *Confessions*, 70, 71
Augustus, Emperor: final words of, 105n27
Aulus Gellius: *Noctes Atticae*, 137; on pedantry, 150n81
Ausonius, 266
authority: of apostolic succession, 116; ascetic, 61; versus celebrity, 32–33; in Christian late antiquity, 63; Epiphanius's, 33, 59, 63, 99, 119, 122n97, 273; Epiphanius's celebrity and, 35; episcopal, 77, 92, 119, 271; functioning of, 33; in late ancient Christianity, 32; personal, 63; of Roman Empire, 155; secular, 32
Ayres, Lewis, 179n11, 184n31

Baker, Joseph Ellis, 244n87
Bardesan (heretic), social ties of, 81
Barnabas, Joseph: veneration of, 124n101
Basilides (heresiarch), 144; on evil, 193n69
Basil of Caesarea: *Contra Eunomium*, 183n25; correspondence with Epiphanius, 14, 41–42, 177n2; on Nicene Creed, 180n15
Benjamin (patriarch), 168–69; in Epiphanius's conversion narratives, 93–94

Bergermann, Marc, 19, 21
Bible: in *Ancoratus*, 140–43, 175; antiallegorical reading of, 133–35; antiquarian readings of, 138, 139, 154, 175; coherence of, 145–46; Epiphanius's literalism concerning, 133n3, 134; Epiphanius's use of, 132–35; historical authority of, 155; linguistic layers of, 147–48; Origen's use of, 132–33; in *Panarion*, 144–45, 175; reconfiguration of, 169; and Roman literature, 141; in *On Twelve Gems*, 162–73, 175; unity of, 157, 169; in *On Weights and Measures*, 154–62, 175
Bible translations: boundaries of, 67–68; Greek, 65–67; linguistic borders of, 67, 68; post-Septuagintal, 148–50; spread across empire, 68; transformation through, 69
biblical interpretation, Epiphanius's: allegory in, 140n35, 160; antiquarianism in, 145–48, 167n148; compilation in, 140; digression in, 152–53; disorganization in, 141; ethnographic knowledge in, 143; genealogy in, 151; geographic knowledge in, 143, 144; heresiology in, 143–44; and Roman antiquarianism, 174; spiritual truth in, 150–51; use of Origen's Hexapla, 150
Bigham, Steven, 241n76
bishops, late antique: expulsion of Gnostics, 98–99; monk-, 60, 76; rise to prominence, 33n7. *See also* episcopacy
Blake, Robert, 24, 25
blind and lame thieves, parable of, 146n62, 186–87, 188, 209, 218
bloodstone, imagery of, 165
Bloomer, W. Martin, 104n26
body: church discipline over, 108–14; in Epiphanius's theology, 182, 185–86, 212, 213–20; and human history, 214; monastic theology of, 219n170; moral continuity of, 219; moral unity and, 216; salvation and, 214; as site of transformation, 219
body and soul: of Christ, 190–93; commonality of, 186–88; and divine justice, 214; *enhypostatoi*, 193; final reward of, 210; judgment of, 186–87; moral agency of, 212–13; and moral selves, 214; moral unity of, 187–88, 189, 201, 218; recovery of God's image, 213; resurrection of, 213, 217; salvation and, 214; separability of, 188; Shenoute on, 217; Theophilus on, 215–16; unity of, 180–81, 212–14
books: Christian, 54n79; Epiphanius's, 26–27; Gnostics', 27n85, 98, 147n63; Origen's, 27
Boorstin, Daniel: on celebrity, 35–36, 37, 63
borderlands theory, on late antiquity, 69n15
borders, in antiquity, 69. *See also* frontier zones
borders, religious, 76–77; in Bible translations, 67; control of, 78–81; heretics' crossing of, 81–82; Jewish-Christian, 88; of orthodoxy, 81; self and other in, 69
boundaries: of community, 69; of identity, 69; personal, 84
boundaries, geographical: of Bible translations, 68; of empires, 73; porous, 80
boundaries, religious: of Christian Roman Empire, 87; clergy/laity, 76–77; collapse of, 74; Epiphanius's control of, 81; in Epiphanius's conversion narratives, 67; improper maintenance of, 85; of late antiquity, 67, 68; of orthodoxy, 67–68, 81, 85; policing of, 96; of religious status, 76; in *Vita Epiphanii*, 240
Bowersock, G. W., 268n17
Boyarin, Daniel, 88

Brakke, David, 219n170; on Gnosticism, 97n2
Braudy, Leo, 37, 39n30; on fame, 40n32
British Empire, expansion of, 243
Brown, Peter, 267n15; on ascetic logic, 108n35; on Christian empire, 269n22; on Epiphanius's imagination of place, 211; on Gibbon, 266n11; on holy men, 221, 223; influence of, 265; on "new men," 277; study of the poor, 277n45. Works: *Augustine of Hippo*, 5, 6; "The Rise and Function of the Holy Man in Late Antiquity," 32n4; *The World of Late Antiquity*, 274–75
Bryner, A.A.M., 122n96
Burrus, Virginia, 225; on nineteenth-century religious politics, 243n83
Byzantine Empire, Roman-Christian fusing in, 224n9
Byzantine studies, Anglo-American marginalization of, 275–76

Cain, Andrew, 80n56
Cambridge Ancient History, late antiquity in, 266n9
Cameron, Averil, 107n32, 140n34; on Byzantine studies, 275
Canaan: curse of, 151; oath breaking in, 142, 143n45
canon, biblical: as antiquarian device, 147; correct theology in, 146n58; Epiphanius's respect for, 146–47
Cappadocians, 3; metaphysical theology of, 189
Castiglione, Baldassare, 131
castration, voluntary: discursive phenomenon of, 61n100; excommunication for, 61; Valesians', 109n46
Catharites, 117; inflexible asceticism of, 115
Catholic Popular Library series, 244nn88–89
Cave, William, 241n79

celebrity: audience of, 38, 42; and authenticity, 38; versus authority, 32–33; biography, 46n54; commodification of, 38, 62; continuity in, 63; and culture, 27, 37–38, 45–62; episcopal, 271; versus fame, 36; function of, 27, 36, 37; immediacy of, 33; imperviousness to fixity, 62; origins of, 37; role in cultural production, 37; as social phenomenon, 38; social production of, 42; and society, 40–45; versus status, 36; theorists of, 46; transience of, 33; types of, 63
celebrity, Epiphanius's: among pro-Nicenes, 43; appeals to, 44; Christian authority and, 35; commodification of, 47; in conception of *askesis*, 46, 47, 56–62; in conception of *imperium*, 46–47, 48–52, 62; in conception of *paideia*, 46, 47, 52–56; in controversies, 40; cultural effects of, 45–46, 62, 63–64; cultural production through, 46; discipline in, 47; function of, 40, 56, 63; and his accomplishments, 62; iconic, 33, 62–64; knowledge in, 47; as opportunity, 40; power in, 47; social networks of, 43, 44; social production of, 45; in sociocultural critique, 40; use in cultural critique, 38
celebrity, modern, 35–36; contents of, 46; in media, 36n13, 38n24, 39n27; of movie stars, 38; origins of, 39n27; in popular culture, 36n16; as pseudo-event, 35, 36; sociocultural sites of, 40; structures undergirding, 39
celibacy, clerical, 115, 117
Certeau, Michel de, 226
Chadwick, Henry, 2
chalcedony, source of, 164
change, anxiety of, 96
Cheery, David, 95
Chidester, David, 73n29

Chin, Catherine, 174, 205
Christ: bloodstone imagery of, 165;
   body and soul of, 190–93; divinity
   of, 186n38; dual nature of, 166; as
   enhypostatos, 189; as *genētos*, 208n120;
   Godhood of, 185; humanity of, 121,
   185n36, 191, 216; *hypostaseis* of, 193; on
   matrimony, 109; miracles of, 152–53;
   particularity of, 181; power against
   magic, 89, 90n93; as soul in the
   person, 195; unified composition of,
   193; uniqueness of, 135. *See also*
   incarnation
Christian culture, late ancient, 3, 5, 13,
   33, 47; deconstruction of, 47; of
   difference, 29; display in, 272;
   Epiphanius's vision of, 273;
   exclusionary, 108; imperial, 131, 154;
   improvisational nature of, 108, 131;
   management of, 273; performance
   in, 272; power in, 175, 272; production
   of, 27–28; Roman aspects of, 6, 9, 28;
   status in, 272; transformation of, 275;
   world knowledge in, 175. *See also*
   culture, late ancient
Christianity, late ancient: absorption
   of Judaism into, 94, 256–59, 260;
   alignment with Rome, 228–30;
   authority in, 32, 63; boundaries of,
   68–69; canon of, 4n8, 6; as example
   for modern society, 269; following
   Council of Nicaea, 4; fractures in,
   6; imperial, 4, 33; of imperial
   household, 240; Jewish otherness
   and, 240; orthodoxy-heresy
   spectrum in, 81–87; otherness in, 7,
   271, 272–74; politics of, 49; power in,
   32–33; relationship to Judaism, 245;
   and Roman imperial tradition,
   224n9, 273; signaling of Roman
   power, 175; status in, 32, 63; tension
   with Rome, 234; theological
   argumentation in, 141;
   understanding of, 5; vulnerability
   to outside influence, 86

Christianity, nineteenth-century:
   muscular, 243. *See also*
   Anglo-Catholicism
Christians, late ancient: ante-Nicene,
   244, 249; ex-Jews, ix, 88–94;
   intellectual particularity of, 5;
   modern historiography on, 5;
   nonmonastic, 206n170, 215;
   relationship to empire, 47;
   remarried, 115; unified moral body
   of, 204–5
Christians, non-Anglican: political
   rights of, 242
Christians, Serbian Orthodox, 235n53
Christology, Monophysite, 14
church, late ancient: human unity in,
   199; institutional rigor of, 129; moral
   unity of, 200, 203; multiple creeds
   of, 203; power relations of, 128;
   purification from heresy, 98; as ship,
   111; staffing needs of, 117; unity of,
   202, 203; in Victorian fiction, 243–46
church and state, in late Victorian era,
   252
Church of Ireland, disestablishment of,
   252n120
Church of the Holy Sepulcher, 250n110
Cicero: on improvisation, 102n15; on
   translation, 16
circumcisions: reversal of, 67n5;
   second, 66
Clark, Elizabeth A., 59n94; on
   construction of past, 276; on
   Epiphanius's antiallegorism, 134n11;
   on Epiphanius's anti-Origenism,
   126n113; on moral continuity, 211; on
   Origenist controversy, 205–6,
   207n113, 209; on Theophilus, 216n156
clergy: allocation of resources, 80;
   commodification of offices, 80n56;
   lapsed, 114n59; reintegration from
   heresy, 80; sexual requirements for,
   117–18; social class of, 80
Clovis, conversion of, 74
Collatz, Christian-Friedrich, 21

Collectio Avellana, Epiphanius in, 24
colonialism, and religious emancipation, 243n84
community, boundaries of, 69
community, Christian: fracturing of, 81
Constantia (Salamis): Epiphanius's ordination at, 9, 76n39; pilgrimage to, 10; refounding of, 9n22
Constantia (Tomis), 24n73
Constantine, Emperor: conversion of, 74; Easter celebration under, 202; in Epiphanius's conversion narratives, 89; in Mossman's *Epiphanius*, 250, 251–52, 253; in *Vita Epiphanii*, 230n32
Constantinople, Epiphanius's travel to, 12, 155
Constantius II, Emperor: anti-Nicene empire of, 34n10
consubstantiality: in Epiphanius's Trinitarianism, 180, 188, 199–200, 217; of Father and Son, 148; in Nicene Trinitarianism, 176, 188, 204–5
conversion, religious: within Christian hierarchy, 88; as colonial discourse, 72, 91; exteriority of, 70, 73–74, 94; forced, 70; frontier zones of, 73; genealogical layers of, 94; to heresy, 81–87; hermeneutics of, 72n24; as interior introspective process, 70, 71–72, 73–74; from Judaism, 88; modern understandings of, 70; in secret, 91; as social process, 70, 94; socio-cultural locations of, 71–72; spectrum of, 74; state power and, 72; theorists of, 70
conversion narratives, Epiphanius's, 28, 65–67, 88–94; Benjamin the patriarch in, 93–94; boundaries in, 67; Constantine in, 89; difference in, 73; Ebionites in, 91, 92; ex-Jews in, 88–94; forced ordinations in, 75–77; frontier zones in, 90; Hillel the patriarch in, 89, 90–91; individuality in, 91; interiority in, 91; on Joseph of Tiberias, 88–91, 92; Paul the apostle in, 92–94; selective incorporation in, 91; status in, 73, 74–81; transformation in, 88; in *On Twelve Gems*, 93–94; types of conversion in, 74
corporeality, problem for monasticism, 214n145. *See also* body
correspondence, Epiphanius's, 13–18; with Athanasius, 14n36, 15, 41; authenticity of, 14; with Basil of Caesarea, 14, 41–42, 177n2; on date of Easter, 41n36; with episcopal colleagues, 41, 43; fragmentary, 14; with John of Jerusalem, 15–16, 74–78, 126, 207, 210; manuscript tradition of, 15n39; survival of, 10, 13–14, 17–18; from Syedra, 43; in Syriac, 14, 18; with Theodosius (purported), 9n18, 17; with Theophilus of Alexandria, 42–43
Council of Chalcedon, Trinitarianism of, 190n55
Council of Constantinople (381), 11, 13; condemnation of Apollinarius, 123n98; controversies preceding, 43; Epiphanius's absence from, 13, 34n11, 122; Meletius at, 122n96; revised Nicene Creed of, 204; signatories at, 34n11, 122
Council of Ephesus (401), on Cypriot autonomy, 124n101
Council of Nicaea (325): Arius following, 87; fifth canon of, 122n95; imperial Christianity following, 4
creeds, multiplicity of, 203
Crouzel, Henri, 116n65
cultural production: celebrity in, 37; role of institutions in, 105
cultural production, late ancient, 266–67; disruption in, 272; through Epiphanius's celebrity, 46
culture, late ancient, 4, 5; canonical figures of, 270; compatibility with modern culture, 269n20; creativity

culture *(continued)*
of, 274; Epiphanius and, 271–77;
reflexivity of, 267. *See also* Christian
culture, late ancient
culture, Roman: antiquarian, 136–38;
performative, 105; totalizing
knowledge of, 136–37;
transformation by Christianity, 221
Cyprianus Gallus, *Heptateuchos*, 173n176
Cyprus: banning of heresy in, 232n43;
dominance among eastern bishops,
127n118; forcible ordination in, 77,
125, 127n116; monasteries of, 58,
220n171; Nicenes of, 34n9;
Valentinus in, 81
Cyril of Alexandria, 190n53, 217

Damasus (bishop of Rome), 11–12
Daniel, book of, 167
Davidson, Ivor, 106n31
Davis, Stephen, 216–17
Dean, James Elmer, 22, 23
Dechow, Jon, 33n8; on *Ancoratus*,
215n150; on Epiphanius's paradise,
133n7; on Epiphanius's theology,
185n35; on Origenism, 206, 207n112,
208n119; on problem of corporeality,
214n146; on reactions to
Epiphanius, 1n1
declamation, Roman, 102nn13–14. *See
also* rhetoric, Latin
De incarnatione (Epiphanius of Cyprus),
152n88
DelCogliano, Mark, 194–95
Demetrius, *De elocutione*, 104n25
the devil, in Epiphanius's theology,
210–11
Didascalia apostolorum, 117n70
dietary restrictions, 118
difference, Jewish, 236; and Catholic
truth, 260
difference, religious: Christian
cultures of, 29; in Epiphanius's
conversion narratives, 73;
Epiphanius's deployment of, 7, 271,
272, 275; in late antiquity, 277;
management of, 28, 260, 271; in
Mossman's *Epiphanius*, 259, 260–61;
and national identity, 243;
performance of, 274; power and, 223;
saints' management of, 260
Dimoirites (disciples of Apollinarius),
Epiphanius's refutation of, 121
Diocletian, Emperor: tetrarchy of,
106n30
Diodore (bishop of Tyre), 23
Dioscurus, excommunication of, 51
discipline, bodily: by church, 108–14;
Massalians' lack of, 128–29; in
Panarion, 109–12, 113–14
discipline, church: bodily, 108–14;
boundaries of, 99; Epiphanius and,
114–28; in Epiphanius's celebrity, 47;
Epiphanius's interventions in,
118–28, 131; Epiphanius's style of, 99,
101, 113, 128–31, 271–72; flexibility in,
114–19; improvisational quality of,
104, 123, 127, 128–29; over communal
body, 108, 114–28; over individual
body, 108–14; rigidity of, 107; rules
of, 117
discontinuity, aesthetics of, 174
Disraeli, Benjamin, 259
Donatists, forced conversions of, 70
Douglas, Mary, 267
Dummer, Jürgen, 21, 147n65

early church novels, Victorian, 243–46;
bibliography of, 245n91; conversion
in, 254n127; death in, 257n144;
Epiphanius in, 246; hagiographic
figures in, 245; Judaism and
Christianity in, 254; Judaism and
empire in, 248n105; martyrdom in,
257n144
Easter, date of, 34, 41n36, 202
Ebionites (heretics): incorporation
issues concerning, 91; in *Panarion*,
34n10, 91; use of Hebrew New
Testament, 89n92

education. See *paideia*
Egypt: "gnostic" sects of, 97n1; monasticism in, 9, 59–60, 206n111, 214n144, 215; nomes of, 144–45; Origenist movement in, 178; theological controversies in, 12
Egyptians, despoiling by Israelites, 141–42
Ehrman, Bart, 2
Eleutheropolis, monastery near, 79
Elijah (prophet), 166, 167; feeding by ravens, 258
Elliott, Mark, 133n3
Elsner, Jás, 222, 260
embodiment, human: and image of God, 215n149. *See also* body
emerald, 164, 173; properties of, 168
Emmel, Stephen, 217n161
empires: boundaries of, 73; limits of, 94. See also *imperium*; Roman Empire
Encratites (heretics), use of noncanonical texts, 147n63
encyclopedic tradition, Roman, 136n15, 137
Englezakis, Benedict, 124n101
Epiphanides, 241n78
Epiphanius (Syrian philosopher): conversion of, 238n68; debate with Epiphanius of Cyprus, 226
Epiphanius of Cyprus, ix
—anthropology and, 28, 190–91, 206
—antiallegorism of, 133–35, 211
—allegory in writings of, 140n35, 160
—ascetic flexibility of, 112–14, 115–19
—*askesis* of, 33, 46, 47, 56–62
—as Athanasius's successor, 183n25
—authority of, 33, 59, 63, 119, 122n97, 273
—biblical interpretation by, 28, 139
—Byzantine aspects of, 276
—character, 263–64, 271; anti-intellectualism, 2; celebrity, 27–28, 33, 221, 261; commodification of persona, 47; dishonesty, 273–74; intolerance, 2; intransigence, 2; negativity, 276; as problem-solver,

130; traditionalism, 275; women's attraction to, 97n2
—and church discipline, 114–28
—connection with Hilarion, 34n8
—contrast with Origen, 132
—controversies, 1–2, 9, 10, 118–28, 176; with Anomoians, 148–49, 201–2; Antioch episcopacy, 11, 34, 41n45, 42n40, 46n53, 119–24, 126, 177n2, 178; with Apollinarians, 120, 123; Arianism, 122n94; celebrity in, 40; date of Easter, 34; with Dimoirites, 121; in Egypt, 12; with Eutychius, 10n23; with Gnostics, 27n85, 97–99, 119; with John Chrysostom, 34n11, 50–51, 127n119, 178n9; with John of Jerusalem, 12, 31–32, 49, 74–78, 125–26; with Manichaeans, 151; with Marcellus of Ancyra, 179–80; with Massalians, 128; in Mount of Olives dispute, 42n40; Origenist, ix, 12, 17, 34, 42, 51, 54, 75, 83n66, 132–35, 181, 207–13, 220; in Palestine, 12; with Paul of Samosata, 149; virginity of Mary, 15, 20, 41, 109n39
—conversions under, 88
—disciplinary style of, 99, 101, 113, 128–31, 271–72
—early detractors of, 8n15
—and Empress Eudoxia, 50
—engagement with *paideia*, 84n70, 85, 108n34
—episcopacy: authority of, 27; duties, 122, 177–78; ecclesiastical meeting attendance, 120–21, 122–23; meetings with Antiochene claimants, 120–24; ordination, 9, 76n39; reform of Cyprus churches, 34; synod in Cyprus, 122n95; tenure, 17, 60
—and Eusebius of Vercelli, 9n21, 34n10, 178n5
—forcible ordination by, 75–77, 125–26, 127, 233n48
—hagiographies of, 28–29, 88n88, 221, 222, 261

—historical figure of, 221, 261
—imagination of place, 211–12
—improvisational style, 101, 108, 113, 123–24, 127, 128–31, 274
—in *Apopthegmata Patrum*, 48n57, 54, 56–57, 61
—in early Christian novels, 246
—influence, 4, 5; on Byzantine heresiology, 276n42; on Egyptian monasticism, 215n150; on Shenoute, 217
—in Palestine, 9, 12, 23, 27, 34n8, 78
—in Victorian fiction, 223
—Jewishness of, ix, 9, 29, 88n88, 223, 234–40
—kinds of expertise, 52
—knowledge: of languages, 147, 148–49; of Tall Brothers, 55
—library of, 26–27
—life, 8–10, 13; birth of, 9, 79n52; Canaanite identity of, 255; conversion, 223, 241; death of, 9n22, 10, 12, 34n11, 50, 224n11; education of, 8n17, 9, 84n70; erudition of, 52–56; rise to prominence, 33–34; tomb of, 10
—management of status, 7
—materialist preaching of, 211n136
—miraculous works of, 33n7, 63
—and modern conception of late antiquity, 264–65
—modern historiography on, ix–x, 1–8, 263–65
—monasteries: in Palestine, 125; near Eleutheropolis, 79
—as monk-bishop, 60–61
—Nicene partisanship of, 34n10, 122, 176–77
—on abstinence, 115n61
—on marriage, 109, 110n43, 111, 112, 115, 116, 117
—and Paula (ascetic), 57–59, 112–14
—performance of knowledge, 149
—philosophical capacity of, 206
—prebaptismal teaching of, 220n172
—public appearances of, 34n11
—rhetoric of, 3, 197
—role in Christian identity, 271
—sainthood of, 221–22, 223, 258n150, 259, 260–61, 263
—self-representation of, 127n115, 128
—sources of, 146n59
—standing in antiquity, 8–13, 42
—and totalizing discourse, 8n14
—travel: to Constantinople, 12, 49n60, 50, 155, 224n11; to Palestine, 23; to Rome, 11–12, 57, 124n102, 224n11
—use as source, 1, 2n2
—use in iconoclast controversy, 16, 17n47, 63, 241
—worldview of, 271
—writings, 10–11, 13–27; allegorical interpretation in, 140n35; Coptic, 215n150; denunciation of classical culture in, 83n70; dictated, 129–30, 151n86; dissemination of, 26; haste in, 11; and his celebrity, 45; on his selfhood, 78; legacy of, 18; letters, 10, 13–18, 41–43; literalism of, 133n3, 134, 140, 205–6, 220; manuscript tradition, 22n67; plagiarism charges against, 56; pro-Nicene, 34n10; pseudepigrapha, 25–27; requests for, 20, 43, 183, 184; self-presentation in, 26; sermons, 26; simplicity in, 53–54; spontaneous language of, 130; style of, 53–54; treatises, 18–25, 44–45; use of Bible, 132–35; use of noncanonical works, 146–47. *See also* antiquarianism, Epiphanius's; celebrity, Epiphanius's; heresiology, Epiphanius's; monasticism, Epiphanius's; theology, Epiphanius's; Trinitarianism, Epiphanius's

episcopacy: asceticism and, 59, 60–61, 108n35; authority of, 77, 92, 119, 271; celebrity of, 271; combative confrontation in, 129n126; ecclesiastical councils of, 122n95;

flexibility and, 118; improvisational style of, 106; instability of, 88; in Nicene controversies, 120; Roman models of, 106
episcopacy, Antiochene: Athanasius of Alexandria and, 120n82; claimants to, 119–21; contested, 11, 34, 41n35, 42n40, 46n53, 119–24, 126, 177n2, 178
Epistula Acacii et Pauli. See Acacius; Paul
Epistula ad Arabos (Epiphanius of Cyprus), 18; virginity controversy in, 15, 20
Epistula ad Ioannem Hierosolymitanum (Epiphanius of Cyprus), 15–16; authenticity of, 16; Latin copies of, 16n44
Erastianism, 242n82
Ervine, Roberta, 22
ethnography: descendants of Noah in, 142n44; in Epiphanius's writings, 143, 153, 171; Hellenistic, 136
etymology, antiquarian, 166n141; of Golgotha, 144; metaphysical truth in, 161n118; specious, 160
Eudoxia, Empress: conflict with John Chrysostom, 233–34; and Epiphanius, 50, 51
Eugnomon (Roman), Epiphanius's freeing of in *Vita Epiphanii*, 229n30
Euphrates River, Epiphanius on, 134
Eusebius of Caesarea: *Historia ecclesiastica*, 85n73; *Onomasticon*, 161, 170n164
Eusebius of Vercelli, Epiphanius and, 9n21, 34n10, 178n5
Eutactus (heretic), 80
Eutychius, dispute with Epiphanius, 10n23
Evagrius Ponticus, Origenist theologies of, 210n128
Exodus, in *On Twelve Gems*, 154
Ezekiel, secret book of, 186–87

Facundus of Hermiane, 23n71
fans and fandom, 39n26

Farrar, Frederic William: *Gathering Clouds*, 246n95
Fatti, Federico, 127n118
fiction, Victorian: pro- and anti-Catholic, 244–45, 252. *See also* early church novels, Victorian
Flavian (bishop of Antioch), 123n98
florilegia, Epiphanius's letters in, 14
Foucault, Michel: on "author-function," 37n18; influence on asceticism studies, 269n20
Francis of Assisi, Victorian biography of, 248n103
Fredriksen, Paula, 70n18
free will, in Origenist controversy, 212
French, Todd Edison, 225n13
frontier zones: control of, 78; of conversion, 73; intercultural relations in, 73n29; between Judaism and Christianity, 90, 94; loss of containment, 80; power in, 73n29; Roman, 95; theoretical work on, 95n113. *See also* borders

Galvão-Sobrinho, Carlos R., 129n126
Geertz, Clifford: and study of early Christianity, 267n14
gemmological treatises, Greek, 163n125
gems: allegorical properties of, 166n145; spiritual interpretations of, 164. See also *On Twelve Gems* (Epiphanius of Cyprus)
Genesis: Epiphanius on, 133–34; reality of, 208
George of Alexandria, 176
Georghallides, G. S., 122n96
Gervaise, François-Armand: use of *Vita Epiphanii*, 242
Giardina, Andrea, 266n9, 267n12, 268n16
Gibbon, Edward: anti-Christianity of, 245, 269; on late ancient culture, 266
Gleede, Benjamin, 190n53
Gnostics: bishops' expulsion of, 98–99; books of, 27n85, 98, 147n63;

Gnostics *(continued)*
  Epiphanius's exposure of, 97–99, 119; honey-pot stratagem of, 98n4; ignorance of Hebrew, 147; names for, 97n2; seductiveness of women, 98
God: anthropomorphite ideas about, 215n149; benevolence of, 141, 159–60; body of, 195n74; correction of fallen souls, 94; creation of world, 159–60; as *enhypostatos*, 189; as form, 195; justice of, 142; multiplicity of, 185; *ousia* of, 185; relationship with humanity, 195n76, 205, 259; righteous judgment of, 188; Trinitarian nature of, 184; unity of, 135, 185, 199, 200, 202, 210
Godhead: composite unity of, 207, 210, 213; moral unity of, 203
Golgotha, etymology of, 144
Gospels, Epiphanius's harmonizing of, 152–53
Gould, Carol S., 100n8
Grafton, Anthony, 68n12
Great Britain: established religion of, 242; and "primitive" church, 249n109. *See also* Anglo-Catholicism
Greek Orthodoxy Church, American: Epiphanius's life in, 235n53
Greenblatt, Stephen, 130–31
Gunderson, Erik, 138n24, 139; on Gellius, 150n81; on improvisation, 105n28
Günther, Otto, 24n73

Habinek, Thomas, 39–40, 105n28
Hadrian, Emperor: Jerusalem temples of, 249, 250; renaming of Jerusalem, 68n8
hagiography, 221–23; boundaries in, 260; as discourse of virtues, 222n3; East-West transmission of, 225n13; extraction of social history from, 222n2; sexuality in, 225n14; space in, 226; transgressive elements of, 222. *See also Vita Epiphanii*

Hanson, R.P.C., 178
Hebrew language: Epiphanius's knowledge of, 147–48, 258; heretics' ignorance of, 147–48; letters of alphabet, 160
Helena (mother of Constantine), 249–50
heresiarchs: biography of, 83–87; errors in Hebrew, 147–48; linguistic errors of, 147–48
heresiography, totalizing, 197
heresiology, Epiphanius's, 6, 28, 33, 45, 196–98, 261; in biblical interpretation, 143–44; celebrity in, 44; Christian history and, 198; dishonesty in, 273; moral unity and, 207; otherness in, 273–74; in *Panarion*, 21, 83–87, 196; rhetorical strategy of, 197; role in Christian community, 81
heresy: ancient debates about, 1–2; *Ancoratus* on, 20; boundaries of, 67; Byzantine, 276; catalogues of, 197n82; causes of, 81, 83; conversion to, 81–87; crypto-pagan, 197; external life events in, 81; and failure of empire, 87; Gnostic, 78; Latin handbooks on, 198n84; myths of, 108n34; sexual libertinism in, 109; in spectrum with orthodoxy, 81; as theater, 108n34; theological "others" in, 197; uniformity in, 111; use of noncanonical texts in, 147n63; in *Vita Epiphanii*, 261; weed symbolism of, 98
Hesychius, Epiphanius and, 57n88
Hieracas (Egyptian heretic), 81, 186, 240n75; sexual abstinence of, 109
hierarchy, ecclesiastical: of Jerusalem see, 127; status change in, 74–81, 95; Victorian debates about, 245
Hilarion: *askesis* of, 57; death of, 14; Epiphanius and, 34n8, 57; Jerome's life of, 9n19; in Mossman's *Epiphanius*, 258

Hillel (Jewish patriarch), deathbed conversion of, 89, 90–91
Hippolytus, 196; *Elenchos*, 197
historicism, rise of, 245n92
historiography, late ancient, 265–70; Anglo-American, 265; anthropological aspects of, 267, 269; Augustine of Hippo in, 6; continental thought in, 265n5; on Epiphanius, ix-x, 1–8, 263–65; North American conferences on, 265n7; positive models of, 267; reflection of modern values, 268; sociocultural studies, 266, 274
history, sacred: eternal truths of, 258
Holl, Karl, 17, 19; edition of *Panarion*, 21; on Epiphanius's manuscript tradition, 21n64
Holy Spirit: in *Ancoratus*, 203; Athanasius on, 183n25, 185; as breath, 195; as *enhypostatos*, 189; Epiphanius's defense of, 183; Godhead of, 43; role in salvation, 185
homiletics, early Christian: improvisation in, 106n31
homilies, attributed to Epiphanius, 25–26
Honorius, Emperor: in *Vita Epiphanii*, 230, 231
household manuals, ancient, 106
humanity: dual nature of, 135; embodied difference of, 191; God's contract with, 259; incorruptibility of, 214; moral unity of, 28, 181, 182–96, 198–99, 210, 211; unity in church, 199; unity with God, 198
human persons: composite nature of, 188n49, 192, 195–96, 199, 206–7, 210; continuity of, 208, 213; divine and human parts of, 195; image of God in, 191, 194–96; as models of divine activity, 196; moral continuity of, 196, 207, 211; moral responsibility of, 182, 212; unified reality of, 194
Hypatius (amanuensis), 130n127

Hypatius (monk), request for *Ancoratus*, 183

iconoclast controversies (eighth-ninth centuries), 17; Epiphanius's use in, 16, 17n47, 63, 241
icons, 107; saints depicted on, 64
identity, boundaries of, 69, 95
identity, Christian: Epiphanius's role in, 271; interpenetration with Roman identity, 224; management of, 271; problem of, 272
identity, European: following fall of Rome, 95
identity, national: linguistic heritage in, 255n132; in Victorian discourse, 243
identity, racial: nineteenth-century, 255n132
immoderation, Epiphanius on, 110
imperium: Epiphanius's celebrity and, 46–47, 48–52, 62; Epiphanius's involvement with, 85; late antique Christian relationship to, 47; Socrates (historian) on, 49, 50; Sozomen on, 49, 50–51; susceptibility of orthodoxy to, 51
improvisation, 101–8; audience appreciation of, 103–5; basis for, 100n9; in Christian imperial culture, 131; and church discipline, 104; cultural value of, 100; dangers of, 128; in early Christian homiletics, 106n31; in Epiphanius's style, 101, 108, 113, 123–24, 127, 128–31, 274; in episcopacy, 106; familiar models for, 105; in imperial power, 106; of institutional power, 105–6, 129; in jazz, 101; in Latin rhetoric, 102–3; as *mimesis*, 101; mimic, 104; in oratory, 101; in *paideia*, 101–2; perception of, 104; performative mode of, 99–100; power relations in, 104–5, 106; preparation behind, 131; Renaissance, 131; rules of, 100;

improvisation *(continued)*
  spontaneity in, 105; style of, 100; as tool of domination, 131; in Western imperial power, 130–31. *See also* performance
incarnation, 199, 204; in *Ancoratus*, 135, 192, 203; divinity and humanity in, 217; in Epiphanius's theology, 185; in Nicene Creed, 204; Shenoute on, 217; Theophilus's defense of, 216n152; and unity with church, 196. *See also* Christ; Word incarnate
Inglebert, Hervé, 268n18
Inglis, Fred, 39n27
institutional control, Epiphanius on, 28
institutions: inflexibility of, 107; role in cultural production, 105
intellectuals, Christian: dissemination of works, 26
Irenaeus, 196; *Against Heresies*, 20, 198; on Jewish proselytes, 66n3
Isaiah (prophet), 166
Isidore of Seville, antiquarian writing of, 136
Israel, tribes of, 164–65, 170–71, 172

Jacob, sons of, 164–65, 169–70
James, William: on introspection, 70; on unification of self, 94
jazz, improvisational, 101
Jericho, fall of, 151
Jerome: anti-Origenism of, 127n115; ascetic teaching of, 113; and Atarbius, 178n8; defense of Epiphanius, 49; depiction of Epiphanius, 51; on Epiphanius's *askesis*, 57–59; on Epiphanius's authority, 59; on Epiphanius's erudition, 53; on Epiphanius's linguistic prowess, 147n65; at Epiphanius's preaching, 26n81; learned simplicity of, 59; letter to Fabiola, 23n69; on Origen, 84n72; and Origenist controversy, 16n42; on *paideia*, 56; Palestine monastery of, 125; on Paula (ascetic), 58, 112–13; on Paulinian, 75n36, 77n46; translation of Theophilus, 215–16; translations from Greek, 15–16; travel with Epiphanius, 11–12, 34n11; on *On Twelve Gems*, 23. Works: *Adversus Iovinianum*, 109n39; *Against John of Jerusalem*, 12n30, 31, 49, 50, 54; *Apology against Rufinus*, 56; *Epitaphium Paulae*, 12n28; *On Famous Men*, 53; *Vita Hilarionis*, 9n19
Jerusalem: as bride of Christ, 198; ecclesiastical hierarchy of, 127; Hadrian's temples in, 249, 250
Jewishness: Epiphanius's, ix, 9, 29, 88n88, 223, 234–40; as marker of social difference, 236; Paul's, 92
Jewish Temple, destruction of, 236n62
Jews: in British political life, 242–43, 255; Christian attitudes toward, ix; converted, ix, 88–94
John (bishop of Jerusalem), 26n81; accusations of heresy against, 77; approach to church discipline, 127; clerical borders of, 77; conflict with Epiphanius, 12, 31–32, 49, 74–78, 125–26; Epiphanius's letter to, 15–16, 74–78, 126, 207, 210; monastic jurisdiction of, 75, 77, 126n114; Origenism of, 126, 210; Theophilus's mediation for, 178n8
John Chrysostom, 3; conflict with Epiphanius, 34n11, 50–51, 127n119, 178n9; conflict with Eudoxia, 233–34; deposition of, 46n53, 50, 232–33; in *Vita Epiphanii*, 238
John Lydus, antiquarian writing of, 136, 138n26
Johnson, Maria Poggi, 245n92
John the Baptist, 168
Joseph (the patriarch), 170n162; cup of, 169
Joseph of Tiberias, conversion of, 88–91, 92
Josephus, *Antiquitates*, 164n134

Jovinian (western monk), 109n39
Jubilees, book of: Epiphanius's use of, 142n44, 146
Judaism: absorption into Christianity, 94, 256–59, 260; Christian attitudes toward, ix; conversion from, ix, 88–94; relationship to Christianity, 245
Julian the Apostate, 129
Justinian, Emperor: Christian empire of, 138n26
Justin Martyr, 196, 197n81; conversion of, 71n21; *Dialogue with Trypho the Jew*, 237n67, 257n143

Kaldellis, Anthony, 224n9
Kaster, Robert, 101n12
Kaulakau (archon), 147n66
Keaton, Kenneth, 100n8
Keble, John: "National Apostasy," 242n82
Kim, Young Richard, 19, 34n9; on Antiochene controversy, 121n93; on Epiphanius's importance, 264–65; on improper ordination, 126n115; on John of Jerusalem, 75n33, 126n113; on *Panarion*, 83; on Theophilus, 50n64
Kingsley, Charles: *Hypatia*, 243–44; rejection of rationalist past, 245
Kitzinger, Ernest, 64
knowledge: antiquarian, 136–38; performance of, 149; power of, 28; totalizing, 136; worldly, 52
knowledge, Roman: imperial, 138; totalizing, 136; in triumphal processions, 143n48
Koll, Karl, 17
König, Jason, 138
Konops (cleric), request for *Ancoratus*, 183
Kösters, Oliver, 19, 184
Kuefler, Mathew, 6n100

laity, sexual activity of, 116

Lang, Andrew: on early Christian novels, 243n85
lapidary, classical tradition of, 163. *See also* gems
late antiquity: anthropological study of, 267, 269; antiquarianism in, 135–39; borderlands theory concerning, 69n15; Christian culture of, 3, 5, 13, 33, 47; continuity in, 32; cultural biography of, 29; cultural construction of, 264; difference in, 277; holy women in, 239; "jeweled style" of, 173–74; liminal spaces of, 68; material turn of, 64; and modern cultural concerns, 268, 277; modern historiography of, 263, 265–70; North American conferences on, 265n7; poetic sensibility of, 173–74; religious boundaries of, 67, 68; rhetoric of, 3, 102–3; social scientific studies, 266; sociocultural study of, 266, 274; status changes in, 28, 74–81; transformative aspects of, 5, 32, 268; women's history in, 277n45
leadership, early Christian: in sociocultural fabric, 32n4. *See also* episcopacy
Lebon, Joseph, 14; on Epiphanius's correspondence, 18n49
lemniscus, 155, 156; medical origins of, 157n102
Lenski, Noel, 80n56
Lenten fasts, 202; flexibility concerning, 118
leptologēmata, Epiphanius's use of, 179n12
Leyerle, Blake, 103n18
"The Life and Conduct of Our Holy Father Epiphanius." *See Vita Epiphanii*
Life of Antony, 225
Life of Pelagia, 239
ligure, 166–67; harvesting of, 163–64
literalism, Epiphanius's, 133n3, 134, 140, 205–6, 220

Lives of the Prophets (pseudepigraphic work), 25
Lofland, John, 71n21
Lucian, on improvisation, 104
Lucifer of Cagliari, 119n80
Lyman, J. Rebecca, 84n70

Maas, P., 16n44
Maguseans (Persian sect), 177n2
Mani: biography of, 83n65; as comic writer, 108n34; Epiphanius's refutation of, 151
Manichaeans, 151
Manukyan, Arthur, 24, 25
Marcella (ascetic), 58n90
Marcellus of Ancyra: controversies with Epiphanius, 179–80; legacy of, 180; orthodoxy of, 177; Trinitarianism of, 189n50
Marcion, 67; biblical interpretation of, 146
Marcionites, 20
marriage, Epiphanius on, 109, 110n43, 111, 112, 115, 116, 117
Marshall, David, 39n27
martyrs, confession of, 236n61
Mary, Virgin: in Mossman's *Epiphanius*, 257; virginity controversies concerning, 15, 20, 41
Massalians: Epiphanius's refutation of, 128; lack of bodily discipline, 128–29; outdoor worship by, 128
master-disciple relationships, 57n89; Epiphanius's, 114
measurement, allegorical, 160n116. See also *On Weights and Measures* (Epiphanius of Cyprus)
medical practitioners, Roman: in extemporaneous performance, 103n17
Mediterranean, late ancient: social scientific study of, 266
Meier, Christel, 172n174
Melania the Elder, 55n83

Melania the Younger, 76n38
Meletius of Antioch: claim to see of Antioch, 11, 119; at Council of Constantinople, 122n96; death of, 123n98; exile of, 119n79, 124n102
Melitians, Arius and, 200n92
Melitius of Egypt, and lapsed clerics, 114n59
Meltzer, Françoise, 222, 260
Methodius, *De resurrectione*, 209
Migne, J.-P.: *Patrologia Graeca*, 25
Miller, Patricia Cox, 64, 174; on Epiphanius's imagination of place, 211–12; on *Life of Pelagia*, 239
Milner, Murray, Jr., 36n14
mime, ancient, 103; scripting in, 104n22. See also theater, Roman
mimesis, improvisation in, 101
modernity, postcolonial: parallels with late antiquity, 268
modius (sacred measurement), 159–60; numerical interpretation of, 160
Momigliano, Arnaldo, 136
monasteries: of Cyprus, 58, 220n171; Epiphanius's supervision of, 79, 125; outside episcopal authority, 77
monasticism: conservatism of, 214n144; in Cyprus, 58; flexibility concerning, 118; personhood in, 269; problem of corporeality, 214n145
monasticism, Egyptian, 9, 59–60, 214n144, 215; Epiphanius in, 9, 34n8, 224n111; philosophy in, 206n111; Shenoute's, 218, 219. See also Shenoute
monasticism, Epiphanius's, 13, 59–60, 108, 223; authority of, 61–62; celebrity in, 56; in Egypt, 9, 34n8, 224n111; in his theology, 214, 216, 220; in Palestine, 27, 34n8; in *Vita Epiphanii*, 237
monk-bishops: *mythos* of, 76; rise of, 60
monks: anti-philosophical, 206; long-haired, 118n76; Origenist, 214

monks, Palestinian, 59–60; disputes among, 177n2; of Mount of Olives, 42n40
Montanists, opposition to marriage, 112
moral agency: in conception of the divine, 212; in Epiphanius's theology, 186, 206; in Origenist controversy, 213
moral justice, human continuity and, 208
moral transformation, theology of, 205
moral unity, 28; of body and soul, 187–88, 189, 201, 218; of church, 200, 203; continuous, 212; and Epiphanius's heresiology, 207, 208; in Epiphanius's Trinitarianism, 182, 188, 196; in God's image, 195, 212; and human body, 216; of humanity, 28, 181, 182–96, 198–99, 210, 211; multiple instances of, 202; of Nicene Creed, 203; in *Panarion*, 186–87; through orthodoxy, 202, 204
Mossman, Thomas Wimberley: knowledge of Epiphanius's heresiology, 261n153; reading of Epiphanius, 261n153; skepticism of miracles, 248n103, 250; use of Panarion, 247, 53n126, 261; use of *Vita Epiphanii*, 247–48
—*Epiphanius*, 29, 246–59; Christian Roman Empire in, 249–54; chronology of, 249n107; church and empire in, 250–54; Cleobius the Christian in, 247n100, 255; Constantine in, 250, 251–52, 253; empire in, 259; Epiphanius's conversion in, 247, 251, 254, 257–58; Epiphanius's death in, 247n101; Epiphanius's early life in, 247; Epiphanius's Jewishness in, 248, 254–59, 259; Epiphanius's sainthood in, 258n150, 259; Epiphanius's sister (Callitrope) in, 248; father's funeral in, 248, 255; female gnostics in, 247, 253; geography in, 249n108; Hebrew language in, 258; heresy in, 253, 254, 259; Hilarion in, 258; introduction to, 246–47; Jacob the Jew in, 255; Jerome in, 258n150; Jerusalem in, 249–50; Jewish past/Catholic present in, 256; Laetus (monk) in, 248; Lucian (monk) in, 256; martyrdom in, 251; messianic prophecies in, 257; miracles in, 248, 250; missionaries in, 252; *mithlakkachath* (verb) in, 258; monasticism in, 253; national/racial identities in, 255; persecution in, 251, 252; pilgrims in, 252; religious absorption in, 256–59; religious difference in, 259, 260–61; religious ritual in, 248; Roman Empire in, 248; Saracens in, 247n100; setting of, 249; sign of the cross in, 257; Spanhydrion monastery in, 247n100; Tryphon in, 247, 256–57; Tryphon's daughter in, 248, 257, 258n149; Virgin Mary in, 257
Mount Ebal, tribes of Israel on, 170, 171
Mount Gerizim, tribes of Israel on, 170–71, 173
Mount of Olives, monks of, 42n40
Moutsoulas, E., 22, 23
Muldoon, James, 74
Murphy, Trevor, 136n15; on triumphal processions, 143n48

Nahum (prophet), 166
Nasareans, Epiphanius on, 143
Nashon (Book of Numbers), 151
Nasrallah, Laura, 72
nativity narratives, Epiphanius's reconciling of, 152, 153
Nautin, Pierre, 1n1, 23n70, 116n65; on Epiphanius's death, 9n22
Nero, Emperor: in *On Twelve Gems*, 163
Nettl, Bruno, 100n9

Newman, John Henry, 242n82; ante-Nicene martyrs of, 249; *Callista*, 244; rejection of rationalist past, 245
New Testament: affinity with Old Testament, 151, 167; Hebrew translations of, 89, 90
Nicene Creed, 202–5; as antidote to heresy, 202–3; Epiphanius's adherence to, 122; Epiphanius's proposals for, 180n15, 203; incarnation in, 204; moral continuity of, 205; moral unity of, 203; revisions to, 204; as rhetorical performance, 203; suggested additions to, 177n2
Nicenes: of Cyprus, 34n9; Epiphanius's celebrity among, 43
Nicene theology: episcopal controversies in, 120; *ousia* in, 189; proponents of, 177; soteriology in, 184n31; Trinitarianism of, 119n79
Nicephorus of Constantinople: on *Epistula ad Ioannem*, 16; in iconoclast controversy, 17n47, 241
Nicolaitans (heretics), ignorance of Hebrew, 147
Noah: descendants of, 142–43; sons of, 142n44, 151
Noah's ark, remains of, 143
Nock, Arthur Darby, 70, 94
Noetians, patripassionist, 190n54
Noetus, biblical criticism of, 145–46
noncanonical works: Epiphanius's use of, 146–47; heretics' use of, 147n63
Norton, Peter, 76n37
Novatianists, inflexible asceticism of, 115

oath breaking: Canaan's, 142, 143n45; divine punishment for, 142
Old Testament: affinity with New Testament, 151, 167; twenty-two books of, 160
Oliphant, Margaret: *Saint Francis*, 248n103

Olympias (ascetic), 59
On Twelve Gems (Epiphanius of Cyprus), 12; agate in, 164; allegory in, 172n170; amethyst in, 163; antiquarianism of, 162, 173; antiquarian knowledge in, 154, 173; Armenian version of, 172n170; Babylon in, 165; Benjamin in, 168–69; Bible in, 162–73, 175; biblical analogues in, 45; biblical intertextuality in, 166; biblical wisdom in, 166; bloodstone in, 165; book of Daniel in, 167; breastplate imagery of, 163, 173; chalcedony in, 164; commentarial style of, 172; composition of, 23; conversion narratives in, 93–94; Coptic translation of, 93, 94n109, 169n160, 172n171; date of, 23, 93n103; digressions in, 170; dry measurements in, 159; editions of, 24; Elijah in, 166, 167; Elisha in, 167; emerald in, 164, 168, 173; ethnography in, 171; Exodus in, 154; four Jesuses in, 165; Gad in, 166–67; geography in, 166–67, 170–71; intertextuality of, 93, 169; Isaiah in, 166; jacinth in, 166; Jacob's blessing in, 165; John the Baptist in, 168; Joseph in, 169, 170n162; Judas Iscariot in, 168, 169; Latin version of, 172n173; ligure in, 163–64, 166–67; literalism of, 133n3; minerology in, 167; Moses in, 165, 166, 170; Mount Ebal in, 170, 171; Mount Gerizim in, 170–71, 173; Nahum in, 166; naturalist section of, 164, 172n170; Nero on, 163; Old Georgian version, 24–25, 164n133, 171; Old/New Testament in, 167; onyx in, 168–69; orderings in, 169–70, 171, 172; origins of, 23, 93n103; pairs in, 169; Paul in, 168–69; Pharisees in, 168; and *Physiologus*, 25n79; priestly figures in, 167; resurrection body in, 173;

Reuben (son of Jacob) in, 164–65; river Pishon in, 164, 166; Samaritans in, 171, 172; sapphire in, 163, 166; sardion in, 163, 164; Shechem in, 171; Simeon in, 169; sources of, 163n125; Stephen in, 166; survival of, 23–24; Thecla in, 167; topaz in, 163, 167–68; transformation in, 94; transmission history of, 163n124, 172; tribes of Israel in, 164–65, 170–71, 172; unity of Bible in, 169; Zebulon (son of Jacob) in, 164–65

On Weights and Measures (Epiphanius of Cyprus), 12, 22–23; allegories of, 192n63; ark of the covenant in, 192n63; asterisk in, 155, 156; Augustine's familiarity with, 53n72; bath (oil measure) in, 159; Bible in, 154–62, 159, 175; Bible translations in, 65, 157–58; biblical place-names in, 155, 161–62; boundaries in, 65–68; cardinal directions in, 162; chronology of, 157–58; composition of, 49n60, 154n95; constellations in, 162; currencies in, 161; date of, 22, 44n51, 65n1, 154n95; on diacritical marks, 155–56; dry measures of, 158; fall of empires in, 161; four winds in, 162; geography in, 161–62; Greek in, 158nn108,110; imperial order in, 159, 160; land areas in, 158; lemniscus in, 155, 156; measures of flour, 160n116; modern historians' use of, 158n107; *modius* in, 159–60; monetary amounts in, 158; multiple measurement forms of, 159; nonbiblical measures in, 158; numerology in, 160; obelus in, 155–56; Origen's Hexapla in, 150, 156, 157; Origen's Octapla in, 157; origins of, 22, 44n51, 65n1, 154n95; post-Septuagintal translators in, 149n74; Ptolemies in, 157; on punctuation, 155, 156–57; religious conversions in, 65–67; request for, 44; Roman emperors in, 157–58; Syriac translation of, 155; text-critical marks in, 155–56

onyx, cups made of, 168–69

oratory: improvisation in, 101; physical space of, 103n21

ordinations, forcible, 75–77, 125–26, 233n48; in support of church, 127

Origenist controversy: anti-intellectualism of, 273; charges of plagiarism in, 55; in Egypt, 178; Epiphanius in, ix, 12, 17, 34, 42, 51, 54, 75, 84n66, 132–35, 181, 207–13, 220; Evagrius Ponticus in, 210n128; free will in, 212; Jerome and, 16n42; John of Jerusalem in, 126, 210; moral agency in, 213; morality in, 212; ordination of Vitalius in, 124n103; otherness in, 273; in Palestine, 178, 232n44; Theophilus's motives in, 216n155; in *Vita Epiphanii*, 232

Origen of Alexandria: Ambrose and, 84–85; antiquarianism of, 145, 174; Bible of, 139, 174; biblical knowledge of, 145; on body and soul, 218; commentary on first Psalm, 150; contrast with Epiphanius, 132; on the devil, 210; engagement with body, 209, 212–13; Epiphanius's biography of, 83–85; Epiphanius's use of, 150; erudition of, 83, 85; exegetical criticism of, 85; *On First Principles*, 207n116; on first Psalm, 208; Hexapla of, 22, 68, 150, 156; library of, 27; on materiality, 209; metaphysics of, 220; monastic interpreters of, 212n138; neurological castration by, 84; orthodoxy of, 85; on paradise, 133–35, 207; on resurrection body, 207–8; role of empire for, 84n73; textual criticism of, 85; theology of, 34, 207, 208; use of allegory, 134, 207; use of Bible, 132–33; use of drugs, 84; use of "enhypostatos," 190n53; use of proof-texts, 141; worldly influences on, 85

Orlandi, Tito, 217n162
Orthodox Church, American: Epiphanius's life in, 235n53
orthodoxy: ancient debates about, 1–2; boundaries of, 67–68, 81, 85; of converts from Judaism, 92; front line (*stiphos*) of, 200–201; imperial power and, 254; institutionalism of, 129; late ancient culture of, 272; moral unity through, 202, 204; Origin's fall from, 84; prevailing over chaos, 98; and Roman imperial politics, 130; susceptibility to *imperium*, 51; unity in, 200
otherness: in Epiphanius's hagiographies, 261; Epiphanius's view of, 7, 271, 272–74; Jewish, 240; persistence of, 273
Oxford Movement, 242n82

paideia: formation of social class, 102; Hellenistic, 84n70; improvisation in, 101–2; intellectual violence in, 84; persona in, 104
paideia, Christian: appropriate bounds of, 52; content and style of, 54; Epiphanius's celebrity and, 46, 47, 52–56; Epiphanius's engagement with, 84n70, 85, 108n34; multiple forms of, 47; social effects of, 54n75
Palestine: Epiphanius in, 9, 12, 23, 27, 34n8, 78; monks of, 59–60, 177n1, 214n144; Origenist heresy in, 178, 232n44; Phoenicia as, 235; theological controversies in, 12
Palladius (author): on Epiphanius's monasticism, 59; on Melania the Elder, 55n83
Palladius (monk): request for *Ancoratus*, 183, 184
Panarion (Epiphanius of Cyprus), 2; Aerius's followers in, 129n125; Alogi in, 152–53; *Anakephalaioses* (summaries) of, 25, 198n84; *Ancoratus* material in, 20; Anomoians in, 201–2; Antiochene controversy in, 120; antiquarianism in, 144–49, 175; Apollinarians in, 120, 186; Arianism in, 122n94; Arius in, 85–87, 200; on asceticism, 109; Audians in, 194n74; Bible in, 144–45, 175; bodily discipline in, 109–12, 113–14; calendars in, 153; Christian culture in, 182; Christian documents in, 20; church discipline in, 114–16, 117–19; circulation of, 21; compilation in, 140; composition of, 10, 20, 44n48, 182n19; consubstantial Trinity in, 199–200; culturally productive aspects of, 182n21; date of, 20, 182n19; *De fide* treatise, 11, 21, 116n68, 118–19, 130n127, 198; on destiny of humanity, 198; detail in, 99; difference in, 7; digressions in, 144–45, 152–53; discussion *peri thesmōn*, 116n68; divorce in, 2n4; earlier heresiography and, 197; Ebionites in, 34n10, 89n92, 91; editions of, 21; effect on Epiphanius's reputation, 264; Epiphanius's theology in, 181; flexibility in, 119; geography in, 68; goals of, 7–8; Greek philosophies in, 21; heresiography of, 21, 83–87, 196; human error in, 198; human history in, 198, 207; incarnation in, 185n35; intolerance in, 107; lists in, 144n51, 153; Mani in, 151; manuscript tradition of, 21; mendacity of, 99n6; moral panic in, 201; moral unity in, 182, 186–87, 196; Mossman's use of, 247, 253n126, 261; naturalist literature in, 144n52; Nicene theologians in, 177; noncanonical works in, 146–47; Origen in, 141, 208–9; paganism in, 153; paradise in, 134; on Phibionites, 2; polemics of, 181; pre-Christian heresy in, 152n88; purification in, 98; readership of, 11; refutation of Marcion's Bible, 20; religious frontiers of, 81;

resurrection in, 185n35, 193n66; Roman consulships in, 153; Sethians in, 146n59; ship metaphor of, 111–12; Song of Songs metaphor of, 21; sources for, 27; style of, 20; summaries of, 25; "Summary and True Account of the Catholic and Apostolic Faith of the Church," 116; Trinitarianism in, 176, 177, 199, 200–202; truth and error in, 198; virginity of Mary in, 41n34

papa (title), early use of, 59n93

paradise: in *Ancoratus*, 133; Origen on, 133–35, 207; in *Panarion*, 134; reality of, 133–34

Parliament, British: anti-Ritualist legislation, 252n120; religious freedom acts, 242

past, late ancient: historical construction of, 276–77

Pastis, Jacqueline Z., 237n67

patristics, golden age of, 3, 4

patron-client relations, social context of, 70n16

Paul (apostle): authentic Jewishness of, 92; on Christian unity, 201; conversion of, 70n16, 92–94; on flexibility, 112; letters of, 201; on long hair, 118n76; metaphor of body, 111; in parable of gems, 93; in *On Twelve Gems*, 168–69

Paul (cleric): identity of, 44n47; request for *Ancoratus*, 20, 43

Paula (ascetic): Epiphanius and, 57–59, 112–14; Epiphanius's eulogy for, 112; Jerome on, 58

Paulinian (brother of Jerome): diaconate of, 77n41; forcible ordination of, 75–77, 125; residence in Cyprus, 77n46; sources for, 75n36, 125n104

Paulinus of Antioch, 124n102; accusation of Vitalius, 120n81; claim to see of Antioch, 119–21; disciples of, 123n98; Epiphanius and, 120, 178;

episcopal controversy of, 11, 34n11; Nicene faction of, 23n71; orthodoxy of, 120; Sabellianism accusations against, 119; theological affidavit of, 120, 123; travel to Rome, 124n102; in Trinitarian controversy, 119n80

Paul of Samosata, Epiphanius's controversy with, 149

performance: of difference, 274; disciplinary function of, 104; fluency in, 100n8; in late ancient culture, 272; power dynamics of, 105n27; as spectacle, 105. *See also* improvisation

personas: in declamation, 102n13; in *paideia*, 104; popular, 39–40

Pétau, Denis, 247n99; *Life of Epiphanius*, 25

Peter (heretic monk), 78; Epiphanius's rebuke to, 79; monastic expulsion of, 79; teachings of, 80

Pharisees, 168; sexual abstinence among, 109

philologoi (antiquarians), 145n54. *See also* antiquarianism

philosophy: in Egyptian monasticism, 206n111; Greek, 21; moral self of, 206

Philostratus, *Vitae sophistarum*, 102n16

Photius, on Epiphanius's style, 54n76

Physiologus (pseudepigraphic work), 25; and *On Twelve Gems*, 25n79

Piacenza pilgrim, on Constantia, 10n25

Pinian (husband of Melania the Younger), escape from ordination, 76n38

Plato, speculative tradition of, 206

Pliny the Elder, antiquarian writing of, 136

Pneumatomachoi, 43n46; *in Ancoratus*, 182n20, 192n61; Epiphanius's refutation of, 202

poetry, late antique: construction and production of, 173–74; discontinuous aesthetic of, 174

pop art, Warholian, 38n24

Pourkier, Aline: on golden age of patristics, 3, 4
power: in frontier zones, 73n29; improvised, 104–6, 129, 130–31; institutionalized, 105–6; in late ancient Christianity, 32–33; relationship to piety, 223
power, imperial: and Christian religion, 175, 260; improvisational style of, 106
power, institutional: improvisation of, 105–6, 129
power, Western: improvisational quality of, 130–31
power relations: in improvisation, 104–5, 106; of Roman households, 105–6; of Theodosian-era church, 128
priesthood, requirements for, 117. *See also* clergy
Proclianus (Christian), 183n25
proof-texts: of *Ancoratus*, 140–41; Origen's use of, 141; polemical, 141n39; of Trinitarian controversies, 141n37
Protoevangelium of James, 146
Proverbs 8:22, 147n71, 192, 200
pseudepigrapha, Epiphanius's, 25–27
Ptolemy, *Letter to Flora*, 20
Pummer, Reinhard, 66n5

Quintilian, on improvisation, 102n15
Quodvultdeus, request to Augustine, 53n72

Ranke, Leopold von: positivist history of, 276
Rapp, Claudia, 46n54; on Epiphanius's life, 225n12; on forcible ordination, 76n37; on *Vita Epiphanii*, 223n8, 235n54
religion: cultural ideas about, 72; nineteenth-century politics of, 242–43
religion, late ancient: centrality of values, 268n18; creativity of, 274; historiography of, 267, 268–69; modern historiography on, 267. *See also* borders, religious; Christianity, late ancient; conversion, religious; difference, religious; heresy; status, religious; transformation, religious
renown, Roman desire for, 40n32. *See also* celebrity
renunciation, Christian desire for, 40n32
resurrection: in *Ancoratus*, 184; of composite body and soul, 188n49, 213, 217; in Epiphanius's theology, 140n35, 141, 181, 184, 185n35, 196, 215; as hope of salvation, 216; human continuity in, 207; in *Panarion*, 193n66; Pauline, 213; Shenoute on, 219; of whole body, 209
resurrection body, 185, 215; Origen on, 207–8; reality of, 208; in *On Twelve Gems*, 173
rhetoric, Latin: improvisation in, 102–3; theater and, 102n13, 103
Rhodes, Royal W., 248n103, 249n107; *The Lion and the Cross*, 243n85
Riegl, Alois, 267; on late ancient art, 268
Riggi, Calogero, 2n4, 116n65; on *Ancoratus*, 220n172; on Epiphanius's flexibility, 118n77
ritual, Victorian debates about, 245
Roberts, Michael, 173–74
Roman Empire: alignment of Christianity with, 228–30; barbarians in, 227n24; Christianization of, 227, 251; conflict with Persia, 229; creative tendencies of, 275; frontiers of, 95; as ideological system, 227; improvisatory aspects of, 106n30; naturalized authority of, 155; political/cultural ethos of, 136; Romanization of provincials, 227; in sacred space, 250; self-promotion in, 39n29; tension with Christianity,

234, 240; totalizing knowledge in, 136–37; in Victorian thought, 223
Roman Empire, Christian: boundaries of, 87; colonial discourse analysis of, 72; crossings in, 96; culture of, 13, 33; Epiphanius's celebrity and, 48–52; imperial authority of, 155; individual alienation in, 70n17; key figures of, 50; in Mossman's *Epiphanius*, 248, 249–54; peace in, 49; personalities of, 40; power in, 48n57; religious ambiguity in, 47; religious transformation in, 73; secular foundations of, 85; sociocultural identity in, 40; sociopolitical space of, 74; totalized power in, 8; totalizing discourse of, 107; transition from paganism, 6, 48; unity of, 202
romanitas, and *christianitas*, 224n9
Roman literature, early Christian Bible and, 141. *See also* antiquarian writing, Roman
Roman Republic, political/cultural ethos of, 136
Rufinus of Aquileia, 125n111; and Atarbius, 178n8; on Epiphanius's erudition, 55–56; on *paideia*, 56. Works: *Commentary on the Apostles' Creed*, 205; *Historia ecclesiastica*, 23n71
Russell, Norman, 124n101

Sabbath: Epiphanius on, 151; flexibility concerning, 118
Sabellians, Trinitarianism of, 190
saints: depiction on icons, 64; embodiment of cultural uncertainty, 223; flamboyant, 223; imitation of, 222; institutional norms and, 222n4; lives of, 221–23; as transgressive figures, 222, 260; virtue of, 222
salvation: of Adam, 143–44; body and soul and, 214; in Epiphanius's theology, 184, 185, 212, 219, 272;

human body and, 214; and human morality, 199; monastic view of, 214; reality of, 212; resurrection as hope of, 216; role of Holy Spirit in, 185; Trinitarianism and, 184
Samaritans, in *On Twelve Gems*, 171, 172
Sanders, Andrew, 245n94
sapphire: allegory of, 166; healing power of, 163
sardion: healing power of, 163; source of, 164
Schor, Adam, 119n78
Scott, Alan, 25n79
Scott, Walter, 245n92
Scripture: aid to weakness, 112n54; truth of, 150–51
self: moral continuity of, 216; Roman, 105n28; technologies of, 269, 271
selfhood, Christian: boundaries of, 76; limits of, 222n4
self-mastery, Christian, 28
Seneca the Elder, *Controversiae*, 101n11
Seneca the Younger, 139; celebrity of, 39
Septuagint: pentateuchs of, 156; primacy of, 147; Seventy-Two translators of, 156; text-critical marks of, 155–56
Serapion, Bishop: Athanasius's correspondence with, 183n25, 185
sermons: dissemination of, 26; Epiphanius's, 26
Sethians (gnostic group), 97n1, 146n59
Severan emperors, governance of, 106n30
Severians (ascetics), 109–10
Severus of Antioch: *Contra impium Grammaticum*, 14; Monophysite Christology of, 14
Shenoute (archimandrite): affirmation of the *homoousion*, 218n164; anti-Origenism of, 217n162; ascetic discipline of, 219; on body and soul, 217; Christology of, 216–17; on communal participation, 219;

Shenoute (archimandrite) *(continued)* concern for moral unity, 218; cultural value of, 270; Egyptian theology of, 216–19; *I Am Amazed*, 217–18; on incarnation, 217; incipits of, 217n161; on individual accountability, 219; on "Jesus prayer," 218n163; lacunae in, 218n163; modern scholarship on, 270; monasticism of, 218, 219; on resurrection, 219; Trinitarianism of, 218

Shoulson, Jeffrey, 71, 72

Shroeder, Caroline, 219

signs, psychological theories of, 71n20

Simelidis, Christos, 1n1

Simeon (son of Jacob), association with treachery, 168n152

Simon Metaphrastes, 246, 247n99

Simon the Pharisee, 168n152

Smith, Geoffrey S., 197n81

Smith, Philip: *The History of the Christian Church during the First Ten Centuries*, 242n81

Socrates (historian): on anthropomorphite God, 215n149; *Church History*, 50; on Cyprus synod, 122n95; Epiphanius's celebrity in, 46, 49, 60; on Epiphanius's character, 54; on extracanonical ordination, 127n119; on *imperium*, 49, 50

solitaries (*monazontōn*), among church staff, 117n71

sophists, improvisational performance of, 102–3

sōphrōn, in New Testament, 115n61

soteriology: Athanasius's, 185n34; cosmology of, 184n31. *See also* salvation

soul: God's correction of, 94; reality of, 193. *See also* body and soul

Sozomen, 10n22, 34n8, 234n52; on Cyprus synod, 122n95; on Epiphanius's *askesis*, 59–60; Epiphanius's celebrity in, 46, 49, 50–51; on Epiphanius's character, 55; on Hesychius, 57n88; on *imperium*, 49, 50–51; sympathy for Eudoxia, 51

Stark, Rodney, 71n21

state, sexual violence of, 83

status: versus celebrity, 36; in late antiquity, 28, 74–81

status, religious: boundaries of, 76; changes in, 74–81, 95; community instability and, 81; in Epiphanius's conversion narratives, 73, 74–81; failures of, 81; as form of management, 81; in late ancient Christianity, 32, 63; in late ancient culture, 272; transformations to, 78

Stephen (saint), 166

Stone, Michael, 22

Sulpicius Severus, *Vita Martini*, 225n13

Surius, Laurentius, 247n99

Swete, Henry, 66n3

Syedra (Pamphylia), correspondence from, 43, 183–84

Symmachus (Bible translator), 65, 66–67, 149, 157; conversion to Judaism, 66

Tall Brothers (Origenists), 51; works of, 55

Tatian: abstinence of, 109n46; on Adam, 143–44; conversion of, 71n21

texts, Christian: social scientific historical studies of, 222n2

theater, late ancient: social historical context of, 103n18

theater, Roman: improvisation in, 103; physical space of, 103n21; rhetoric and, 102n13, 103. *See also* mime

Theodoret: *Historia ecclesiastica*, 46n53, 119n78; knowledge of Epiphanius, 46n53

Theodosius, Emperor: Epiphanius's letter to (purported), 9n18, 17; in *Vita Epiphanii*, 231, 234

Theodotion (Bible translator), 65, 149–50, 157; conversion to Judaism, 67

Theodotus (heretic), 81

theology: metaphysical, 189, 206; of moral transformation, 205

theology, Epiphanius's: alternative discourse of, 180; in *Ancoratus*, 181, 183–86; anti-Arian, 181n17; authority of, 123–24; bodily morality in, 216; body and soul in, 180–81, 186–88, 217; the devil in, 210–11; diversity of, 196–205; divine unity in, 213; goal of, 209; the *homoousion* in, 181; human body in, 182, 185–86, 212, 213–20; image of God in, 205, 212; incarnation in, 185, 192; modern opinion on, 178–79; monasticism in, 214, 216, 220; moral agency in, 186, 206; moral concepts in, 180, 213, 272; moral consistency in, 209; multiple concerns of, 196; Nicene partisanship of, 34n10, 122, 176–77; nonmonastic Christians and, 215; orthodoxy, 51; reactionary aspects of, 180; relation to Origenist theology, 212; resurrection in, 140n35, 141, 181, 184, 185n35, 196, 215; salvation in, 184, 185, 212, 219, 272; Shenoute and, 218, 219; terminology of, 180; in tradition of Athanasius, 178–79. *See also* moral unity; Trinitarianism

Theophilus of Alexandria: anti-Origenism of, 178n8, 216n155; on the body, 216n156; correspondence with Epiphanius, 42–43; death of, 216; defense of incarnation, 216n152; on Epiphanius, 51; and Epiphanius's Constantinople journey, 50; festal letters of, 215–16; monastic context of, 216n151; transmission of Epiphanius, 215–16

Theophrastus: Epiphanius's use of, 111–12; on shipbuilding, 112n52

topaz, 167; for eye disorders, 163; Theban, 168

transformation, religious: ancient technologies of, 71; body as site of, 219; borders in, 95; in Christian Roman Empire, 73; control over, 95; social becoming in, 95; to status, 78; through translation, 69; in *On Twelve Gems*, 94

treatises, Epiphanius's, 18–25; biblical commentaries in, 21–22; his preference for, 18; in Syriac, 22

Trinitarianism: Arian, 190; of Council of Chalcedon, 190n55; post-Nicene, 176; proof-texts of, 141n37; of Sabellians, 190; salvation and, 184; Shenoute's, 218

Trinitarianism, Epiphanius's, 135, 176, 188–96; anti-Origenist, 180–81; consubstantiality of, 180, 188, 199–200, 217; distinctiveness of, 191; incarnate body in, 192; language of conjoining in, 190–91; moral unity in, 182, 188, 196; one- and three-*hypostasis*, 180n16, 191n57; in *Panarion*, 176, 177, 199, 200–202; unity of, 191

Trinitarianism, Nicene, 119n79, 189n50; *homoousios* (consubstantial), 176, 188, 204–5

Trinity: coequal, 216; debates over, 129; distinctiveness of, 191; as *enhypostatos*, 189–90, 195, 196; gendered filiation of, 204n100; measurement allegory of, 160n116; relationship with church, 199; three *hypostaseis* (realities) of, 190n54; unity of, 189, 191, 194, 196, 207, 208n118, 218

Turner, Graeme, 37, 38n22

universalism, Origenist, 225n13

Valantasis, Richard, 264n3

Valens, Emperor: death of, 124n102; Epiphanius and, 49; exile of Meletius, 119n79
Valentinian, Emperor, 266n11
Valentinus (heretic), 81
Valesians (ascetics), voluntary castration of, 109n46
Velimirovic, Nikolai, 235n53
Vesey, Mark, 26n82
virginity, Epiphanius on, 108–9
Vis, Henri de, 24, 25
Viswanathan, Gauri, 72, 91
Vita Epiphanii (fifth century), 28–29, 46n54, 223–43; alignment of Christianity and Rome in, 231, 234; Aquila (Alexandrian Jew) in, 237; Arcadius in, 230, 231, 233n49; audience of, 231; boundary maintenance in, 240; civilizing of Saracens in, 227, 229; civilizing values in, 227, 234; Cleobius (Christian) in, 235; Constantine in, 230n32; Constantinople episodes in, 231, 233; contemplative space of, 240; conversation with animals in, 226; conversions in, 230–32, 236–40; date of, 223n8; debate about law in, 237; demonic possession in, 238n70; divine power in, 226; divine visions in, 226, 234; doubles in, 238n70; Epiphanius's death in, 234, 238; Epiphanius's early life in, 235–36; Epiphanius's education in, 237, 238n69; Epiphanius's Jewishness in, 234–40; Epiphanius's monasticism in, 237; Epiphanius's sister in, 237; Epiphanius the Syrian in, 238nn68,70; Eudaimon the philosopher in, 238n68; Eudoxia in, 233–34; exorcism in, 228, 229n30, 235n56; Faustinianus (pagan) in, 231–32; French translation of, 240n74; geographic movement in, 226; healing in, 225–26, 230, 231; heresy in, 226, 261; Honorius in, 230, 231; imperial family in, 230–31, 234; influences on, 225; Isaac (Jew) in, 238; James (Jew) in, 235; John Chrysostom in, 238; John the Saracen in, 227n23, 238n68; Latin translation of, 247n99; loyalty to Rome in, 229–30; medieval circulation of, 241; metrical sections of, 228; miracles in, 225–26, 227, 230, 238–39, 261; modern historiography on, 240; Origenist controversy in, 232; Persians in, 228–29, 230; poetic source of, 228n27; political issues in, 224, 229; in post-Reformation church histories, 241–42; Proklianē in, 230n35; religious difference in, 229; Roman-Persian conflict in, 229; Theodosius in, 231, 234; Trypho in, 236, 237

Vitalius: claim to see of Antioch, 119, 121, 123; Epiphanius's questioning of, 121–22, 123; following Antiochene controversy, 124n102; heresy of, 121; ordination of, 119, 124n103

Ward-Perkins, Bryan, 268n16
Washburn, D. A., 88n89
Webb, Ruth, 103, 105n27
Weber, Max: on charisma, 36n14; on status, 36
Whitmarsh, Tim, 102n16, 138; on postclassicism, 267n13
will, psychological theories of, 71n20
Williams, Frank, 150; on Epiphanius's character, 2; on *monazontōn*, 117n71; on Origen, 132; on *Panarion*, 11
Williams, Megan, 68n12
wine drinking: abstinence from, 110; Epiphanius on, 112–13
Wiseman, Nicholas: ante-Nicene martyrs of, 249; *Fabiola*, 244, 245n94; rejection of rationalist past, 245

wood, metaphors of, 111–12
Woolf, Greg, 106n30
Word incarnate, 192, 193–94; full humanity of, 186. *See also* incarnation
Wyschogrod, Edith, 222n4

Xenocrates, *Lithognomion*, 168n151

Young, Frances, 7n13

Zebulon (son of Jacob), tribal allotment of, 164–65

www.ingramcontent.com/pod-product-compliance
Lightning Source LLC
Chambersburg PA
CBHW030520230426
43665CB00010B/693